# REMEMBER US

## Letters from Stalin's Gulag (1930-37)
## Volume One: *The Regehr Family*

Ruth Derksen Siemens

Library and Archives Canada Cataloguing in Publication

Remember us : letters from Stalin's Gulag (1930-37) / [compiled by] Ruth Derksen Siemens.

Letters translated from German.
Includes bibliographical references.
Contents: v.1. The Regehr family
ISBN 978-1-894710-82-4 (v. 1)

1. Mennonites--Soviet Union--Correspondence. 2. Concentration camp inmates--Soviet Union--Correspondence. 3. Mennonites--Soviet Union--History--20th century. 4. Concentration camps--Soviet Union--History. 5. Soviet Union--History--1925-1953. I. Siemens, Ruth Derksen

BX8141.R44 2008 947.0088'2897 C2008-900892-8

REMEMBER US. LETTERS FROM STALIN'S GULAG. VOLUME ONE: THE REGEHR FAMILY.

Published by Pandora Press
33 Kent Avenue
Kitchener, Ontario N2G 3R2


**Credits**

Map on pages 21and 397 used with permission from Thurston, Robert. *Life and Terror in Stalin's Russia 1934-1941*. New Haven and London: Yale University Press, 1996. p. 64.

Maps on pages 24, 398 and 399 used with permission from Schroeder, William and Helmut T. Huebert. *Mennonite Historical Atlas*. 2nd ed. Winnipeg: Springfield Publishers, 1996. pp. 14 and 16.

All photographs used with permission from Bargen, Anne and Peter. *From Russia with Tears*. Kelowna, British Columbia: Private Publication, 1991. Preface, Section I, Section II, p. 180.

Book cover design and photography by Karl Griffiths-Fulton.
Book contents designed by Christian Snyder.

www.gulagletters.com
www.pandorapress.com
All Pandora Press publications are printed on Eco-Logic certified paper.

10 09 08 07 06 05 04 03 02 01 07 08 09 10 11 12 13 14 15

*To all those who lived the story of the letters.*
*We will remember.*

# CONTENTS

# PREFACE

It is August 1989, and Frank Bargen is cleaning out the attic of his Manitoba home. He has been storing some of his parents' belongings since they died twelve years earlier. Among the possessions is an old Campbell's Soup box. In casual conversation with his younger brother Peter Bargen and his wife Anne who are visiting, Frank refers to "a box of old letters" in the attic that are "just cluttering up the place." Peter finds the box, opens it up, and discovers hundreds of faded letters, some little more than scraps of paper. They are written in German gothic script and dated as early as 1930. To Peter's surprise, his mother had kept all of these letters from Russia until she died.

The correspondence is from aunts and uncles, grandparents and cousins, neighbours and friends, who by choice or fateful chance remained behind in the former Soviet Union. Their letters describe the inhumane conditions under which millions lived and died: from the mother dividing meagre portions of black bread among her starving children to the father prepared to freeze to death in order to provide for his children. Although the writers' words reveal human flaws and frailties, they also bring to light an elemental faith that united the Mennonite people for over 400 years.

It was only when the cardboard box emerged from the attic in 1989 that Peter began to comprehend the suffering of his people. For three years, he and Anne organized and translated 463 of the "pre-war" letters (1930-38). Peter learned of the events that took place in the hours immediately following his family's flight in 1929, and the unthinkable horrors experienced by those left behind in Soviet Russia. Peter and Anne wanted their children, grandchildren, and extended family to know their own story, so they printed one hundred copies of the 463-letter collection in 1991.

Significantly, research has confirmed that the letters from Stalin's Gulag comprise the largest international corpus of its kind to date. Also noteworthy is that these letters were written "in the moment." Unlike many published memoirs written years later, after memory and the passage of time have possibly eroded the experience, (e.g. Alexsandr Solzhenitsyn, Eugenia Ginsburg, Kseniia Medvededskaia) these letters capture the experiences of prisoners and villagers in actual time.

Clandestinely carried out of the country, the letters offer a rare glimpse into the bleakest chapter in the Soviet Union's history. They open a previously obscured window into both the day-to-day existence in Stalin's prison camps and the suffering of oppressed people in their home villages. Yet the letters also evoke the human spirit's most enduring quality: hope.

## Translation of the Letters

Translating the letters presented numerous challenges for Peter and Anne Bargen. In their 1991 published collection, they note the following:

1. Many letters are unsigned and undated. We have done our best to estimate by whom and at what time they were written.

2. Many words, phrases and sentences are illegible because of faint writing, faulty spelling, abbreviations, smudging and unknown Russian expressions. We have tried to express the substance of the communication accurately.

3. Many unknown or illegible "place names" in either German or Russian language are used by the correspondents and are written as they appear to the translator; they may be grossly misspelled (i).

The Bargens explain that they tried to reflect the essence of the letters as precisely as possible and did not "sanitize" the story. It is also my intention to present the letters accurately and to preserve the integrity of the writers. In publishing this book, I have insisted on keeping the letters intact. The writers do not need to be censored once again. However, to guide the reader, I provide contextual information, clarify family relations, and define some Russian terms and ethnic expressions. Most spellings of geographical locations follow the Germanic-Mennonite conventions used by the letter writers. In some cases, Library of Congress spellings (in non-Cyrillic alphabet) are used to represent Russian words used by the writers. Ellipses generally indicate either words that are missing in the original letter or handwriting that is impossible to decipher.

## Overview

This volume begins with an introduction to the Mennonite people. It describes their journey from parts of Europe in the sixteenth century to Russia in the eighteenth century. It also narrates the odyssey of Mennonites from a golden age of relative peace and prosperity to the dark prisons of the Gulag in the twentieth century.

Chapter One includes the early letters of Jasch and Maria Regehr and their six children, recounting their arrest in 1930, imprisonment, and exile. Chapter Two presents the letters written from various prison camps to which the Regehr family was transported (1932-33). Chapter Three contains letters written in the following year (1933-34) which reflect a loss of hope after several deaths in the family. The number of letters drops dramatically after 1934; those in Chapter Four reveal the increasing vulnerability of the remaining family members. The letters stop in 1937. Decades of silence follow.

Then, after more than fifty years, two surviving sisters, Lena and Mariechen, “fill in the blanks.” Their letters are included in Chapter Five. Renewal is evident in this chapter, which recounts a meeting with Lena in 2005 in Cologne, Germany. The only remaining survivor of the Regehr family – the little girl who wrote a letter from her cramped space in a prison barrack, the woman who embodies the pain of an oppressed people – now radiates with hope for her daughter and two granddaughters. The Epilogue invites readers to respond to Jasch and Maria's plea: "Remember us."

# Acknowledgments

Without my sister Lois Derksen Hall, who handed me a privately published book of letters in a coffee shop in 1999, I might never have known about the letters translated by Peter and Anne Bargen. I thank her, and I thank Peter Bargen, who met and corresponded with me many times before his death in 2004. Neil and Elsie Bargen of Edmonton, Alberta also provided valuable information and support.

I also thank the three letter writers in the corpus, all first cousins, who survived their Soviet experiences: Lena Regehr Dirksen (Cologne, Germany), John Regehr (Kelowna, British Columbia), and Maria Bargen Mantler (Winnipeg, Manitoba). This is their story. Interviews with them and with other survivors have been essential in shaping my perspective.

I have also corresponded with Anne Applebaum, Dr. Terry Martin, Dr. Lewis Siegelbaum, and other distinguished scholars who have expanded my understanding of the Gulag. Dr. Tatiana Teslenko of the University of British Columbia provided vital assistance with the translation and contextual framework of Russian terms.

Thanks is also extended to the Bakhtin Centre in the Russian Slavonic Studies Centre at the University of Sheffield, where I conducted research on the letters in fulfillment of my PhD.

Alf Redekop and staff at the Mennonite Heritage Centre in Winnipeg, and the staff at the Mennonite Historical Society in Abbotsford, British Columbia have also provided valuable support. Thank you.

# GLOSSARY

*Artel:* a centrally-controlled cooperative (*Kolkhoz*) that embraced the socialist collective economy and involved fishing, mining, and logging enterprises

*Cydomeins, Cyodomnm, Cyddomen, Cydomnmer*: Russian terms used to describe the place of additional work (noun), or the act of performing additional work (verb). In addition to their regular tasks, exiled workers were expected to provide "free" or "added" work as a gift to the Motherland.

"Degrees of frost": an expression used by the letter writers to indicate temperatures below freezing.

*Dessiatine*: a measurement of land. One dessiatine is 2.65 acres.

*Geschwister:* a German term meaning brothers and sisters but often used to address extended family members and friends. Used as the salutation in most letters.

GPU: a local branch of the political police force in the USSR, *Gosudarstvennoye Politicheskoye Upravlenie*. The larger Soviet police force was the OGPU, active from 1922 to 1934. Initially known as the *Cheka* during the era of the Civil War, this police force was responsible for state security, arrests of dissidents, and administration of the Gulag system. In 1934, the organization evolved to become the NKVD (*Narodny Komissariat Vnutrennikh Del*), and finally the more well-known KGB (*Komitet Gosudarstvennoy Bezopasnosti*). Fear of the GPU is evident in the words of the writers. In masked language they refer to "the three letters" (*die drei Buchstaben*) who are responsible for the arrest and torture of prisoners.

Gulag: an acronym for *Glavnoe Upravlenie Lagerei*, literally "Main Camp Administration," commonly known as the state administered system of forced labour camps in the Soviet Union (1930-55).

*Kolkhoz, Kolchos:* a collective farm or industry.

*Komsomol:* a Communist youth organization whose members were often recruited to guard prisoners and assist in camp management.

*Kulak:* originally defined as "a prosperous peasant," the term took on the connotation of "enemy of the people" during the Bolshevik Revolution. In the 1930s, *kulak* was broadened to include anyone ideologically resisting Soviet policies and authority.

NKVD: See GPU above.

Numbered Villages: Russian Mennonite villages were assigned numbers as well as names. For example, Peter Bargen was born in Tiege, No. 8. Letter writers often refer to village numbers, such as "The teacher in N.7 can do a lot." The map of Mennonite villages in Appendix A includes both names and numbers of villages.

*Plawen:* a Russian term meaning marshy and unstable delta lands near rivers or seas.

*Pripps:* a German term used to describe a drink made from roasted wheat; a coffee substitute.

*Pud*: a measurement of weight; approximately 36 pounds or 16 kilograms.

*Ruble*: the chief monetary unit of Russia and several former republics of the USSR. It was also the currency of the former Russian Empire prior to its dispersion. The ruble is subdivided into 100 *kopeks*. A letter writer reports that the family bought "porridge, rice and oil for 1r. [*ruble*] 75k. [*kopeks*], one *pud* flour for 1r. 32k., oil for 50k., rice for 26k., porridge for 26k., and fish for 10k." It is almost impossible to provide equivalencies for the ruble or kopek during the 1930s. The cost of living was extremely unstable, since many products were simply not available. In such cases, the ruble had minimal buying power.

SHIZO: an acronym for *shtrafnoi izolyator,* which were punishment cells in a prison camp constructed to hold prisoners accused of serious crimes.

*Torgsin*: an acronym for "Trade with Foreigners." State-controlled *Torgsin* stores were set up in heavily populated areas. Before prisoners were given a parcel, the contents were searched for contraband items and a *Cnpulsa* (certificate) was granted.

*Trudodnie*: points earned for work, which could be redeemed for supplies at the *Torgsin* store.

*Werst*: a measurement of distance; approximately four-fifths of a mile.

*Zek*: a prisoner.

# Introduction

## From a Golden Age to the Gulag

Little Lena is on her knees, leaning over a crude wooden trunk. Her hair falls over her eyes, the ribbons too torn to hold the blonde strands. She tries to focus. Noise distracts her, and her baby brother bumps her elbow. The pencil is dull and the thin paper tears easily.

"Dear Aunt Liese ... " Two men below her are fighting, and her father is coughing. "I really do not like writing letters. Our Papa is so sick he can no longer get up. If our dear Papa should die, what will become of us?"

What is happening? Where is this little girl? Why is she in this noisy, crowded place, writing on a wooden trunk? Why is her father so sick? Where is the doctor? Where is Aunt Liese?

### Transport

In the former Soviet Union, during Joseph Stalin's first wave of arrests in 1930, children, women, and men were crammed into cattle cars for the long journey to remote northern regions of the Soviet empire. The first prisoners were dropped into the frozen wasteland and given picks, shovels, and lumber to construct their barracks. Death was their companion. As prisoners died, trains deposited new workers. For little Lena, her parents, siblings, and young uncle Abram, prison camp shattered communal customs and religious practices observed in Russia for more than one hundred and forty years. Jasch and Maria (Goosen) Regehr with their six children had become part of the Gulag: a chaotic, complex system of forced labour camps and prisons that held millions of "criminals" captive.

Lena's barrack is a three-storey wooden building around an open space. Every day she and her family stand outside for the daily census of prisoners. She is guilty without trial. But for what crime has she been arrested, and what justifies this prison sentence? One historian reports that arrests were made for "reading forbidden philosophical, political, or religious books, posting up notices, putting up a flag, demanding religious instruction for children, or undertaking a private commercial initiative" (Shifrin, 4). How could little Lena have been capable of such crimes?

The Gulag system included children's camps, women's camps, psychiatric prisons, and political prisons. It stretched across the vast northern regions of the former Soviet Union, from Finland in the west to the Bering Sea in the east; an area one-and-a-half times the width of Canada. Two thousand prison camps were active during Stalin's regime (1929 to 1953).[1] The largest camp held one million prisoners; life expectancy was one winter. Specific ethnic groups[2], dissident intellectuals, members of political factions, and "criminals"– including children – were incarcerated. For the Russian people, places like Karganda, Archangelsk, Tarabunka, Magadan, Vorkuta, Kolyma, and Kolschim evoked an icy fear. For the writers of the letters and their recipients, Lunowka, Aynebka, and Polowinka were synonyms of horror.

However, for Stalin and his state officials, the Gulag "settlements" industrialized the northern regions of the expanding Soviet Union. Free labour provided by prisoners was intended to usher in a new world order. Although some workers were employed by the state, the burden of industrialization was the yoke of millions of prisoners transported from their homes. Prisoners such as the Regehr family executed Stalin's Five-Year Plan for agriculture, mining, forestry, and fishing. They constructed rail lines, dams, bridges, and hydroelectric power plants. Lena, her sisters, and her brothers were expected to contribute to the leader's ambitious plan. Lena's childhood in the peaceful Mennonite village of Altonau had been destroyed.

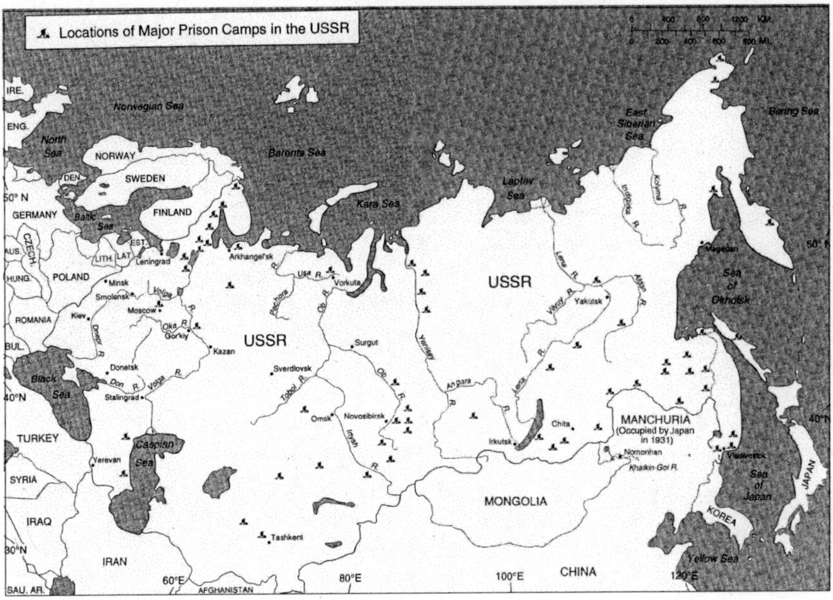


*Location of Major Prison Camps in the Former USSR in 1939 (Thurston 64).*
*For enlarged map see Appendix C.*

## Tranquility to Terror

How did this Mennonite family happen to call Russia "home" in the first place? Why did they settle in the plains of the southern Russian steppes? They were neither Russian nor German, yet they spoke Russian and German. The narrative of the family begins during the Protestant Reformation in sixteenth-century Europe. Since the Reformation, the saga of the Mennonites has been one of disruption and migration. They were Anabaptists, a religious community defined by the rejection of infant baptism and by the re-baptising of adults who committed themselves to a new life of faith. Communities were first established in Zurich, Switzerland in the 1520s and then spread to present-day Belgium, the Netherlands, and northern Germany. From these regions, many individuals and family groups fled from their homelands and state-controlled religions to begin a community that sought to live by its religious convictions.

Central to the faith and practice of the Anabaptists was a belief in the voluntary baptism of adults; a pacifist, nonviolent worldview; rejection of the oath; and resistance to hierarchical structures to which they had been subjected within the Roman Catholic tradition.[2] Anabaptists were a threat to church and state authorities who were intolerant of religious diversity. Many were arrested and became martyrs for their faith. Those who did not conform to state religious practices (Catholic or Protestant) were imprisoned, burned at the stake, or drowned. Persecution and prejudice resulted in migration. Resettlement strengthened the Mennonites' singularity, and they saw themselves as a people separated from "the world" and its influences. Successive generations continued to generally live apart from the surrounding societies. Sharing a loyalty to the teachings of Menno Simons (1496-1561), a young Catholic priest from the Netherlands, members of this separatist sect became known as "Mennists" or "Mennonites."[3]

Thus, a distinctive leader, a shared culture, a unique language, and a specific belief system created a fusion that unified Mennonites in an ethnic identity. It has been argued that Mennonites are not an ethnic group, but are of Swiss, Dutch, or German nationality. However, long-held misconceptions have recently been challenged, and persuasive evidence supports the concept of a distinct Mennonite ethnic identity.[4] Mennonite people have shared a common and unique culture, religion, tradition, and language for more than four hundred years. Wherever they settled, they lived as a minority within a larger society. Until the mid-twentieth century, Mennonites did not easily assimilate into the societies surrounding them.

Although a passive and private people, Mennonites continued to pose a threat to authorities. Many fled to Prussia (presently Poland) in the sixteenth century to escape imprisonment and live within their religious creed. The tolerance of the Prussian monarch attracted them to the Vistula River region and the City of Danzig.[5] On these lands, they drained the marshes, farmed the land, and built churches and schools. Here they experienced religious freedom and economic opportunities long denied them. From the Netherlands, Switzerland, and Moravia, followers of Menno Simons found a refuge and homeland in the Vistula delta.[6]

It was in this Prussian location that a Mennonite identity was more distinctly formed. Not only were their liturgy, farming practices, housing, manner of dress, and culinary customs unique, their language also reflected their exclusiveness. Initially, Dutch was the language most commonly used, particularly in church services. However, Low German, or Plautdietsch,[7] was the oral language of the people, and a unique (often humorous and irreverent) colloquialism developed in their storytelling tradition and folklore. High German, because of its use in judicial, political, and educational spheres in Prussia, soon became the more formal and liturgical language.[8]

But the Mennonites' distinct practices and resistance to military participation posed a threat once more. In the late 1780s, at the invitation of Catherine the Great, many Mennonites left their homes in Prussia and other parts of Europe to establish communities on the fertile Russian grasslands. For over 140 years, they built homes, schools, hospitals, factories, and industries – and enjoyed what can be fairly called a "golden age" in their history as a people.

But the exclusiveness of many Mennonite communities, their perceived prosperity, and their religious practices would attract the attention of Marxist revolutionaries. From 1917 to 1921, their homes were invaded, and hundreds were murdered during the Bolshevik Revolution and the Russian Civil War. Access to food was limited, and famine (exacerbated by government policies in 1921) further weakened these emaciated people. Just as many families were preparing to leave the region, Lenin's New Economic Policy revived their hope.[9] The move from War Communism to new legislation restored some previous rights, primarily the right to own private property and the recognition of national territories in a multi-ethnic State.[10] However, these rights were only a temporary measure.

Many Mennonites sensed the fickle and uncertain nature of Russian policy. Approximately twenty-thousand were able to leave

*Map of Former Mennonite Colonies and Villages (Schroeder and Huebert 14).*
*For enlarged map see Appendix C.*

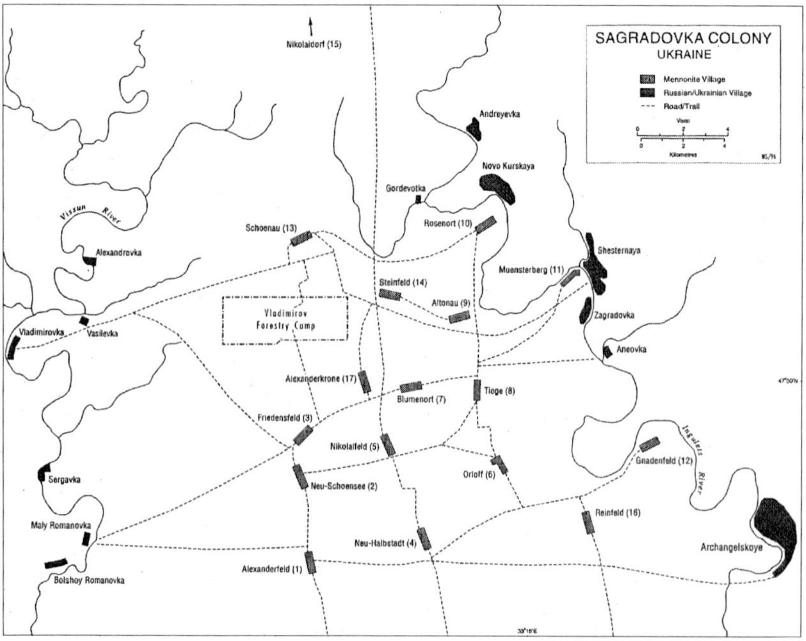


*Map of the Former Mennonite Colony of Sagradowka (Schroeder and Huebert 46).*
*For enlarged map see Appendix C.*

Russia and Ukraine for Canada in the mid-1920s. Following Lenin's death in 1924, Stalin's reclassification of citizens (beginning in 1928) marshaled in a new wave of fear as remaining Mennonites, unable to escape to Canada, were reclassified as *kulaks* or "enemies of the people." A toxic climate of discrimination and betrayal drove many Mennonites to abandon their homeland and flee for their lives. The last trains rolled out of Moscow, passed through the Red Gate, and entered into the free West through Latvia in December 1929.

One of those trains carried Lena Regehr's cousin Peter Bargen and his family: sister Lieschen (Betty), brother Frank, sister Meka (Mary) and parents (Franz and Liese). By a margin of a few hours, the Bargen family escaped Stalin's snare.

Lena, her parents, siblings, and frail grandparents delayed their flight for twelve hours – too late to flee the ravages of Soviet Communism. They were stopped at the railway station. The borders had closed.

*Passport photo of Bargen family taken just before their departure from Moscow in 1929 (Bargen 11). From left to right: Meka (Mary) Bargen Kroeker, age 4; Mother Liese Regehr Bargen, age 33; Peter Bargen, age 7; Lieschen (Betty) Bargen Gerish, age 10; Frank Bargen, age 12; and Father Franz Bargen, 35.*

## Box Cars and Barracks

One year later, on October 30, 1930, the Regehr family was arrested. Lena's father Jasch and her mother Maria, her young uncle Abram, and her five siblings had their rights as citizens removed and their possessions confiscated. Her father was arrested without trial, and the entire family was evicted from their home in Altonau, Sagradowka (near the Black Sea in present-day Ukraine). After wandering from place to place for seven months – it was illegal to house *kulaks* – the entire family was arrested, packed into railway cattle cars with hundreds of other prisoners, and transported into the northern Ural Mountains in June 1931.

This family became part of a massive wave of arrests during the first of Stalin's purges in the 1930s. The Gulag was not a simple system. In a multi-tiered and poorly administered scheme, prisoners with lighter sentences worked in industrial settlements (*spetsposeleniia*) while prisoners with longer sentences were ordered to harsher, multiple-industry camps. "Punishment blocks" or shizo (*shtrafnoi izolyator*) were for prisoners accused of serious crimes (Applebaum 218; 224ff). All members of the Regehr family, children and adults, were sentenced to all three levels of incarceration throughout their long exile. Wherever prisoners were held, the circumstances of confinement were similar. Captives worked without pay, were restricted to a *zona* marked by a fence, and were guarded by dogs (Applebaum, 186). Prisoners could travel only with a permit, and they had to report regularly to the "Kommandant."

In some respects, references in the letters make some camps appear ordinary – almost "normal." The larger camps contain administrative centres, stations for supplies, a *Torgsin* store for approved items, a post office, a medical centre with a doctor, and a "suburb" of barracks. But there is another aspect that was far more unpleasant. Behind the façade of normality, Lena and her sisters scavenge for potato peelings in the garbage heap behind the officers' quarters. Prison guards read Lena's letter, and check every word, every name and address. Letters can be mailed only inside the Soviet Union. Wherever Lena walks, she is watched by guards with dogs. She and her family cannot leave the *zona* without a permit. The doctor – if he agrees to see her – does not practice the Hippocratic Oath.

Under the ruthless direction of the NKVD, arrests and imprisonment became a colossal exercise in the 1930s. Aleksandr Solzhenitsyn names this mass migration of *kulaks* "The Prison Industry" and reports that millions were driven to their deaths in uninhabited northern territories (24).[11] Although the number of deaths during Stalin's reign is not explainable by simple addition or subtraction, and scholars warn that estimating the number remains a matter of skilled guesswork, we err on the side of folly by not examining the numbers. We are warned that "no death figures compiled by Gulag authorities can ever be considered completely reliable," since "individual camp commanders had a vested interest in lying about how many prisoners had died" (Applebaum, 583).

Robert Conquest estimates that in the purge of 1937 to 1938 alone, seven million people were arrested (1968, 485). One of the first camps established in 1921 in the Archangelsk area contained 30,000 prisoners. The barracks were built by the first ones who arrived by train in the frozen wasteland. Other camps operated at Kotlas, Murmansk, Vologda, Karaganda, Taymyr, Novaya Zemlya, and Magadan in the Kolyma basin – almost as large in area as all of Ukraine (454-80). In camps around the White Sea, "the average lifetime between 1929 and 1934 did not exceed one or two years" (454). The camp in the Vorkuta coal-mine district in the basin of the Pechora River, the largest single concentration of forced labour in Russia, registered more than a million prisoners (480). Conquest places the number of Gulag prisoners in 1938 at eight million (1990, 485-86).

In attempting to assess the victims, Antonov Ovseenko estimates that in 1938 the camp population was sixteen million (212). Another recent publication estimates that in the Gulag alone, twenty million people were victims of Stalin's penal empire (Pohl, 5). However, the most distressing figure in D.M. Thomas' biography of Solzhenitsyn (see Appendix A), is an estimate of sixty million deaths. Another estimate is that "at least 45 million died during the duration of Stalin's reign" (442-43). The numbers are overwhelming and the chaos in the former USSR makes assessment difficult. It was a time of horror regardless of the method used to tally the victims.

Astonishingly, Lena Regehr and several of her siblings survived. Years later in Cologne, away from the censors' gaze, Lena describes her family's imprisonment:

> Then they brought train box cars along side and we were all ordered into them. The cars were then locked and the train headed for the Urals. We drove for 9 days and it was intolerable. . . . When we arrived at our destination in the Urals we were ordered to get out. There were many people there already. There were very large barracks there. The village was called *Lunowka*. It was rumored that in the days of the Czars, prisoners were kept here. There were 2 or 3 storey barracks. We, Papa and Mama, Uncle Abram and 6 children got one corner 5 feet long and the same width.[12]

The cramped space in the barracks became their home – the handmade wooden travel trunk their only possession. Within a few days, Lena's older brother Peter and sister Liese were sent 70 miles away to a timber camp near Ustupil. Here they waded through miles of muskeg and snow to cut timber in the frozen forest. At first living in snow caves, they built huts which became their home for many months. Lena remembers that "[we] younger children stayed with our parents in the Lunowka barracks." This was the exception. Most children arrested with their mothers could remain only until they were weaned in their first year, "at which point they had to put them in orphanages" (Applebaum, 317). Little Lena knew that her time with her parents was at risk. She saw other children being separated from their parents. She also knew that she had to be very careful: she did not talk to others, she did not make eye contact, and she did not walk alone. Writing to her Aunt Liese in Canada, Lena knew that her words would be seen by many eyes, some of them sinister.

Mailing letters to locations inside the Soviet Union was permitted, but mailing letters directly to Canada was not. Documents of the NKVD declared that state officials across the Soviet Union had the authority to arrest or execute, without trial, any person who had "contacts abroad." Addresses, letters, or even casual conversations with neighbours about contacts in forbidden regions in Europe and North America were perceived as criminal (Conquest 1990, 257-58).[13]

Gulag survivors are often incredulous that so many letters from a prison camp in the Urals reached their destination in Carlyle, Saskatchewan, a small prairie town in Canada. Peter Plett remembers a knock on the door that came after midnight one day in 1936 in his Mennonite village not far from Altonau.[14] The NKVD entered and searched the house. On the top level of open shelves, hidden between books, they found a letter sent from Yarrow, British Columbia. The father was abruptly arrested and taken to prison in nearby Kherson. He died from disease and malnutrition three years later.

Lena's parents were careful. They rarely sent letters directly to Canada. Most letters travelled to Lena's grandparents (Kornelius and Liese Regehr) in Altonau, her former home village. From this place, with no stamps, often no envelopes, and only a sparse address, the letters somehow found a safe corridor to the forbidden West.

Now we have little nine-year-old Lena's letter. We can even hold the fragile paper in our hands. We can see her large, carefully-crafted child's printing in pencil. We can also see a letter from her twelve-year-old sister Tina, from her older siblings, from her parents, and from friends. Despite the risks and volatile journey, these scraps of paper reached the home of Lena's Aunt Liese and Uncle Franz Bargen in a tiny town in Saskatchewan.

## A Campbell's Soup Box

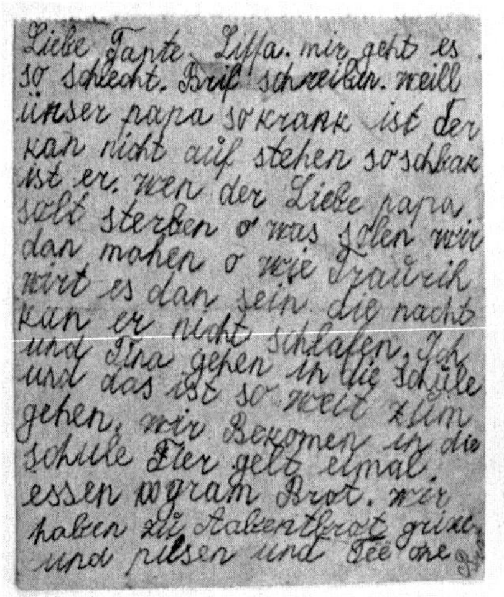
Liebe Tante Liffa. mir geht es
so schlecht. Brif schreiben. weill
unser papa so krank ist der
kan nicht auf stehen so schwach
ist er. wen der Liebe papa
solt sterben o was solen wir
dan mahen o wie traurih
wirt es dan sein die nacht
kan er nicht schlafen, Ich
und Tina gehen in die schule
und das ist so weit zum
gehen, wir bekomen in die
schule Tee gelt einmal.
essen wgram Brot. wir
haben zu abentbrot grize
und pilsen und Tee ohne

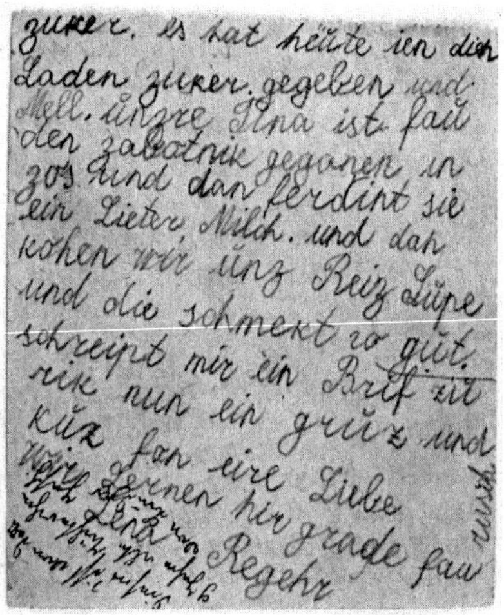
zuker. es hat heute ein dieh
Laden zuker. gegeben und
Mell. unzre Tina ist faw
den zabotnik gegangen in
203 und dan ferdint sie
ein Liter, Milch. und dan
kohen wir unz Reiz Supe
und die schmekt so gut.
schreipt mir ein Brif zu
rük nun ein grüz und
Kuz fon eure Liebe
wir lernen hir grade faw
Lena Regehr

The flimsy cardboard box that once contained soup cans captivated Peter and Anne Bargen. For three years, they worked at their kitchen table, reading, translating, and crying at the fate of their family. They were uniquely qualified for the translation task, since both could read the German Gothic script and both were of Russian Mennonite descent. But their work was complicated by the faded ink and the torn paper, the illegible writing and smudging, and the strange spellings, numerous abbreviations, and unfamiliar Russian expressions. Often the date and writer could be identified only from the context. Many messages were also masked. The writers knew the risks of making contact with the West: extended prison terms or execution. Many readers, some friendly and some hostile, would read these words. Prison guards, censors, and informers were numerous, but sympathetic readers could pass the letters along and try to find a secure passage for them out of the USSR. One writer says she is writing "through the flowers as if two are present." She is masking her message to avoid the censor's eye; she knows her intended reader in Canada will correctly interpret the message among the flowery words.

Although Peter and Anne did not always understand the writers' words, they continued their massive task of translating so that "this drama could be preserved for you, our children and grandchildren, as well as for others." In his preface to the translation, Peter explains their motivation:

> We have tried to be faithful to the substance of the letters, and to reflect as accurately as possible the nuances as well as the emotional tenor of the words. [...] What a disturbing yet inspiring experience it has been! The letters are heart wrenching, and we are persistently struck by the extreme tragedy that overwhelmed our people. Even 60 years later it is unsettling to read their first-hand accounts. We have again and again affirmed our determination that this rich and brave yet terrible history of our immediate ancestors be made available to our children and grandchildren – to Catharine and David, to Shawna and Nicole, to Benjamin and Michael. If such compilations as these are not undertaken, the knowledge could be lost. Unless something has been written, only fragments would be remembered and our past would become a misty dream shot through by only a few rays of light. Some of our own recollections of childhood in Russia have been altered and enriched by these letters. We have gained an increased appreciation of who our ancestors were and what sustained them during times of affliction. We marvel anew at how personal faith, shorn of all earthly hope, can still stand triumphant amidst the wreckage of the material world.

## Through the Red Gate

Peter Bargen remembers the last day in their home in the villiage of Tiege. He was seven years old. It was November 7, 1929, and the family was just sitting down to an early evening meal. Their home was a modest yet comfortable place. Father Franz burst through the door and exclaimed, "We have to go! We have to go now! They have a warrant for my arrest." A friend, the secretary of the local Soviet authority, had issued the warning. He managed to delay processing the arrest warrant as long as possible to give Franz a chance to escape. Food stayed on the table, the dog remained on its chain, and the family fled for their lives.

The news, though frightening, was not unexpected. Franz Bargen and his family were property owners. They had occasionally hired extra help to assist them. And they were Mennonites, a suspect ethno-religious group that was resistant to Soviet Marxist ideology and collectivization. Like other Mennonite officials in the region, Franz was removed from his post as village mayor by the new Bolshevik regime. The previous election was declared illegal. He was re-classified as a *kulak*. Franz states in his memoirs that "From that day forward I knew that my days of freedom were numbered. My great concern now was how I could flee with my family and leave Russia forever." After his removal as mayor, Franz had surreptitiously sold enough of the family's property to finance their passage to Moscow and, hopefully, out of the country.

Within two hours of the family's dinner, NKVD officials arrived to arrest Bargen. They found the horses in the barn, the dog on its chain, and food on the table. Thinking the family had briefly stepped out, the police questioned neighbours, grandparents, and relatives but received no information. The officials decided to return the next morning to make their arrest. They were too late. The night before, Franz and Liese and their four children had fled across the fields, their horses and *droschka* [wagon] bouncing across the ruts. They stopped briefly to say good-bye to their elderly parents (Kornelius and Liese Regehr) and to share a meal.[15] In the cover of darkness and undetected by neighbours, they slipped away to a distant train station. By the time the authorities had solved the puzzle, Franz and Liese and their young family were on their way to Moscow.

However, their terrifying journey was far from over. In Moscow they joined an enormous throng of twenty thousand refugees clamouring to leave Russia. For one month they hid in a shantytown shack owned by a Jewish tailor. One side housed the Bargen family, the other side a prostitute. When Soviet authorities arrived to arrest Franz Bargen, this "fallen" woman distracted them and saved their lives.

Of the thousands of desperate people who gathered in Moscow in 1929, only about five thousand escaped. Those left behind suffered various fates: some were arrested and sent into the northern prisons in Stalin's Gulag; some were executed; others were sent back to their home villages, only to be dispossessed of all their belongings and citizenship. Peter Bargen, with his sisters, brother, and parents, was among the few who narrowly escaped. After many official inspections and delays, the train crept forward, moving west. Many trains reversed their movement and traveled east. Many of the passengers were arrested and sent into the prison camps of the Gulag.

The Bargen family did not know their fate until their train passed through the Red Gate into Latvia. A Red Cross nurse opened the door and announced: "Ladies and Gentlemen, welcome to Latvia!" The entire train load of exhausted travelers burst spontaneously into song – a hymn of jubilation. They tumbled out, kissing the ground with elation. Christmas 1929 was celebrated in a refugee camp in Prenzlau, Germany. On February 23, 1930, the Bargen family was safe in Canada, with promises of work as hired help on a farm in Carlyle, Saskatchewan.

But their parents, brothers and sisters, extended family members, and friends were not free. Some were allowed to remain in their villages and work on collective farms established by the Soviet regime. But some, like little Lena Regehr and her family, were sent into the Gulag network of forced labour camps in the remote northern regions of Siberia. Most prisoners did not survive. Yet their voices live on. The letters written on the crude wooden travel trunk in the five-foot-square barrack space recount the Regehr family's experiences. All 463 letters stored in the Campbell's Soup box in an attic in Canada tell the story of those left behind.

## A Tenuous Lifeline

Although it is difficult to comprehend, a subversive network of mail delivery must have been in place at some point in the letters' journey. Otherwise how could Lena's letter travel overseas? Gulag survivors recall the risks of sending letters outside the USSR's borders. Whether they stayed in their home village or not, fear resided in every word they wrote. Ida Kempler[16] remembers the house searches in her village in Sagradowka. State officials searched dresser drawers, closets, and cupboards looking for addresses or letters from outside the Soviet Union. Ida knew that finding one meant prison or death. In another case, a woman grieved the separation from her parents and siblings who had left for Europe in 1914. Walter Loewen[17] recalls his mother's longing to connect with her family. But for fear of the consequences, she did not write letters or communicate with them for twenty-five years. Her anxiety was not unfounded.

*The Red Gate between the former USSR and Latvia (Bargen corpus).*

A Canadian whose father was arrested in his home in Russia substantiates the risk of possessing foreign correspondence or any visible evidence of contact with the West. Walter Wiebe[18] was ten years old when his father was arrested.

> On December 17, 1937, several armed police officers came to our door. They knocked. Why they didn't simply break down the door is a mystery. They always knocked. All the men in our village of Chortiza were waiting for the knock. They always came at night. When they searched our house, they found several letters from Canada in a dresser drawer. They had been written in the late 1920s and the 1930s. My mother always kept those letters in this place. All the letters had foreign addresses and stamps. This was the reason they used to arrest our father. We watched him go and never saw him again. We never found out what happened to him.

Not only did the writers risk discovery of foreign letters, but writing materials were almost impossible to find. Letters in the Bargen corpus are written on accountants' ledger paper, cigarette paper, Soviet postcards, scraps of newsprint, or old shipping orders.[19] Some pieces of paper are marked with previously printed official markers, addresses, and instructions for another recipient. Among the most ironic letters are those written on red Soviet propaganda postcards. One postcard depicts a group of liberated Soviet women happily working with heavy road construction equipment. On the reverse side, Lena's mother Maria writes in splatters of grief: "Will we ever be free?" She and her children will die if food does not arrive soon. The red postcard is her lifeline. Prisoners often had to choose whether to eat their rations of bread or to exchange them for paper, pencil, or ink. Writers also begged their readers for paper, pens, and stamps. Most letters arrived at the Bargens' house in Canada marked "postage due."

Adding to their precarious journey, many letters have no specific salutation, no complimentary close identifying the sender, and no return address. We can only speculate on their route. Gulag survivors recall that many letters were passed from person to person. Aleksandr Solzhenitsyn describes notes being dropped through the cracks of moving box cars as prisoners were transported. When found, the notes could be submitted to the state police for a reward or passed along, hidden in the soles of shoes or the seams of a shirt, in hope they would reach the intended families.[20] Variations among levels of bureaucracy and prison camp officials sometimes resulted in letters slipping through the system. Some guards were delinquent or lazy in their censorship, and some Kommandants were more sympathetic and generous with their supervision of the mail. Rigorous censorship could be enforced in some regions, while other districts enjoyed more freedom. It is not surprising that maintaining a consistent standard across a vast, expanding nation was almost impossible, particularly in the early stages of a new political regime. A letter from the NKVD in 1939 provides a possible explanation for the safe passage of some of the Regehr family letters:

> There have been cases of prisoners sending letters and various statements to their families [...]. Such slanderous letters are used for anti-Soviet purposes and to spread provocative rumours about the methods of investigation and conditions in the camps. Such letters make it outside, avoiding censorship, via unescorted prisoners and free camp workers. Please take measures to prevent the sending of letters without the knowledge of the camp censors. (Khlevniuk, 329)

Lena's mother was acutely aware of the risks of writing and receiving mail. In the family's first year of exile (1931), Maria confirms that "I received all the clippings you sent in the last letter" but warns that "There was no danger until now." Despite her warning, the letters continue to travel and find a safe place in a Canadian attic. Somehow, a network of mail delivery was functioning. Letters were sent and received, and parcels with bits of food, scraps of paper and, occasionally, money arrived in the Regehr's prison camp. Written with cautiously masked messages, these letters formed a tenuous lifeline of material, moral, and spiritual support.

But was the trickle of aid from overseas enough? How long could the fragile link be sustained?

## Notes

1 According to Robert Conquest in *The Great Terror: Stalin's Purge of the Thirties* (1968), one of the first camps established in 1921 was in the Archangelsk area. One camp in this area contained 30,000 prisoners, and was built by the first prisoners who arrived by train and were deposited in the wasteland to build their own barracks. Other camps operated at Kotlas, Murmansk, Vologda, Karaganda, Taymyr, Novaya Zemlya, Magadan in the Kolyma basin – almost as large in area as all of Ukraine (Conquest 1968, 454-80). Conquest notes that in the camps around the White Sea "the average lifetime between 1929 and 1934 did not exceed one or two years" (454). The camp in the Vorkuta coal-mine district in the basin of the Pechora River was the largest single concentration of forced labour in Russia. This camp registered a population of more than a million prisoners (480). Although many names of camps no longer appear on maps, letters published in Mennonite periodicals (*Mennonitische Rundschau* and *Der Bote*) identify camps such as Ivdel, Novaya Lyalya, Nizhnii Tagil, Severouralsk, Krasnoturinsk, Berezniki, Prokopievsk, and Novokuznetsketc.

2 James Urry, *None but Saints: The Transformation of Mennonite Life in Russia, 1789-1889* (1989),34-40.

3 Henry Smith, *The Story of the Mennonites* (1957), 85-113.

4 A persuasive argument that Mennonites are an ethnic group is provided by John Redekop, *A People Apart: Ethnicity and the Mennonite Brethren* (1987). Among his thirteen references, the most convincing is the detailed definition found in the *Harvard Encyclopedia of American Ethnic Groups*, S. Thernstrom (ed.), 1980. Not understanding the distinction, historians have often included the Mennonite experience within that of the German colonists of the Soviet Union. This perspective (although historically useful in some aspects) is evident in the title and content of Fleischhauer and Pinkus's *The Soviet Germans: Past and Present* (1986). For further discussions of ethnicity, see Fredrik Barth's *Ethnic Groups and Boundaries* (1969), and G.C. Bentley's "Ethnicity and Practice" (1987).

5 The overview of sixteenth-century settlement patterns of the Mennonites is a compilation of information from several sources: James Urry (1989), John B. Toews (1982), Henry Smith (1957), P.M. Friesen (1978), and the *Mennonite Encyclopedia*.

6 L. Klippenstein in, "The Mennonite Migration to Russia 1786-1806," observes that the first Mennonite settlers in the Vistula Delta in the sixteenth century were particularly valued by the aristocracy because of their ability to drain the swamps in the northern lowlands of Prussia (13).

7 Low German is a language shared with the Anglos, Saxons, and Jutes who settled in Britain before the Norman Conquest in 1066. Resonances of this language are evident in the East Midland dialect of the Middle English used by Chaucer. The language more closely resembles Middle English than German (Smith, 751-52).

8 Smith, 752.

9 In March 1921, Lenin proposed a New Economic Policy (NEP) to the Tenth Party Congress. The NEP was designed to stimulate economic recovery. Although it was often described as a "retreat to capitalism," Lenin was convinced that "changes were needed to restore the economy of Russia before a forward movement toward socialism could be contemplated" (John M. Thompson, "Russia and the Soviet Union," 210).

10 See Terry Martin's *The Affirmative Action Empire: Nations and Nationalism in the Soviet Union, 1923-1939.*

11 Referring to a report by Merle Fainsod, Nicholas Riasanovsky in *A History of Russia* notes that "The arrests mounted into the millions; the testimony of the survivors is unanimous regarding crowded prison cells and teeming forced labor camps. Most of the prisoners were utterly bewildered by the fate which had befallen them. The vast resources of the NKVD were concentrated on one objective – to document the existence of a huge conspiracy to undermine Soviet power. The extraction of real confession to imaginary crimes became a major industry. Under the zealous and ruthless ministrations of NKVD examiners, millions of innocents were transformed into traitors, terrorists, and enemies of the people"(505).

12 Lena provided additional information about her years in prison camps in a post-war letter to Peter Bargen, and during an interview with Ruth Derksen Siemens in Cologne, Germany in October 2005.

13 In *The Great Terror: A Reassessment* (1990), Robert Conquest substantiates that the NKVD listed categories that identified "hostile elements" to the success of Party's mandate. Such a list gave local authorities the occasion to arrest "all remaining elements expected of not being reconciled to the regime" (257). The various headings were:

| | |
|---|---|
| AS | anti-Soviet element |
| TS | active member of the Church |
| S | member of a religious sect |
| P | rebel – anyone who in the past was in any way involved in Soviet uprisings |
| SI | anyone with contacts abroad |

The category of "contacts abroad" would have implicated anyone with a foreign address in their possession, or anyone corresponding with a recipient outside of the Soviet Union. As Conquest notes, these categories "automatically made those listed as natural suspects automatic victims when an NKVD branch was called upon to show its merits by mass arrests" (258).

14 Interview, 2007.

15 Maria Bargen Mantler recalls that last meal with her uncle, aunt and cousins. She remembers the fear, but she also recalls the food on the table and the seating arrangement (Interview, 2006).

16 Interview, 2002.

17 Interview, 2001.

18 Interview, 2003.

19 Many letters are also undated. If a date does appear it is often the day but not the year. Perhaps the writers were assuming the reader's knowledge. Or perhaps space was at such a premium that a date would be considered superfluous. For clarity in this publication, approximate dates are placed in square brackets at the beginning of each letter.

20 One of the more poignant accounts of the obstacles to mail delivery in the Gulag is recorded in the memoirs of Aleksandr Solzhenitsyn. During his imprisonment (1945-53) there was a mailbox in the yard, but pencils or paper were almost impossible to find. A fortunate prisoner might find a "makhorka [rough shag tobacco] wrapper" or a sugar packet wrapper, smooth the folds, find a pencil among the prisoners, and write "in an undecipherable scrawl" to let their family know of their whereabouts (Solzhenitsyn, *The Gulag Archipelago 1918-1956*, 549). But a prisoner in transit had to be much more ingenuous.

> [Y]ou might find someone with a piece of pencil lead half an inch long and a piece of crumpled paper. Making sure the convoy doesn't see you from the corridor ... you write to your family between lurches of the car, that you have suddenly been taken from where you were and [are] being taken somewhere else, and you might only be able to send a letter once a year from your new destination, so let them be prepared for this eventuality. You have to fold your letter into a triangle and carry it to the toilet in the hope of a lucky break ... you can quickly press down on the flush pedal and, using your body as a shield, throw the letter into the hole. It will get wet and soiled, but it might fall through and land between the rails. Or it might get through dry, and the draft beneath the car will catch and whirl it, and it will fall under the wheels or miss them and land on the downward slope of the embankment. Perhaps it will lie there until it rains, until it snows, until it disintegrates, but perhaps a human hand will pick it up. And if this person isn't a stickler for the Party line, he will make the address legible, he will straighten out the letters, or perhaps put it in an envelope, and perhaps the letter will even reach its destination. Sometimes such letters do arrive – postage due, half-blurred, washed out, crumpled, but carrying a clearly defined splash of grief (514-16).

# Chapter One

## What Will Become of Us? 1929 - 32

### Early Letters (1929-30)

With hardly enough time to settle in Canada, Franz and Liese Bargen soon begin receiving letters in their new homeland. With their four children (Frank, Lieschen, Peter, and Mary), they find work as hired help on a farm in Carlyle, Saskatchewan. The "Dirty Thirties" – with crop failures and dust storms – are imminent. Farm owners Charlie and Margaret Clark are generous, but they need workers. Time to rest and recuperate from a harrowing escape from Russia is not an option for the Bargen family. Rent is due, children are hungry, and winter clothes are needed. Yet the plight of family and friends left behind disturbs them deeply. Liese loves her older brother Jasch and his family.[1] She is heartsick about their plight. She sends money saved from her family's meagre earnings to help her aging parents and extended family in Russia.

Before their arrest Jasch and Maria are still fairly young (45 and 39). As long as they are in their home village of Altonau in southern Russia, they can work and plant their own crops. The oldest four children, Liese (18), Peter (16), Mariechen (14), and Tina (11) are also able to help. The youngest children, Lena (8) and Jascha (2), are oblivious to much of the hardship, but also more vulnerable.

As long as everyone remains healthy, the family can find enough food to stay alive. But it is never enough to satisfy their hunger and provide a balanced diet. In the summer of 1930, finding food is becoming an obsession. Sources of protein are particularly sparse. Catching mice and insects for food is not unusual. Dogs and cats no longer wander the streets. But the corn crop is ripe. Some of the Regehr children are "gleaning" – a hazardous venture forbidden by law. The Soviet authorities assume that if gleaning is allowed, harvesters will deliberately leave more grain and corn in the fields. The penalty for gleaning is harsh: a ten-year prison sentence or death.

*Jasch Regehr in 1916 as an officer in the Medical Corps during WW1.*

*Maria and some of the Regehr children in exile in 1934. Their clothing has been borrowed from a German family.*
*From left to right: Jascha (6 years old); Mariechen (17); Mother Maria (43); Tina (14) and Lena (12).*

*In this first letter purchasing food is inordinately expensive and the "spirit of our times" is overwhelming many villagers.*

[1930]

In Lepcon u Kpubou-Pox there are stores where you can buy anything for dollars, and quite cheaply too. In comparison everything is terribly expensive in Russian money. [...] now costs 10 to 12 rubles. Boots cost 100 to 150 rubles, and everything like that. I bought 4 geese and we are raising them for the meat. We have no pig to slaughter. Those four geese cost us 36 rubles. To be able to feed the geese my Marie and Nuta one day put on some boots and went gleaning, as the Russians used to do. They gleaned among the corn stalks and brought home a bit of corn. For bread we still have 63 Pud rye, 75 Pud millet and 25 Pud beans, some maize, and then the wheat which is now being threshed.

According to some letters it is going much better in Bouorga; it is said they also are allowed more rights. In the Urals the wife of Jakob Isaac, N. 2, is said to have died. Old Herbold, N. 5, Kronau, has also died. They always ask about you when I am there. They also send warm greetings. The spirit of our times is completely engulfing Sofie Siemens and her children – this is what I have been told. Old Unruh and his son-in-law, Becker, are now our neighbours. Well, now we have written to you of all the essential things. Please forgive my imperfections and write us long letters.

With hearty greetings, and with our signature,
Your Geschwister [*relatives*] and their children
Jakob and Marie

[*Written around the edges*] Mother is well, only she does not care for the meagre rations. She likes good nourishing food. We are all poor.

*In the same season, Mother Maria continues to crave for food, but she is now alone with her children. Jasch has been arrested and is imprisoned in the nearby town of Kherson. Maria can talk to him only through a distant window. She brings a basket of food. Jasch's haggard, gaunt appearance shocks and disturbs her. Yet she must carry on. The pressure is mounting on Maria to work with a road construction crew, but this would mean separation from her children. To her peril, she refuses.*

[1930]

Dearly beloved Geschwister Franz and Liese,
I want to send a small sign of love to you in that far away America. Oh, how I have missed you, dear Liese. Who would have thought that we would all be scattered abroad as we are? Papa always felt so privileged that he had his whole family together. And now you are in America, and Tina will probably go to Paraguay. They wrote they would probably leave May 12th for Paraguay. And who knows where our home will be.

The way things are here, our future looks very dark. They are now going about and giving contracts for grain and on all that has been seeded, Welch Korn, sunflower seeds, wheat, etc. They came here and wanted me to sign that I would also provide forced labour fixing the road. You just would not believe how the devil inspires them to find ways to torment us. We are here only as objects of derision and contempt. You have escaped so many horrid things since you left. My ways are not your ways, and my thoughts are not your thoughts, says our God. Read Lamentations 3:31 to the end of the chapter. In my present situation I have often found comfort there. But I want to be silent and not complain because the time will surely come when we will sing Psalm 126 from our hearts.

Dear Liese, you ask where Mr. Nikkel and H.F. are. They are still at home. No one bothers them because the old man has a foreigner as a wife. When they forced us out, the old man was also on the list. Then they had said they could stay and continue to work and they would report it to headquarters. Until today they have left her completely in peace. On May 3rd Nickolai Regehrs' little son Nicka was buried. He was 6 years old, their only son; he died of typhus.

They just refuse to be comforted. She now has a boil on her finger. Liese goes to milk at their place, morning and evening, and gets milk as payment.

Dear Liese, you write you are eating so well that even Gen. and Irg. will not have eaten so well. In comparison, we are eating as poorly as never before in our lives. If this goes on for long, we have no idea of how we will get by. If only my dear Jasch was home again and they would give us our freedom, then all things would work out. I drove down there to bring him some food. We were only allowed to speak to each other from a distance through his window. Actually, even that was not allowed, but I still went and asked the Molitz [*Police*] if I could talk to my husband. Then he asked what I wanted to talk to him about and I said, "About flour, I have none anymore."Then he said: "Absolutely not." I begged and pleaded, but he just would not allow it. Then I walked sadly to the wagon, got the basket with food, and went back and gave it to them. They searched through every single thing.

If you could see him you would be astonished. He is very pale and thin, unshaven and unkempt, long hair and beard. He looks like a stranger. Once he had seen a doctor who had written him a prescription for medicine and a powder. Two men with guns had escorted him. My heart just aches when I go visit him and have to go home. I cannot, dear Geschwister, even begin to tell you how I feel. It was a great comfort to me that P.B. had included a small page for us and wrote, "No hair will fall from our head without God's will." And if God has really allowed all the misery that we are going through, then surely the time will come when our prayers will be answered. I firmly believe that.

Yesterday we had a village assembly meeting. Many wanted Walter to write something so that Jasch would be set free. Others said it was useless because the GPU arrested him and sentenced him to 3 months in prison. Brother Pankratz was set free yesterday – he was released without a trial. The rumour is that all prisoners will be set free, as well as all those in exile. I do not know if that is true. There are so many rumours floating around one does not know what one can believe and what are lies. Warkentins are said to have written that they have been set free and are only waiting for their papers. We believe there may be some sort of change in the wind. The prisoners and exiles from Siberia have all returned. Only Wilhelm Dueckmann is not back yet. We are told that he is so weak he cannot walk alone anymore and they have admitted him to a hospital.

Dear Liese, you ask if the sewing kept us back. You know very well I did not delay very long, because our Liese was with you until Wednesday and we left on Sunday. On Thursday we were in N. 9 at the time when you went back to check on your place. We said then that we wanted to leave Friday or Saturday. Then Papa cried so much and said to Jasch, "Liese and Tina are leaving already, and you want to leave me alone too?" We remember it very well when you said, "Without you, Papa, I will not go." No one else expressed themselves like that! We do not want to find fault because nothing happens by chance – is that not so? We, who are still here, so often now say that we all want to stay together. However, it is impossible to know what will happen.

Today the day has been very dark and cloudy, and yesterday it rained heavily. The grain is standing nicely, the harvest could be a good one. But if things remain as they are, it will not be for us. Please greet Joh. Mar., Jakob M. and grandfather's Tina who is at Paul Koops'. Have you been there already? Isaac Hueberts live in Klaas Loewen's place. She had said the old guy now had no business hanging around there, it was now their place. Just think of it, those are the kind of people who are to remain here when things have settled down. Our horses run free in the fields day and night. If horses are needed, they are caught and used. Cows are milked wherever. I will have much to tell you when we can speak face to face. We used to own 65 dessiatine [*one dessiatine is 2.65 acres*] of land before the war, and Papa had 100 dessiatine, and our production quotas are now being set on those amounts of land. May God be with you until we meet again.

Your loving sister, Marie.

*Somewhat later, a letter from the Wiebe family in New York arrives – an illustration of the practice of exchanging letters among family and friends. Maria uses the postcard they have sent to thank her benefactors for their gift of six dollars. She can now buy basic food supplies. Although her husband remains in prison, this mother has little time to be upset. Little Lena has had a harrowing incident, and Maria must find medical help.*

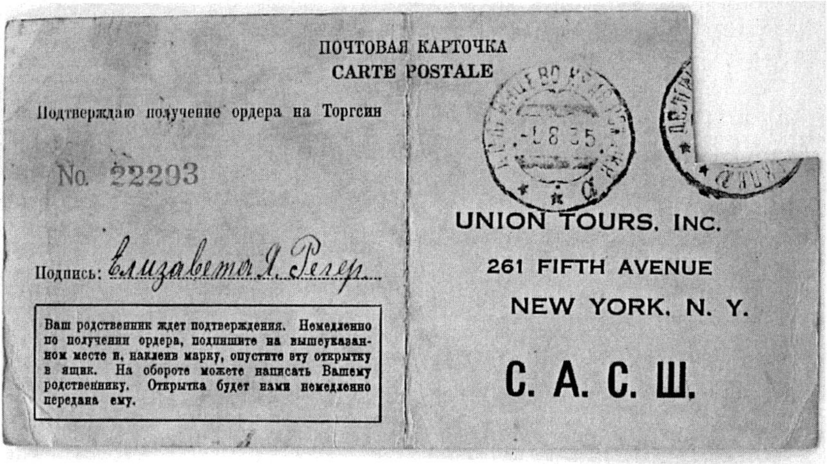

ПОЧТОВАЯ КАРТОЧКА
CARTE POSTALE

Подтверждаю получение ордера на Торгсин

No. 22293

Подпись:

Ваш родственник ждет подтверждения. Немедленно по получении ордера, подпишите на вышеуказанном месте и, наклеив марку, опустите эту открытку в ящик. На обороте можете написать Вашему родственнику. Открытка будет нами немедленно передана ему.

UNION TOURS, INC.
261 FIFTH AVENUE
NEW YORK, N. Y.

С. А. С. Ш.

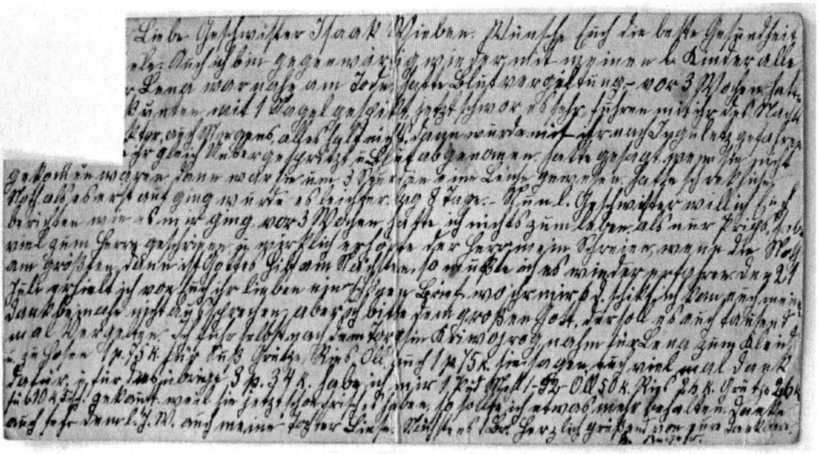

August 4 [1930]

Dear friends Isaac Wiebes,
We wish you the best of health in body and soul. At this time our family is also very well. Our daughter Lena was close to death after she stepped on a nail, got a severe infection and developed blood poisoning. It was at night and we drove her to N. 8 to the doctor. Nothing seemed to help, and they took her to Inguletz to another doctor who tested her blood and gave her an injection. He told us that if we had not come when we did, she would have been dead in 3 hours. She was in great pain until the boil opened up and then things got easier for her, but she had to stay in bed for 8 days.

And now let me tell you what happened to me 3 weeks ago. I had nothing to live on, only Pripps [*a coffee substitute made from roasted wheat*]. I cried to God and God heard my cries. When trouble is the greatest God is the nearest, and this I experienced again. On July 21 I received a nice letter from you in which you sent me 6 dollars. I cannot express my thanks and gratefulness enough, and I pray that God shall reward you a thousandfold. I drove to the store in Krivoy Rog and got some dress material for Lena, 1 ruble 75 kopek, pants material for Susie, porridge, rice and oil, also for 1r. 75k. They send many thanks to you. For the remaining 3r. 34k. I got 1 'Pud' flour for 1r. 32k., oil 50k., rice 26k., porridge 26k., and 10k. for fish, since they had some fresh ones now. And so I should have a little extra left over. Thank also J.W. and your daughter Liese.

A hearty thank you from M. Regehr

*But the gift of six dollars and the ability to purchase food and fabric soon diminish. A much more distressing concern envelops the Regehr family. In a letter with no date and no address or salutation, Jasch recounts recent events.*

## Eviction

[1930/31]

Today is Sunday. I want to go to N. 7 for the night. There I hope to meet Henry Friesen and we want to discuss how to go on from here. I have a summons from Odessa, and also one from Moscow, to the Kolkoz [*Collective*] – there where our men had to work in past years. God knows how He has determined this in His holy plans. I was so happy about my dear Marie. She said, "Let us be completely at ease, this will be a lonesome road we must travel." Yes, the poet sings, "Simply believe every day; believe even if it storms always."

After those hooligans evicted us, I did not have a kopek. As I just stood there in that despairing hour and wondered where to now?– without money, without clothes, without bread – a dear brother came and pressed something into my hand as well as into the hand of my dear Marie. We put it very quietly into our pockets so as not to be noticed. When we were away from there we counted it up and it came to 100 rubles! Then you can see that there are some very caring people here. May God reward them a hundredfold.

I was summoned to the GPU – there were 2 representatives from Kherson. They urged me to become an informer against our people so that they would, once and for all, get the stupid idea of emigrating out of their heads and never again consider leaving Russia. They made great promises of how good things were going to get in this country – all rights would again be restored to us. Three times they offered me this opportunity. Finally I said that if they would restore to us all our old Germanic rights, then I would do it, otherwise I could not. This they refused. Then I withdrew my offer as well. I am glad that God knew that He could keep me faithful in this situation and I would not yield to their threats. I really desire to hold high the principles and precepts of our forefathers, even in the face of persecution.

Did you receive my dear Marie's letter? Send our letters to the address of Ab. Martens N. 9, to be given to Liese Reg. We love you always.

Your Geschwister J. and M. Regehr

*Although Jasch is unaware of it in the moment, his refusal to cooperate will cost him and his family dearly. The Regehrs have been allowed to return to their home, and they think the worst is over. They are wrong. In the middle of winter and during a fierce snowstorm, unwelcome guests arrive.*

Feb 7 [1931]

Beloved Geschwister,
I am hardly in a condition to write a letter, I feel so troubled I could burst. I feel exactly as it says in Psalm 35. On Feb 3, at 12 noon, it was a very cold day – about 22 degrees of frost and storming out of every corner of the sky – I went to visit my elderly father and told him about the great unrest in the streets. He comforted me and told me not to be disturbed, but rather put my trust in God.

I went home and told my dear Marie, who was just busy getting the noon meal on the table. We were about to sit down to eat. Then 2 sleighs, with about 10 people in them, drove onto our yard – Torwaertzer [*literally "gate warts"*]. When they entered our home they swore and yelled at us in full voice: "Get ready, you have to leave this village in 20 minutes. You devils are obstructing us in this village!" Our children started to cry. I begged that they should at least allow us to stay in the village because it was winter. Where should we go with our little ones? They kicked me with their boots and hit me with their fists and swore a blue streak. My dear little wife collapsed. When she again became conscious she dropped to her knees before the mob, put her arms around their legs, and pleaded as desperately as Genevieve pleaded for her life with the murderers in the forest. But it got unremittingly worse. In a cold sweat I cried, "Why do you treat us like this?" Then they told us what we were allowed to take along: a little flour, 1 pillow for 2 people, 1 spoon and 1 fork, and nothing more! Everything else they took away from us. Then they loaded us up and drove us out of the village. There they freed us to go to another C/c [*meaning unknown*].

We went to Goosen's, N. 6, and my family stayed there for the night. However, I continued on to N. 1 and stayed there for the night. The next day I went with H.F. to Utupona to find work! But I did not find work. For 3 nights now I have been at Hans's in his cellar – and often in his loft – hiding, in order not to be caught. My dear Marie visited me yesterday evening. For night she drove back to N. 6 again. The little children are all scattered and are with various families in the village. Our little Jascha misses us so much that he did not eat all day yesterday; before mother came yesterday they brought him to Hans. When he saw me, he threw his little arms around my neck and kissed and hugged me. We both wept with joy. Suddenly Marie walked in – then you should have seen the scene – then the other children came in too. In such an hour the heart of a mother almost wants to break.

It is so hard to believe that all things work together for good for those who love God. Jesus says:"When you hear of these tribulations, then lift up your heads, and be joyful, for your salvation draweth nigh." To remain worthy in such hours is almost impossible. Then you ask God: "What about your promises, since you say heaven and earth shall pass away, but my Word shall not pass away?" Thousands, and many times a thousand, are crying and pleading for deliverance today. But there does not seem to be any deliverance for them. Tina's Cornusha writes that he read in the New Testament: "How could God not hear His chosen ones who cry to Him day and night?" I said, here in our situation that is a comfort to us. Maybe God will answer the prayers of the little ones – our little children.

Our people are so "verstrickt" [*inflicted, enslaved*] they let themselves be used for whatever is demanded of them. The current situation is being used as a Ruhe Kissen [*comfort cushion*] in the hopes that foreign countries can and will help. Then, according to my understanding, only those who are now in this tribulation and are being persecuted will have remained free of this plague. Jak. Barg. and F.M. were forcibly evicted with us. Aron R. works in the Noss brigade. They demand another two thousand Pud of grain from N. 7. People are being brutalized without end. Our dear parents were also evicted – also H.F.! The parents are at G. Siemens, N. 6 – Abram just came from there – but today they were ordered away from there as well. Probably they will be driven to N. 1. Our father will probably die on the way. Boldt is home also, and as I read in a letter yesterday, he has not allowed himself to be sucked into the vortex of the Zeitgeist [*Spirit of the Times*]. No, no.

Will close. Your J. and M. Regehr

I really wanted to stop writing, but I read an article in a paper that a Commission from America investigated the situation in Russia, to determine if the exported wood, which is sent to foreign countries, is the product of forced labour. The Commission states firmly that it is a gross lie. But I attest herewith, that it is forced labour only that produces the product. The worker does not want to work any more at all because of the poor and meagre diet. From our Mennonite villages there are at least 200 men working at forced labour. The Commission should go to the German [*Mennonite*] Colonies and ask!

Yesterday I and H.F. drove to Moscow, and at one location we saw 15 men pick-axing dirt from a mountain and throwing the dirt into a big gully. We stopped and asked what this all meant. Then they started to talk in German. Then we asked them in German what they were really working at. Then they said they were supposed to fill up this big Prawulja [*cavernous pit*], and then by spring they must still work 500 square metres of dirt out of it. They wept and told how hard their work was and how badly they were being treated. They had to sleep in unheated barracks, got only very poor food, had to wear their own clothes, and lost their rights to buy more. They were in rags, without shoes, and asked us if there were any prospects from overseas. Many, many languish and will perish if help is not soon forthcoming. These are working at forced labour because of their religious beliefs and have been disenfranchised. The

Commission members should get a picture from this perspective instead of from that of the authorities! They should listen directly to us!

In some places there have been worker uprisings – they want meat! Here, however, it is being taken away. Most people have to surrender their last cow. Our Liese had also bought a heifer for 200 rubles – she had to surrender it to them. It was so hard on the children to give up this heifer, since they had already been without milk for a year; it was as if they had to carry their mother to the cemetery. There is only lamentation in our house.

I will close. Just now Wilh. B. was here and told us they had officially recorded all his possessions, even the dishes that were standing on the dinner table and all the dirty laundry (they did this at our place too). W.B. is also one of those who would not be hurt by foreign intervention. If he does not deliver 85 pud wheat by tomorrow, everything he owns will be sold. If he fails to deliver, the sum is then increased so that his entire estate is not enough to pay for the debt they ascribe to him. Then such a malicious "non-payer" is dragged into court and is sentenced to months or years of forced labour.

From Mupora to Fanobka the whole Plawen [*marsh land*] is being planted with cabbage. There are over 1000 hectares. For that the government needs 3 thousand workers. The goal is to use only forced labour so that they can sell their products more cheaply – just like they are doing with our grain. With such measures they increase their foreign capital, which is here then heralded as a great victory for us. If this is not soon stopped, the plague will soon come over to you. Our country is poor and longs for deliverance.

That which was impossible 10 years ago is easily possible today. The people are fed up, and more than fed up. When foreign countries make more and more demands of us, our situation continually worsens and gets more difficult. For us it is: Either, or! May God through the Voelkerlage [*People's Movement*] achieve His ends so that many, many could freely determine their destiny. If there are new developments, please do not keep silent. We would not like to be put to shame in our suffering, in our waiting, in our hope nor in our faith. Just now 6 fully loaded sleighs drove from here to N. 13 to pry some more grain out of the farmers. It will not be long before most of us will be out of bread – then they intend to open a communal kitchen. How long will our tribulation be? My dear M. is in N. 6, and I am here. We are both hiding out. May God be with us. Please forgive me that I wrote so much. Please report if there is any chance of deliverance – if there are any prospects of saving us!

*Jasch is hiding and the family is scattered. Yet he finds time and paper to write to his nine-year-old nephew in Canada. Little "Petroosha" (Peter Bargen) must have been a well-loved nephew to receive such a warm letter.*

[1931]

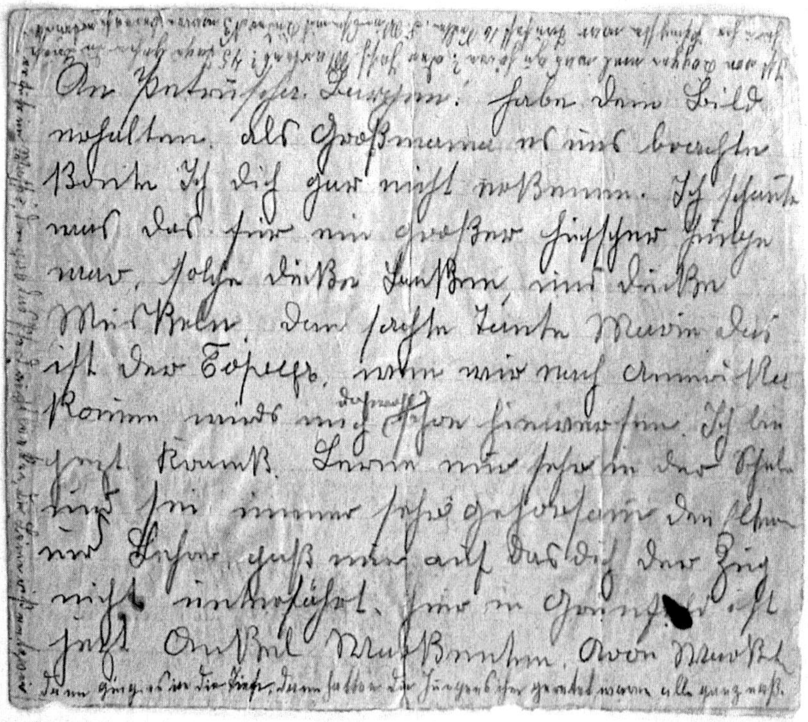

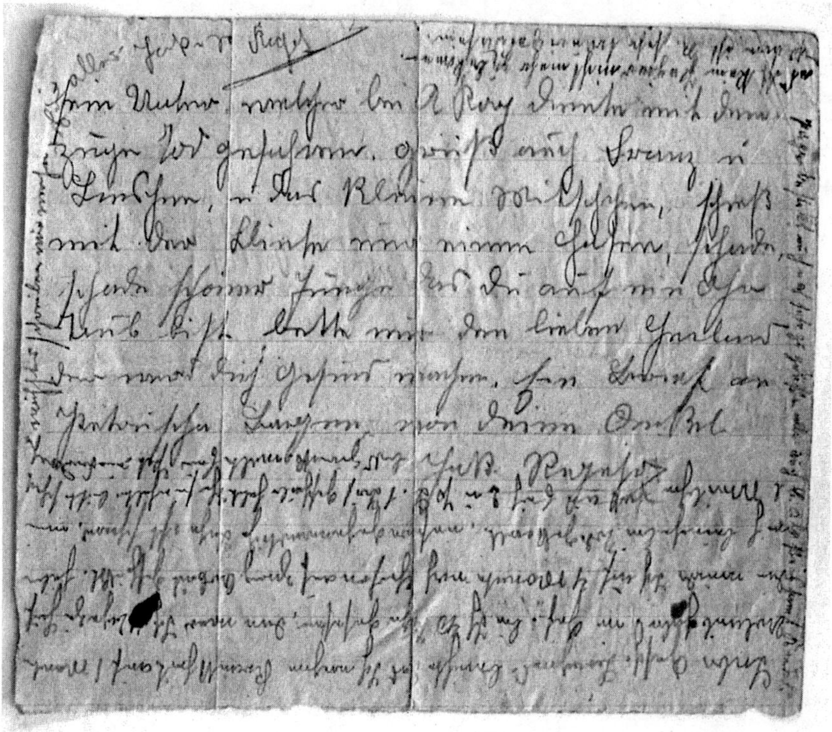

To Petroosha Bargen!
We received your picture. When grandmama brought it to us, I could not recognize you. I looked at it and wondered what kind of a big, beautiful boy was on the picture! Such fat cheeks, fat muscles. Then Aunt Marie said, that is the "Topeyr." When we come to America, you will probably be able to throw me down. I am sick now. Study hard in school, and be very obedient to your parents and teachers. Watch out that the train does not run you down. Here in Gruenfeld a Mr. Warkentin has been killed by a train – he was Aron Warkentin's father, who worked at A. Reg. Give greetings to Franz and Lieschen and that little Mariechen. Shoot a rabbit with that gun. It is so sad, so sad, dear boy, that you are deaf in that one ear. Pray to our dear God to make you better. A letter to Petroosha Bargen from his uncle Jak. Regehr.

*In the same letter, a message to Peter's parents is embedded.*

Dear Geschwister Bargen,
I report that because of my illness I have furlough. I have been released from my incarceration for 1 month. I was incarcerated for 40 days. Then I was home for 4 weeks. Then I was sent to Kherson to do forced labour for 4 months. They almost tortured me to death. Our present circumstances are hard. My little wife sent 2 letters to you and 1 to P.B. Did you receive them? Do you ever hear anything from Koops? Jasch Martens? The [...] have gone back and forth for 45 days. On the day of Pentecost we had baptism – 16 souls.

F. Wienses and children from N. 3 were almost drowned. He was driving through deep water, when the horse would not be guided and the rein tore apart. However, the boys rescued him but everyone was soaked. Next time we will write more. Papa sends greetings to everyone, also to B. Klassens. We cannot get any paper anymore. Russia is so poor! What a miserable existence!

Jak and M. Regehr

## Exile and Prison (1930-32)

*From their intimate knowledge of the Regehr family, letter editors Peter and Anne Bargen tell us that the whole family was disenfranchised (deprived of all civil rights of citizenship), labeled as* kulaks, *and evicted from their small farm and house in October 1930. Father Jasch, separated from the family and sentenced to a punishment cell, was released seven months later. On May 21, 1931 this weakened, emaciated father joined his family only to be arrested again, this time together with his entire household. Jasch's youngest brother Abram Regehr (only sixteen) was also arrested in place of his aging, frail father Kornelius. Scrap wood was found and quickly nailed together to construct a trunk[2] – the permissible contents were one pillow for two people, one spoon, one fork, some clothes, and a little food. A granary became their prison until the train arrived. In a crowded cattle car, for seven days (with no beds, no toilets, a little water, and rations of soup) they moved north to a prison camp in the Ural Mountains. The whole family, with young children, adolescents, parents and uncle, is now caught in a prison system of unparalleled size and brutality.*

*The family is fortunate to survive the seven-day journey, packed shoulder to shoulder with other prisoners. They are also fortunate to move to a ready-built barrack. Not all prisoners have this luxury – living in the open air and foraging for building materials is a common fate. The three-storey barrack space in Kizel in the northern Urals measures 1-½ metres (5 feet) square for the family of nine. Layers of sleeping platforms line the walls, and the handmade wooden trunk fills the centre.*

*The trickle of aid from overseas is hardly sufficient to keep the starving, frozen, exhausted prisoners alive. Pleas from the Regehr family begin in the first letter from father Jasch. In the late summer of 1931, he pleads for his six children, from three-year-old Jascha to nineteen-year-old Liese. The oldest two, Liese and Peter, cut frozen timber for export and live in a hut three days' journey away. Mariechen, now fifteen, works in an unknown location; we know only that she has not come "home" for five days. Tina, just twelve, shovels slag in an iron-ore smelter.*

*When not at work the family lives in their cramped space in the three-storey barrack. Sound travels freely between thin walls. Bed bugs and lice are their companions. From floor to ceiling, bunks crowd the perimeter of their room.*

*Work dominates their lives. While some of their assigned labour is life-threatening, other jobs appear to be part of a normal day. Jasch's description sounds typical and ordinary – almost normal. But the services of the doctor, the store, and the post office are available only for those workers on a payroll who voluntarily move to these regions. The Regehr family receives perfunctory visits from the doctor at best. Behind the façade of normality, their letters are censored, and they are monitored by guards and dogs as they work.*

*Writing on the wooden trunk, father Jasch narrates their lives on a scrap of paper torn from an accountant's ledger. He writes in German Gothic script, a style of writing not likely legible to a Soviet prison guard or official mail censor. Wasting space is intolerable, so he adds fragments of thoughts in the margins and upside-down between sentences.*

[1931]

Tina goes to work each day in the Commune. We have applied for acceptance into the Commune as well. I was always against this, but the situation is getting worse all the time and we have to work in the Commune anyway! If we belong then we get credited with work days, and in fall we get some produce – if available. We so much want to stay alive and that [*acceptance*], in addition to the parcels we get, would help so much. I go to work for 5 or 6 hours almost every day. We can buy milk, and for butter we pay 2 rubles while Liese pays 1 ruble for butter – and so there is a difference in everything.

One day we deported ones were each ordered to attach a Kolendar [*porch*] to our barracks. We would get horses, wood and nails. All are now nearly done – ours too. The Ural region is being built up, but the displaced persons are dealt with more sternly and denied essentials. The post office, a doctor's clinic, a store, and a Cmanoba [unknown word] is in the barracks close to us, but all this will be moved to the other end where the volunteers are living. It does not look like they will let us go soon but will work us as long as they can.

You ask about J R's children. We know little of them – we are far away from there. They are all still alive and do get many parcels – that is what we have heard. A few days ago I spoke to Peters who live in the same house with them. We are glad for them. H.F. get many things sent to them too – and often in money. They have 40 rubles of credit in the Torgsin [*a Soviet-sanctioned store*] and several money orders. They have received many products – many sent by those Klassens. They must be extremely rich people. Too bad that Kroebel will not listen to our pleas. We have received the address of that Mrs. Klassen. Too bad they are so poor. Received a package from that Hoellig from Germany but have received no answer to our letter.

How privileged your children are compared to ours. Yours can learn and enjoy all good things – and ours go down to ruin. – Liese and Peter are completely overworked! Every time they come home from work they complain that they ache all over. Mariechen is gone for the 5th day, which seems rather long to me. It is said that they must work there for 1 month – but that could well become a year.

*Jasch's next letter exposes the inadequacy of his writing materials. The paper is a four-by-four-inch scrap torn from a larger piece. One side contains an address with numbers and geographical locations inside Russia (Aynebka and Dniepr) in the region of the Ural Mountains, indicating the letter's journey inside the Soviet Union. The other side is covered with previously printed Russian script and with Jasch's small writing.*

[1931]

You will have to excuse me that I do not have better paper on which to write, but there is none here. It would cost me 10 kopek – that is what the communists tell me. It is almost impossible to write with ink on this paper. Well, if you cannot read it, do not worry. Our children send warm greetings to your children, Franz, Liese, and you, nice Peter. Please write a letter too. My children cannot write letters because of lack of schooling. Many are suffering from famine here.

*Not only are his children hungry, their minds are starving too. Literacy has been very important to Mennonites for centuries. Beginning with the Reformation, reading, writing, and private study of sacred texts were central to their religious beliefs. For Jasch and Maria, the salvation of their children's souls is linked with their level of literacy. But when their children scavenge in the garbage behind the officers' barrack for potato peelings, these parents know that literacy cannot be their primary concern.*

*Yet leaning over the wooden trunk in the cramped barrack, with noise rising from the layers of prisoners stacked in their cages and with her three-year-old brother bumping her arm, Lena writes a letter to her Aunt Liese. The large, careful script of a young child bears witness to Lena's age. At nine years old, her childhood innocence has been shattered. Her father is dying and she is hungry. She attends "school" with her sister Tina, but it is not like the school in her home village. This is a school where the children of imprisoned* kulaks *are re-educated; where a new ideology replaces the values of their previous culture. Soviet authorities enforce four hours of schooling and four hours of work for children. Older children work eight hours with two hours of school. It is in such a school that Lena and her sister Tina, the little* kulak *students, are sometimes refused food while they watch other children eat. Here Lena is questioned: Do your parents criticize communism? Do they write letters? Do they talk about God? And here, several years later, Lena and her classmates will be told to wave goodbye to their mothers as armed guards transport them to harsher prisons. But here in her crowded barrack space, little Lena's pencil moves across the fragile paper:*

[1931]

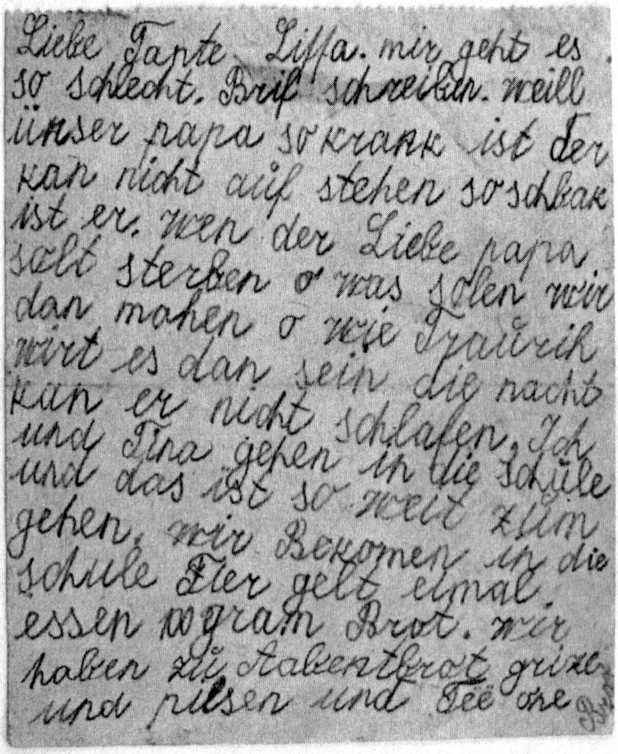
Liebe Tante Liffa. mir geht es
so schlecht. Brif schreiben. weill
ünser papa so krank ist der
kan nicht auf stehen so schlak
ist er. wen der Liebe papa
salt sterben o was solen wir
dan mahen o wie traürih
wirt es dan sein die nacht
kan er nicht schlafen. Ich
und Tina gehen in die Schüle
und das ist so weit züm
gehen. wir Bekomen in die
schule Eier gelt elmal
essen 100 gram Brot. wir
haben zü Abentbrot grize
und pilsen und Tee one

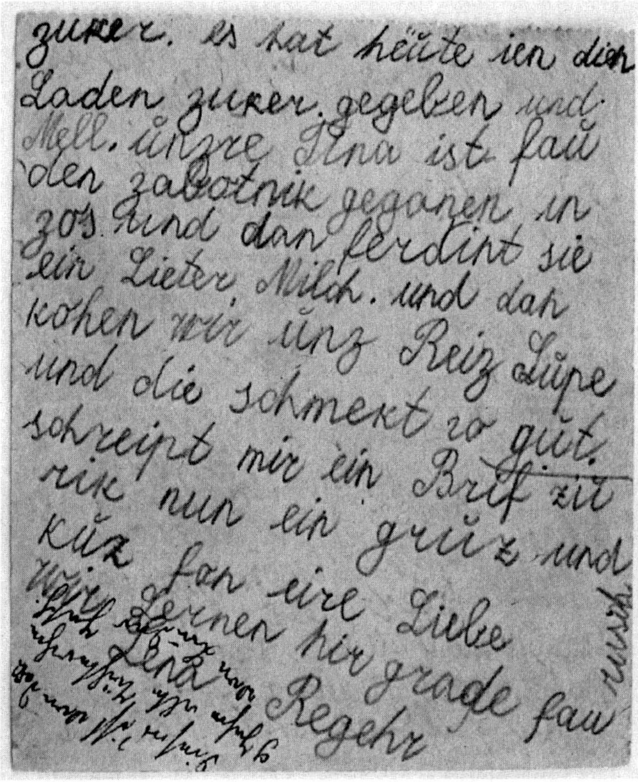
zuker. es hat häüte ien dien
Laden zuker gegeben und
Mell. ünzre Tina ist fau
den zabotnik gegangen in
zo's und dan ferdint sie
ein Lieter. Milch. und dan
kohen wir ünz Reiz Züpe
und die schmekt zo güt.
schreipt mir ein Brif zü
rik nun ein grüz und
küz fan üre Liebe
Lena Regehr
Wir lernen hir grade fau rusich

Dear Aunt Liese,

I really do not like writing letters. Our Papa is so sick he can no longer get up. If our dear Papa should die, what will become of us? How sad that would be. He just cannot sleep during the night. Tina and I go to school and it is so far to walk. For those that pay the school provides 1 meal a day – 100 grams of bread. For supper we have porridge and mushrooms and tea, without bread or sugar. Today, in the store, they actually had flour and sugar for sale. Our Tina went to the Soviet very early this morning and earned 1 litre milk. Now maybe we can cook rice soup, and that tastes so very good. Write me a letter too. Greetings and a kiss from your dear niece,

Lena Regehr

*Some time later, from the same cramped quarters, mother Maria writes a letter to her parents in Altonau. In this first year of their prison term, she is careful not to name herself. However, her mother and father will know these are the words of their daughter, longing to be rescued. They will know this is her expression of a faith that sustains her. Not only her parents but also those family members who eventually receive her letter in Canada will know this writer. Small and faded, the handwriting is difficult to read; some words are illegible and some messages are heavily masked.*

[1931]

Dear Loved Ones, since we didn't send greetings before, I will write to you now. At present I am alone in the [...]. The others have all left for home. The time is exactly 8 o'clock and I have washed the dishes and cleaned up. It is so quiet you could hear a mouse. Since there is hardly any water the plants are wilted and the [...] is red as fire, just like people want to [...] at other places. In like manner my heart and head want to [...]. I have too many thoughts, but I do not wish to complain since the almighty and great God is leading me in better ways than I deserve, and He will certainly continue to be with me. I am journeying through this life with Jesus, day by day – directly through the camp of His enemies. Even through danger I will follow Him since His nail-pierced hand is holding mine. He alone is my only support. Actually it seems that fear is my lot, although I do not fear as much as when I first came. But it would be wonderful to be free again. To be a free person!! Therefore, I ask all of you to be good enough to do what you can – write what you know and what we have to endure to whoever can help.

My dear Geschwister Ab. and Lena, are you still living in the old place? All of you, please write to me – I have not had any communication from you for so long. What is my dear Mama and my dear brother Hans doing? Read something with them – comfort them for me and let them do what they can. I will try not to complain. Please forgive me that I am pleading so much. Well, enough of that.

I will have borscht for supper and tea with lemons – I would love to eat them together with you. Of course we have as much as we want. Good night, the time is 10 o'clock.

*Maria's satirical description of the abundance of food would not escape the attention of her readers in Canada. But the truth of this mother's search for food and her struggle to keep her family alive is apparent on this scrap of paper.*

[1931]

He is our refuge, otherwise we have none. I have sold my blue dress for 50r., my gold ring for 20r. and 1 pail of potatoes, the golden dinner ring for 8 kilo rye flour and 4 kilo grits, and many other things – just to stay alive. Too bad that all our things that could be sold are now gone. We had all new underclothes and such nice new quilts. If we had them here, we could live better. We did not know the future. Well, the great God has everything in His hand. When we have reached the end of our own resources, maybe then His help will break forth so that we do not perish. We trust in God!

*On a larger piece of paper without a date, salutation, or initial greeting, Jasch recalls the events that led to his family's arrest and imprisonment.*

[June 1931]

We were shoved into another Kammer [*room*] where there were another 60 men like us. Then it did not take long and the streets were filled with women and children. They cried and screamed – it was heart-rending. Then during this fearful time a policeman entered and said to one of his acquaintances that a telegram had arrived [...]. It did not take too many minutes, then everyone knew. Then many dropped to their knees and thanked God for their marvelous deliverance. (The policeman was relieved of his position in 2 days.)

But we were brutalized for another 3 weeks. Our captors and guards had the authority to vent their anger and frustration on us as they pleased. We were awakened on the night of June 20 and told to get ready, for we would be taken to the station. It did not take long and we were called out one by one and loaded onto wagons. I alone remained in the Kammer. They locked and barred the door. Then I thought: Are you one of the more fortunate ones who will be allowed to remain behind? After a few minutes the guard came and took me outside to a Droschka [*wagon*] where I alone had to get in. Then 2 policemen sat beside me and away we went, escorted by armed riders and wagons. The scene was much like in the year '19 in N. 11.

When we got to the station [...], I suddenly saw my whole family locked up in a granary. Oh, then there was weeping and wailing, and little Jascha screamed loudly: "Papa, Papa!" The police locked us up too, and so we lay there for 2 days. Then we were loaded into cattle cars, 40 people to one car, and the car was locked. The train took off – no one knew our destination. So we traveled in the train for 7 days and nights until we got to Kizel in the northern Ural Mountains. There we were unloaded and were taken to a large barracks. We were the first ones there. Abram and little Peter were sent 60 km further to work in the forest. They strapped a bundle on each of their backs and away they went on foot to their workplace. There are many swamps here. Liese got a position 8 km from here as [...]. Michi must work in the forest for the Punjab, for only 1 quota of bread, 2 teaspoons granulated sugar and 1 dried fish.

We are thankful, dear Geschwister, that we can get bread here. Those who are unfit for work only get ¾ of the quota of bread and nothing else. If only you could invite us to your place for a visit, how gladly we would come. According to the newspapers ½ million people are being sent here. Then you can imagine what will happen here. Many children are dying in our barracks. Yesterday one died and today another died. The poor children only get that sour black bread – no milk, no oil or fat, no sugar! If help does not come soon many, many will find their grave here. Should our brothers forget us completely? Please help, Franz and Peter – we are here in the far north, without bread, without clothes, without money!

There are many like us here. And what is the reason? Because in the last 3 years we rented some land and hired workers during the threshing season. That Rempel has done his worst to us. Oh, if we could ever get together there would be so much to tell – things I do not want to commit to paper. There are 12 Mennonite families here. H. Voth, H. Friesen, H. Wiebe N. 3, J. Reg. N. 9, Joh. Reg. N. 7, Jakob Derksen, Joh. Wiens, J. Brauns and Pet. Loewens N. 7, and Abram and Peter Dueckmanns of N. 8! If you, dear friends and relatives, want to correspond with us, then please send us paper and stamps and envelopes because they are unavailable here. It seems rather futile to send this address to you because we will be sent further very shortly. Our address is [*illegible Russian*].

If we stay here for any length of time we will all perish. Please send news of us to Goosens and Truda [*Maria Regehr's sister*]. I cannot write to all. I was not even allowed to say goodbye to our parents and Geschwister. Brother Johann is in very bad shape.

*In the next letter, on paper previously used as a shipping order, Maria writes about millet and cabbage. Finding enough food consumes the entire family. It is summer, but even then food is scarce. This resourceful mother finds innovative ways to cook with seeds, grasses, moss, and worms. Anything that moves provides protein. With scraps of garbage the children find behind the guards' kitchen, and with the contents of parcels, Maria makes soups, stews, and pancakes. On a red Soviet postcard that Lena has brought home from school, Maria records her hopes that the family can soon work in the Commune and collect "Trudodnie" (reward points for food). Jasch is too sick to work, and they do not get milk if they do not work. But unexpected sources of food arrive.*

[1931]

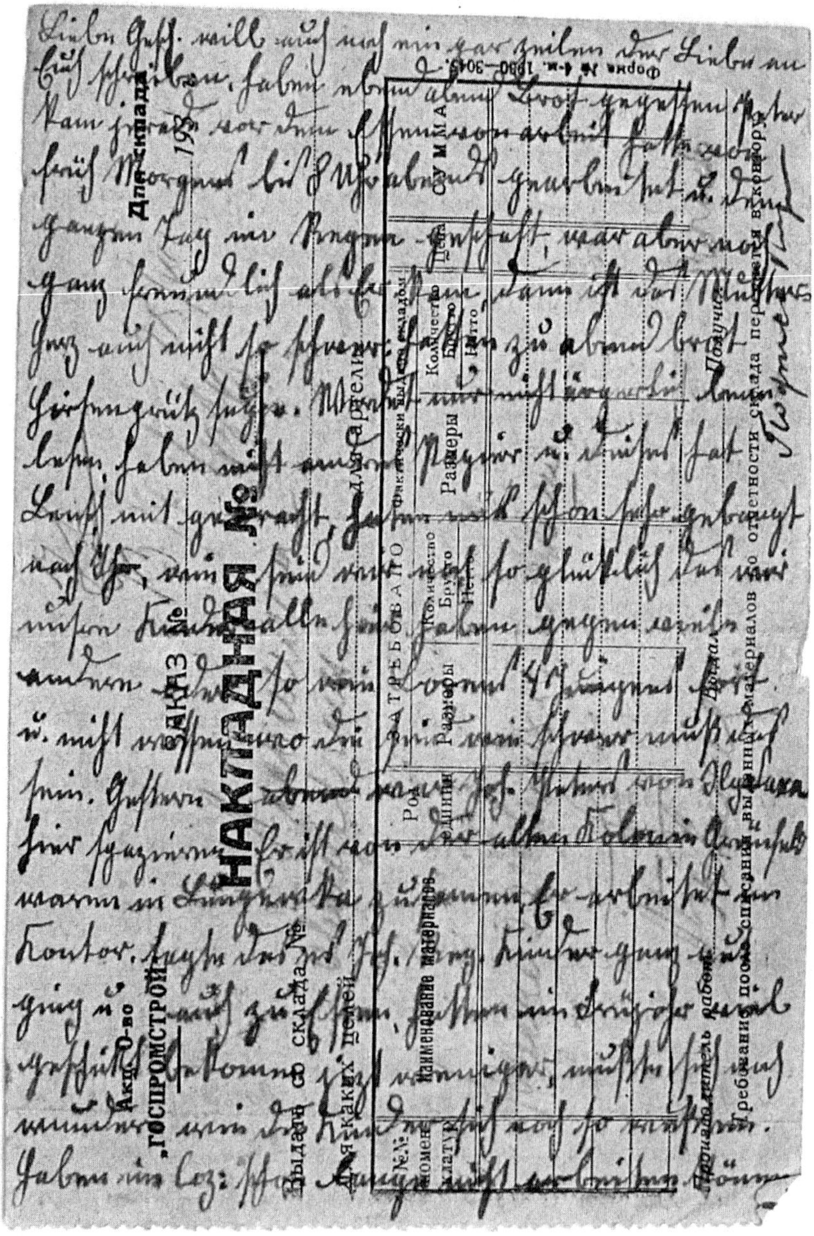
Акц. О-во
„ГОСПРОМСТРОЙ"
ЗАКАЗ №
НАКЛАДНАЯ №
Выдать со склада №
Наименование материалов
Размеры
Сумма
Получил

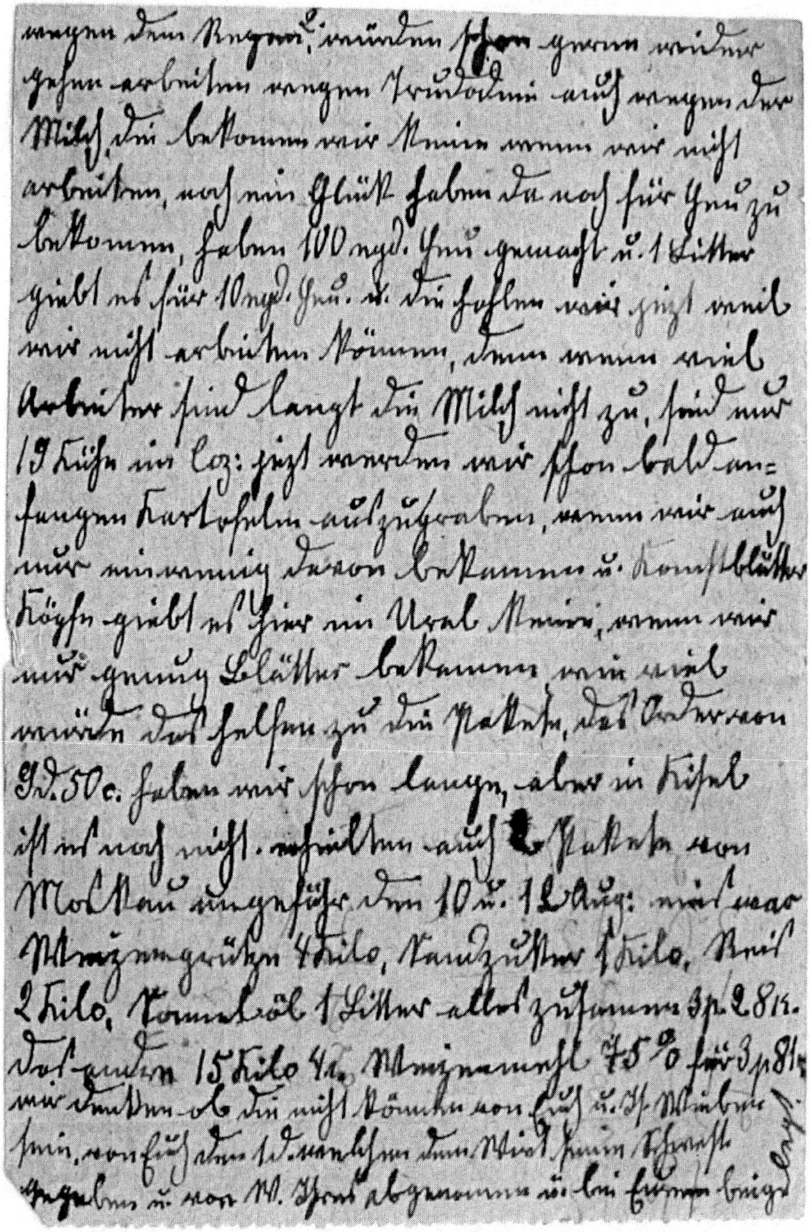

wegen dem Regen, würden schon gern wieder
gehen arbeiten wegen Verdienen auch wegen der
Milch, die bekommen wir keine wenn wir nicht
arbeiten, noch ein Glück haben da noch für Heu zu
bekommen, haben 100 rgd. Heu gemacht u. 1 Liter
giebt es für 10 rgd. Heu. u. die holen wir jetzt weil
wir nicht arbeiten können, denn wenn viel
Arbeiter sind langt die Milch nicht zu, sind nur
19 Kühe im Koz: jetzt werden wir schon bald an-
fangen Kartoffeln aufzugraben, wenn wir auch
nur ein wenig davon bekommen u. Krautblätter
Köpfe giebt es hier im Ural keine, wenn wir
nur genug Blätter bekommen wir viel
würde das helfen zu die Pakete, das andere von
9 d. 50 c. haben wir schon lange, aber in Kisel
ist es noch nicht. erhalten auch 2 Pakete von
Moskau ungefähr den 10 u. 12 Aug: mit was
Weizengrützen 4 Kilo, Sandzucker 1 Kilo, Reis
2 Kilo, [illegible] 1 Liter alles zusammen 3 p. 28 K.
das andere 15 Kilo 4 a. Weizenmehl 75% für 3 p. 81 k.
wir denken ob du nicht könntest von Euch u. ich [illegible]
sein, von Euch den 1 d. welchen den Brief sein Schrift
angeben u. von M. Ihm abgenommen u. bei Euren bringt
[illegible]

Dear Geschwister,
I also want to write a few lines of love to you. We have just eaten supper. Peter came home from work just before supper. He had worked from early in the morning until 8 P.M.– the whole day in pouring rain. However, in spite of this he was quite cheerful – of course then the heart of this mother does not feel so heavy either. For supper we had millet meal soup. Do not get impatient with reading this – I have no other paper and Lena brought this along.

We have been very lonely here. How fortunate we are to have all our children still with us. We are very fortunate compared to so many others, like the Loewens – their 4 boys were taken and the parents do not know where they are. How hard that must be.

Yesterday evening Joh. Peters from [...] was visiting here. He is from Gruenfeld in the old colony. We were together in Lungawka. He works in the office. He said that things were going reasonably well with Joh. Regehr's children [*recently orphaned*] since they did have some food. They had received many parcels in spring, but fewer now! He had been surprised how the children were able to cope. They have one worry: For a long time now they have been prevented from working because of the rain.

We would really like to work again because of the Trudodnie [reward points] and the milk, which we do not get if we do not work. We are fortunate that we can get milk for hay. We made 100 [...] of hay, and we get 1 litre of milk for 10 [...] hay – and now that we cannot work we have to fetch it. If there are many workers there is not enough milk – the Commune has only 19 cows.

We will soon begin digging potatoes, even if we only get a small part of them. Cabbage is not available here in the Urals. If only we could get a few cabbage leaves, it would help so much when supplemented by the packages we receive.

*Packages have an even more precarious journey than letters. Many are stolen or damaged. Some arrive with few of their original contents, having been sorted by censoring guards who monitor contraband materials. The thought of misplaced or undelivered packages haunts Maria.*

Long ago we received notice of the 9r. 50k., but it has not yet arrived in Kizel. On about the 10th and the 13th of August we also received 2 parcels from Moscow, one was wheat-porridge 4 kilo, sugar 1 kilo, rice 2 kilo, sunflower oil 1 litre, all together 3r. 28k. The other one was 15 kilo – 4k. 75% wheat flour for 3r. 81k. We wonder if that was sent by you and Isaac Wiebes. We received the 1 dollar from your landlord's sister [...].

*Lena remembers these days. In a letter written more than fifty years later (1989, in Germany), she describes their existence. Her father was sick and "he stayed with Mama and us in the barracks. The rest of us children could stay with the parents because we were very young." The older children had to walk to Ustupil every day to cut timber for export:*

> The road to Ustupil was muddy and mostly muskeg. You could not drive there with wagons. You could only walk there. You received a little bundle of 400 grams of frozen bread, tied it to your back and set off on foot. It was a very hard road to walk. But when you arrived there it was even sadder. The barracks were cold, no beds, nothing warm to put on your feet and no warm clothing to put on your body. People were hungry but there was no food and the cold was terrible. You just felt you could not live much less work there in the forest.

*The journey to Ustupil ends, and the family is scattered further. The eldest children, Peter and Liese, are "taken away." In July 1931 Jasch is consumed with grief and almost collapses under the weight of his family's misery.*

Ural, the 6 July 1931

Dear Geschwister and friends away in that great distance,
Since I have recently been robbed of my freedom it became impossible

to write to you, but I will try to do so today. If I can maintain the right mood, I will try to tell you of our life and condition. It is impossible to describe our current circumstances. My dear little wife has covered her head and weeps for the loss of both our oldest children. Yes, tears are our food day and night, for here is a gorge and there is an abyss, the depths thunder and the waves and wild breakers swoop over us. Yes, if God had not been with us, we would have perished long ago.

*On the same page, Jasch recounts the night of terror in their home village one year ago.*

It was on the night of the 7th of May. Around 1 o'clock there was a knocking on our window. It was the GPU. We opened the door and let them in. [*An officer*] arrested me and took me along as far as the [...]. There he took me into an auto and off we went to the "Forsterei" in the woods [*barracks in the forestry reserve where Mennonite men had worked as an alternative service in pre-communist Russia*]. Spasms of fear and terror convulsed through my body. Shrouded with the fear of death I cried to God. And God heard. From there they then went back to Kronau and I was locked up for 43 [...].

In the Kammer where I sat there were 31 men. The Kammer was 17 feet long and 13 ft. wide, with only one very tiny window – you can imagine how much room we all had. We were allowed out once a day for 15 minutes but during that time we never got a single piece of bread from the government. For days we went without water and almost perished. My dear wife brought me some food every week. Eight times I was questioned at an interrogation, usually at night. It was on the last holiday of Pentecost when we got a little note inside a bread, telling us that this night would be a bloody night. Then there was great confusion in our Kammer. Many cried aloud to God, others ran around in utter despair. Our room was guarded by Komsomol [*Young Communist League*][3] and Molitz [*police*] – in all about 60 men with loaded weapons.

*Although the bleakness of their existence often overcomes Jasch, hope also emerges. In the barracks of Kizel, he escapes through an imaginative journey. He is able to transcend his circumstances and travel to another place and time. With eloquent language, he revisits sumptuous meals shared during long visits with his extended family in the security of their home village.*

Aug. 22, 1931

Dear Geschwister Bargens,
Since such a great longing is welling up in my breast, we have decided to visit you by letter. Oh, dear Geschwister, could you look into our place for a few moments I absolutely know you would not be able to say a word, only just stand there and cry and cry again. But even so, do not be burdened by this too much; our way has been so determined. It is going through the night unto the light. Even knowing this is a comfort. This change of climate, along with the unhealthy diets, means a burdensome life for us.

How often I see you in spirit, dear Geschwister, driving up to our place. One horse runs full gallop and the other trots as if riding on the wind. Often you would not stay very long, only long enough to invite us for a meal – roast duck or filled pancakes made so deliciously with all the trimmings, and you made certain that there were always 3-5 pieces remaining in the plate as overflow. It was always so nice to exchange visits with you. And today the change is so drastic that it can hardly be described. You, loved ones, are away in that great distance – and we are here in this desolate exile. Well, God knows if we will ever meet again. Our daily plea, oh Father, is that we once again see our entire family. We want to believe that our deliverance is near. So many prayers are being said for us here – at your place as well.

H. Wiebe received a letter from Joh. M. on June 28, saying that in a few days you will have prayer sessions when people will pray especially for us here. When we read that there are still children of God who think of us and make intercession for us before the

Throne of God, then we could just shout for joy; then we forget all the calamities which have struck us. Here we are a small handful of Mennonites. (I have written the names to you.) They all feel thankful to you that you remember us and work day and night to get us out of here. Yes, dear Geschwister, often we experience hours when we feel forgotten by God and man. Do you ever hear from your house friend [*a previous house guest, Johann Toews*]? It is reported here by the families who went to Germany, that he may have died – or could he be with them?

Isaac Warkentin writes that the situation in the land where he came from is improving, only he hopes that there may be a chance that we will meet you all again. If we read this, and believe it, we hope to be first in line. Oh, may that hour strike soon when we all are set free from this prison.

Elder Jakob Janzen, N. 4, and Kroeker, N. 6, have been sentenced for 1 ½ years in exile to an island in the Black Sea. They have to catch fish. Regarding the [...] which Driediger gave them to submit at the time, he would not release the papers unless he received a specific sum of money and a signed promissory note. The money he gave him shortly before they departed but he did not give him the promissory note. And now the talk is that he tried to bribe him. That is why these two men are being punished.

*Injustice is not the exclusive possession of those in prisons. The suffering of people left behind in their home villages increases under Stalin's Five-Year Plan, a radical program of industrialization and collectivization inaugurated in October 1928. Nevertheless, Jasch and his family are piteously dependent on the parcels and letters from Canada and from Altonau.*

Unrighteousness is taking over everywhere. From home the report is that those who are single are taxed more than 5 times what the harvest yields. If this continues, our situation this year will become very critical. But when our need is greatest, then help is nearest. It has to be like this, so that all those who were always so ready to raise their hands should realize what it really means to live in the land of freedom.

The weather is cold here and rainy. I guess winter will close in soon. I am very concerned about both of our 2 children, Liese and Peter – and also brother Braun. They are so very far away from us – more than 100 Werst [*80 miles*]. Liese had a good position in the office, worked there for 1 month, then the Komsomol realized she was one of the disenfranchised and she was forced to leave her position. She came home for a few days. Then she walked to the [...] and in three days she had walked 111 Werst – the whole way through the forest, walking on tree stumps and tree roots, in bog and muskeg, and carrying a 1 ½ [...] burden on her back. When she got there, her back and feet were completely soaked. But the next day she had to report to work immediately to cook for the boys there.

Liese wrote us a little bit about her work in the last few days. They were sent to a river and had to cut wood for the winter and float the logs onto the water. The house in which they live is also on the water and floats along with the logs. They have to heat the house every day, since it is so cold on the water. The boys have to work with the logs from early until late (about 17 hours) and are wet the entire day. They are not allowed to go and change clothes. It often happens that they fall into the water, but that makes no difference – there is no halting, no slowing down, always forward! The logs jam where the water is shallow. They must loosen the jam with dynamite, and many times serious accidents occur in the process. Large pieces of log fly high into the air and at times the little house is damaged. My dear little wife just cannot get over it, and intends to walk there and see for herself. Mrs. Wiebe, N. 9, has already walked there and we expect her to return on foot tomorrow. We are very anxious to hear what she will tell us. The workers get only 1 ¼ [...] black bread, 1 fish, and 2 cups sugarless tea, per day! And nothing more! They suffer terribly from malnutrition. Children, especially young children ages 2-4, die here every day.

Well, dear Geschwister, we trust you will help us! What do you think? We have been brought into a region where almost nothing is available. Here a pail of potatoes costs 5-7 rubles – a cucumber costs 35-50 k., a bunch of onions no larger than walnuts cost 10 kop. per bunch. Then you get a small idea how costly life is here – and we are without money. We received packages from Germany. We have had little news from home. We only heard that Hans will not be allowed to go for those baths because his father has been too wealthy. Did you receive our letter? It was the third one sent from here, one to Benjamin. We also enclosed one to brother Peter, greet him heartily from us; they should let us hear more of them! We will write to them next time. My dear Marie will complete this letter when she comes. She went to town for [...], which is 15 Werst from here. She hoped to buy 1 [...] of potatoes; she took along a few wild raspberries which our children picked in the forest. Well, stay well until we meet again.

Your Geschwister, J. and M. Regehr

*In this land of tears, winter arrives early. Even in August, the forests and rivers are cold. Liese and Peter, still adolescents, work in the forestry and logging industry. Sharing the same paper, Maria finds time and space in the crowded barrack to write to her family in Canada. Providing as much of their ongoing saga as she can under the censor's gaze, she reflects on the richness of their past when food was plentiful and their needs were satisfied. Like her husband, she clings to hope, and pleads with her readers to keep her from sinking into despair.*

[1931]

Dear Geschwister Franz and Liese and children,
Yes, it is really as Jasch writes, we long for the former times when we were all together – when we were full of food and had everything. We often say: Our dear God draws us through His goodness even when illness draws near to our dwelling. At your place it was the opposite; you, dear Liese, had to be sick so often, and I often questioned myself: Will we get through life so easily or will our Saviour yet walk very deep ways with us? Now we realize that a

different way, which we did not know of before, was destined for us. It is a hard road, and we cannot understand it, but we believe because: "All things work together for the good to them that love God" (Rom 8:28). So we are comforted and do not despair!

We are still here where we were in the beginning – in the barracks. Life is very hard here because you cannot get anything. We cannot get any potatoes and things like that – cannot get any other things either. The hardest part of all is that we cannot be together with our children. The poor children have to be so unfortunate in their young years. Liese still says, "Why did you not let me go away with Aunt Liese and Uncle Franz? Then I would not be in this awful place!" Well, our dear God will be able to care for His dear children even when things look so dark.

It rains here almost every day and we always get wet while we cook. We are told it stays rainy for a month, then everything freezes up. What we will do then, we do not know yet. The houses, which are supposed to be built for us, are not ready yet. But for the winter we are supposed to go to a new location which is 101 Werst away. We are anxiously waiting for the time to come when we can be together with our children and Abram, and have a little room to ourselves. Here you have to have nerves of steel or you would lose your mind. The day is filled with horribly alarming noises and the rail cars clatter and clang all night. We must rise early in the morning to go to work. My dear Jasch is not left in peace anymore either. He absolutely cannot work anymore – much less walk 111 Werst with a pack on his back. I long so much to receive encouragement and hope from you. Destruction is descending on us with giant strides. Jasch is completely grey and I have a lot of grey hair too.

What are you doing? How is the harvest there? Do your children all go to school? Do you ever hear anything of J.G. and Truda? Greet P.B. heartily; did they receive our letters? I cannot comprehend that you are there and we are here – and our other loved ones are in our lovely homeland – we are all scattered. Papa said to me before we were sent into exile: "The ways of the Lord are right."

May God keep you, your praying Geschwister, J. and M. Regehr

*The losses are many. Simply enduring from day to day is a test of every resource the Regehr family possesses. Jasch, Marie, and their children cling to life. Their remarkable faith sustains them, and their hope remains alive: hope for being released; hope for reuniting with their family and friends in their home village; and, ultimately, hope for emigrating to Canada to join Franz and Liese Bargen. Maria dreams of the day when she and Jasch will be liberated from their oppressors. Yet another kind of hope is evident, one that transcends their circumstances. If they are not set free, Jasch and Maria express the paramount hope of re-uniting with their families after death. Such thoughts sustain them, and give them purpose and strength to endure. But for how long? How does Lena manage to survive, and what happens to her family?*

[1931]

"As a hart crieth for fresh water, so crieth my soul unto God" (Psalm 42). And so we believe that our great God will soon answer the cries of His children and not leave the righteous in turmoil. Are B.K. visiting you and Hans Martens for the first time now? How come Liese and Tina do not write at all? We have received only 2 letters from them. We have written several times to them – even without stamps; maybe that is the reason they do not write. Or is the reason that we asked them to send us something if it was possible? We always hold so very tightly to earthly things. Did they not say anything when they visited you? They have received so many letters from us. His brother Isaac is also sent into exile – 2 of Isaac's sons starved to death. Mrs. Bosch. once wrote that Isaac himself starved to death, but this turned out to be untrue. They wrote to F. Friesen that they should send them parcels. However, they cannot since they themselves are without bread. I wonder if Banmann sent them something?

I thank you, Geschwister, that you have again sent me paper and envelopes! We are completely without paper – and you cannot get any either. I feel so sorry for you, dear Geschwister, that you also are so poor, and above all, that you are so sick. Yes, our dear God wants to educate and train us for heaven so that one day we shall be with Him. Who knows what would have happened to us if we had always had good days? But even these dark days were all in God's plan before we were born – also our poor Liese's way, dear Geschwister!

We regret, dear Geschwister, that you must pay "Postage due" on our letters – we cannot afford the stamps. We thought you received them like that. Truda wrote also that brother John received our letters without having to pay extra. But when we receive money for our work we will always put stamps on the letters. They do not send us any money from home either – outside of Hans, who sent us 15 rubles! Hans had sold our sheep for 30 rubles and got 25 rubles which a Loewen from N. 5 still owed us! A.B. sold Liese's coat for 55 rubles – and Ab. R. sold Jascha's mitts for 1.45 rubles – but they do not send any of it even though they know how desperate we are. Mama wrote that A.B. are living in the summer room by Hans. We are very happy that 4 German [*Mennonite*] families are allowed to live in one little house – at least then the Russians are not always at our place.

This little house is 8 metres long and 6 metres wide, a little stove in the middle on which the 4 families cook. There is enough wood for heating. We get as much wood as we want but must fetch it ourselves. Much work has already been done here – all by exiles! What would happen if suddenly word came down: You are free? I wonder if even one person would stay here? I do not believe so! What a moment that would be! May God give us much grace to endure and to remain faithful until the hour comes when we receive our reward and thank our Saviour with glorified tongues. Yes, my heartily beloved sister Liese, if it is not God's will that I see you again here on earth, then I will see you there and throw my arms around you.

Your praying Geschwister who will never forget you,
Jasch and Marie and children

## Always Winter, Never Christmas

*In the northern Ural Mountains, summer is short and winter is endless. Christmas celebrations of the past are a transient dream. Clothing, shoes, blankets, fuel, and food are never adequate. The writers plead continually, yet are ashamed of their constant neediness. But death by starvation is horrific. Their hair prematurely turns grey and falls out; their skin becomes infected and their stomachs swell. A former friend and now fellow prisoner is dying of malnutrition. His abdominal swelling and his inability to digest food is an ominous sign to those sharing his barrack. Jasch recovers enough to work again, and will now qualify for his ration of food if the local supply is consistent. While surviving the cold and avoiding starvation is a central concern, monitoring the journey of letters and parcels also remains critical.*

[1931]

Have not had a letter from Bargens for a long time. Mrs. Joh. Regehr has already received 17 parcels from America. They are all healthy and living quite well. Joh. Wiens of N. 4 is very swollen because of the poor diet. Do you have food to eat? You cannot buy anything for dollars here. We have already traded our golden rings and now we need the money that people owe us. We hope to be reimbursed as soon as possible. Tomorrow Peter and I must begin to go to work. We get no bread for our family today, and we do not know when we will get any more. May God save us from death by starvation. Well, maybe all things work together for good. Is Joh. Warkentin N. 7 home already? The talk here is that all those from Boraga have been moved away. Well, all of you stay in God's protection, pray for us, give greetings to Ab. Regehrs. Did they receive our letter?

Jakob and M. Regehr

*Jasch's recovery is short-lived. He has typhus, a menacing disease transmitted by fleas and lice that are abundant in the camps. The prisoners have few opportunities to wash themselves or their clothing, and body lice thrive.*

*The cold weather draws the lice indoors and the crowding encourages their propagation. Jasch faces days of fever, an irritating purple rash, intestinal inflammation, and severe muscle spasms. Without treatment, his heart and brain will swell and cause his death. But he continues to work, driven by desperation.*

*With her husband becoming sicker, Maria finds her responsibilities increasing. She must walk long distances in the cold wilderness to find food. She is aware that Christmas is approaching, and memories of past celebrations haunt her. Celebrating Christmas is a crime, and work continues as usual. Yet Maria is relieved that Tina, now twelve years old, has been granted leave from railroad construction to attend school. While it is not a conventional school, choices for prisoners are limited and Tina is fortunate to have this option.*

*Although their surroundings are desolate, Maria finds humour in the unexpected "folly" (pregnancy) of an aging couple in their home village – if only they had followed the instructions in "The Golden Book." Evidently, publications about birth control were accessible to the Russian Mennonite community. Everyone in the barrack has gone to sleep. Maria finds paper and pencil, bends over the trunk, and writes.*

[1931]

I too want to send a few lines of love to you. It is now evening, everyone has gone to rest. Everyone is tired from work and I am tired too. Today I walked to Aynebka twice. I got 35 kilo cabbage for 35k. per kilo. A Mrs. Fast and I went with a little sleigh. We had loaded 72 kilo on it and pulled it. It is about 5 to 6 Werst away and the road is up and down hill. We dragged it home, had a bite to eat, and went back and each got a jar containing 15 kilo of tomato pulp for 20r. We shopped for the winter.

But that beautiful money does not want to stretch far enough. I am always astounded by our son Peter. He hands over all his money so we can buy food. Compare that with Jasch F. who gives up none of his money; he has already saved up 500r. but claims he too must give up all his wages. But the difference between Friesen and my dear Jasch is also great. He is healthy and strong while my Jasch is sick. My Jasch is a watchman, which is very hard for him. He earns 50r. per month compared to J.F. who earns up to 318r. per month. I feel so sorry for my Jasch when he goes to work early in the morning or at 10 o'clock at night. Many a moan rises from him to God, but our suffering stays as it was – and no end in sight.

When will the time come when we will see each other face to face? I have such a great desire to see you all again, as well as B. Kl. At times I am so dejected that B. Kl. do not even write us a letter. We love them too, they are our Geschwister. Is Dietrich married yet? Please write about this. Dear Geschwister, how can we ever repay you for all the deeds of kindness that you, dear souls, do for us? Again you sent off a parcel – and with your last funds. If God will only bring it into our hands quickly and undamaged, we will thank Him and you! Who could ever have imagined that we would stand here so helpless and poor? How hard it is to understand the road God makes us travel. I always remember the words our dear Papa used to say, even in his last letter: "The ways of the Lord are right!" If we can always believe that, it supports and maintains us.

Tomorrow we will be cleaning our barracks. It is now yellow and discolored by smoke. Our stove smokes a lot – it just does not seem to draw – so we must clean. Soon, soon the lovely days of Christmas will upon us. How will you celebrate them, compared to us? If only we could again experience them as we once did.

Dear Liese, you wrote something very interesting about P.B. How can it be possible? They were already so smart in their younger years, and besides, they took along "Das Goldene F. Buch" [*a reproductive and birth-control manual*]. And now to commit such folly in their old age. It never would have entered our minds. H.F. said, "If P. had been here with us in the Urals, it never would have entered his mind." That will not be one they wished for. If we would all be together, as in olden days, what laughter there would be, right? From my heart I wish them joy, and I am not jealous – not a bit!

My sister Truta writes she will probably marry a B. Epp. She has done much for us too; she sent 35 dollars for us to the Torgsin, and also 2 parcels. She writes her landlords are very good but they cannot send anything. They wish only the best for my sister. I did not receive the letter with the picture. What kind of picture was it? I am so sorry. I received all the clippings in the last letter. No danger until now. Please write often and lots. For us it is always too long before a letter arrives.

What are your little children doing? Our Tina goes to school now too. She is so happy that she is away from the railroad. Well, a warm greeting and in my spirit I kiss you.

From your Geschwister who never forget you, J. & M.

*The risks of writing and receiving mail are increasing. Although Jasch and Marie track their correspondence, desperately needed letters and packages are missing more often.*

[1931/32]

.... the reasons for the unrest of which you write; if only they did not go lost. We believe and pray that God will let them come into our hands. Warkentin writes from Walogda that he had a package all ready to send to his wife, and just as he was trying to send it a telegram arrived saying no packages were to be sent until the 1st of May. Maybe our situation will change in time? Imagine, we have experienced 2 famines in 13 years in this great expansive Russia – and at the time of a rich harvest! Is that not so? Just think, dear Geschwister, how can such a thing be?

We received a letter from home on April 2nd. Mama and Papa wrote. Papa writes that he still hopes to get well! Hans is joyfully looking forward to the days when the sun will beat warmly into his home. He wants to lie in the sun, for the sun can do miracles! Pray every day that God might spare their lives and give us the occasion to see each other again. We wrote a letter to you last Sunday in which we described our trip. Probably you received the letter. We thought we might get a better place but it seems that everything stays the same – we certainly will not walk on roses here either. We would not really mind, if only we would get bread! How nice the black bread tastes – far nicer than the nicest Vereniki [*filled dumplings*] used to taste. On Aug. 22 we received a letter from J. Goosens. They write that they are sending us a package – and three times Truda has sent us 5 dollars. May God reward the poor orphans and my dear youngest sister and bless them. Too bad that Peter B. dealt that way with the 5 dollars which they sent through him. We can hardly get over it.

*In heavily masked language, Jasch and Marie describe the fate of their oldest daughter Liese. She has escaped from her prison camp and subversively returned to her home village of Altonau. Well-meaning family members and friends persuade her to apply for a position in the Commune. To do this, she must report her return to the local headquarters and ask for an issue of new, clean clothes. Naively, she consents. She is immediately arrested and sent to a punishment cell in a northern prison.*

We find it hard to cope with the many obstacles which are thrown in our path – and the most difficult is that it has to strike our poor child. Why did everyone at home encourage her to go to the regional office and tell her then she would be set free? And she believed them – and now? – and only because her clothes were soiled. Things here are going as in Naboth's Vineyard, right? [*An Old Testament narrative recorded in 1 Kings 21.*] Oh, my heart bleeds and weeps, my thoughts are with her in prison. How shall I bear it all? How that poor child will already have begged and wept – if only she does not sink into the depths of despair. Not only is her body being ruined but her whole being, soul and spirit, are being brutalized and killed. Is this also the Liebesabsichten [*a sacrifice, motivated by love*] of my Saviour?

*On the last day of January 1932, in forty-two degrees below freezing and a metre of snow, Jasch notes the change in their location. Although he warns that they may be moved again in a few days, he also verifies the existence of an underground network of information and mail delivery; he appears confident that "parcels ... will find us anywhere."*

Aynebka 31/1/32

Dear Parents and Geschwister!
We send you greetings of love; we want to send you a sign of our love again. Today is Sunday and parcels are being distributed. That is done on Sunday because the workers have no time on working days. Friesens again got one with fruit, butter, and Christmas presents. They got nice things. They got the 12r. from their Geschwister. Then we rejoice with those who rejoice – but without emotion or participation. We are especially worried about Abram. Lena and Mariechen have forgotten their brother and us very quickly. Abram is the only one here who has not received anything.

Well enough – God will awaken some ravens here or there who will provide for Abram and for us. But both Mariechen and Lena do too little for him. We are in a situation where we are selling our clothes, pillows and shoes etc., to be able to get some money. My dear Marie took the woolen scarves to the bazaar in Kizel to sell, but she did not sell any – it was just too cold during those days. At night she stayed at the bazaar and came home the next day quite exhausted. We have more than a metre of snow. It snows almost every night. Yesterday we had 42 degrees of frost. It was very quiet but cutting cold. Our dear Liese got her feet frozen. Today she went to see the doctor and he wanted to remove her big toe. We have cried a lot here. Peter is still at Tcmohnun – have not heard from him for a long time. He has a very hard lot and lives in terrible conditions there. For 7 months he has been living only from that small piece of bread he receives daily. We hear he is very pale and thin. We also sent him something from the parcel we received from our good friends and that, of course, makes our situation even more critical.

Abram still works in the forest 8 Werst away from here. He is well. Tuesday he wants to go to the bazaar in Kizel to sell his things. You get no money for your work. You cannot buy any potatoes – actually you can buy nothing – that is why we are so concerned about Abram. He should get something sent to him from the Koops. The time may come when Abram could work to repay them. I have submitted his name in several places and he will probably get a parcel sent to him by friends or even strangers. There are still some sympathetic people.

We will probably be shipped to another place in the next few days – to the place where Peter is. Tomorrow 53 families will be moved – we cannot guess where to. The German [Mennonite] families stay here – we, H. Friesens, Joh. Regehrs and J. Wiens. We regret that we are again being torn apart, but we want to remain true. If only we could retain our health and have patience and courage, maybe it will not last very long. But our future looms dark before us, especially in regard to the supply of bread. However, it is a small thing for God to change the situation.

I have not been at work for several days. The Kommandant ordered me to appear before him a few times but I was always released again. He has thrown many like me into jail. Cor. Thielmann is in prison for the 4th day already. Tell Ab. Regehr, if he has not already done so, not to send any heavy parcels before we notify you when we will be sent further, because that lifting is very difficult for him – rather send it through the mail, then it will find us anywhere. We have written to Rg. and also to H. Goosen. Have they received the letters? We write a lot but we receive very few letters.

How do things look with the health of all of you? Is Hans' health improving? Have you already killed a sparrow for food? We are very sorry, Mama, that you did not send us some tomatoes – that is what adds flavour to the soup. Well, I will close – may you all remain in God's care. Our children send warm regards. Marie will write further. We have no stamps. Abram is at work – his day of rest is Tuesday. He gets every 6th day. Brother Hans, send us some money – at least half. And what does it help if someone wants to send something and does not have the money for it? Please do it, dear brother. Boldt should send me the 55 rubles for the overcoat. We desperately need it!

*Maria again shares the paper, reporting on the state of their clothes and pleading for food.*

Dearly beloved parents,
It is with some anxiety that we desire to know how things are with your health. I take pen in hand to report to you that we are still alive. Oh, dear parents, when will the time come when we can see each other face to face? Here it seems that they want to evacuate everything by February 18th. They gave out Pejok [*possible meaning: points for work*] until the 1st, when ordinarily they would always give it for 14 days. We ran out of wood and coal so that for 2 days we could barely cook our meals. In the barracks it is severely cold. It seems as if everything is collapsing around us. Greetings to Franz Voths and Abr. Regehrs, Liese, Hans and Sonja. If we should be allowed to come back we would have no house. Would you allow us into your house and give us something to eat? Or do you not have anything yourselves? Tell us! Jascha often says he wants to go home and drink some milk. Is your cow fresh already? Then spread some butter on your bread so that you will grow tall. Give warm greetings to your Papa and Mama. Do not be offended that we send this letter without stamps – there are none to be found.

Do you hear anything there about the possibility of our coming home? Jasch must load barley and oats at the station and deliver it today. For this he earns his piece of bread. Abram certainly does not get fat either from the little piece of daily bread which he gets. Has Boldt already looked for Zakaznou B. Oblihazia? Yesterday H. Friesen received a parcel with Christmas presents – they celebrated Christmas today. Boschmanns still have of everything. When we observe all that, then the commandment "Thou shalt not covet" is so hard to keep. May the great God send us times when we will again be able to celebrate Christmas as in former days. The lining in

Abram's underpants is completely torn – I just do not know what to do with them. I also gave him the new stockings to wear underneath so that he would not freeze his feet.

*On a Soviet postcard, a red broom sweeps away unwanted filth: a member of the clergy (figure with a halo), a member of the intelligentsia (figure with glasses), and a* kulak *(large, overweight figure). The large red "BOH" screams "Go Away!" Across these images, a despairing father pleads for his family.*

[1931/32]

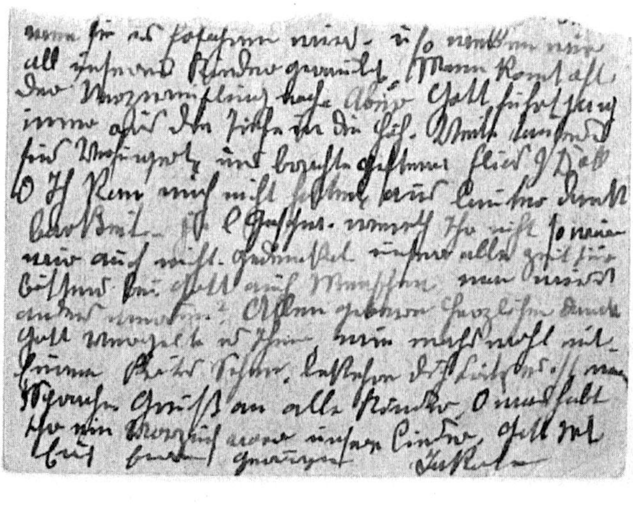

...when she will experience it. And so we are robbed of all our children. One often gets close to despair. But God always leads out of the depths onto the heights. Many thousands have starved. Yesterday we received the 9 dollars from you. Oh, I just cannot restrain myself out of sheer thankfulness. Yes, dear siblings, if you were not here we would no longer be here either.

"Remember us at all times" is our cry to God as well as to people. When will things change? Hearty thanks to all those who have given. May God reward them. How are things with your Peter? Fritz, be saved while there is time. Greetings to all the children. Oh what advantages your children have over ours! God be with you.

Your humble Jacob

My Marie just said we have no more flour. The dollar is worth about 1r. 37 k. Things are looking very very bad for our Peter. Help, Geschwister, please. We can hardly carry our burden any longer. He can no longer walk. On June 27th we reported the news from grandfather to you. This night I dreamt a lot about him. Aufwiedersehen.

Your humble, Jacob

*Sitting beside her daughter Tina, Maria describes their conditions and thinks about cabbage, bread, and watery soup.*

Today is the 12 of January [1932]

Dear Geschwister Franz and Liese,
I just want to visit with you in this evening hour. I am sitting at our small table on a wooden block. Tina is sitting beside me and is drawing pictures. Will enclose it. She should study, but there is so much noise in the barracks that you cannot hear yourself speak. You have to have good nerves to concentrate and write a letter. A week ago I wrote you a letter and also answered the letter written on Nov. 30. I presume you have received them. How happy we are every time we receive a letter from you. Write often, and write the

good news: that there will be help for us here! But we do believe "Our help comes from the Lord!" It could happen overnight – when it is God's time!

We believe it will be soon because we have run out of everything here. There is almost nothing to buy – and what you can buy is so expensive that it is prohibitive. 1 kilo herring, 5 ruble, 1 litre oil, 40r., 1 loaf of bread from 20 to 30r. and a pud flour costs 130r. Those who do not earn a lot of money can start nothing. Our family has not received any money for 3 months and so the mantle of worry and sorrow wants to dominate our life. How happy we are that in the darkest hours we can run to Jesus who cares – there we can leave every worry! The future is very dark – we are especially worried about bread. The salary workers are all in the Cmanobua [*canteen or dining hall*] and get 1 kilo bread a day, but in the last week it was irregular and they received no bread for 2 days. Several days they got only 100 grams per meal but must still work very hard.

How happy and thankful we are that you have sent so much to us and to many others! If this were not so we would no longer be here. Oh yes, God knew how to care for us and keep us alive. Brother Hans also sent us 5 dollars here to Perm. We got 2 kilo 75% flour, 2 kilo rye porridge, and bought products for the rest of the money – but always they take half of everything for shipping costs. Yes, God has blessed those dollars so. We received that parcel with tears. We look forward so much to receiving the parcel you are sending via Moscow – it seems so slow in getting here. Oh, if only it would not go missing. We always pray that nothing will go lost and that God personally protect the things being sent to us.

Did you specify the kind of material for Liese's dress? And what else? We are so excited. Sister Truta also sent us a parcel via Iceland. The card was from Dec. 6. It should actually be here. I wonder what my little sister is sending? One of our bosses is reputed to have said, "In spring the famine will be so great that people will lie on the roads like the railway ties that are now being laid." Then I shudder to think of the future. When will all this misery end? We firmly believe that our great God will end this misery soon and call a halt to these deeds of brutality.

Well, what are you doing? I am so glad that you, dear Liese, send me such nice recipes. Too bad we cannot get cabbage or anything else here – we only get that which arrives in parcels. In 8 months we have only made thin watery soups – and it costs a lot – and there is never enough bread. Too bad that grain is so very cheap in your country. If the grain had a decent price, many might be able to help us here in our distress. Well, God will look after us whatever the future may bring.

Your Geschwister, Jasch and Marie Regehr

*Parcels from southern Ukraine are becoming less frequent, and packages from "America"(North America) are becoming scarce. Another kind of desperation is occurring in the West. Unknown to Jasch and Maria, in October 1929 prosperity ground to a halt with the stock market collapse in New York, Toronto, Montreal, and around the world. The crash set off a chain of events that plunged the continent and the world into a decade-long depression. It was the beginning of the "Dirty Thirties." The Great Depression caused Canadian workers extreme hardship. Prices deflated rapidly and business activity fell sharply. Massive unemployment – twenty-seven percent at the height of the Depression in 1933 – resulted, and families lost most of their assets. All of North America suffered, but farming communities were most affected. Grain-growing areas experienced the greatest decrease in per capita income between 1928 and 1933. Although Jasch and Maria are aware of some of the hardships of their Canadian readers, relative to the desperation in the prison camps, the North Americans appear prosperous.*

[January 1932]

Dearly beloved Geschwister,
We received your most welcome letter of 27 and 31 December, on 22 January. We have received all your letters, even those two, dear Liese, which you wrote in the hospital. We read them and sent them

to our home as you asked. We are so happy that the letters go so regularly. We answer all letters but are so concerned for you, dear Liese, that you are not well. If only you could get well again. We thought you were completely well!

Dear Liese, it is not good for your health to worry so about us. You should be happy and joyful with your family and enjoy the good days that God has given you. And do not be sad! God will definitely help us – that is our faith. He gives strength to the weak and courage to the helpless. We have all experienced that. Let us leave these problems with our great God. Let us have faith that He will give you health, sustain us in our tribulation, and give us all the gift of again seeing each other in this life. That is the assurance we live by.

You write that you hope our misery will soon end. J.K. from there also wrote to H.S. that the families should stay together. Is there any truth in that? L. and A. [*Liese and Abram*] are primarily concerned with looking for distance [*a masked message that indicates they want to flee*]. We want to make some money by selling pillows, and then let them go – everything is coming to an end here. They just cannot live on the one piece of bread they get for working an entire day. The little children must give up some of their bread so that the adults, who work so hard, can survive. So, if they move further away and find work, at least their pay will be food. And we can then improve our chances as well. We thought in the beginning A., L, and P. [*Jasch's brother Abram, and children Liese and Peter*] would be a real support, but now it is just the opposite. It is not easy for us to encourage them to leave, but we can see that staying here is wrong for them – we will all die of starvation. And if they go somewhere – to the Duezstroj [*unknown word*] or some other place – they may even be able to send us something. Many young men have left here and they get by.

We wrote and asked if Liese could go to [...]. If we get an answer she will be gone – as well as A. Here they all perish doing forced labour. Imagine, working all day while standing up to your knees in deep snow – always wet. That must end in severe rheumatism. How we worry about our children – and our dear son – who cannot be with us! I am so afraid he will starve to death, or that he will get sick and die! How often have I cried and asked: "Oh God, why? Why such a way?" I cannot understand it. Even though our rations are insufficient for us, we sent something to him with H.V. – some foodstuffs. The poor boy will be happy if he gets it. I have already said: "Our Peter will be able to testify to the greatest hunger anyone has experienced." But dear Liese, do not worry about it. No, just read the letters and then be in a joyful mood again. Maybe your dream that we will see each other again will come true, and we will be able to talk face to face. Then we want to talk and cry together, and praise God for his wonderful help and leading. Those will be wonderful hours!

There are several here whose feet have been frozen – a young lad, whose toes all froze. That happened 3 months ago. Today those toes still look like they have been through a meat grinder. On Sunday a man, with holes in the soles of his shoes, came to the other end of the village. There is a lady shoemaker here, a very good woman. Her husband and her 3 daughters are still with her but all have frozen their feet. They are lying there in the [...] and waiting until transportation is available. And then, would you believe it, they have to pay their own way! That is the way they deal with you when you are "kaput" [*broken*]. They abandon the people with the order, "Now look after yourselves." I feel so very sorry for that woman. She has 3 children – one has died. Her parents moved to Germany in 1918. They write they will request her return to Germany and she should try to keep the family together. We experience many such things here.

We have not had a letter from home for some time – they write very little. A week ago we received a letter from A.R. They write that Papa is getting weaker every day, and Hans is still bedridden and often very distressed. I guess we will not see him again if we have to remain here much longer. How sad about good brother Hans and his poor wife and children – they are still demanding grain from them even though they have given their last long ago. How will Russia ever weather this calamity?

It snows here almost every day but it is not too cold. We discern God's hand in that too. We look with foreboding into the future. But we know what the last year was like and God brought us to the new year, healthy! But we do not know what lies ahead. We would love to be freed!! Saved! – and come to your country. That is our wish! A.R. sent us 2 packages a few weeks ago. They do a lot for us. May the great God bless all those who do good to us. Wishing you, dear loved ones, the very best! And may this letter find you in the best of health.

In love, your ever remembering Geschwister, J. and M. and children

*Liese, now released from her punishment cell and free to work again as a slave labourer, writes to her aunt, uncle, and cousins in Canada. She is twenty years old. Her work cutting trees in the frozen forest requires resolute survival skills. In the darkest days of winter, Christmas has passed without fanfare. In the new atheist regime, religious celebrations and rituals of the past are prohibited. Liese is desperate to escape. Her life is being wasted in the Siberian mountains, and she longs to go home and begin a new life with a new husband. She is tempted to use "the weapons of the rabbits" once again.*

24 Jan. [1932]

Dear Aunt Liese and Uncle Franz and children,
Since it is Sunday today, I will to try to write and answer your very precious letter. When I came home from work yesterday, Lena came to meet me and she was so happy. "You have a letter from America, from Aunt Liese!" Yes, Aunt Liese, I felt proud and privileged over the others to personally receive a letter from you. I value it very highly and am so delighted. It was not meant to be as grim as you seem to interpret it. I regret that I hurt your feelings and will never do it again.

Now I wish all of you the very best of health, which we also enjoy to this very day. Recently Jascha was rather sickly. But we gave him extra "Speck" [*pork fat*] from our meagre rations; now he is quite cheerful. We are so very thankful for that package from you. We exist on a very slim diet. It is so sad that my dear brother's portion has been lost. Peter, that poor fellow, has now been imprisoned for 7 months and daily gets only his little piece of bread for which he must work very hard. He is often very close to despair. He cannot understand why he must suffer so in his best years. He and P.D. and J.F. and H.W. have tried to flee from here, but were caught every time! Elder H. Voth from Melkg. was here last week Sunday, and he told us the last time they were caught they were sent to jail for 3 days without even 1 piece of bread. Then Voth put in a good word for them. They were freed then but literally driven and chased back to their forced labour.

I have a very dangerous and hazardous job as well. I must chop down trees in the forest. It is often very cold and an average of 1 meter deep snow so that you often sink into the snow up to your hips. We are about 20 km away from Aynebka in a barracks filled with nothing but Russians – and we are 9 children of Mennonites. We do not have many joyful experiences here in the Urals. We hope things will change again. Not so long ago a young girl was killed by a falling tree and crushed into the snow so far that only the corner of her dress was visible. And so we are full of fear from one day to the next. I am tempted to use the weapons of the rabbits [*run away*], but who knows if that will happen. Here you cannot live on what you earn! You wrote that Santa Claus was very poor at your house; well, he went right past our place without stopping. We were not even allowed to take a day of rest.

Hearty greeting from your loving L.R.

Now Mama will write too!

*Mother Maria is curious about China. On another piece of paper the same size, she wonders about rumours that have been circulating. In the winter of 1930, a group of Mennonite families living near the Chinese border fled south over the frozen Amur River to China. Other groups followed and escaped to freedom. Somehow the news of this escape route had traveled.*

*Maria's hopes are evident in her words written between the lines of previous script.*

Aynebka, 25 January 1932

Dear Geschwister Franz and Liese,
We bring you a greeting of love. We received your very interesting letter on Dec. 27th. Many thanks. Mrs. Dueckmann is no longer at our place. They are in [...], about 110 km from here. They actually were on the way home [*escaping back to their home village*] but were stopped and their tickets were taken from them and she was sent back. We will see that she gets the letter.

Dear sister, we are happy that your health is improving. It has been our constant prayer to God that you may become well and have a long life, for you are our support in this place. Our situation worsens every day. We have been completely without bread for 2 days, and today we have not eaten anything. Later we will cook rice and eat. But that is the way it must be if our food is to last as long as possible. We must ration our food so that it lasts longer.

Yes, we do not know how our dear God will yet deal with us, but we so much want to believe that help will soon arrive. After all, so many prayers are being said for us everywhere. If only we could get some money from someplace we would send our L. [*Liese*] away from here. My dear Marie will go to the bazaar to sell some pillows. The work that Liese is forced to do here she just cannot do much longer. They must fell trees – 50 trees per day per person. The trees have thick trunks about 8-16 [*inches*] in diameter, and many are even thicker. They are up to 185 [*feet*] high. When it is windy the work is very dangerous, since you cannot control where the tree will fall. Several men have been killed. A few days ago a girl was killed at work. Let Barg. P. continue his efforts so that she can come over.

Peter is still in the Dopper [*prison*]. Our heart almost breaks – the burden lies so heavily on our hearts. He has lived only on black bread and fish for 7 months now, and then only 300-400 grams of bread a day. Now we have sent him some food from that which you have sent us. May God bless you a hundredfold. Please continue to remember us! We can only see dark and hard times before us. We have written to Kroeker about our life to this point; please ask and report if he has received it. If we get any parcels from him, we will let you know immediately. May God bless him that he should care for us strangers. Surely it is a result of your work, and I just do not know how we can thank you enough. We will leave it to our heavenly Father. He will surely reward you. Why do B's not write? Please send greetings to them as well as to your landlords.

Your Geschwister, Jak. and M.R.

[*Written around the edges and in between sentences*] Write us what is happening in China. Could it come to us too? Mr Nickel died in Kherson on 7 Jan. His wife did not go there. Oma has made a very tragic mistake in her life because she got divorced. She should help carry the burden but now she is alone and has fallen into the pit. She was one flesh and soul with war. Very, very sad that it happened like this. She should have endured for this short time – "until death do you part."

## "Writing through the flowers"

*Although previous letters include masked messages, no letter is as confusing as the next one. Only a very specific reader would understand the intended meaning of "Papa," the "garden," and the activities of baking bread and selling plums. Jasch would not send this carefully crafted message to his elderly parents in Altonau if he was not in danger. Someone is sitting across the street with a gun. His words need to bypass this hostile reader. Only an allied recipient of the letter would understand his encoded message. His mother understands. She adds her own message around the edges of the paper: she explains that her son is writing "through the flowers as if 2 are present." She knows he uses flowery language to distract unwelcome eyes. Mother Liese sends the letter to her other children in Canada, where it is read, interpreted, and placed in the Campbell's Soup box.*

Thursday, 4 /II/1932. At the same place.

Dearly beloved Fr. Hans R. J.R. A L M,
Since loneliness and love for you drives us to write, we will send you a small sign of life and love. We are all very well, which we also wish for you with all our hearts. We arrived home safely from our trip. Everything is in the best order. We were welcomed very much. At 11 o'clock I went back to my usual work. Today we have a day of rest. I am sitting beside Papa [*likely a guard*] in the garden and writing. Where she is I do not know, probably visiting around some place. Our P. and N. were fearful that we would get a different place, but we are very happy that we could come home once again. When I went to work yesterday, I was given a paper that I should report to [...] on the 4th. This morning I went there early. The place is in a dark cellar. Such things go on here, one after the other. How long I will have to learn I do not know. [*Time in prison is often referred to euphemistically in other letters as "receiving an education."*] I always go there after work! Ber[...] is sitting across the street concealing himself and ready to shoot me. It is hard. It is enough!

Otherwise everything here is as before. We and our dear old parents are baking a lot of bread to send to H.R.M. We wanted to take our Ma here, but it is a little too late, because here they have already distributed the bread for 3 months. Now papa says we will send her money, 10-15 rubles every month, and when 2 ½ months have passed then he will bring her here. If only our old Ma does not become discouraged; things will not stay like this. We will send off the "Pas" as soon as possible, or if possible you can bring Mama some plums to sell. Ten plums cost her 1 ½ rubles. Then you, dear people, visit us at the same time. You shall have it good at that time, Papa says. Papa suggests you buy a return ticket so that you would have a good return trip and still be able to buy a number of things.

Dear Mariechen, be so kind and visit us. Just write us when you will be coming, and we will wait for you at the station. When you get this letter, then write back immediately if you can come. But do not refuse this request. Demonstrate your love to us. How do things look with that dear Hans Regehr? Are they still all alive? Tell him if he cannot write, then his dear Susie should write. Would love to hear from them and also from you. Greet Abram Boldt and his wife warmly. Regehrs want to write to them shortly. They are just too busy at the moment. Well, I must close. Hope to get an answer soon. Asking you please to visit us. Ade. Ade. [*Adieu*]

In love, we remain your friends, J.R.

[*Written around the edges*] We will send you what we can, only be patient. Greet all our friends J. M. M. N. M. W. J. W. S. W. all of them. Oh dear loved ones, we miss our dear loved one – like never before. If it is possible, visit us now! I am sending you the address of our "dear heart." He is quite well, just as we read of the youngest son Benjamin. [*Readers familiar with the Old Testament story of Joseph and Benjamin will know that Jasch is being sacrificed for a greater political cause.*] He wants to come home on October 1st for 14 days. God is caring for us. I have nothing more to do with the blood, only my womb is coming out on me. [*This elderly woman obviously suffers from uterine dysfunction.*] He always writes durch die Blumen [*through the flowers*] as if 2 are present. Peter, Liese, Michi shall also come to him if they can. P. Ungers are the ones who came to J. Wiebes in N. 8. Not converted.

*Descriptions of food are easier to understand. Writing through the flowers does not appear to be necessary. Hunger does not need to be masked. In the frost of February, the only life that seems to thrive is lice and bedbugs. The Regehr family (now only the youngest children with their parents) remains in the same region of the Ural Mountains, but they have moved once more: "shuffled around from one place to another like old furniture." This letter identifies Lunowka as the region where they now live.*

Lunowka, 5/II/32

Dear Geschwister Klassen and children,
We come to you with a greeting of love. We received your most precious letter. Many thanks for the same. You, dear brother-in-law, because of your brother Isaak, ask whether there are any people here from Siberia. No, there are only Ukrainians, Germans and those from Sagradowka here. I think those from Siberia have been sent even further north. The entire population is mobilized and dispersed. Many Tatars from Asia and further, together with their horses, are mobilized for a period of 4 months.

It is like that at home too. They had to go to the Krim [*Crimea*] for work to dig out cotton plants. No person is any longer his own master. We are shuffled around from one place to another like old furniture. We were told 65 families will be sent on to Bursia, and then only 4 families of our people will remain here, Wiens of N. 4 and Mrs. Joh. Regehr – you probably know that he died on the 6th of January. H. Friesens and we are already very afraid we will all be separated and dispersed even further. We would much rather remain here on the "Naren" until our salvation comes. Will it come soon? When we see how things are going we feel it could be soon. At times they do not even distribute any bread, and we have now been without bread for 4 days. He who does not have something else, like beans or other things, has had to starve for 4 days.

We have not been able to satisfy our hunger for such a very long time. The bread is always measured and apportioned, but only on those days when it is distributed. Such workers as Abram get, if they are working, 300-400 grams of bread per day – and nothing else! On Sundays no one gets anything! Or, if you stay home one day – nothing to eat! Then you can imagine how the worker here lives. The other family members get, or should get, at most, 200 gr. per day – but even this is seldom given – and then for 4 days nothing is distributed. On the average the children eat a ¼ p. bread a day and then such wet, heavy and sour bread – not made with wheat flour but from rye or barley. The thought of wheat flour is beyond our imagination.

Our children look very pale. Once a day they eat a rice soup from the supply which F. Bargens sent us, but it does not last very long – soon it is also gone! The future looks so dark. We really believed, dear little sister and brother-in-law, that you would send us something. But you, dear brother-in-law, write you are poor. If you are poor, or even poorer, and could see our situation, you would say, "How rich we are and how fortunate in comparison with them!" Well, dear Geschwister, have mercy on Abram and send him something. No one here has yet received anything that has been sent through the Board. If it is sent by individuals it does get here. We received something from J. Wiebes. Did you encourage them, dear sister? May God bless you. He also included in the parcel powdered milk so that we can eat rice with milk now. Our Geschwister Bargens have sent 5 parcels from there: one to Johann Regehr, one to Dueckmanns of N. 8, two to us, and our brother Abram received one. May God reward our Geschwister a hundredfold, and He will do it too.

We fully realize how much they spend on doctors and how much they give away – and in spite of that they still have a harvest. That is the kind of blessing that our dear Papa used to speak about, right? Our wish and prayer is that we can endure and keep the faith. Often we are led into the desert and believe now it is all over – there is no answer to prayer. Suddenly we realize that the answer is there already, but quite differently than we had expected it. We received one letter from home, and it is very hard there too. It has been a long time for our old parents to be without even one piece of bread. They are living on potatoes and cabbage, and anything that good people give to them.

Papa's situation is deteriorating. Since Hans Regehr went to Sagradowka [*the Mennonite colony in which the home village of Altonau is situated*], he has not been out of his bed. He will have a hard time to survive. What are John Martens doing? Are they still alive? We never hear anything of them. We wrote to them – I wonder it they received the letter? We definitely believed that good Agatha and that good John would do Samaritan services for us sufferers. We loved each other so much and visited each other so often when they still lived here in Russia. Oh, dear relatives and friends. do not forget us here. If we do not soon get help – and food is impossible to get here – then we are staring death in the face. Our Peter still is not to be found, and we have no idea where he is. Someone just came from where Peter is supposed to be and he knows nothing of him. Should that poor boy perish somewhere? Oh, that makes our situation so very depressing that we cannot sleep day or night.

Liese has frozen her feet. The doctor wanted to remove her big toe immediately. She would not allow this! But now we do not know how it will develop without the amputation. She seems to be recovering. Michi [*Mariechen*] is quite grown up. She does not go to work now because she is registered as somewhat younger. Tina, Lena and Jascha sit all day long on the "Naren" [...]. Outside it is too cold. It is very cold outside – up to 42 degrees frost and very much snow – over 1 metre on average. My dear Marie knits and mends all day, or kills lice – there are very many of those here, as well as bed-bugs, and they do not let us sleep at night....

Your loving Geschwister, J. and M. Regehr

## Isolation and Confusion

*Although hunger and disease consume them, this family also hungers for knowledge. They crave to know about events beyond their prison camp. Rumours and speculation circulate. Jasch hears that something is happening in China, but he is "in a sack" – isolated from news of national and global events.*

Lunowka 25/II. [1932]

Dear Geschwister F. and Liese and children,
Today, dear Geschwister, we want to honour you with this: "We are not worthy of all the kindnesses you do unto us." We received the parcels from A. Kroeker. We have written our deepest thanks.

However, a big thank-you is for you too; it was you who sent our names to him. Our thanks are but empty phrases; but we call to you the very words of our Saviour: "I was hungry and you gave me food." Matthew 25:34-36.

Dear Geschwister, we have often been envious of your good traits; if only we had them too. I have often, very often I must confess, hindered my dear little wife when she wanted to give something to someone. When she would ask me, or tell me she felt the urge to give so and so a sack of flour or wheat, then I would first discuss it with the human side of my nature – and in the end nothing was done. I now confess that I have done great wrong in this regard. She gave away much, but often quietly and only told me a little later. May God reward her and may He forgive me. I have made a promise to God, and to my dear Marie, never, but never to hinder but rather to support. Therein lies a great blessing. Is that not right, dear Geschwister? God will certainly reward you, and even more so your children as well. Those are God's promises. If even a cold drink of water will not go unrewarded, how much more all this that you have done, and still will do for us – just as you have written, dear Liese. You are setting a good example for your children.

How are things with your health, sister? We have not had a letter from you for a long while; we were surprised but wonder if letters may have gone lost. We sent our last letter off on 12/II. Did you receive the one from our dear Peter? Oh, that poor boy is still somewhere in the forest, if he is still alive. People are beginning to swell and some have already died. Yesterday an adult died of "Hungertifus" [*hunger typhus*] and 2 children from a neighbouring barracks died of malnutrition. Those who must subsist solely on what they receive here do not survive, it is just not enough.

Much is being said here that there are K. who are fighting with those who have long pigtails [*Chinese*]. Is that true? We don't get to hear anything – we are as if in a sack. No newspapers are allowed to reach us. We would even be satisfied not to know what is going on if only our deliverance would come quickly; many thousands are waiting for that with indescribable longing. Many of the younger people have escaped from here. Our Abram is also toying with the idea. When he has saved enough money, he will leave. I really do not want him to leave; I feel that the poor boy will get himself into a squeeze, but of course he hopes to get through. Besides, he can't go home, he would still have to be on the move and hiding out in his attempt to save his life. If you want to send something to him, then send it in Peter's name or in my dear Marie's name. When he is gone and should a parcel arrive in his name, they would not give it to us. We would send it to him as soon as we had his address.

Last night the Kommandant read the rules to us. He especially emphasized the fact that we had been sent here for 5 years, and if we would be on good behaviour in these years we would again be enfranchised! Ach, I thought, what a long road we still have before us. Then all kinds of questions were asked of him. Finally he said, "Today we have sunshine and tomorrow we have frost." And that is also the way we believe it will happen; it can happen today or tomorrow. God will answer the prayers of His children.

We received a letter from Aron Regehrs [*close relatives of the recipients in Canada: Franz Bargen's sister Katherina is married to Liese Bargen's cousin Aron*]. The future looms forebodingly before them as well. The boys are working. Peter works in the Commune and Hein, I believe, in Kherson. Jakob was conscripted. They live in J.'s little house, but he is allowed to be home. They have already traded their gold rings for flour. I believe they got 1 pud flour per ring. Many are doing this just to remain alive. My dear little wife will go to see if she can trade hers for flour. But I do not have one. But nothing seems to go very far. One "nyg" of flour is only enough for baking twice. Then it too is gone. Many have traded their clothes, and even their bedding, for bread. For a good pillow you can get 2 pails of potatoes. And so, the people soon run out of goods, and finally are completely out of bread! This happens mostly among Russians.

Our people have all received some help. When we see these goings on, we cry out again and again: "Thou preparest a table before me, in the presence of my enemies." Oh, how good it makes us feel that there are still people who think of us, and love us. How much we would like to share with you, verbally, all our grief and woe. If peace should ever come, then many new things will appear.

Well, dear Geschwister, what are you and your dear children doing? Fritz and Liese are probably all grown up. And that good Peter, is probably so well behaved that he never sneaks up to the loft to get sunflower seeds. Is he still slightly deaf? And that little Meka, what is that little one doing? Please children, write to our children, they would love a letter; they get pretty despondent here, especially when they do not get even one piece of black bread a day. Be very obedient to your mama and papa, and thank God that He has restored your mama's health – as far as we know. Our children cannot go to any school. Our Michi and Tina started to go to school, even had a German teacher, but it did not take many days and she was removed from the school and Cossacks were installed as teachers. Our children also had to stay home. We are so sorry that they are not allowed to learn. Mama cannot even teach them to sew or knit since we have no materials. Often they sit and cry that they cannot learn anything.

We received a letter from home [*Altonau*]. Papa is rapidly going down hill. They have almost nothing to eat except potatoes. Hans is still in bed. They have eaten only three loaves of bread since Christmas, and these were given to them by some kind people. However, Mama's health is somewhat better. Their pig has also been confiscated. Their cow is fresh but only gives a bit of milk. They have no butter. Their cow will probably be confiscated as well. The cows are all to be gathered together at J. Martens. Already 32 horses have died and the rest are not fit for work. Currently things are going very much against the disenfranchised in the towns.

Well, I must close. Again, many thanks for everything you have done. Continue to remember us. My Marie will write more.

Your Geschwister who will never forget you,

J. and M. Regehr and children

*Again, Maria shares the paper with Jasch. Although her own state is desperate, she cares deeply for her sister-in-law Liese's health.*

Lunowka, 2 March [1932]

Dearest Geschwister Franz and Liese and children!
May the great and almighty God, who holds everything in His hands, who leads and directs everything as He pleases, who commands life and death, protect you and comfort you in the severe sufferings which have been ordained for you, precious sister, by our God. Yesterday we received your very welcome letter of Feb. 4th., but when we read it we were not happy. In your previous letter, dear Liese, you sounded so hopeful, but in this letter it seems to be the opposite. How can that be possible, dear Geschwister? Is your body swollen from the treatments or can the swelling envelope your heart so that death could still claim you? No, let us hope that is not the case. Do we not have a God who helps and a God who can save from death? How often have you experienced that, dear Geschwister – and now He should not help? Dear Liese, do not overtax yourself, and do not burden yourself so much with your loved ones here in R. Our God will know how to sustain us no matter how dark the future may be.

You, dear sister, write that the war is already on – otherwise we will probably not be helped. We only wish that things would happen more quickly so that the great tribulation here in R. would end. Almost the entire country is being ravaged by typhus – many people will yet die. Could it be the time of which the prophet Jeremiah speaks: That in the last days people will be destroyed by the sword, starvation and pestilence?

I am so distressed today – I really do not know what I should write. Yesterday we received that letter from you. Dear loved ones, it really brought us no joy. We also received one from our dear son. He writes very despondently – typhus has broken out there. And how will it be with the medical services there? No doctor or medical personnel, so many people crowded into one house, the people crawling with lice, and they cannot change their clothes because they have no more. And our Peter has already been alone for 8 months! What must he look like by now? He only has one blanket and no pillow, because the road was difficult and he had to carry it all – it was too much.

Cleanliness is of greater importance than medicine during a typhus outbreak. My head almost comes apart when I think on everything. In spirit I can see him lying there, whimpering and in his last throes – and then to think that he is not converted! My heart almost breaks. If we should lose this poor boy in this manner – then I do not know – I cannot think on it! Several times he has mentioned in a letter: "You do not know how hungry I am." And he writes that he has given up all hope of ever seeing us again. I was going to enclose his letter, but it is so dear to me that I want to keep it.

I am completely out of control. I did not wish to make things harder for you, but not to write anything about it is beyond my strength, even though that would be better for you, dear Liese. But do not be too concerned, we want to see you, yes, all of you, again in this life. We hope that by now you are well again. How nice it would be if we all could live close together again and visit with each other. How gladly I would like to sit by your bed and share joy and sorrow with you. How happy that would have made us, right? May God grant us such times again.

How are things at home now? We are very anxious to know. Lena and Mariechen [*Jasch's sisters in Altonau*] do not write. Susie is occupied with those who are ill – only Mama writes. In the last letter Hans also wrote. If only he could get well. I will close for this time.

We remain your praying Geschwister in exile,

J. and M. Regehr

Because my dear little wife has already written, I too will write a little about our existence here. Everything has become much more restrictive here since the first of March. Everyone who can walk must go to work. I too was forcibly driven out. We do not know why they must treat us in this way – but I am sure we will have to endure still more.

We got a very sad letter from our dear Peter. He says that on the day he is writing he has not had anything to eat. There are 18 men in their barracks, and of these 15 are down with typhus. He is not feeling well either. Then in closing he signs:"Your lost son Peter!" Oh, Geschwister, I cannot describe how we have already wept for our son. Thousands of tears have already flowed from his dear mother's eyes. Typhus without beds – and in addition, absolutely no bread. We would so much like to send something to him, but that is practically impossible. If at all possible we want to send him a few pounds of rye flour. You will say that is not for those suffering from typhus. Yes, dear Geschwister, but we cannot do any more.

Will God deliver us soon? We have no news yet from Liese; we believe her trip will have gone well [*she has attempted another escape*]. The Wiens girls also left one night. Yesterday Wiens had to appear before the Kommandant because of it. They immediately incarcerated him because he had not reported that they were gone. It was impossible that those poor girls could stay here. The snow is 1 ½ metres deep and it snows almost every day. Then those poor girls had to go into such snow and fell trees. Hungertyphus has broken out in many places. If help is not soon forthcoming, R. will experience a great tragedy. Report often how things are there. Could a change be coming?

Oh, Geschwister, spare no effort or work to support us here as much as you can. If only we could live through this and come to you – you shall receive our praise and thanks! However, the best reward will be given by Him who sees and knows everything. May God give you complete health, dear sister. We still have not received anything from the Board. It seems to get here faster if it is sent by private persons. Pet. B letter with Truda's has been received. It will be a nice parcel – Truda's 5 dollars and Bargen's 3 dollars, and the expenses. May God reward them.

Oh, that poor Truda, she does so many good things for her siblings. Dear brother-in-law, if someone sends parcels to us, please send us their addresses immediately; then I can describe our situation to them. It is with regret, dear siblings, that we decry our lot to you, but we would so much like to survive this ordeal by the help you send. Maybe we will be able to write letters of joy soon. That will be much more satisfying. Please accept everything in love. We only get bad news from home – they have no more bread. Well, I hurry to a close. Write often and lots, also of news from there.

Your humble Jak. and M. Regehr and children

*From this place of desolation, a young girl ignores the distractions around her and sketches. Twelve-year-old Tina is the artist in the family, always looking for paper and pencils. But an object of beauty is not her current subject; rather it is an austere, towering smelter where she works in order to get "a bigger piece of bread."*

*Tina is thrilled to receive a letter from her cousin Lieschen in Canada. March 8 has been declared "Women's Day" in the new Soviet Regime, and theoretically Tina has the day off. But instead of celebrating the new status of women, she is consumed with hunger and embarrassed with her tattered green dress. However, she excels in school. Russian is not her first language, yet she receives the "Ydaprin," a socialist certificate with a photo of Stalin given to students for outstanding achievement. She appears proud of this award. In the crowded barrack, she finds space on the wooden trunk to write and sketch.*

March 8. [1932]

Dear Lieschen,

Finally I have received a letter from you, dear cousin. This is the second letter I have received from you here in the Urals. I go to the mail every day and always I walk home without a letter. But today I finally got one. Received two parcels from Cbepdrobck, one with flour and one with porridge and one kilo sugar. That takes a very long time to get here. I go to the Russian school and am in the 3rd group. It is very hard for me to learn when only Russian is spoken. I am "Ydaprin" in school. It is very beautiful outside and the frost has melted off the windows.

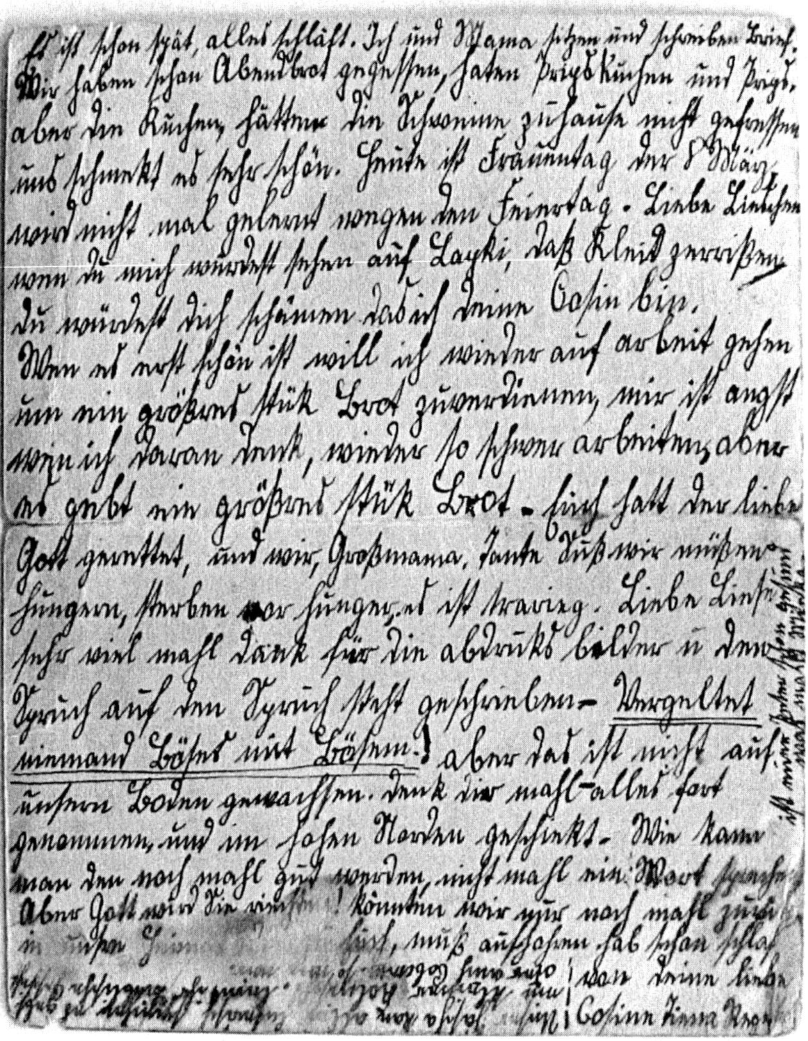

Es ist schon spät, alles schläft. Ich und Mama sitzen und schreiben Briefe.
Wir haben schon Abendbrot gegessen, haben [illegible] Kuchen und [illegible].
aber die Kuchen hätten die Schweine zuhause nicht gefressen
und schmeckt es sehr schön. Heute ist Frauentag der 8 März
wird nicht mal gefeiert wegen dem Feiertag. Liebe Lieschen
wenn du mich würdest sehen auf Lagki, das Kleid zerrissen
du würdest dich schämen daß ich deine Cosin bin.
Wenn es noch schön ist will ich wieder auf arbeit gehen
um ein größeres Stük Brot zuverdienen, mir ist angst
wenn ich daran denk, wieder so schwere arbeiten, aber
es gibt ein größeres Stük Brot. Euch hat der liebe
Gott gerettet, und wir, Großmama, Tante Dus wir müssen
hungern, sterben vor hunger, es ist traurig. Liebe Lies
sehr viel mals dank für die abdrucks bilder u den
Spruch auf den Spruch steht geschrieben – Vergeltet
niemand Böses mit Bösem. – aber das ist nicht auf
unseren Boden gewachsen. dank dir mals alles fort
genommen, und in hohen Norden geschickt. Wie kann
man dan noch mals gut werden, nicht mals ein Wort sprechen
Aber Gott wird die richten! könnten wir nur noch mals zusammen
in unser [illegible] muß aufhören hab schon schlaf
[illegible]
von deiner lieben
Cosinne Anna [illegible]

[illegible]

*Liebe Lieschen, dieses habe ich selber gemahlt aus freier Hand.* ["Dear Lieschen, this I have drawn myself with a free hand."]

My family is at work – all of them. Papa has been taken. Here about 50% have been taken because of the bread. The government has no more. One horse's head costs 40 rubles and one pound of butter 25 rubles. If we had not received parcels we would have starved to death long ago. Many people die around here. Uncle Hans has died too. Aunt Susie and the children have typhus and nothing to eat [*her relatives in Altonau*]. It is very sad in this Russia and everyone is without bread. We never have enough to eat, and it is so terrible to be hungry all the time.

Dear Lieschen, I thought you might be able to collect money from your fellow students and send me money for a dress. I have only one green dress and that is already so very torn that I am sure you would never wear it. But even more than that, I would like a package of food. Send it via Finland and addressed to me. Jascha was overjoyed to receive those Abdrucksbilder [*pictures*]. I do not know what else to write and had better close. A greeting and a kiss from your cousin, Tina Regehr.

It is already late and everyone is sleeping. I and Mama are sitting and writing letters. We have had supper. We had Pripps and cookies – but the cookies are the ones the pigs refused to eat. They tasted good to us. Today is March 8th and is "Ladies Day" and a holiday. Dear Lieschen, if you would see me in my torn dress you would be embarrassed to call me cousin. When the weather is nicer I will go to work again, because then I can get a bigger piece of bread. God has saved you from this country and we, grandmama, Aunt Susie and our family must starve; it is so sad!

Dear Lieschen, thanks so much for those Abdrucksbilder and the verse which says, "Never return evil with evil." That verse does not flourish in this soil! Imagine – we have been robbed of absolutely everything and then sent into the high North. How can we ever be reconciled to this? One cannot even say a word in protest against such treatment! But God will judge them! If only we could get together in our homeland. Well, I had better close. Have a nice sleep. Our Jascha can speak everything in laterisch [*Latin*], a budding little kolonist. Are you learning Bible stories or also Cobemez [*Communist propaganda*] like we are?

Your cousin, Tina

Dear Franz, you must also write a letter sometime. Miechi has just come from work. I have to go for bread tomorrow and again stand in a line-up from 6 until 9 to get it. What a verschisseness [*shitty*] Russia!

*In this foul place, the family is still receiving mail delivery from their former home in Altonau. News of various families and of their parents continues to arrive. For now, the circuitous route of mail delivery from the prison camp to the home village and then on to Canada is functioning.*

March 20, 1932

Dearly beloved Geschwister Franz, Liese and children,
May the God of peace comfort you and make you rejoice in good health. May He give you what you need in this life. We are all still well, praise God. It is Sunday today, but it does not feel like Sunday since all the people have gone to work! Even my dear Jasch went to work early. He has to walk 5 Werst one way. When he gets back in the evening he is always so very tired. Oh, when will this slavery ever end?

We received your very nice letter which you, dear brother-in-law Franz, wrote on Feb 18. You suggest that the letters may be coming too thick and fast. In no way is that the case! We always wait impatiently for letters and are so happy that we can still receive letters. We wonder if they will continue to go if R. [*Russia*] should get involved. Now at least we still get to hear something from others, even though it may be sparse.

And how, dear Geschwister, is it with your health now? You, dear Liese, I believe are probably very ill because you did not write yourself. How can it be that your body is so swollen for such a long time? Can the cancer really be dead, or do you dear ones only want to spare us the bad news? Oh, may God grant that you, dear Liese, would already be well and that we soon would receive good news from you, dear loved ones! Dear Liese, I feel so sorry for you, knowing what suffering you went through even here in R., and at the time you fled from here. When you were first in Canada, it appeared as if you had fully recovered and were free from all suffering. We all thanked God and praised Him for the help He had given you. But now we pray again and again that He may restore your health. And we believe that He will do it too, for we have His promise that if we pray in His name He will give us what we ask if we ask with our whole heart.

Oh, we have also experienced that God answers prayer. When we were completely at an end, He sent help at the right time. God has prepared willing hearts over there in order to help us, otherwise we would no longer be alive. May our great God reward them, as well as you dear Geschwister, a thousandfold, for it is through you that we receive the packages. Today J.R. again received 2 packages, both were from a certain Klassen; he has already received 6 packages – and all because of you. Everything arrived in perfect condition, much Fett und Speck [*fat and bacon*]. We received a card from Germany, sent on March 9, notifying us that there would be a package arriving from my dear sister Truda. She wrote that she wanted to send us one. On Feb 6th she paid 5 dollars to the "Board" for us.

On March 18th we received a letter from our dear parents. Mama and Susie had written that they called the doctor to see our dear brother Hans. The doctor said that he was completely well in the lungs, heart and kidneys, only the left hip bone was rotting – but there was still hope. Papa is also very weak and has been bedridden for 4 days, but is now up a bit and resting on the oven-bench. Mama has also had great pain. How sad it is over there. Often we just cannot understand the ways of God. Why is our entire family afflicted so? We comfort ourselves with the words: "The afflictions of these times are not worthy to be compared with the overwhelming glory that is awaiting us" [*2 Corinthians 4:16 & 17*] if we remain faithful until we have completed our pilgrimage here on earth. Jasch just came home from work.

*Among the afflictions of these parents is separation from their children. Some are sent into distant forests or mines; others like Liese, attempt another escape. Yet Maria's faith endures. She sends a sacred poem to her brother and sister in law in Canada.*

[March 1932]

Dear siblings Franz and Liese and children,

> My God always intends my good,
> Even if my cross is painful.
> He only wants my very best,
> So I shall follow in his steps.

Dear Liese, I write this to you as a comfort because you will often feel despondent in your great suffering, as well as over the circumstances that your dear parents and siblings are in here in Russia. But be of great confidence and in a joyful mood so that you do not damage your physical health by worrying. You can still get well, and it could be possible that we will all see you again even in this life. We believe that God will soon rescue us from this great distress.

We have not received a letter from you for a long time – the last was written in December. We just do not know – do the letters go lost or have you not written? We are looking forward to your next letter with longing. You, dear loved ones, we are anxious to know how circumstances are with you – especially with your health, dear Liese! You wrote that by the end of January you must return for an examination to see if your cancer is completely gone or not. May our great God give grace in this situation! That is our daily prayer to God.

We received a letter from home on Feb. 14! Mama and Hans had written. It is very sad there too. No bread and no money! They subsist on what good people give to them. And still our brother Hans writes that he is one of the privileged ones. They even allow him to live in his own home. Yes, by his suffering our dear brother Hans has been prepared by God in the smelting furnace of tribulation. It is hard to understand the difficulties he describes! But he hopes for health too, and he would like to see all his siblings again during his life. He writes that his stiff hand is actually writing the letter while he is sitting in his bed!

Mama writes that things are not better with her – the operation did not seem to correct her condition. And Papa is deteriorating very fast. He is so very skinny it is quite impossible to imagine. He desires to die, if only he could see all of his children once more. And our wish is that he may see his Saviour soon, where there is no parting, no suffering, and no hunger! They have suffered so much here in this world – in their old age. Who would have imagined that we would be scattered all across the globe, and live so far apart that we hardly know anything of each other? It was so nice when we all lived close beside each other and could visit so easily and were so happy.

And now every family is torn apart; our joy in family is shattered – ! We are not allowed to be with our own children, and this is very hard on us. Finally received one letter from our dear son. He is still well and alive, but must do very hard work. For the work he gets 1 kilo bread, 100 gram fish, 20 gram sugar per day. However, he still feels hungry all the time. But he is not allowed to come and see us. How happy we were to finally get word from him! Yes, dear siblings, one load has been lifted from our hearts by this letter – but only to be replaced by another one, which is no easier to bear.

You will know that our daughter Liese was driven away from here. We wrote it to P.B. a few days ago. We believe you will read that letter also. On Feb. 13 she drove away from here – very secretly and at night. A. went with her to the station Kopi, about 8 km from here. There she took a ticket to Perm. On Feb. 22 we received a letter from her. You just cannot imagine how hard it was for us to go this route – and we did this trusting God. But the situation here was just becoming impossible. It was hardly possible to do the work here! She already had severe rheumatism.

We talked long about what to do and how to counsel her. The trip cost 80 rubles and we did not have the money. We acquired money by selling those woolen scarves you sent – and those shining forks and spoons. We sold whatever possible, and in this way we were able to get her a ticket. She wept so much when she said goodbye to us. Before she left she wanted to see her brother! But that was impossible. We feel as the old patriarch Jakob in the Bible says:"You rob me of all my children." We will go to our grave very early. We will write to you the beginning of her letter which she wrote on the way to Moscow:

*The parents copy their daughter Liese's words into their own letter, but only "the beginning." We can only speculate on the reasons for their action. But we do know that, somehow, Liese has the means to write and post a brief note on her escape route, and that her parents have received it.*

Dear Parents,
Is it not heart-rending when you put yourselves into our place? I am here in this far away evil world rolling towards Moscow, and you must stay in a slave labour camp in Siberia. And my dear brother is perishing in a different slave camp. Oh, what a jumble of thoughts are rushing into my brain on this trip. But I do not regret having left, even though my heart is heavy when it realizes that I will not see you for a long time! Or maybe never again – ! Oh, I just cannot think of that or I dissolve in tears. But I certainly do not miss the work I was forced to do, and even if I feel sad at missing you, I feel so sorry for all those young children who must give up their youth to such hard work.

*Maria continues Liese's saga in her own words:*

For 5 days she had to stay in Perm and was not able to get a ticket to Moscow. We believe she will already have some job. We really wanted to get the [...] home too, to sneak him home for a few days; but even with all our thinking we cannot do it. We believe it is God's will. Many have fled this camp! For 3 weeks we were without a [...]. No one cares about us here! Now is the time to leave! J.R's Lena has also fled. It was very hard to let her leave. And the mother is alone with the young children. There is much talk here of K. and that we may be returned to the land – or maybe we will be returned to our homes? It seems very hard to believe! It isn't time yet. How very happy we would be if we should ever be set free again and could see all our loved ones.

We are still at our old place and it is still the same work. Mariechen and I have been mending clothes. Now Mariechen and Tina are darning stockings. My Jasch just got up from a noon nap. Lena and Jascha are playing outside, but it is quite cold outside yet. What are you doing all the time? You will probably be getting ready for seeding. And you, dear Liese, will have your hands full in the house. Thank you, dear siblings, that you are really helping us so much. May God reward you. May God be with you until we meet again! We can never forget you, our siblings,

J.M. and children

[*A postscript written around the edges*] There have been 5 boys conscripted here now. We are told that they will conscript up to the 40-year-olds. People are saying there is war.

*On the reverse side of an already fragile paper, Jasch includes his words. The script is difficult to read, but adequate writing materials are rare. Clearly, Jasch's concern for his imprisoned son Peter and fugitive daughter Liese is escalating.*

March 21, 1932

Dearly beloved Geschwister Franz, Liese, and children,
We wish you the best of health and a joyous spirit in all your ways. We learn from your letters that you are really quite busy because

of us, writing and answering letters, sending parcels, enlisting and recruiting others on our behalf. Dear brother-in-law, if a drink of cold water shall be rewarded, how much more will the things you are doing for us. I have to tell you again and again that we count you among the especially fortunate. What profound paths God has already traveled with you! You have had tremendous expenses, you have done so much good to us and others, and the good Lord has given you special blessings: enough bread, nice clothes and especially talented children. Those are all blessings from God.

Oh, may God restore Liese back to health! How very sorry we feel for her, and our daily prayer is that she may become well again. We are also well as usual. Today is Monday, a day of rest, and I do not have to go to work today. My daily work in the vast forest is to shovel snow to clear a path in order that the trees and logs may be dragged out. The walk to work is a bit far – about 6 km each way. At work I do not over-exert myself, but the walking is very difficult because of our meagre and inadequate diet; but he who wants to get the 1p. of bread per day has to work. Oh, we owe you so many thanks. You again report that two more parcels have been sent on their way.

Yes, dear Geschwister, if I may beg of you, then please also remember our lost son; maybe somewhere there is also a compassionate heart for him. Send out a call for help for him. The address is the same as ours, only write [...] beside it. How thankful that boy would be! Or send it to us and we will forward it to him. Well, do as you can. If only he could soon come home to us! How we have already cried for him. We rarely get any news from him, but we would so much like to have him in our midst! Yes, dear Geschwister, if you had not expressed your concern in practical ways, who knows if we would still be alive. God reward you a thousandfold. Please do not forget us.

Dear Geschwister, as long as we have been here in this great tribulation we have not yet received anything from P.B. When you are alone with him, ask him to put a few dollars into the letter – then we could buy something here. We will keep this confidential and not write to him about it. We believe that he will gladly do it. You write that Peter again has applied concerning Liese [*He must be attempting to sponsor Liese to come to Canada*]. May God grant that it happens. Her health would allow her to come over. Please report all you can about the political situation. We do not know where Liese is now. The last we heard was that she was arrested and imprisoned in Kronau. We are hoping for news of her today and will let you know as soon as we hear. My dear Marie is almost perishing with worry. Dear Geschwister, pray that God would change our situation.

J. and M. and children

*In his desperation, Jasch sends a formal appeal to Canada, hoping it will reach someone with the political authority to help them. On this thin scrap he does not include either his address or his name in the closing comment. He hopes those in Canada and the United States will direct his petition to the most effective authorities.*

[1932]

Dear Brother-in-Law,
Please send this petition to the place it should go. Sign my name, and write our correct address. May God bless it. Our future is very dark. A horse's head is priced at 30 rubles. Dear brother-in-law, help us and send us Hoellig's address, we would be ever so thankful – the one that was quartered at our parents for 10 months. Rescue us, help us, otherwise we perish. Write if you receive this. Yours.

*Abram, like other prisoners, risks traveling outside the perimeters of his camp to beg in a nearby village. Although he is already eighteen years old, he still occasionally shares the same barrack space with his older brother Jasch, his nieces and nephews. But this barrack may not be theirs for long. Rumours of the family being transported again are threatening to become a reality. Transportation is dreaded by prisoners. Although their conditions in the present camp are bleak, moving to a new prison camp is unpredictable and formidable. Wagons and trains are crowded, and guards are cruel. Food and water are withheld to avoid the inconvenience of stopping for toilet breaks. Days of travel result in exhaustion, disorientation, disease, and often death.*

Lunowka, April 10, 1932

Deeply beloved Geschwister Franz and Liese and children,
We wish you God's richest blessings on all your ways. Not many days have passed since we wrote to you. Our Peter wrote to you too. Do not get tired of our many letters; we write so often because we love you so and know that you love us too. You really show such concern about us. We received those packages from Kroeker. We have already notified him and described something of our trip. We sent a letter to him and told him how thankful we were.

Our letters may go lost. Peter Bargen [*This is not the young Peter Bargen who escapes with his parents Franz and Liese in 1929 and finds the letters in the attic. This is Franz Bargen's older brother, who came to Canada in 1925 and settled in Carlyle, Saskatchewan with their children*.] mentions there is something coming from the "Board" – but nothing has arrived until this day. Every day we get our ration of bread, weighed out exactly. For our family we get 4 [...] bread in 8 days. In actuality that is enough bread to satisfy one's hunger for one day – but not for 8 days and for an entire family. For 2 days now Abram has gone to the village begging for bread. He gets enough handed to him to keep him alive. He can hardly go to work any more. His fingers got frozen. Now the doctor has cut away his frozen skin, and that is the way the poor boy must go to work – and at 40 degrees frost. He was not excused from work for even 1 day. He does not get any remuneration either. If I had the money, I would send him away from here. He has worked very hard for 7 months and has not received a red cent.

In reality we do not care about the money either. If only we could get some rye bread for what is owed to him we could eat enough one time to satisfy our hunger. We are very careful with the Posilkas [*parcels*] since they must last a long time. We eat our rye soup without bread. But every time we eat, we speak of you. May God reward you a hundredfold. We will not be able to repay you for everything you have done for us. My dear little wife says: "Next time we will get 2 parcels from P. Bargens." I have no idea where she gets this conviction from. Oh, may she only be right! Many children as well as old people are very ill. It is because of the poor quality of the food – or no food at all.

In the store rye flour costs 60 rubles per Pud, and there were only 3 Pud to be had in the entire store. Money is getting so scarce because the government puts so little into circulation. If it continues like this, it will be a repeat of the year 1921. Many, many will succumb. Our writing and pleading is only "Please help!" Even though you cannot change things, by helping you do so very much. We have seen it! But we realize fully that you cannot do more. We are completely dependent upon you and P. Bargens. You shall bring us through as long as it is possible. We just do not wish to die of starvation.

Actually, we believe we will be sent even further into the north – we have no idea where. Sunday 65 persons were sent 50 Werst further. At least 90 people were squashed into cattle cars and away they went. By this you can see how they deal with people here. Tatars and Asians and Cossacks rule over us, and we are regarded as an internal disease. Especially bad are those 16-year-old members of the Komsomol. They have the controls in their hands.

Abram has gone to sell the wool scarves to make a little money. We want to send our Liese away from here so she can earn more money. Here she can earn nothing. It is also better that she gets work that is indoors, even if she only works for her food. Here the girls just waste away. There already has been snow for a month, and even then the girls are sent into the forest to root out trees.

*Since Liese has already left and is now a fugitive, this is a puzzling comment. Perhaps it is meant to circumvent a censor. Meanwhile, in the Regehr family's former home village, Soviet authorities are demanding exorbitant amounts of grain. The "Red Broom Brigade"*[5] *sweeps through the entire countryside looking for hidden stashes of food. Although the Regehr family's conditions in prison are desperate, the lives of those left behind in the home villages have also been radically altered. The elderly parents of Jasch and Maria, and countless others, are homeless and without rights. It is illegal to house "enemies of the people," so they live in sheds, barns, granaries, and churches. Small children and the elderly are most vulnerable; many die of starvation and from a typhoid epidemic. The forced collectivization instituted by Stalin in his Five-Year Plan to finance his political scheme and subjugate the "peasantry" has had a disastrous effect on agriculture. He has doubled the demand for grain quotas from the farmers. The high quotas and forced collectivization leave very little grain for the villagers. Anyone who does not look gaunt and malnourished is suspected of hoarding grain.*

*Chaos results, crime is rampant, and desperation increases as millions perish in Ukraine, northern Caucasus, and the lower Volga River region. Named the "Holodomor" (an "intentional genocide" from 1931 to 1933),*[6] *the enforced famine is accompanied by a purge of the Russian intelligentsia and the Russian Communist Party itself. The combined factors break the peoples' will to resist and leave vast regions politically, socially, and psychologically traumatized. To intensify the political scheme, the GPU issues a system of internal passports that prevents individuals from leaving. Villagers became prisoners in their own towns.*

*Jasch and Marie do not fully comprehend the desperate conditions in Altonau. However, when parcels and letters arrive, both writers pour a profusion of gratitude onto paper. Such deliveries to their prison camp keep them alive and strengthen the tenuous lifeline of the postal delivery route.*

G. Friesen got a letter from Joh. Voth yesterday. He reports that Papa is losing so much weight, is very skinny. Brother Hans has been confined to his bed since the time of his arrest. It is somewhat better with Mama but they have no bread; that is probably the reason why Papa is deteriorating so quickly. They live only on potatoes. Brother-in-law Koop writes to Abram that as long as they have bread our parents will have bread also. But to flee from there is impossible. Mrs. Voth writes that 38 horses have died on the Commune. And the ones living are unable to work. The straw and chaff must be threshed twice by the Commune. The village is ordered to deliver 8 thousand Pud grain and the entire village is without bread. A communal kitchen is to be established. There are many wares in the stores now, but you can only buy them with grain. The wares are moved from store to store to show the people how many products are available. Many horses are slaughtered for food; actually they are only bags of bones. Cattle and sheep are gone; now they can suck on horse bones – and the 5 yr. plan is completed.

Well, how are things with the Zoepfigen [*those with pigtails*]? Are the Schafpelze [*sheep coats*] included as well? Report it to us please. Well, dear Geschwister, what are you doing? How are things with Liese? Will she get well? We are anxiously waiting for letters. We got one today. Have heard nothing from Bargens for a long time. Do they receive our letters?

Just a minute ago a Russian came in with a message from our Peter. He is still alive in the forest work. He is almost starved to death. This morning L. [*Liese*] is away from here. If she will get away is a big question. Received a letter from home. Everything is as usual – without bread and without money. But Papa comforts us a lot, and so things remain as they were. It is very hard to understand how God leads. In many places in N. 13 they raided the cellars and the pantries at night. There are 3 people who have not had bread for 14 days [...].

*Obsession with parcels and letters is understandable. Some fellow prisoners receive more than the Regehr family, and Jasch stifles his envy. But soon other matters become more urgent. Their previous fears have been confirmed. With only two hours notice, the family is transported from Lunowka to Ulaxma (60 km. further north) in an unheated cattle train during the frigid night.*

April 17, 1932

Dear Geschwister Franz and Liese Bargen and children,
Since we have received no word from you or from Bargens for

over a month, we would like to know how things are with you. Are you all still alive? Oh, how often you are in our mind. Maybe something happened? Oh, may God have mercy on you and restore you to health, this is our daily prayer to God. With Him all things are possible. He is the Lord of life and death.

We have not heard from home for a very long time either. For weeks, we have not had any letters here. We do not know what the reason is. There is a great lack of bread here and each day it gets more severe. For 8 days now I have not received my quota of bread for my work. The family has been without bread for a very long time. We live on water soup, and even for that we are thankful to God. In many places people are dying of starvation. What is happening in this lovely "Red Paradise" is just horrible! If it is not stopped, it will be much worse than the previous years of famine!

Our children are extremely pale. Having only soup is not enough for people. Our dear Peter came home ill and is presently sick. He had typhus at his forced labour location. He was allowed to come home to recover. But when it gets dark at night, he is completely blind. The doctor says he is anemic and should get nourishing food. Then he would improve. But, alas, we cannot give the lad anything, even though we will give our last to help him. We have not yet received the package you mention, dear brother-in-law.

Oh, how thankful we are to you, Geschwister, for all the supportive things you do for us! You will certainly be rewarded in heaven. Geschwister, we count on God for our entire future – and on you. With God's help please do not forget us, or we will not make it. My dear Marie is as skinny as Mrs. Joh. Bargen was. Then you can imagine. So dear Geschwister, I am sure you will not be surprised if we always come to you with the same requests: "Help us and help us again!" Do what is possible.

Abram's address is no longer to be used. He is gone from here. We do not know where he is. It is said here that he was at home for a day. He is just like Cain, a fugitive and a wanderer. It was the severe hunger that drove him to escape. If you, dear brother-in-law, could generate some help for our Peter, maybe he could be saved.

He wrote telling you how he got sick – I even corrected the letter because he cannot see and his writing is hard to read. He is almost blind. Did you receive the letter?

Our children say that if they can make it through this period of famine and are allowed to come to you, they will all work to repay you for everything you are doing for them and us. Mrs. Joh. Regehr has received 17 parcels through you. She is living quite well. She also got lots of bacon and lard from home – an amount of 82 kilo. She also got a lot of money sent to her from different churches. Yesterday she got a package from Friedensfeld, some money from the church at Nicolaiovna and from other places. Yes, dear Geschwister, God has blessed your work and He will continue to do so.

I have often said that God had a reason for bringing you over to that country. Maybe many people are being kept alive because of your efforts. We have received nothing from Peter Bargens. How come? We are rather disappointed. We believed we would receive something from him too. The package from Truda Goosen, in which she sent 5 dollars to Peter Bargens, and then Bargens added 3 dollars and sent it to Susie without duty, has been received.

The parcel contained 10 m. flour and ½ kilo rice and 1 kilo bacon. I guess something must have happened to it. Or did it come in 2 parcels? That which John Goosens sent us for 3 dollars and 60 cents contains more products. I wrote this to Bargen and asked if he sent it in 2 packages. Perhaps the other may yet arrive. It was heavy, and with the box together it weighed 4 kilo. We were especially happy for this package. Was it for 8 dollars, not counting sending costs? We would be very, very sorry, if this should be all and the other package is lost. Or maybe an error has been made by the senders or in Germany? We have described everything in the letter written to Bargens and have enclosed the invoice.

The package of which you write, sent by Doctor Thiessen, was not received by us but by Mrs. Regehr. There was very much in it – for 6.90 dollars. There were 10 metres flannel, the same pattern on both sides, a pair of stockings, and sugar and lard and bacon.

Dear Geschwister, now a little about our lives. We are no longer in Lunjanrika [*Lunowka*] but 60 km further at [...] Ulaxma N. 2 since April 15. I still have to go to work. At 11 A.M. Lena came and said I should come home immediately, because in 2 hours we would be moved further away. I threw everything down and went to the office. There things were already being hurried along, and everything was quickly carried outside for transport to the station. Things were very busy. We carried our possessions outside. The sleighs were already waiting and the goods were loaded onto them and taken to the station. At 6 P.M. we, like poor cattle, were loaded into a red railway car without heat. At night we nearly froze to death. It is still so cold at night – we get 15 degrees of frost. There is still much snow.

We are now at a new location for the 2nd day. We have received no bread so far. We now must build a roadbed for the railway line. It will be hard work. The ground is very hard loam and still frozen – and further down is water. What will they finally do with us? Is there a rescue coming for us? Write us if you hear of any! How we long for freedom! Are there no nations who are working on our behalf? Have the elections in Germany been held? And how did they turn out? Please let us know. In closing, a plea: Dear Geschwister, do what is or lies in your power. Maybe God will be merciful to us and save us through your hands. From the bottom of my heart I wish see you all again. My dear little wife will also write.

*Despite her inhumane treatment, Maria expresses concern for her sick sister-in-law in Canada.*

Dear Geschwister Franz and Liese and children,
May the almighty God protect you and keep you in His care and give you what you need, complete health. Oh, how are things with you, dearly beloved and true Liese? Oh, how much we think of you and pray for you. We have not heard from you for a long time. You loved ones, we do not even know if you are still alive or not. Yes,

dear Geschwister, we hope to God that all things are in order. I trust He will not allow you to die, dear Liese, and leave your poor little children as orphans.

As you can see, we are now moved to another place. Our bodies had to tolerate many a knock, especially I – I am completely broken. When we arrived here, we expected to be allowed into the barracks immediately. But no! First everyone had to be unloaded – and then there was no water. They said there would be water in an hour. But that hour lasted from morning until late evening. We arrived in the morning – frozen!

April 24, Ulaxma N. 2 [1932]

Dear Geschwister Franz and Liese and children!
I want to send to you, dear loved ones, a small sign of life. Before I continue I wish you the peace of God and the best of health; and for you, dear Liese, that God may make your pains disappear and also restore your health. Dear loved ones, do not lose courage. Look to our Saviour for comfort, He who has done everything for us. We too are all quite well and still alive, for which we thank and praise God.

Today is Sunday, but what kind of a Sunday do we have? Just like any other day – everyone is at work. Jasch and Peter are at work every day too. It is very hard for them both. But what shall we do? Our great need drives us on, since they get a bigger piece of bread then. Michi must also go to work, otherwise we just cannot make ends meet. I said to my dear husband Jasch: I would like to go to work too if only I would get a piece of bread as well. Today we went to register ourselves in the Cmaniobka [*communal farm*], but they will not accept any more names until May 1st. They said there was still bread for today and then there was no more. We have not received bread since April 18th. They said there is no flour and no bread. What will happen in the future looms so dark before us.

Yesterday we received 2 letters from you, dear Geschwister – one where Franz alone had written on March 24th, and another from April 2nd, where you, dearly beloved sister Liese, had also written. Oh, how happy we were to see your handwriting. We always feared that we would suddenly get news of your death, dear Liese. You would not believe how happy we were. I too believe that our great and almighty God will make you well again, even if people cannot help you, as you wrote.

This morning I read John 11 with the children, the story of how our Saviour awakens Lazarus from death. In the minds of Lazarus' sisters it was also impossible when the Saviour said "He shall rise again." That is exactly how we often experience it too – we are often brought to shame. Let us always pray and believe – believe steadfastly. God can and will help, making you well and freeing us from this exile. So I said to my children, "Our Saviour can also give health to your Aunt Liese just like that."

Your letter of March 24th arrived here at the Germans'. We went to get it from there. Here in the post office they find it very interesting that we Germans [*Mennonites*] have also been exiled and that is why they took the letters there. The [*ethnic*] Germans have a kitchen for themselves, but there you still do not see any shortages. They still have of everything, even white baked goods. Mrs. Friesen and I went in there once, but they do not give even a black piece of bread to others. If only that time would come again when we and our children could satisfy our hunger. What riches that would be for us! When we sit in the evening and talk of what we used to own and how we used to eat, then our children Lena and Jascha say, "Tell us more." Our little Jascha watches so carefully that he does not get a smaller piece of bread than the others.

If only the parcels would arrive soon. Have received 3 cards from March 21, 24, and 26 that parcels have been sent to us. We have been waiting for over a month and they still are not here. Have received 2 N. which had traveled for 11 days, the others 19 or 20 days, but none as slow as these. What [....]

*Jasch continues to work, but his tasks are for a healthy, robust male, not one suffering from hunger and typhus. An increased bread ration for his family is his reward. Concern for his children overwhelms him: Liese has been arrested again; she is prison in Charikona. Peter has typhus and is losing his eyesight, and the little ones are begging for bread. It has been six days since their last ration.*

Dear Geschwister, I actually did not want to write since I am very tired and just came from work. All winter long we have worked outdoors in the forest felling trees. Now the Mecozarojobrra [*required ration*] has been filled and we must crush rocks and carry them up a steep mountain. Our son Peter and I work together. It is very hard but as you, dear sister, write, accounts will be settled with Dora. [*According to letter editors Peter and Anne Bargen, this unscrupulous, devious woman compiled names of Mennonites for Soviet authorities. Here it is suggested that she may have contributed to the imprisonment of Jasch Regehr and the exile of his family.*] That is also our prayer to God – and maybe then it will be different.

We are completely out of bread. We only eat soups but have to do very strenuous work, so that one feels like lying down and dying. But if only we could remain healthy and escape that gruesome death by starvation. It is very sad here. If things stay as they are today and no help comes, then hundreds and thousands will miserably perish. One loaf of black bread costs 25 rubles but is often not available. Yesterday we wanted to buy 1 kilo Mannaca for drinking tea. It costs 4r. 50k., but then we were also required to take 3 rubles worth of pictures – so we could not possibly afford to buy it. These times are much worse than those starvation years. In those days one could occasionally buy some things. That is now completely impossible. We believe that here there are many [...] but they are so weak and hungry they couldn't begin to do anything. Well, whatever God has decided – but the way we feel the time is right now.

The letter written by Franz alone had been delivered to the German engineers by the postman. They had read it. Was there just one page inside? Where we are now, there are many German nationals. They live quite well but several of them want to return to Oma. Their brothers, however, were not allowed across. The voluntary workers earn quite a bit of money in the coal mines. There are many of them here. There is much wealth in the Ural region. We received a letter from our Liese from the Charikona jail. It is very hard for her – she abhors it. Who knows if we will ever get to see that child again?

At times we just cannot understand the leading of God, and still we believe that His ways are right and we do not become discouraged. Please continue to pray for us. Our situation is desperate: We are without bread, without money, in exile, considered sheep for the slaughter, required to work hard! And our children: Liese in prison in Charikona, Peter suffering much from typhus and in his eyes (I wrote you of this), the little ones crying and begging for bread!

Today is the 6th day without bread. Then our efforts to stay quiet before God, and to trust in God, are put to the acid test. Often there are hours when we are submerged in despair, but we believe that the prayers of God's children protect us and support us so that the burden does not become too great to carry. There are many here who have despaired of God's help. Write to us often and write much, dear Geschwister. And how things are with Ivan? We get fresh courage when we read and hear of the things you wrote in your last letter.

Dear Liese, if only you could regain your health again. We certainly were aware of the fact that you were very sick again. So we prayed for you a lot. We get few letters from home. If you should be preparing packages for Abram, send them in our names. He does not get them here because he is gone.

Well, again hearty greetings and kisses from your Geschwister,

J. and M. Regehr and children

*At first glance, it is hard to determine who is writing the next letter. But from the context we can ascertain that Maria is the writer. It is clear that the family's fate has not changed; work never ends and hunger is never satisfied. Liese is still in prison, but Peter is home again. Despite his failing eyesight, he has made a little bench and a table. Maria is grateful.*

[Summer 1932]

Dear Geschwister Frank and Liese and children,
Oh, if only we would get some news of you, Liese. Is your illness getting worse or better? May our great God give you health. He has the power over life and death, and the power to soften and direct the hearts of those that rule over us and over our poor Liese [*Maria's daughter*].

Who can understand the ways of God? It often appears to me that God's way with us is far too severe – is what we have already been through not enough? We have one letter from Liese from [...], but from the prison where she is now, no news. I pray hourly that God should not let her despair but draw her closer to Him. Don't you get upset, dear Liese; it is enough if I sorrow so that I almost collapse. Your personal suffering is great enough. I really did not want to write of this and it would have been better for you, but my heart is so crushed. If only I could speak to you for an hour, dear Liese. Oh, if only God would give us such a time again!

We are now at another place. We already wrote to you about it. I wonder if you did not receive that letter. We are happy to have left the other place. At least we are not together with the Russians, and that alone is an improvement. From 5 in the morning until late at night they urge us to volunteer for work in the Artel [*cooperative*] after we complete our regular work. Our family members work from 6 A.M. until 3 or 3:30 P.M. The evening gets so long without any food. We all wait until everyone gets home from work. But Jascha and Lena can hardly endure it until the little bit of food is at last on the table.

Once I too went to work – there were 5 of us then: Jasch, I, Peter, Michi, and Tina. Then they gave us a very thin soup with a few kernels of barley in it, and a small piece of bread of 100 gr. which we had to pay for with 20k. The footpath led far into the forest about 2 Werst to a small level place. There we had to dig out the trees. The women and girls had to gather the wood after it had been sawed into pieces, and pile it into heaps and burn it. They are preparing the land for planting potatoes. Huge amounts of wood are being burned here. The Commune is made up of banished or exiled ones, but no Germans [*Mennonites*] have joined it. We would rather suffer than enjoy the fleeting pleasures of sin.

God will reward us if only we can persevere. And that is our daily prayer. How glorious the reunion will be on that day (if we do not meet here again) – so full of joy and jubilation. All those whom we loved so much even here, will be there. When will we finally get word from you? We have not heard from you for over a month – no letter. We are not sure – do the letters not get here or are they stopped somewhere? Or do you really write so little? We would love to get more news of you. Mama wrote us and told us that on the day she wrote her letter she had received a letter from B.K. She wrote that Tina had been visiting at your place. How happy you had all been together. Your Lieschen had made the whole meal and cleaned up everything like a big girl. How happy we too would be if we could see you face to face! Will it ever happen in this life? God knows!!

Dear Liese, I am sure you will be longing for your home in heaven. Maybe you even asked the Saviour for release from your suffering? Even if it is very hard for you to leave your dear Frank and little children, and even if I do not have such bodily ailments as you, still I feel along with you. I too have such deep heartaches, first with our dear son that he could not be with us for 9 months and we had no news of him. He had to live through typhus and now has almost lost his eyesight. And add to that our poor daughter. It almost breaks my heart. We only had good motives, and did not act without asking God, and we prayed a lot about it. We got the conviction it was His will. And now to see the misery here every day – how the poor children must go to work from early morning till late, with 40 degrees of frost, and how they must walk in very deep snow to work. And now this!

Oh, where shall I, poor miserable one, find comfort? It is true, if we did not have a Saviour, where could we go?! We would long ago have despaired in our misery. I feel like the Psalmist David: My visage has changed to sadness, and I have become old. Day and night my thoughts are of my dear child – why did they [*villagers in Altonau*] tell her to report to the authorities? At times we cannot understand the ways of the heavenly Father! Why did it have to be like that?

Dear Geschwister, how glorious it will be when we are at the throne of God and we will all see each other again, if only we remain true and keep our faith. We always come to you, dear Geschwister, with thankful hearts for your love and kindness and your efforts on our behalf. You have done so much and still continue to help. May God bless you and your work now and in the future. It is very necessary to help again and again! Our situation worsens from day to day. We would no longer be living if you had not had pity on us. How a mother's heart hurts when the children plead and cry for bread is known only to someone who has experienced it. It is hardest with our little son Jascha. He cannot grasp the fact that we do not have any food. When he gets up in the morning, he can hardly wait till he gets his portion. How joyful we will be when the time comes and we can once again each have our little piece of bread in peace!

I am sitting on a little bench at our little table, which Peter made, and am writing this letter to you. Outside it is raining fiercely, but we must go to work in spite of that. Peter and Michi just came home, wet through and through. At 6 A.M. today, with a heavy heart, I went to sell Michi as a slave [*to work for a room and food*]; then she gets a larger piece of bread. We have been forced to go through many hard situations here. And what is still to come? When will the time come when we will be free from all this misery?

How are things with you? Please write us more, dear Geschwister. Mama writes she received notices that several packages were on the way. How happy we are for that. May God make many more hearts willing to help, for our situation is critical. I remain one who loves you and who prays for you.

Your Geschwister Jasch and Marie and children

Dear Geschwister,
We notice that [...] also plays its role over there. I want to report that through your writing we have received 10 dollars from Dr. Hofer for our poor son Peter. He has reported that it has been sent to [...] to the [...]. We received a catalogue sent from him so that we ourselves can write to [...] telling them what we needed most. We have ordered the cheapest products. Flour 75%, 20 [...], 20k. per kilo. When we get it we will report to you. Please write our thanks to Hofer for us – we have no address for him or we would do it. Please do it if you have the time and love.

Now a bit about our situation. It gets worse from day to day. If you are in contact with Kroebel who used to live in Russia in our homeland and who depicted our situation so accurately, write it to him as well as to Hofer, since we do not have their address. At that time I was the Oberschulze [*Mayor or Reeve*] and we stood ready to serve them in any way. But do not write that to him. Maybe God will reveal to them how needy we are and they might help us along. If we could only last until the new harvest. Write to them also about our Peter. Send us their addresses. We trust in God and believe that you, dear dear Geschwister, will succeed in doing something on our behalf. May God bless you. Keep it to yourselves. I will report more later.

Warm greetings to all from Jasch and Marie and Children

Send him our present address, please.

*Three scraps of torn paper used by Jasch and then by Maria reflect their fragile state. Yet this avenue of communication is their only hope.*

[May 1932]

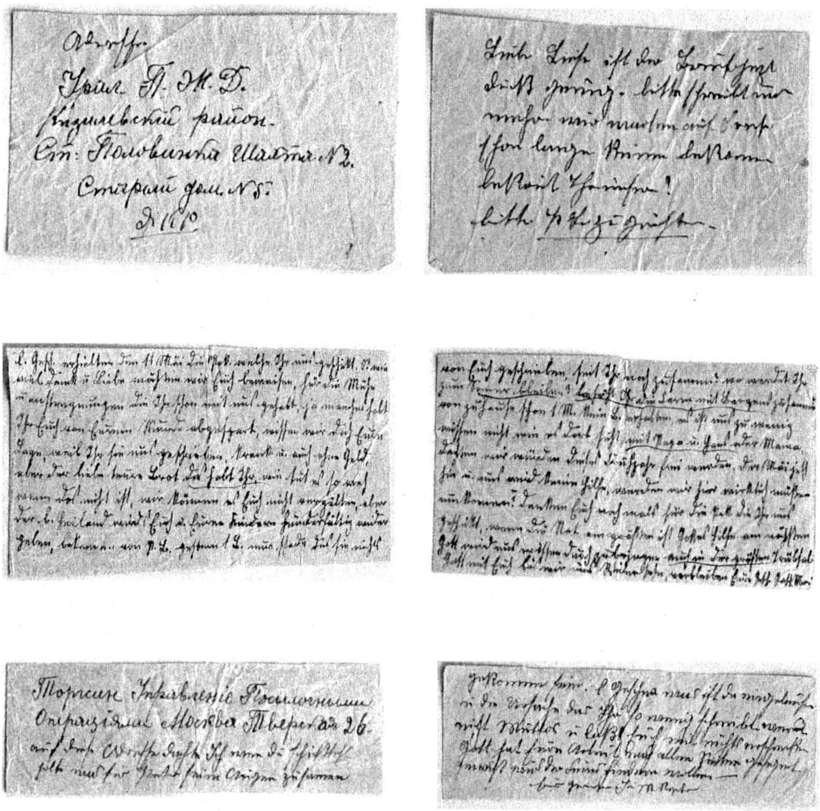

I wonder if you would send something to this address for Peter's eyes. Dear Geschwister, just what is the reason that you write so very little? Do not lose courage and do not be frightened away; God has blessed your work on all sides. Of course our arch-enemy will try to hinder at all times.

Your humble Geschwister, M. and J. Regehr

Dear Liese, is the letter fat enough now? Please write more. We wait for letters. There has not been one for a long time. Do you get our letters? Please give regards to P. and L.

Dear Geschwister, we received the parcels you sent on May 11th. Many thanks. We would like to show you much love for the trouble you have had and the efforts you have made on our behalf. Yes, we are sure you have deprived yourselves in order to provide for us! We know your situation, for you have written to us. You are sick and without money. But you do have enough of that precious bread. How it hurts when one does not have bread. We can never repay you, but our God will repay you and your children a hundredfold.

Yesterday we received a letter from P.B. but too bad they wrote nothing of you. Do you still live together? Where will you be for the summer? Do you seed that farm together with Bargens? We have not had a letter from home [*Altonau*] for over a month. It is just too little. We have no idea how things are there, with Papa and Hans and Mama. We thought we would be set free this spring. May is almost gone, and there is no help for us. Will we really have to perish here? Thank you again for the packages that you sent to us. When the need is the very greatest, God's help is the very nearest. God will know ways to bring us through even in this great tribulation. God be with you until we meet again.

Your Geschwister, Jasch and Marie

*The volume of letters continues. More than half of those found in the Campbell's Soup box were written in 1932 and 1933 (See Appendix B). But how long will the lifeline of letters and parcels sustain the Regehrs, and how long will their hope endure? Will they ever meet lost family and friends again? And will they eventually find freedom from Stalin's brutality?*

## Notes

1 Liese was related to Jasch and Maria Regehr by both birth and marriage. Jasch Regehr was Liese's older brother. Maria Regehr's sister Susie was married to Jasch's brother Johann.

2 Lena remembers this trunk. It measured ½ m. by ½ m. by 1 m. (18" by 18" by 3.3'), and was held shut with two bent nails.

3 The *Komsomol* (Young Communist League) was the youth organization of the Communist Party in the Soviet Union. Members ranged in age from fifteen to twenty-six (Thurston 21; 287).

4 This letter is out of sequence in the Bargens' publication and included here because of the date of writing.

5 The "Red Broom Brigade" was the common moniker for the Soviet-initiated campaign to sweep across the Ukraine and north Caucasus and brush away all grain and all *kulaks* (Interview, Louise Bergen Price, 2006).

6 In a lecture series about the Holodomor, held in Toronto in 2003, Bohdan Klid reported that "Toward the end of 1932, Molotov, Kaganovich and Postyshev met with the head of the secret police in Ukraine, Vsevolod Balytsky, to undertake severe repressive actions, which were justified as measures to prevent the sabotage of grain procurements. On December 5, for example, Balytsky issued a directive to 'destroy the counterrevolutionary underground and to land a decisive blow against all counterrevolutionary kulak-Petliura elements in the village.'"

In another lecture, Dr. Yuri Shapoval listed the measures taken against Ukrainian villages: (1) fines in kind (especially meat and potatoes) levied against individual households for not fulfilling grain procurement orders, while higher penalties were levied against entire collective farms for alleged theft of collective farm property by individuals; (2) prohibition of trade in potatoes, meat, and animals; (3) prohibition of commercial products procurement (e.g., matches, salt, and kerosene); (4) establishment of a food blockade of Ukraine's borders by interior ministry troops and police (preventing peasants from fleeing famine zones, plus prohibiting the importation of foodstuffs from Russia without special permission); (5) institution of an internal passport system that excluded villagers, further restricting their mobility to flee the famine; (6) distress sales of valuables by villagers to special shops in exchange for food. The amount of intake in these shops increased dramatically from 1931 to 1933. While the famine raged, the cover-up began. Village councils were ordered not to list the cause of death upon registration. All entities were forbidden to register incidents of bloating or deaths caused by famine, except for officials of the GPU. (Bohdan Klid, Canadian Institute of Ukrainian Studies [CIUS], Toronto, Canada, December 12, 2003)

# Chapter Two

## Remember Us as We Remember You
## 1932 - 33

Hope remains alive as long as the Regehr family feels they are remembered. They have moved again – to Tarabunka. Although this place name does not exist on modern maps, interviews with survivors confirm that the Regehrs were still in the region of the northern Urals, near Perm. Over and over again, Maria and Jasch plead, "Remember us" and "Do not forget us." But more important than being remembered, they want to be free. Like the Hebrew slaves in the land of Egypt, Jasch longs for "a Moses" to liberate them.

### We Yearn for Release from Here

Tarabunka, May 11, 1932

My dear Geschwister Franz and Liese and family,
We thank God and you with heart and mouth! Today we received two packages from you and with tears of joy we think of and remember you. You should just see how happy our children are today. Our little Jascha just leaped and skipped for joy. In his excitement he ran to meet me when I came from work and eagerly told me what Auntie Liese had sent us. How shall we ever repay you, dear Geschwister? We will have to leave it to Him who will repay you better than we ever could. Oh, we are so thankful that God is blessing your life, and through you is blessing us. We look and see God's hand in this. You put a light on the path for someone – and so we do not lose courage and hope.

The situation is what it is, and it is the way it will be. You are welcome to publish, in the newspapers, the letters we wrote to you describing in words our situation here. After all, they are only too true – in fact, things are actually even worse than we can describe them. Our Peter has lost his eyesight and can see some things in daylight but nothing in twilight. They diagnose it as Bulgarian typhus as a result of malnutrition and anemia. But we wrote you about this before and, should someone there want to send him a few dollars, please encourage them to do so. Please, dear brother-in-law, send it to Moscow to [...] and the goods will be sent from there to us. I guess they shop for us there. Please send something to heal his eyes.

If you do this, then please mention the items they should send to us. They have sent us a catalogue with the price of products marked: Flour, 20 rubles per kilo; [...], 20 rubles per kilo; [...], 40 rubles per kilo. This is the easiest and cheapest way to help us. To send the parcel to us costs 8 ½ rubles per kilo [...]. That will cost 25.50 rubles. For the other money you can get products [...]. These firms have been opened all over Russia. They have allowed all these imports because they do not want so many people to die of starvation.

We have received a letter from John Wiens, and he writes that many grown men have died in the last little while. They have been without bread or food for a long time. Then the people went to [...], which is 8 km away, to get some potatoes – potatoes that had been thrown out in the fall because they were too small. The potatoes have been rotting in a pile of garbage all winter and were stinking badly, but they were washed and eaten. Many get sick and die. If we had not received that help from you, we would have done the very same thing. In most of the time before May we were always without bread. Then my dear Marie got some flour and made soup with some greens, and we ate until we were full. But we will never get fat that way. I just have not the words to describe it, and if you have not experienced it you cannot imagine what I am writing about.

L. still is not here – she is on the way and might not make it. May God have His special way with her. My dear Marie just worries so much, and she is so emaciated. I often ask God, "Why must you lead us in such deep and painful ways?" Who can give me courage and hope? Oh, how we yearn for release from here! Is there courage and hope to be found anywhere? How is it that lately you do not write? Did something happen to you, and has death played his gruesome game with you as well? Do not be shocked at what the devil does to God's children as soon as they do some good deeds. He will do everything to prevent you from writing or continuing in your good work. Alas, if only we could come to your country and help you.

We received 2 letters from B. Klassens. Liese, are you getting better? Are the children well? It seems that B. Klassens are very poor and cannot help us at all. That is rather interesting. Have you, dear brother-in-law ever written to [...] or [...]Regehr? On one parcel there is a return address from Holland. How can that be? Do our pleas for help even reach that country? We are relatively well, but Peter has problems with his eyes.

We go to work every day and today I will work 10 hours laying a railroad track. It is very hard work. In this area the water table is so high that when we dig, the water is right there. We must first clear the forest in a 40-metre-wide strip, remove every tree, and then build the road bed. We feel exactly like the Israelites in Egypt even to the point where we have to gather our own straw. Why does not a Moses reveal himself here? We have not heard from home in a long time. Do you ever hear anything of Br. Abram? We have just learned that they have arrested Liese because of her clothes, the reason being that she had more than she needed. We must accept this as God's way with us. Please pray for us that we do not despair since it is all so hard to understand! Well, I will close. God bless you all, and remember us as we remember you.

Jakob and Marie Regehr

*Remembering is critical, but maintaining communication links is difficult. Oddly, the extended family in Canada receives a letter from Liese. Uncle*

*Franz and Aunt Liese Bargen learn that another attempt by Liese to "use the weapons of the rabbits" has failed. She has been caught. Her punishment is prison in Moscow with 500 other fugitives and then prison camp in Kizel. But where is Peter? She wonders if he is in Canada.*

*Liese has lost her family connections. She needs to contact her parents, and they are desperate to find their daughter. Perhaps Franz and Liese in Canada hold the key. This letter has had an extraordinary journey – a testament to the circuitous communication route.*

Sunday, May 15 [1932]

Dear Grandparents and Uncles and Aunts, who are all so far across the sea,
Probably you have waited a long time for a letter. But I did not want to write before I was settled. My health is fragile but I am almost well. I trust that you are well too. I am in a slave labour camp at Kizel – for how long I do not know. I work on the 3rd level from 6 to 2 o'clock, then we are free. The work is very hard. While in prison I languished very much because my thoughts would not give me any peace. We get 700 grams bread, and 3 times a day we get soup, so that currently we are satisfied with the food.

Only one thing is so hard for me: I have no idea where all my loved ones are! Are they still alive, or is one already lying under the earth? Only God knows. Please send me their addresses; maybe they are quite near to me and I do not even know it. Is Peter with you? And what about Abr. and Lena Regehr? Have they been lucky or are they also in misery somewhere? I have experienced many, many things on this my sad journey. Oh, how many people like myself did I meet when I was in jail! 500 of us were sent away from Mosk [*Moscow*] – all were those who had tried to escape. Conditions in the jail in Mosk are now good: Bread 500 grams, good porridge twice a day, and one tea. But once I am free I do not want to linger here very long.

Send me the address immediately – and write in Russian, and very little, or I will not get it. I will post this letter right away. For the 3rd month I am among Russians only. But maybe better times are in store for us as well. Please write to my parents immediately and inform them of my circumstances.

Hearty greetings from Liese Regehr

*It is no wonder that Liese cannot find her parents. Again, this defenseless family has been transported. Tarabunka, a location not found on maps of the former USSR, appears to be a colossal site in the northern Ural Mountains. In one day 350 prisoners arrive, and 1,000 more are expected.*

*Amid the throng of prisoners, Jasch and Maria cannot stop worrying about their two oldest children. Still having no news of Liese, they are grateful that a woman has seen their daughter in prison. If only they could all be free. Perhaps an escape route through China is still possible. Jasch inquires again about "those with pigtails."*

Tarabunka, 16 May 1932

Dearly beloved Geschwister Franz and Liese and children,
May God bless you and may you experience His grace and mercy your entire life! Dear siblings, do not get cross that we so often come to you. You deserve our praise and our thankfulness. Yes, we can never repay you. That will be done by our dear God according to Matthew 25:34-40. That is a blessing that will remain eternally.

Yes, what is this life but misery and distress? Oh, that we experience anew again and again. Sometimes the temptation to doubt gets so great we can hardly bear it. But supported by God's Word our strength is always renewed. He never deserts His own. We have again experienced this in the last few days. We were sitting there, without bread for several days, when your parcels arrived. Oh, dear Franz and Liese, I cannot describe what then happened in our home. Our little children praised God and you. Yes, if in such dark or, put more accurately, terrible hours, such help comes to us, then literally we can see God's help.

Currently our situation is very grave indeed, especially that we get no news from our Liese. A month ago we were given a letter by a Russian woman who had been together with Liese in prison at [...]. We got no further news. Our Peter's eyes are still not better. If it gets dark, he cannot see at all. If our diet would be more nutritious, he would get well too. He is very anemic but nevertheless has to go to work everyday. It rained all day yesterday, but in spite of that he had to work his 10 hours. He came home soaked to the bone. Such things also contribute to misery.

I have received 6 days of leave. I am quite sick from everything that has overwhelmed us. It is especially hard for dear mother when so much is demanded of her. The children beg and cry for bread, and Mama cannot give them anything. Such a thing, dear Geschwister, has to be experienced to be understood. Many more workers are being brought here. Today 350 exiled families are to arrive at our station – from where I do not know. And 1,000 condemned prisoners are expected in the next few days. We thought things might change this month, but it certainly does not look that way.

What do you hear at your place? What do you read in the papers from "Ivan"? Please write. They are saying today that a Russian in France is supposed to have shot the President. Is that true? Yes, may the dear Lord find ways to free His people. How do things look with the Zoepfigen [*the Chinese, "those with pigtails"*]? Ach, if only it could change here overnight! Today we were notified that every able worker shall dig up 850 square Faden [*one Faden is six feet*] of tundra and prepare the field for planting potatoes. The situation is always getting worse. Maybe the affliction will soon be at its greatest and God's help will come.

Pray much for us, dear Geschwister.

God answers prayer. That you will also have experienced many times in your suffering, is that not right, Liese? How is it with your illness? We just received a letter from Bargens and they did not mention anything about it. We are very anxious to know. Let us know. We have not had any letter from you for a long time. Do you think someone is stopping the mail? Or are you very busy with seeding? We would love to read a letter from you every week. We have received only 2 letters from Benj. Klassens – and no packages. It seems to be too little to expect from a sister. With such frugality or thrift they will not accumulate very much.

Dear Geschwister, do not do more for us than you are able. Your situation is so much worse than Klassens. God will return to you 100 fold, and you will see you will get as much saved as the others, even if medical care costs you many dollars. We have often talked of you, what a fortunate family you are! You have such gifted children and have always had enough of everything. May God bless your fields this year a hundredfold.

It is reported to us that the fields here are not being seeded by a long shot. The people are running around like wild beasts, driven by hunger – and in addition there is no seed available. The time will come when Russia will need Mithilfe [*foreign aid*] even more than now. What have those wicked people accomplished? It is reported from home that a shipload of bread arrived in Kherson. But our Russians did not want to accept it – after all, did he not have enough bread for his own people? So it was all postponed till May 7. How it will turn out we do not know, but the future will tell. Well, we trust it will all turn out well.

One night the police took Peter Enns N. 8. Many of these heroes just go missing. Schufer N. 4, remember, who took away our fur coats and other things, also absconded with Papa's fur coat. Graf also stays home very little. The reason our Liese is in such a situation is because Graf, together with Schufer, stole all her clothes. His evil conscience now does not leave him in peace. Our curtains were also taken by Graf, and so were sundry other things which, if converted to money, would be well over 1,000 rubles.

It says in God's Word: "Boys will rule over you and the land will become desert and empty." Most of the horses are dispersed and ruined. They write from N. 14 that of 85 horses only 30 are left, and all of them are unable to work. I could tell you many more things like this, but it is better to keep silent. My dear little wife is also supposed to dig up 800 sq. ft. to plant potatoes. There is no more

Zugkraft [pulling power, such as horse power] and now starving people must do that work.

Where is Moses? Is he already floating on the water?

Just now my dear Marie came in from the store. She had been able to get a bar of soap on my work book for 29k. Here that seldom happens. At the bazaar, a piece of soap like this would cost up to 5 rubles. There are things that used to cost 3k. a package that now cost 2-3 rubles. And so it is with everything. I write this so you will have an idea of how all things have improved here! But in spite of that, things are not available. We have just eaten dinner. We were at Franz Bargens for dinner [*obviously an imaginary meal*]. We had rice. Many thank-you's, Fritz and Liese. Continue to remember us, do not get tired. Just now the mail came – again no letter – it seems too long for me.

We got a letter from home. My dear little wife will report on it. Our dear Papa is probably already in eternity. In wonderful ways our dear God knew how to sustain our parents, even though many were jealous or even worked against it.

*Maria continues the letter from this point.*

How happy we are that finally some help came for our dear parents too. We felt so sorry that they too had to starve so – besides being so very sick. How God had blessed our dear parents. They had such nice possessions, even into their older years, and now in the last days they must almost starve to death. It is almost impossible to accept! If one thinks on all these things: May God reward those who have done this to us according to their deeds.

We got a letter from Mama which she had written on May 7th. She writes that by the time we get this letter our dear Papa will not be among the living. Oh! It is a deep sorrow for all of us. We have all cried about him as if he were dead; but we cannot be sure if he is dead or still alive. We are [*not only*] very sorry to lose him; we certainly will miss him and his counsel. If we should ever get back and start working again, he would help us with advice and example, but we are happy for him in his peace and rest. He has had to experience much difficulty and many heartaches in his last years; and no guilty one has been found, and this he has had to take to his grave. Well, you know of this situation. I always thought someone would come forward and confess his guilt.

Well, God in glory will reward our Papa with a crown. He will shine and be glorious as a Sunday teacher. I am convinced of this. He was faithful and used his talent for God, and now he returns it to Him with interest. Matthew 25:21.

How are things with you, dearly beloved Liese? Will God completely rid you of your illness? We certainly have the promise that whatever we ask for in His name, He will do for us – and how many Geschwister you have who are praying for you in His name! And how many others too – and God should not hear our pleas? His arm is not shortened so that He cannot help. His ears are not stopped up that He does not hear. Let us only believe and not doubt!

They sent us the letter, dear brother-in-law, where you wrote that your dear Liese almost died on March 10th. You wrote the letter on March 28th. We are so interested to hear how things are now. It just seems to take so long. Did you receive the letter of May 13th? On April 23rd we received your last letter, which you wrote on the 28th of March.

*Jasch regrets writing another "song of lamentation" and longs for the golden days of the past. He pines for food but also hungers for knowledge of the outside world. What is happening in Russia? In Poland? In Germany? The claustrophobia of the camps stifles the prisoners' knowledge as well as their freedom.*

Tarabunka, May 30, 1932

Dear siblings Franz and Liese and children,
With this writing I confirm that on April 7th we received two of your letters. Thank you! Please write often and lots, especially of

these times and the goings on in the outside world. We wish so much to know, and we become curious about what one or another has seen or experienced. Time carries the burden, and that is how it is here also.

Our future becomes ever darker. Much work is demanded of the worker now. One has to work 10 hours a day. We received no products in the month of May – except 800 grams of bread per worker per day and 300 for wife and children. Then you can figure out how we eat. The bread is so heavy and wet. In the morning Peter and I go to work around 5 o'clock and we eat half of our allotted bread; we dip it into a little mustard, so it becomes somewhat palatable. Then at 5 in the evening we come home. We have to walk 4 km, but that is not taken into consideration. Then mother has prepared a thin soup, or Pripps is ready, and then we eat the rest of our allotment of bread for the day. Then we wait the passing of time until it is time to go to bed so that sleep can dull the hunger pangs we suffer.

Many people die. For a time their body swells, and soon the swelling turns inward and they die – very often quite suddenly. Johann Wiens, N. 9, died on May 26. Now he sees what he believed. He was terribly swollen and very ill in the last days. It was only for 2 days but it was the result of great hunger. Also a Hoffmann of N. 4, the teacher who had an uncle in N. 9, died. There are many suffering here. If God does not send a change in these times, then many will yet succumb. Today I also missed work. It is very cold today. In the daytime they do not let the fire die here. For a while I was quite swollen too, but thanks to your help it is a bit better now. But I am very weak.

My Marie is so skinny that you would be shocked. When our daughter Liese saw her, she cried, "Mama, what has happened to you?" Well, that is the way it goes with our younger children too. Hard days and times that will have consequences until we are in our grave. Liese was arrested on the 2nd of March. Today she sits in the punishment cell in Kizel. For how long we have no idea. That poor child has suffered so much. Should she be set free, she will write to you, dear Geschwister; that is, if she is not completely discouraged. She was not allowed to take her clothes along, only the dress she was wearing. My dear Marie was able to speak with her yesterday – by permission! She has lost a great deal of weight. Please pray for us, dear siblings, so that Marie and we all do not become bitter. Sometimes it seems that we cannot bear it all!

It is particularly hard to see how our poor children must suffer. Peter can hardly see at night. It seems to be improving somewhat, but he is far from being able to see properly. He is a diligent young boy! They are very pleased with him. He sends warm greetings to you. If only he could see better he would write you a letter too. He has not received the package yet. We go to the post office every day, thinking it will soon be here. May God guide it safely into our hands. I am sure the soap will help the eyes. He is so very anemic! Just now received word that there will be no bread, even for the workers. There is no flour. So again several days without bread.

We received 2 Packages from you, dear siblings, and from Truda Goosen and Hans Goosen – three altogether. Also one from Isaac Wiebe, from Joh. Regehr, from Kroeker and from an Altmann in Holland. May God richly bless all these givers. May they continue to remember all those who suffer. Isaac Wiebe wrote us he would send us another one in spring. H. Goosen wrote us the same. Too bad it takes so long, because it is so necessary now.

Oh, how we wish to be released from this oppression! Maybe the time will come when we can see each other again. In [...] is a Schammij from N. 1 whose release is demanded by Germany. The Hauptmann [*head man*] Pet. G. Unger is questioning him to find out why he wants to get out! Will it soon be possible to be set free in this manner? Then, Geschwister, be on the alert and remember us here. May God grant His blessings to such a development. Does the fact that there is a different government in Germany have any significance for us? You, dear brother-in-law, write that there is unrest at the Polish border. Is this true? Your letter, Peter, seems to indicate this, but other letters are silent on this subject. Sometimes it seems to us that you just cannot be happy when you read our letters, since we only sing songs of lamentation. But reality is worse than that and gets worse from day to day.

How gladly we would write letters of joy. If our situation would improve even slightly, we would be content. We are getting used to eating "Ressoonel" maybe with a little bit of rye – sometimes given instead of bread – then we are content. We have given up any hope of ever eating until we are satisfied. But God could change our horrible situation. Everything is in His hand. We remember that He once fed 5,000 people with 5 loaves of bread and had 12 baskets left over after picking up the leftover bread. Then He can do it also today! Is that not right?

We have read Mrs. Johann Regehr's letter and forwarded it. It is just like Jakob Bargens, N. 7, to write something like that to you. Bargen had [...] he was so sorry for the sister. In Ayrubra it is very sad because of the lack of products. Well, now I have described our circumstances a little. We wish you could come yourselves and see how we live. I am certain you would understand more then. We have not heard from home in a long time, except for a letter from Ab. Regehr who writes that it is the same with our brother Hans and that Papa has great difficulty breathing. They have recently received packages – that is how our God provides for our poor sick parents.

Is Stalin dead or is he gone?

At your place you are probably in the midst of seeding time. May God bless your crops 100 fold this year. I trust that in the future the market will also improve for you, since over here everything, but everything, is gone, and that could be of benefit to you. How are things with your health, sister? Do you have hope to get completely well? We pray every day for you all. We desire so much that you, dear Liese, could stay alive. You and your dear Franz have done so much for us here in S.L. Camp. We still do not know how we can ever repay you. But it will not remain unrewarded – He will repay. He says.

My dear Marie is sitting and mending clothes so that the children can have something warm to tie around them. Oh, where are those beautiful golden times that we once enjoyed? We had enough of everything – and to-day everything is unavailable and we are robbed of what little we have. Greet all your children. I imagine they are all very busy at work. Yes, and our children have already spent 1 year in exile in this slave labour camp. We have thread but no material to sew with. We lack bread.

Your Geschwister, Jasch and Marie Regehr and children

*As Jasch asks his sister and brother-in-law in Canada to "beg for us" to extended family members and friends, he exposes part of the mail delivery route. A passage through Moscow is preferred. But Jasch's instruction only raises more questions. How do letters from Carlyle, Saskatchewan arrive in the prison camp at Tarabunka? How do letters find a safe passage through Germany? Why does Jasch think that mail will travel faster through Moscow? How would a prison guard or censor respond to this instruction? Isn't it risky to write this? Or is it a masked message? A decoy?*

May 31 [1932]

We did not mail the letter yesterday. I thought my dear little wife would also write something, but she will not do so this time. She has become quite discouraged, and is very worried. I also have been burdened for several days, and sick. It is the same with an old person as it is with an old horse: if you only feed it straw, it will not survive in the long run. The young are able to survive somewhat better.

Let me tell you what we ate today. For breakfast we had the residue Pripps grounds. We ate it with spoons until our plates were empty. Then you should see how fast our little Jascha ate his all up in order to make sure he got his share. For lunch we had cabbage soup, without anything. And for supper we had boiled some Pripps. Then you can see, dear siblings – I just want to let you know by writing it to you. Many here eat Brennessel [*stinging nettles*]. They soak them in water one day, then dry them, and then eat them. Many people die of starvation. It gets more tragic from day to day. One asks God,

"How long will You let us be crushed by these corrupt people? Are there no more answers to our prayers available?"

I really had decided not to write of this, but I cannot help it. Is there anything you can do? Please help – but only by getting others involved, since we know you cannot help more. I thought, dear brother-in-law, you could contact all our relatives, like Joh. Regehr, who has sent us a parcel. There is a Heinrich Regehr and some cousins. Encourage them. There are some Funks and Quirings. Yes, dear Liese, you are often inventive. Investigate ways by which you might save us. We thank Peter Bargens very much that they have accepted us and helped us in our bondage. May God reward you all. May He bless your acres and all you have.

Peter has not received anything yet. We have written thank-you letters to all those whose names you sent us. Would it not go faster if it were sent through Russia, in Moscow – rather than through Germany? I mention this because we are again so desperate for the help. I have to admit to you that nothing gets sent from America [*North America*]. Well, dear siblings, the times are so critical. Please beg for us a lot, so that God can sustain us here and we can once again have a Wiedersehen [reunion] with all our loved ones.

We got a letter from Ab. Regehr. He writes that Ab. Regehr, America, sent some dollars to Aron Regehr, and he drove to Kherson to the Torgsin to buy some products. Flour costs 2r. 50k. per Pud, porridge costs 12 k. per kilo, and so for 5 dollars he can buy quite nicely, right? And still it will soon be gone – it does not last long because the need is so great.

It is rumoured here that the preachers will get their homes back. David Wiebe already has received his back. The talk is also that we shall all soon be free and have the rights of ownership restored to us again for 100 [*years*]. But if any of this is true or not, I cannot tell. Time will tell. Is there any rumour of this, in your country – in your papers – that things will go more justly here? Stalin is the fox! Yes, if our deliverance should come, then we want to thank God, and pay our vows to Him. Oh, how much we long again to enter the house of the Lord with all the children of God. "As the hart crieth for fresh water, so crieth my soul to Thee, oh God" [*Psalm 42*]. Here we are not allowed to have church services. We often do not even know when it is Sunday because we must work 5 days a week and have a rest on the 6th day.

Well, remember us in prayers, your siblings who will never forget you,

J. and M. Regehr and children

[*Written between the lines and upside-down*] Have not received the 2 letters from Klassens. They are as if they do not exist. Somehow they can see and cope with all this misery. Write more about the Bargens.

*Yes, Stalin is a fox. But in the intimate space of family relations, Jasch is hurt that his close family members do not help. Katarina (Goosen) Klassen is his wife's sister. This family left Russia in 1929 and arrived in Canada in 1930. Communication over long distances is challenging, even in ideal scenarios. Misunderstandings and tensions can easily escalate.*

*The next letter again reflects the circuitous route of correspondence. Twenty-year-old Liese's letter is addressed to her parents, but it has traveled on to the Bargens in Canada. Although Liese is very sick, she is still expected to fill her quota in the stone quarry. A lovely young woman in her prime is being penalized in the Kizel prison camp for wanting to join her fiance in her home village.*

May 31 [1932]

Dear Parents and Geschwister,
With a heavy heart I will try to visit you by letter, even though these short letter visits are always far too short for me. Following the day when you were here, Mama dear, I became very ill and could not even get up. Today I was supposed to work in the stone quarry. Two men have already died there. Many people here have typhus. If I should get typhus I am sure my days would be numbered, since I am

already terribly weak on my legs and can hardly walk. The doctor, however, told me that there was no sign of typhus at this time but informed me that I was very anemic. But that is no wonder. I have suffered in this camp for three months without a kopek to my name and for two or three days at a time my mouth never tastes bread or food. I cannot write any more. Please do not worry too much about me. They want me in the quarry again.

With friendly greetings, L. Regehr

*A small scrap of paper with miniscule script expresses sorrow and disappointment in friendship, and yet, astonishingly – hope. This writer (either Jasch or Maria) chooses not to include a date, a salutation, or closing signature.*

[1932]

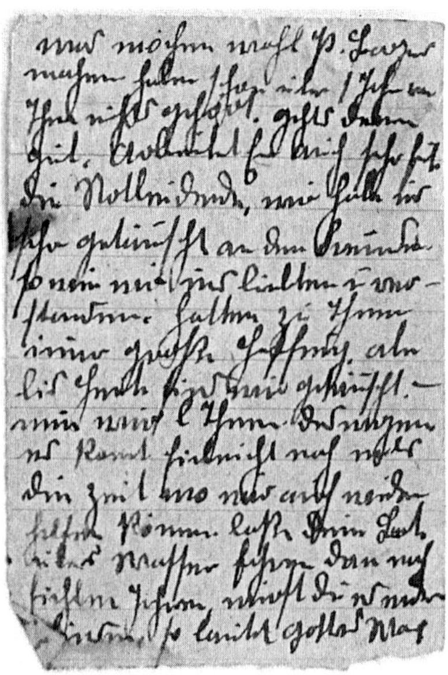

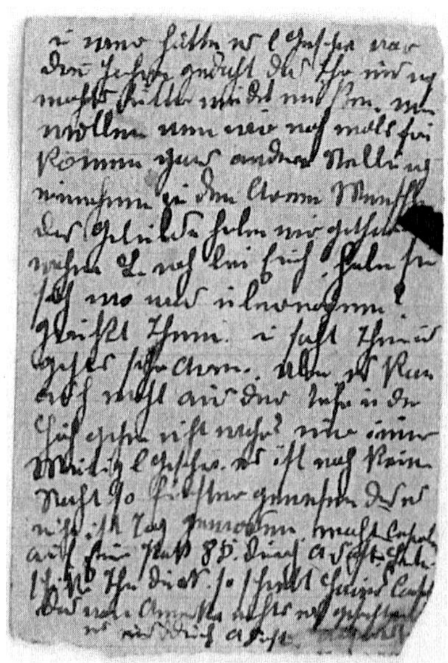

Are P. Bargens living near you? Have not heard from them for over a year. Are things well with them? Is he involved and working for those who are starving and suffering? We have been very disappointed in that friend. We loved each other so much and understood each other so well – and had such hopes in him until today. We are disappointed in him. Still, we love him in spite of this. Maybe the time will come when we too can help someone. Cast your bread upon the waters and it will return to you after many years. That seems to be God's way!

Who would have thought – three years ago – that you would send us more food! If only we could be free again, we would be much more considerate of poor people! We have suffered much. Are they working at the same place you are? Give them our greetings, and tell him we are starving and very poor. But perhaps things will turn around here too – from rock bottom you can only go up! Let us all stay joyful, dear Geschwister. No night has ever been so dark that it is not followed by daylight. For one package we had to pay 8 dollars. Through an A. Fast we were able to get it for 1 dollar. The Americans send parcels through A. Fast.

*The following writer also omits a signature, but "Sister Tina" is clearly Maria's sibling. The plans for daughter Liese are shocking. Is it still possible (in 1932) to be successfully sponsored by a Canadian? Is there a fissure in the Iron Curtain?*

[1932]

Dear Geschwister,
You write that P.B. [*Peter Bargens*] are trying to help get our Liese to Canada. It would please us very much if we would have someone of our family there. You all do so much for us, even sending our addresses far and wide. Dear siblings, all help is needed. Remember how chubby and fat Jakob Doerksen and Mrs. Wiens of N. 4 were? Today they are not more than 3 ½ [...]. Many of the others, not all,

look like sleepwalkers. Do what you can, maybe it will not go on for long. Then we may be helped. Is my sister Tina still alive? We never hear anything from them. We never hear anything of John Martens either. You would be shattered to see how low some people have sunk.

[1932]

You, dear sister Liese, have a good idea when you write that we should write to J. Janzen and you will send him the letter. We have done it. Now you can do your thing. It is very evident to us that you are concerned with devising ways in which we can be helped. May God bless you. No news from Peter [*their son*]. Hope to get news soon. Every time we open a package it is soon empty. Our plea to God is: Give us our own bread so that we no longer have to beg but can give instead. But today such a pleasure has not yet been given to us. Beg for us. Also wrote to P.B.

J. and M. Regehr

*Still existing day-to-day in Tarabunka, the Regehrs are constantly concerned about lost or stolen parcels. A great deal of space on scarce paper is used to track letters and parcels. In some prison camps (like Boworga) food is somewhat more available, but this family's diet remains extremely meagre. Even with so many workers in the family, the food rations are not enough. Father Jasch is also worried about his daughter Liese, who is now in a hospital. His other children cry bitterly.*

Tarabunka, 24th June 1932

You, our dearly beloved Franz and Liese Bargen and children!
We wish you a joyful well-being and God's richest blessings in all your ways. How precious it is that we can still continue to visit each other by letter and can report on our circumstances. If we did

not have this privilege, we would never receive any parcels – and perhaps we would not be around anymore but may have died of starvation. Surely it is proof that God is with and for us, right?

Liese, you write that you mailed 3 dollars to us in [*Kherson Torgsin*] so that we could purchase products. Oh, dear Geschwister, what kind of thank-you can we send to you? We cannot find any more words but God's measure of blessings for you is not yet full. May He reward you according to His pleasure. We continually petition our dear God to richly reward you – which He will surely do. To date we have not received any parcels, for us or for Peter. We do not know why it should take so long. If one should finally arrive, we will immediately report it to you and to the others who helped. What a tragedy it would be if some parcels should be lost! We pray daily that the parcels should come into our hands because our need is so great – and compassionate hearts have sent them.

We have written once to A. Wiens at the time he arranged for a parcel to be sent to our Peter. Did he receive it? We will do it again, immediately. Please continue to send us those addresses. We still have not received those notifications regarding Peter. But to send the dollars to the [*Torgsin*] is the best, I believe, for then we get it a bit sooner and get a bit more. If sent via Moscow the remittance is 8 ½r. for 50r. [...]. Too bad that they deduct this from the dollars and we lose a portion of the products.

How is it, dear sister, that you write only on half a page of a letter? Is it because you are ill and do not have the energy to write more? We regret very much that Franz does not write at all. Write more. My dear Marie [*now sixteen years old*] is standing in line to get bread, but it is still a question whether any will be available. Today is a very cold day. We have made a fire in the stove. Today we salted down fish; we received 2 Vinno for the months of May and June. It is not very much for 2 months for 7 people. However, we are very happy for every little bit.

Peter is working on the railway line and the work is very hard, but nothing can be done about it – he who is a slave is treated like a slave. Often he comes home utterly tired and hungry and complains about his lot in life. We can find no words to give him comfort. Miechi [*fifteen years old*] and Tina [*thirteen*] must go to work every day at 8 in the morning. When they see and hear how many children live in freedom, they too often cry about the fate which has overtaken them. No rainy weather, no storms are considered – they must regularly go to work, regardless. Now they are again beginning with the "voluntarily" imposed obligations. Peter already had to sign for 35 rubles worth of free voluntary labour – and the same for Mariechi and Tina.

Day by day it is getting worse! When will our deliverance come? Yesterday we received a letter from Joh. Warkentins of Boworga [*another prison camp*]. There it is generally better regarding the availability of goods – they can even buy flour and potatoes, which is not possible here. Many people who are in the same situation as we are being driven past this station. No one knows where they are going – whether they are being sent further into exile, or whether they are being sent home which, of course, would be our preference.

My dear Marie will not write today. She is preparing to visit Liese and it is always a long, difficult way. She must walk 15 km and then in such cold weather. Liese is still in Kizel in the hospital, she is very skinny – only skin and bones. She used to be such a beautiful child. How proud we always were of her – and today? Our hearts bleed, dear Geschwister, when we see how our children must grow up in exile. They have been stripped of all rights – no schools – are treated like slaves. Just like Tina – every day she must go to work, never allowed a day to stay home. Oh God, when will things change? Our intention always was that, if at all possible, all our children should be educated so that they could become useful people. And how is it today?

Oh, how thankful you can be that you have escaped! Your children can at least enjoy their freedom, attend school etc. When we talk of it, we cry and almost dissolve in water. If only we would get enough rights to be able to go back to our home. Just now a fellow was here and urged our Peter and J. Friesen to go work in the mines where they would get good pay and receive privileges. We do not want them to do it. Well, I do not think the boys will want it either – it is dangerous to work in the coal mines. Since the clock is already 8 there will be no bread again today. We will have to comfort our stomach in other ways. Zabupa! [*Russian expletive*]

Yes, dear Geschwister, if we did not have God as our comfort we would have perished long ago. But our trust is in the Shepherd of Israel, who does not sleep nor slumber, but keeps a watchful eye over everything. In spite of all our trials and tribulations we have often experienced God's help. It is especially evident in that He makes you so willing to help. We are often touched to tears by what all of you together do for us – that you still regard us of so much worth. May God bless all the givers as well as the gift, and give us here ever thankful hearts. Everything must come from Him who can do everything and who has everything. We wish you the best of health and ask, please write more – and both write. We are happy to read.

Goodbye, J. and M. Regehr

We sent the last letter on June 19th.

*Maria worries that her readers will tire of the litany of woes. But she also knows that "If you grow weary, then we are lost!"*

*The sun shines warmly now in June. Maria hears rumours that some prisoners have been allowed to return to their homes and work in the local collective farms. But she is only cautiously optimistic. She believes that their region (the colony of Sagradowka) has received harsher treatment than most.*

June 25 [1932]

Dear Geschwister Franz and Liese and children,
[...] is again Sunday, and I get the special longing for our dear homeland and all our loved ones there. Yes, today we have talked much of you all and of the times as they once were. We were sitting

at the end of our little house, Jasch and I, when suddenly Lena came running with great joy and brought us 2 letters and told us that there was also a package. Our joy was so great to again have news of you, and the most important thing, you sent something to quiet our stomachs. May God be praised for your love and your support and help.

We see again and again how God loves us. [...] in that to a degree He has restored the health of my dear Jasch. [...] he again can walk by himself. His feet are almost thin [...] just swollen a little down below; he can now more easily get up and can almost straighten his legs. Before he could only walk on his toes and his legs were all crooked. It was very sad. Also, he does not have such severe pains anymore. If only he could have good food so that he could get completely well. He often sits in the sun and lets the sun warm him. Only it is too bad that usually a cold wind blows here; he still has his felt boots and fur cap on. We really long to see you all again.

Today we received 2 letters from you, written on June 2nd and June 4th. But the [...] clipping under Lena's name has not arrived yet. We wonder if it will come. Dear Liese, if only you knew how much you comfort us. We are so encouraged and full of hope. Oh, if at last the time would come when we could go through the sea with dry feet – just like you write! People are really working on our behalf. But it all takes such a long time. Many, many will not survive, but we long for deliverance. Germany must be aware that those in exile are all doomed and perish in gruesome ways. And the [...] stay alive. Whom do they want to save, then? Everything is taking too long.

I did not finish my letter yesterday. Today is Monday when we should be cooking some Kielki [*meatballs*] for lunch, as was earlier done in so many places. In those days we did not consider them very highly, even when there was delicious fat and ham with them. And today it would be the greatest treat possible, even without the ham. But it is impossible – only soup. How we yearn for something else! Dear Geschwister, do not weep for us. We are now very thankful to

God and all the good people for the gifts sent to us, and hope that our survival needs will also be met in the future; or what do you think? If you grow weary, then we are lost!

Dear Liese, you write you celebrated my birthday – it was on May 26th. How we would love to have been at your place with our entire family. I believe your eyes would have popped out of your heads to see how we would have eaten. We often discuss how it would be to sit at a laden table, and if we would be able to practice moderation. Much is said here about freeing us. From home they write that those who have had trials and been sentenced are out of jail and at home, and it is now our turn. Those who [...] are here, also exiled as we were, are almost all [...] from here. They let them into their homes, take them into the communes [...], and write to those still here that they should only come home [...]. But without freedom. Today we got a letter from H. Goos. N. 6, but there it does not sound like we can come home soon. Many are forcibly driven from their homes, all is sold, and they are being tried and judged. Our region was the very worst and probably carries the greatest responsibility as well.

*A letter from eighteen-year-old Peter would be so valuable. Jasch tells his readers that he has enclosed a copy of his son's letter, but unfortunately it has not been found in the Campbell's Soup box.*

[1932]

Dear Geschwister Franz and Liese,
Our Peter is writing a letter to you, but because he wrote with a pencil and it is very hard to read, I have accurately copied what he wrote. Oh, that poor dear Peter, he weighs so heavily on our hearts. Would to God that he would soon be allowed to come to us. He will degenerate there all by himself. But if the ways of the Lord are right, then we want to remain quiet before Him. Today or

tomorrow they are sending 65 families further to the Burna River. We are still 45 Mennonites who remain behind – we, Wiens N. 4, Joh. Reg., H. Friesen.

J. Regehr

[*Written around the edges*] I do not have my free will with letter writing today. Please accept it as it is, in warm love, Jakob.

*Fear emanates from this writer's words. As we read, we wonder who is restricting his writing and how it is being enforced.*

July 3 [1932]

Dear Geschwister, in the land of peace,
I can report to you that you have visited us [*a veiled reference signifying a letter has been received*]. Oh, how your children have grown, especially Lieschen and Fritz. Oh, that poor Peterchen, I am so sorry that he has to be sick. All the rest of you look very well. We weep about the fact that we did not flee two days earlier. Maybe we could also have escaped and now be living as humans as well. Now we are absolute slaves. The grave beckons us all unless we can get warm clothes and felt boots.

You, whom we love, ask about many things. We have received 3 packages, but have no idea from whom. The post office here just sends us a card with the announcement that a parcel has come; we must sign with our complete name and address and send it off to a teacher, Mr. Fast. We regret that we do not even know who the sender is. In the previous year there was at least a return address on each parcel. There is no sign yet of the 2 dollars you said you had sent – and the 1 dollar written about and sent by someone else has not yet arrived. May God in His mercy protect those dollars!

We received the [...] today, the 3rd of July. You write of sending 10 dollars to the Torgsin. My dear wife will go there tomorrow and do some business. I have written you everything about the big farms. I would write you a "'thank you" from here, but I am not the one who has sent the thank you note to you. May God bless him and all those who have helped and given. Please write again, and God be with you. My dear Marie has been forced to do the slave work. Oh, Franz and Liese, how very fortunate you are! And we are incarcerated and expend our life's strength by working in this camp of slaves. Oh, Weh! It is raining and my fragile wife is still at work. Dear Liese, could you give me one of your tasty baked breads?

Jakob

*We gain some insight into Peter's life in the next letter. We also learn more about Tina. Her work in the smelter continues – inflicting its destruction in her lungs, her skin, and her soul.*

Tarabunka. July 8, 1932

Dear beloved Geschwister Franz and Liese Bargen and children,
The God who loves me be with you and protect you for His eternal life. It is so precious that we have this hope, otherwise we would despair and die. We have come to the place called Marah [*a place of bitter water described in the Old Testament*]. The drink is so bitter, but the almighty God helps at the right time. Even now we wish to travel on – so may God help us and save us from these fetters. May He guide us home to our dear parents and siblings. But it takes so long.

Our situation gets worse from day to day. Today we are without any bread. It is good when we have some packages. But of all those packages promised to Peter and to us, none has arrived. We just cannot imagine why it takes so long. The boy would like to thank those of you who have said that you sent one. We have never written to the addresses before, but by writing to them we hope to receive a parcel. If so we will let you know. Well, I guess many packages get lost too.

When there is no writing on those packages they go better and arrive sooner. We got some cookies but they were filthy and in a mess. There was no address given. We got some products to the value of ten dollars from Moscow. We can order such things as we wish. And we did this. If you, dear brother-in-law, find out who the givers are, please thank them in our name. Then please send us their address so we can thank them as well. If help such as that did not reach us, we would not be here any longer. I would thank everyone in such a loud voice that it would be heard everywhere. Until now you have saved us from death by starvation.

Oh God, please touch other hearts and make them willing to help. May God bless your fields and your herds – and He will do it too! I am a little sick now. I just cannot seem to tolerate this sour brown bread. I went to see the doctor today and he ordered half a litre of milk per day for me, for a period of 2 weeks. If I can get the milk, I think I will feel better. But so often they order things which they know cannot be obtained. I cannot go to work and have already missed several days. My neighbour just cannot stand to see me suffer. Peter goes to work diligently and was highly praised by his boss. They have promised him that they would sell him 1 pud flour per month at 30 rubles – in the store it costs 100 rubles. In the store you pay 20 rubles for a loaf of bread. We live in expensive times, but even then you are unable to get clothes anywhere. If available, a man's used suit costs up to 200 rubles. In the store there are no wares, nothing – everything is gone. Sometimes we believed we would receive [...] there and it seemed so cheap. Did you receive the catalogue we sent you?

Each day we have to carry coal into the smelter furnaces and then carry out all the ashes. Sometimes one can hardly tolerate the dust and ashes that cover you and everything around you. It is agonizing to see how they force the children to work, but in order to live one must work. Tina works every day and must leave for work at 3 A.M. She must do a variety of jobs: put bricks in place around the furnace, clean the furnace, and load coal into the bins. The very young children are still exempt from work, but hundreds and thousands have died here of starvation. Oh, what can we do? May God raise up a Moses to help us! Lena and Jasch are well. My dear wife still wants to go to the store. The time is 7, but her mother's heart just cannot stand it any longer – and her name will shortly be removed from the workers list.

Tina has broken skin on her back. That poor child has to go through all this from May 2 until today [...]. She too is only skin and bones, and when she comes home from this hard work we can only give her black bread. It could happen that a package arrives at the right time – often things have happened that way. Well, we trust that God will help. Everything else is as usual. Many single people escape from here. We have not heard much from home; they do not write any more. They are probably eating fresh potatoes already. Mrs. Boschman wrote that Peter Enns from N. 8 has been sentenced to be shot. He richly deserves it – the pitcher goes to the well until it breaks. [*A very harsh judgment. Some Mennonites became informers for the authorities, and because they had an intimate knowledge of the people and the language they could become more of a threat than Russian-Slavic informers. Peter Enns must have succumbed to the lure of the ruble and betrayed his fellow villagers.*] May God keep you, protect you and bless you.

Your dear siblings, Mariechen and Jasch Regehr

*This writer apologizes for using such inadequate paper. Critical messages keep the fragile lifeline of mail delivery functioning. However, mail sent through Moscow or Germany no longer arrives, and a new route must be found. Small dollar amounts and parcels must be accounted for.*

*The oldest children continue to work, but the youngest two have a different experience. Lena, now ten years old, has been sent away to school – a mixed blessing for her parents. She receives more food, but she is absent from the family and educated in communist ideology in the Soviet school system.*

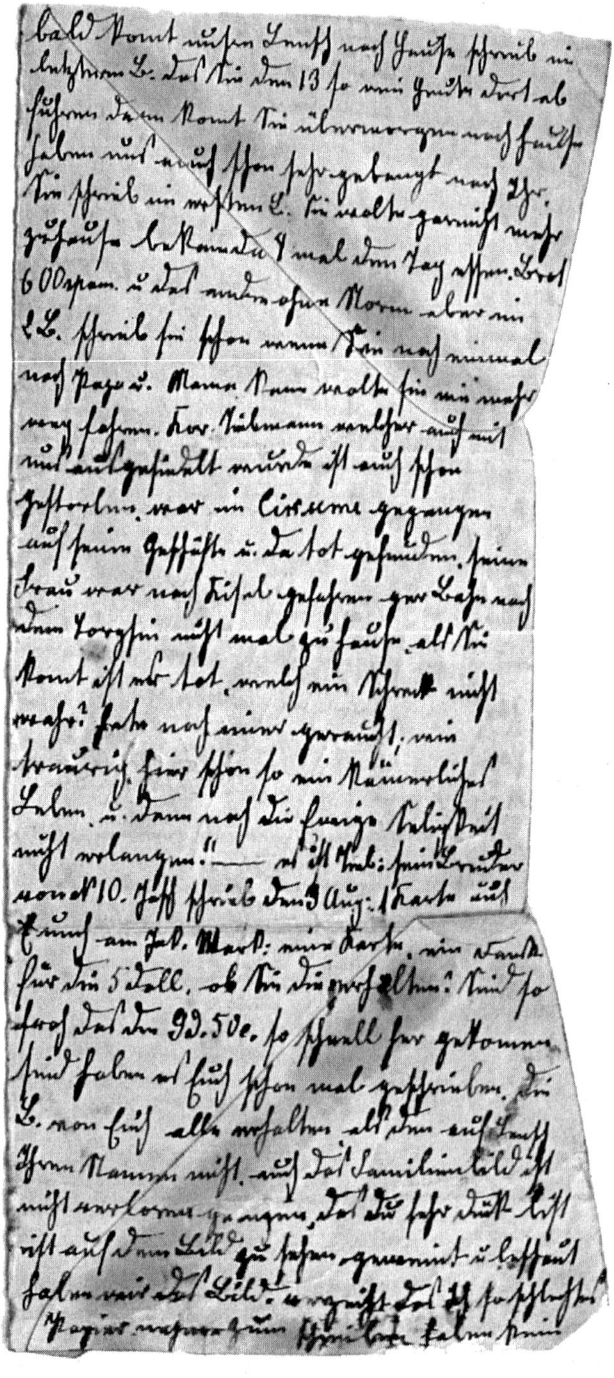

bald kommt unser Fritz nach Hause schreib im
letzten L. daß Sie den 13 so wie heute dort ab
fahren dann kommt Sie übermorgen nach Hause
haben uns auch schon sehr gebangt nach Ihr.
Sie schreibt im nächsten L. Sie wollte garnicht mehr
zuhause bekommen 4 mal den Tag essen. Brot
600 gram. u. das andere essen kann aber im
L. schreib sie schon wenn Sie noch niemal
nach Papa u. Mama kam wollte sie nie mehr
weg gehen. Der Tilmann welcher auch mit
uns ausgesiedelt wurde ist auch schon
gestorben. war in [illegible] gegangen
auch seine Geschäfte u. da tot gefunden. seine
Frau war nach [illegible] gefahren zur Bahn nach
den [illegible] nicht mal zu Hause. als Sie
kommt ist er tot. welch ein Schreck nicht
wahr? hatte noch einen gebraucht. wie
traurig hier schon so ein kümmerliches
Leben u. dann noch die [illegible]
nicht erlangen!! — er ist [illegible] sein Bruder
vom N 10. Jetzt schreib den 3 Aug. 1 Karte auch
[illegible] am [illegible] Markt: eine Karte. wir danken
für den 5 Doll. ob Sie die erhalten? Sind so
froh daß die 93.50 c. so schnell her gekommen
sind haben es Euch schon mal geschrieben. die
L. von Euch alle erhalten als den auch Fritz
Ihren Namen nicht. auch das Familienbild ist
nicht verloren gegangen, daß du sehr dick bist
ist auch dem Bild zu sehen, gemeint u. gestaunt
haben wir das Bild. u vergiß daß ich so schlechtes
Papier [illegible] zum schreiben haben kein

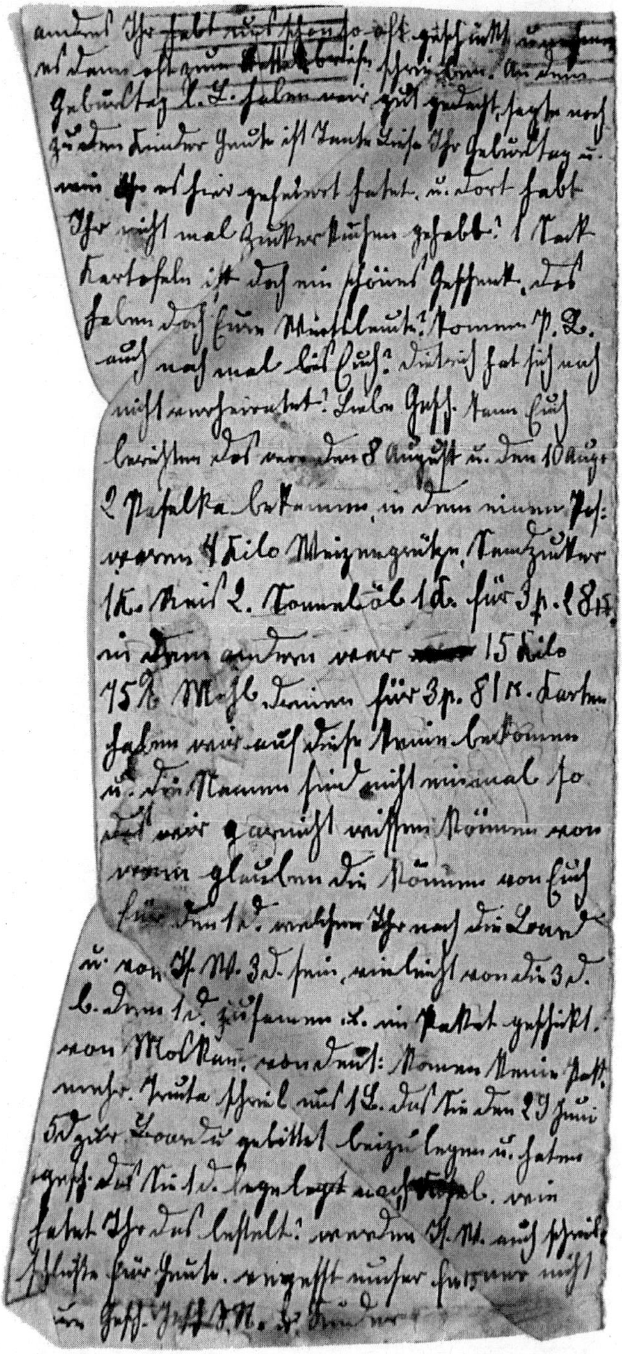

[September 1932]

Soon our Lena will be coming home. I wrote in my last letter that she was leaving there on the 13th. That is today, and she should arrive home the day after tomorrow. We are already very lonesome for her. In her first letter she wrote that she did not want to come home anymore, because where she is they get meals 4 times a day and 600 grams of bread and other food – and no rationing. But in her next letter she wrote if she could get back to Mama and Papa she would never want to leave again.

Kor. Thielman, who was also resettled with us, has already died. He had gone to Cirume to do his business and was found dead there. His wife had taken a train to Kizel to go to the Torgsin and was not at home. When she came home, he was dead! What a fright, nicht wahr [*Is that not so*]? He was still a smoker. How sad to have such a miserable existence here and then not even to attain eternal salvation!!

It is [...] his brother from N. 10, Jasch, wrote a card on the 3rd of August and also a card to Jak. Wark. thanking [*him*] for the 5 [*dollars*]. I wonder if they have received it. We are so happy that the 2.50 got here so quickly, but we have written to you about that before. We have received the letters from you, except the one addressed to Lena. Even the family picture did not go lost. That you are nice and chubby we can see in the picture. We wept and looked and looked at the picture. Please forgive that I write on such poor paper – we have no other. You have already sent us some so often and we often use it to write Bettelbriefe [*begging letters*]. Dear Liese, we did remember your birthday. I even said to the children, today is Aunt Liese's birthday, and talked of how you used to celebrate it here – and there you did not even have Zuckerkuchen [*sugar cookies*]. A sack of potatoes is a marvelous present. I guess that was given to you by your landlords.

Do P.B. come to visit you occasionally? Is Dietrich married yet? Dear Geschwister, I can report that we received 2 parcels on 8 Aug. and 10 Aug. In one parcel there were 4 kilos cream of wheat, sugar, 1 kilo rice, 2 sunflower oil, 1d. for 3r. 28k. In the other there was 15 kilo of 75% flour for 3r. 81k. We have received no cards on these, and there are no names so that we do not know from whom they come. We believe they must come from you. For the 1 dollar which you sent to the Board and from Is. W. the 3d. are perhaps together with the 1d. to send the parcel. We get no more mail from Moscow and from Germany. Truda wrote us a letter that she sent 5 dollars to the Board on 29 June to be included, and they wrote that they included 1d. after [...]. When did you arrange this? Will also write. Is. W. Will close for today. Please do not forget our hunger.

Your Geschwister, Jasch, M. and children

*Accounting for parcels and letters must be so important to the Regehr family that they use scarce writing materials to catalogue their receipts. Newspaper clippings have also arrived, keeping this isolated family somewhat informed.*

[Mid-1932]

The package N. 4434 from April until now has not been received. It could be from Harms. The package from Crebiel has not been received. These packages we did receive: July 17th.

1. Gertrude Goosen
2. Johann Goosen
3. P. Classen – Kansas
4. Peter Penner
5. Franz Bargens
6. Henry Bargen
7. Cornelius Loewens – Kansas

Dear Liese,

Plead for us some more to acquaintances in Germany. Many get help from Germany as well as from America. Maybe you should contact Voigt or Mrs. Klether. Yesterday we wrote and expressed our deepest thanks to all the givers, but maybe they did not receive the letters. Please report it to them through the papers. Report also about those 2 parcels we did not receive. We always report immediately when we receive something, but there may be letters going lost. We are very sorry about those from Harms and Crebiel. From Crebiel there was a 10-dollar package – we were especially happy for that.

But we are happy, dear Liese, that you continue to remember us. A compassionate person sending packages has saved many a life here. And that has been the case with you and us. May God give His blessing. Eight mouths need a lot of food, since the food contains so little nourishment. Only soup and bread – but we are very thankful and happy if we have it. The clipping from P. we have received. Will he have had to [...] as well? Reimer's address received. Thank you. If you have clippings of people being rescued, then do not delay in sending them.

Your Jakob

## When is it Sunday?

*The days become fused into one long winter as the work continues. Stalin is becoming increasingly obsessed with those who might oppose him. He has been warned by the NKVD that millions of Russians support Trostsky and wish to bring him back to power. Stalin's response is to eliminate all those who appear to be Marxist revolutionaries – friends and family are not exempt. Stalin also fears losing Ukraine and wants to repress any revolutionary activity, wherever it is suspected. The massive, enforced famine (the "Holodomor") continues. In the midst of the paranoia and chaos, Maria Regehr tries to be fair to her children as she divides bread and Pripps.*

[1932/33]

Dear Geschwister Franz, Liese and children!
Thank you for that most precious letter which we received from you. We had waited a long time to hear from you, and finally your

letter arrived. We love reading letters much better than writing them. Dear Liese, it is exactly as you write, I do lack that joyfulness. Of course you know me quite well. My dear Jasch likes to write more than I do, but even with him I can notice that writing letters is not easy anymore either. His nerves are so strained by all the stress he has gone through.

Dear loved ones, we wish you God's richest blessing and the best of health. How we rejoice when we get a letter from you stating that you are all well, especially you, dear Liese, because we know how you are suffering. Who would have thought that your health would improve to the degree that it has been restored, even though you are seldom without pain. Oh, how I would love to chat with you – quietly so that even your Franz would not hear us. Many a secret I would lay upon your heart. Well, if it pleases God, such a time may come again. We firmly believe that God will bring us together again.

Here everyone works so hard, as if someone has established a set time when all the work has to be finished. Tunnels are being built everywhere, and one is astonished at how they can accomplish such an elaborate and complex task. We have had up to 48 degrees of frost, but in spite of that the work goes on. My heart is at the breaking point when I help prepare my children to go to work. In former times we did not even go visiting if the weather was so cold, and now they have to work outside for the whole day. Pet. says that it was so cold that they could not work but they still have to remain outside – and eat outside as well. You may well wonder: Is this all true? Your heart would break too, if you could only see! Many have had their hands and feet frozen; no day of rest is given to them, no Sunday is allowed – in fact, we often do not know when it is Sunday. It is a disgrace to admit it, but it is so!

With a deep longing we yearn for a different time. I wonder if our great God will not suddenly call a halt and put an end to this misery and suffering. Yesterday we also received a letter from sister Joh. Baerg. She can also write only of grief and sorrow. Her husband has died. He always felt that the sword would not strike him, but he had to suffer along with many others. [...] where you and Rempel's L. are on has not been received. I guess letters go lost and this we regret very much. It is 10 o'clock and L. has just gone to work. My dear Jasch will soon come home from work, and I am sitting here and writing to you as a symbol of love. In the daytime it is so dark in our little room that we cannot even start anything. The windows are so thickly frosted over that we cannot even see a sprig of green. It is horribly cold. We heat the entire day. But the saddest thing is for our children who must go to work. They have to be out, and we can be inside.

Franz Baerg wrote that there are terrible things going on at home [*in Altonau*]. People are hauled into court, judged, and condemned for the most trifling things – which are not the real reasons for the judgment but the means by which they get more 'forced labour. Mrs. Gerh. Siemens Lena has also been arrested, tried, condemned and sent to jail for 3 years. Just imagine! She certainly won't live through her sentence – and so many enter eternity before their time. Still, we read in the Word that everyone's days have been numbered, and no hair shall be crimped without God's will. In my darkest hours that thought is often of great comfort to me.

Hans Goosen has sent 5 dollars to the Torgsin for us in [...]. For that we ordered millet meal and flour. We received it yesterday – 2 [...] meal and 2 [...] flour for the total amount of money. We had written that they should send it [...]. They did it too and it cost us 29r. 35k., and when they take the delivery expenses from the dollars then exactly half the money remains. Imagine how much we got for it. We are always concerned to get the cheapest so that it will go further. Dear Geschwister, you ask about the parcel you sent off on Oct. 4th. We still have not been notified of it. Jasch wrote a letter to the Torgsin today, asking if there was such a package with the special number which you wrote about and which you personally had ordered. It takes so long; we are waiting for it every day. If only it would not have gone lost! It goes fastest if the order is sent directly to us and we send it to them. Then we usually have it in about 3 weeks from the time we order it and it arrives here. My sister Truda did it this way twice. And then she sent 10 dollars to the Torgsin in Moscow on the 8 June and has received nothing to date. Jasch has written there several times. We wrote to Truda to work and write them from her end.

Oh, dear Geschwister, I am incapable of putting down on paper what you are doing for us. We are so thankful to God that he has given us such dear siblings and that he has spared your life, dear Liese; and if He should grant that we meet again, then we will repay you by our deeds. To survive only on what food is given to us here is impossible. Twice a day, for lunch and supper, I cook soup from what you sent us. For breakfast we have bread and Pripps. I find it most difficult to apportion the food, and I detest doing it. Jasch and Lena feel that they should get as much as the workers, but that is not possible. How nice it used to be when we had enough of everything and the thought of apportioning food never entered our minds. Too bad that B. Kl. are so poor. If only that dear brother-in-law did not have to die too. Tina wanted to write too but said that Lieschen did not write at all.

*Jasch names his younger sister Liese affectionately here. Significantly, he also differentiates their identity from that of the ethnic Germans. The Regehrs and Bargens are of Dutch ancestry from the northern province of Friesland in the Netherlands.*

[1932]

Dear little Sister,
We gather from your letter of March 10th that you wrote to Switzerland, on our behalf, to get some foodstuffs for us. How did you get that idea, do you have friends there? Do you have addresses? Then send them also to us. Dear Liese, you do so much for us, should God not reward you many times over? I say yes, He will, as He promised! But hunger is so painful.

I do not want to make it uncomfortable for you, but is there not somewhere a Dutch Red Cross worker? After all, we are Dutchmen! If so, send us his address. Oh, how long will we still have to beg? Dear siblings, each time we write it is a real struggle for us. Should we write to you and again ask for food? We know how hard it is for you to respond to all those starving ones! But where shall we go? It will not be long now until sweet heavenly music will greet us. Persevere just a little bit longer. Write to us how things are in general. Can we help?

We have not received a letter from Peter Bargens for over a year. We are very surprised that they do not maintain contact with us, especially when we remember what we did for them during the famine [*a reference to the famine of the early 1920s*]. But we believe our dear God will see us through without them. We know very well who is at fault. They have forgotten what it is like to starve. I am happy that Uncle John wants to support Mama and Hans. We were always good friends with Martens. How often they came over for supper! It was so nice, and we wish those times would return again. But we would never have thought that they would completely forget us. But the proverb is true: "A thousand friends in good times, but very, very few in bad times."

How are things going for Bargen's girls? If you can, send us their new address; we would congratulate them. How gladly we would send our Peter to you to work for you. Dear sister, who would not like to be treated so kindly by you and always have enough food? Our wish is: If only we could even get some of the crumbs which fall from the rich lord's table! A thousand thanks for the two dollars sent by your landlord. May He reward them greatly. If only we would get the notification – the package has not arrived yet. We will write immediately upon receipt. The 8-dollar package has not arrived yet either. We will not write letters without stamps anymore. We were sorry to hear that you must pay duty on our stampless letters. Hearty thanks to Franz and Betty and Peter and

Meka for the 25r. Dear children, how gladly we would also like to give you 25 dollars.

Thank you, children. Jasch

*Jasch's other sister, Mariechen, has been more fortunate. She and her husband Hans Koop have not yet been arrested or sent into exile. They also have enough food. But they have lost their home and all of their possessions. Jasch's father has died; his elderly mother is now alone and homeless, wandering from place to place.*

[1932]

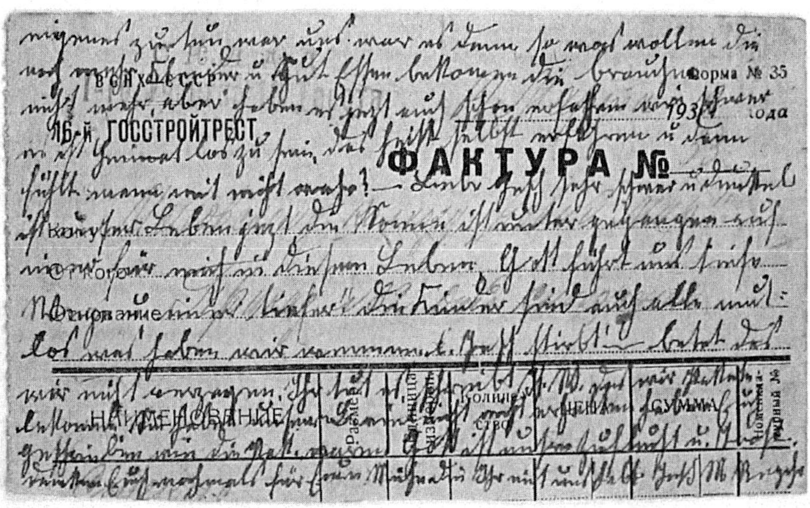

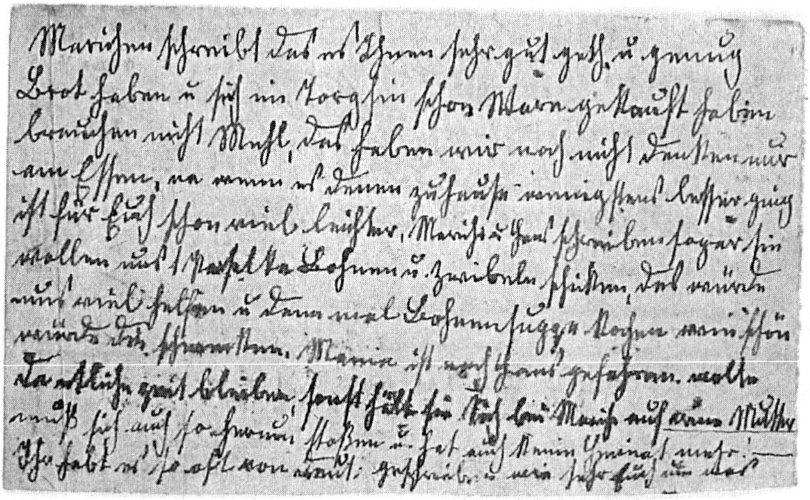

Mariechen [*Jasch's sister who married Hans Koop remained in their home village*] writes that it goes very well with them. They have enough bread, and they can buy some wares in the Torgsin. They do not even need flour. We still are not that far. We only think of food. Well, if things go better at home, then it will be much easier for you. Mariechen and Hans even write they want to send us a parcel of beans and onions. That would help us a lot. Imagine, to be able to cook a bean soup; how tasty that would be.

Mama has gone to Hans, she wanted to stay there a while. Usually she stays with Mariechen. Poor mother. She is forced thither and yon, and has no decent home anywhere! When you were in Germany, you wrote us so often about how concerned you were about us. Then it seemed to us: What more do they need? They have clothes and enough to eat; they do not need any more. But now we too have experienced how hard it is to be homeless. It must be experienced before one can truly sympathize, right?

Dear Geschwister, our life now is very hard and the future is dark. For me, the sun has set forever in this life. God is leading us very deep ways – and ever deeper. The children too are discouraged. What do we have, what do we do, if my dear Jasch dies? Pray that we do not despair. I know you do! Write to W. that we received his parcel. It seems they did not get our letter. We wrote you about how the mail goes. God is our refuge and our comfort. We thank you again for the efforts you exert on our behalf.

Jasch and M. Regehr

*A letter with a location and date is rare, and we value the orientation of time and place. Sometime between July 8th and the following letter dated October 15th, the Regehr family has again been transported. From Tarabunka they have been moved to Polowinka. Perhaps this explains why, in a previous letter, Jasch was not able to "have my free will with letter writing."*

*News arrives that their dear "house friend" (Johann Toews) imprisoned in the far north has died and is now truly "free." In the larger political sphere, the Bolshevik October Revolution has been celebrated and Stalin's Five-Year Plan is approaching its end. Will this usher in a new stability?*

Polowinka, 15 Oct. 1932

Dear Geschwister Franz, Liese and children,

May God, who loves you and us, be with you from day to day. Oh dear friends, every day we count you so fortunate to have escaped from this Wespennest [*hornet's nest*]. Time carries the load, and that is the truth. We have received your card, dear brother-in-law. It was with great joy that we read that Br. Toews is now free. Oh, how our beloved brother will now rejoice!

Oh, that help may soon come to us all, for there are thousands in these death camps who are sorely afflicted and longing for release from their tribulation. We were hoping that during the October Revolution celebrations amnesty would be granted. But the Five-Year Plan is coming to an end and we remain only with our hope. You write that grain is very cheap, but here a loaf of bread costs 14 rubles – if you are lucky enough to find one. I believe that Russia will require foreign aid this year. The land is just not all tilled, and many of the bigger farms are being burned. Evidently a portion of our produce is being sold on the foreign market. We are astonished that the world is silent. The whole world suffers under this [...].

We, as German [*German-speaking Mennonite*] people, are thankful to God and man that He has cleared a way that has saved us and many others from death by starvation, first through Germany and now through Torgsin. All these are ways that God has used; but mostly that He has made hearts willing to help us in our distress. Vogt writes from Germany that they are not allowing any more parcels to be sent from Germany. Is that right? What is the reason for that?

We just received a parcel from Germany, still addressed to Nynibka, sent by a Heinrich Doerksen. I have acknowledged it. I am sending you his address and maybe you can write to him as well. We have received nothing from Kroebel or Isaac Wall, which is doubly regretful because we know them. Please let them know. Maybe they are making Cnpulsa [*a document granting permission to pick up parcels*] and we may still get them. I have written to both of them, but it does happen that letters are lost. If someone sends something through the Torgsin, we never know who is sending it. If you become aware of it there, then notify us of the address so that we can express our thanks to them. We thank you in advance, dear Geschwister. It seems to be a long, slow process.

Truda writes that on the 8th of June she sent 10 dollars through the States, but until today we have received no word. That gift would be so welcome at this time. It is a very rainy day today. It is noon and Peter just came home, wet through and through – had to change shoes and wash everything. Tina is not home yet. She has to produce her quota or she does not get an ounce of bread. Our Tina has cried so much, so much already. But what can we do? Absolutely nothing! We are also homeless!

Oh, dear Lieschen [*Jasch's twelve-year-old niece in Canada*], we thank God every day that you have been able to escape from here. You can go to school, to Sunday school, always eat bread and dress in nice clothes. Our children cannot do those things. They have to work on Sunday as well as during the other days of the week. We eat black, sour bread and not enough of that. Well, we do not want to complain – it has to be so!

We received a letter from home [*Altonau*], and things are very critical with Hans [*He is suffering from malnutrition and tuberculosis of the bone*]. He wrote himself but believes that it could be his last letter. Towards evening he gets such excruciating pains in his hip that he must scream and groan out loud until dawn brings some relief. Every 15 minutes Susie has to turn him, since he cannot do it by himself because he is too weak. But he is altogether calm in his trust in God. Oh, our dear Hans, if only God would call him home, for it is impossible for him to live. His suffering is almost impossible to describe in words. The pains are so severe, and nothing is available to help him.

The Five-Year Plan has robbed us of everything; even matches are unavailable – very sad for those who smoke. Most people are without fire, and so it is with everything. Now the [...] and communist discipline receives priority. They think the least of us need the least food, and even the least becomes too much. There is only one salvation for us – get to a foreign country. But how? They will never allow that to happen. What has developed in Germany? If possible send us information. How is it that so much of the debt is cancelled?

What are the Bargens doing? Have not received a letter from them for months. I guess they are very busy. Do you have the address of Peter Martens from Ufu? Have you any news of Jasch Janzens? We are anxiously awaiting the letter from Liese, which you mentioned in the card you sent. And how is it with your Peter? [Young Peter Bargen, translator of these letters, was kicked in the face by a colt and narrowly escaped death.] We often think of the handsome young lad and hope that he will soon be well. Today it is Sunday, and we do not have the letter finished. It is raining very hard. The children had to go to work today but are home now. Mother is making lunch; some cabbage leaves and water produces a very nice Uralische Borscht [Ural soup], but without any bread. That is our Sunday meal. Oh, if only we had enough even of that.

About the razor, I thought [...] as in the old days, but, dear brother-in law, do not go to extra expense because of it. Oh, how we would like to clean ourselves up, but it is almost impossible here. No hair clippers. I have longer hair than I have ever had in my life. Well, what more shall I write? We are as well as can be expected, and we believe that as long as you accept [us] and care, God will provide for us. The way we sing Klagelieder [songs of lament] about our situation is already a humiliation to us, but what else can we do in this foreign land (Psalm 137)? [*A reference to the verse, "By the rivers of Babylon we sat down and wept when we remembered Zion."*]

Dear Geschwister, should the sun shine upon us again even a little, we will immediately let you know. But there are no prospects except misery and more misery. We hope that you do not weary of us. May God bless you more and more.

Your humble J. and M. Regehr

*Although her husband and daughter have already written, Maria finds another scrap of paper to write about her children and her situation.*

[October 16, 1932]

Dearest Liese,

I already took a small piece of paper, because I do not know what I should write since my dear Jasch and Liese have written everything and have left nothing for me. But I still think I'll send this small sign of love in my own hand and put it into the envelope. We received the card from Franz on October 13. You, dear Liese, wrote on it that you had written us a letter on September 19th. Today it is already October 16th, and the letter still has not arrived. I will write a whole chronicle when I get the letter. I thought for sure the letter would be here today.

Today is Sunday, but what kind of a Sunday do we have? No different from yesterday. Yesterday the children came from work completely wet, and today again – trousers, stockings, foot-rags, shoes, and Lapti [footwear] are then so wet and full of mud. Tina said they were so heavy it was as if she was dragging irons on her legs. She is never happy any more, always depressed. She is in the Yoch [harnessed to labour, with a yoke like an ox] from early till late. Peter also complains, has a lot of pains in his back. I guess they will have to leave their last strength here in the Urals.

What are B.K. doing? They never write, I guess they have completely forgotten us. I guess they are working towards a huge fortune. We would so much like to hear from them. I have just written a letter to Mama and will mail these letters at the same time. If only the time would come when we too would be free, oh, how happy we would be. I always say: I do not want to go back, I only want to go to you, our loved ones. We desire no great fortune, only enough to eat and enough to clothe ourselves – that we would desire to do again.

But just as God wills. Even though we must end our life like this, we still know that this momentary affliction is not worth the glory that will be revealed to us. A better lot is awaiting us there. Papa, parents, and many loved ones are awaiting us there. It will be glorious there. That is where I want to go with my loved ones – to be where all this misery will have an end. I wish you the very best of health, and a good well-being. Would love to see you face to face. May God grant that it will happen soon.

In love we remain your loving Geschwister

What are P.B. doing? Are they still with you?

Polowinka, Oct 21, 1932

Dearly beloved Geschwister Franz and Liese and children.

May God bless you and protect your house and home, plus everything you have. We now see that it is possible to lose all one's possessions in one hour! Even if things are hard out there since the price of your grain is so low, take comfort, dear siblings, as long as you are and remain protected from the pestilence which has hit us.

Security and peace are to be cherished above all things, and if in addition to that you have food and drink, then, dear siblings, be content. We have already had to learn to be content with what we have, and because of that we want to be so in the future. If only we could have enough to eat and enough clothes to wear! But the future looks very dark! Our circumstances become more critical from day to day.

The main thing of interest here is the Keno, the Club [*theatre and pub*] – food is quite secondary. Is that logical?? Our whole Russia has been struck with blindness. Are things unsettled and restless in [...]? We are so deep in the forest here that we never get any news. Actually, we are not even allowed any news. Previously our title was "Kulak," but today you do not hear that word anymore. Today we are called [...], that is the title they yell at us.

Today is Sunday! I was lying in bed or, more correctly, on a bunk, and was thinking what beautiful church services are probably being conducted in America. And they may be praying that we can be set free! And should God not finally answer? Oh, how we look forward to that hour. The time is now 9:30, we just got back from the [...]. We got up very early in the morning. Today we were able to get potatoes – 9k. per worker, 15r. per kilo. It seems so cheap, and if we continue to get them throughout the winter it could become somewhat easier. My Marie has peeled 7 and is cooking them for noon. These are potatoes from our region. There they are stolen and here they provide such joy for us – and that is the way it goes here.

We received your letters, with several news clippings enclosed. This time we have been lucky. But if it really is as you have written and we could get out of here – that could develop into something – it is better not to set our hopes too high. But please always include the most interesting points. It interests us very much when we can read things like that. But we fear that everything will again be covered up and what is really going on in Russia will be suppressed, and thousands of innocent people will have to pay for it with their lives. The devil often comes as a roaring lion, and the next time as an angel of light. And we are precisely dealing with such devils. People are to be shipped further and further, we cannot know where. We have learned that several German [*Mennonite*] families are among them, but who it is we do not know. Oh, we do not even want to think of moving further again, but we would prefer serving our time by working here.

Peter just came from work. For his good work and good conduct he has received a little box of [...]. But it must still be paid for, how much I do not know! Tina has filled her quota by 153%. They have promised her 200 grams of sugar. And that is how they bribe the poor children. We want to keep Tina home next month, if possible. The clothes have given out. Peter and I are without any more. When it begins to freeze and stops raining, we will ask Aanma [a camp authority]. If I wear such things, then I am ashamed of myself. But what can we do? We exist to be the laughingstocks and objects of derision for the Communists!

Friesens received a letter from Boschmanns today. They write threshing is still going on there. Old Mrs. Boschman of N. 7 died. Mr. Heidebrecht is also on his deathbed – he cannot pass water. Peter Siemens of Orloff has also died. In Kherson flour costs 100 rubles a Pud. Things are especially hard for such people as our brother Hans. He is sick and cannot earn anything at the Commune. He gets nothing. That poor brother, he must suffer so very much. Mama is at Boldt's. They will probably remain in the Commune during the winter. Mama wants to stay at home. Little is heard from the Koops, they both work in the Commune. We get only a few letters from them. Maybe they are satisfied with everything.

We have written a letter to Benjamin Klassens. How was the harvest there? We have only received two letters from that dear sister. Franz Friesen is on his deathbed. He has TB and cannot even help himself anymore. Boschman is also bedridden for more than a week. Many of our loved ones we will never meet here again. If my dear Marie gets permission, she will go to Kizel tomorrow. It is rumoured they have fish for sale, and also cabbage. She has to walk 12 Werst and must also go on the [...] . Well, dear siblings, this is our life until today.

What are you doing? We still have not received your letter of Sept 19th. Please write often, especially if there is some significant news. God be with you and bless you. Our children, who consider you as our saviours until this day, send you their warmest greetings.

Your Jakob

Polowinka, Nov. 5, 1932

Dear Geschwister Franz and Liese Bargen,
First we send greetings of love. Oh, how precious it is that we can visit by letters. We can share joy and sorrow. Dear brother-in-law, we received the card in which you speak of a package. Many thanks. Liese's has not arrived yet. We received a letter from Mama yesterday. Hans [*Marie's brother-in-law*] had also written to Liese. He is terribly sick again. He had moaned and sobbed several hours at a stretch. Now that the wound on his back has opened and much pus has drained out, the pains are somewhat less. Mama has sent us Papa's picture [*a photo of Jasch's father in his coffin at the funeral on July 4, 1932*]. He looks like himself, but horribly thin. We do not begrudge him his rest.

Ab. has been home for 7 days. In [...] he is top cook. He had brought Hans some sugar, sausage and bread. He ate well those days. We are well as usual. It is completely winter. Much frost and snow – ½ [...] high. You can hardly walk. However, we all must go to work. Tina would certainly prefer to stay at home, but that is impossible. If she does, she immediately gets no bread. She wrote to Lieschen and the other children. Did you receive the letter? Have you ever heard anything of J. Janzen? We received a parcel, these [recent] days, but we do not know from whom. The Torgsin does not tell us from whom. If you can find out from whom, please let us know at once – and thank them too. God will certainly reward this, we cannot. Please write often.

Your Jakob

[...] of N. 5 walked to Kherson on the tracks. A train came and cut off both legs above the knees.

*Reminiscing about the golden days of the past brings momentary solace, but this writer feels as vulnerable as an ant. Her young daughter Tina wears only "Nanmu" or "Lapti" and sacks on her feet. This footware is made of braided straw or tree bark. Laces bind foot rags or sacks inside the Laptis, insulating the wearer from the cold. In Russia, "Nanmu" has become an offensive term to describe cheap footwear for uneducated peasants.*

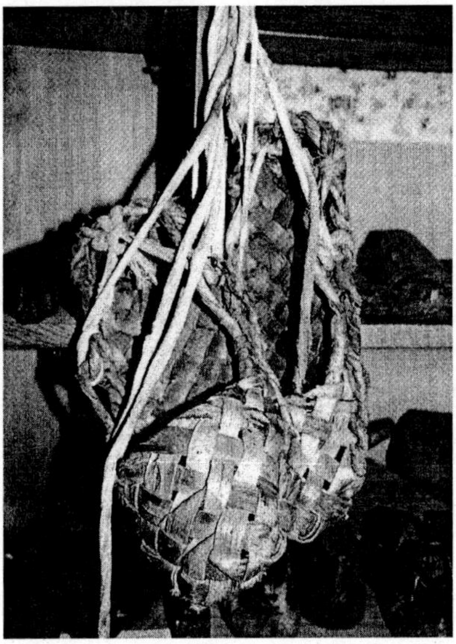

*Nanmu-wearing slave labourers, Peter and Liese have heard rumours about freedom. It is November 7, and the Bolshevik Revolution is being celebrated. The news will be announced at the "Klub." But the surge of hope has been suppressed once more. Only other rumours are confirmed: they will be moved again – even further north.*

Polowinka, 8 Nov. 1932

Dear Geschwister Franz, Liese and children,
First we wish you a greeting of love, as well as the best of health and a happy Dasein [*existence*]. Currently we can say nothing about happy hours; but we always remember the way it was once upon a time, and how it is now.

In those times we gathered together in the family circle, we were happy and enjoyed one another. Sometimes, with our loved ones, we played tricks on one another – but you will remember these things as well. Father, mother, all siblings were together. Yes, those were good and happy days!

Yes, where did those days go? As a puff of smoke they have vanished, everything, everything gone, all are no longer there. You are in America, Papa has died, Mama driven and pursued like a deer, Hans is sick unto death, we are in the far north in exile where there is only woe and misery, starvation stands at the door, and we are almost without clothes and footwear. Such are now our days! We have no joy.

No, these are days of which we can say with justification that we have no pleasure in them. We have been robbed of our children and they must work like slaves. Our Tina [*now 13 years old*] is a fragile child but every day she must go to work very early – 5 o'clock. The ground is frozen hard, and even a strong man can hardly dig through it. A chisel has to be used to break it up, but Tina has to fulfill her quota every day.

Oh, dear Geschwister, one could weep and wail. Imagine yourselves in such a situation. What if your Liese had to dig in this frost every day and pile up one cubic metre of earth, and then only on Nanmu and her feet wrapped only in sacks. For a dress she has a coat that Marie bought from a Russian and then made into a dress for her. The child has already cried so many tears! They eat their lunch in the forest, in all that frost, snow, and rain. We cannot understand why the children must suffer so. Their happy young years they must spend in this primeval forest.

Yesterday evening Liese and Peter wanted to go to the Klub because a Kiesten [*a document declaring freedom for prisoners*] had arrived from Petrograd. They thought that maybe something else had also been brought because it was the 7th of November, the day of the Revolution when many of our people hoped to get their freedom. But they did not allow them to enter – and so it goes everywhere.

Well, we also believed that we would receive encouraging news this day and our lot would be eased.

But no! Nothing! Only that the people will be moved several Werst farther away. There were many Communists who had also been exiled – but they have all been moved and no one knows where to, except deeper into the north, so they say. And we small Ameisen [*ants*] are also so very afraid of this. Our dear dead Papa always said, "The ways of the Lord are right," and if that is so, then we too can trust Him. Yes, we experience again and again that Psalm 23 is confirmed, "You prepare a table for me in the presence of my enemies."

Yesterday we received two nice parcels through the Torgsin. We received 3 kilo rice, 3 kilo butter, 1 kilo porridge, 500 grams soap, 1 kilo pork fat, and 1 box of milk. However, we do not know who sent the parcels to us because the Torgsin does not give us that information. We regret very much that we are not told, so that we could express our deep thanks to them. Perhaps through the Wahrheits Freund [*a German newspaper*] you know who the sender is. If so, please thank them for us and send us their name and address so that we can also thank them. Please spread the word through the newspapers that we cannot ascertain through the Torgsin who the senders are. And thank them again and again in our name, and tell them to let us know, even if through you, who they are. Please, dear brother-in-law, do this immediately – present our plight to them, maybe the Weihnachtsman [*"Christmas man" or Santa Claus*] will bring us something. But as God wills.

How did things turn out with your house friend? Is he free or has he died? We have not had a letter from home in a long time. In the last letter Ab. Regehr wrote that Mama went to Kherson to buy things at the Torgsin. Oh, our poor mother! Ab. Regehrs will probably move into Hans Regehr's Grossestube [*Great Room*]. Jakob Bargen has also been taken to Kronau, so Mrs. Friesen said today. Oh, when will things change? Well, God be with you. Write much and often and pray for all of us that God would help and free us.

Jakob and Marie

[Late 1932]

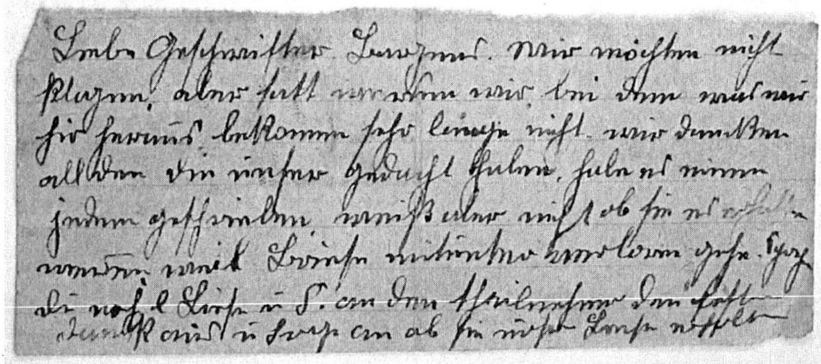

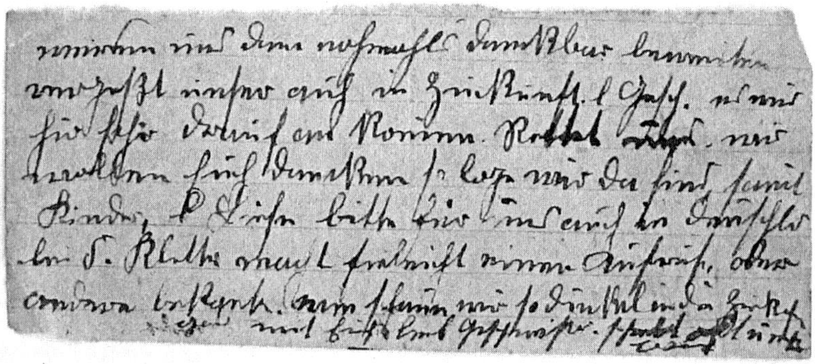

Dear Geschwister Bargens,
We do not want to complain, but our hunger is never fully satisfied with what we get to eat! Not at all. We thank all those who have thought of us and we have written to each one too. But I do not know whether they receive our letters. Some letters just go lost. Dear Liese and Franz, do they still talk there of participating in our tribulation? Check if they have received our address. Do not forget us in the future either, dear Geschwister, because our survival will depend on it. Save us! We and our children will be so thankful. Dear Liese – beg for us, even in Germany, and F. Klassen can perhaps make an appeal for us. Other acquaintances may help. How dark the future looks to us! God be with you, dear Geschwister. Write often.

29/XI/32

Dearly beloved Franz and Liese Bargen and children,
It is almost evening, the time is 7:30, my dear Marie with the children is standing by the oven because it is so cold. And one asks the other, what will we eat for supper tonight? Then it is hard to contain oneself, because we know exactly who has brought us to this state.

It looks to us like things will remain like they are, but we look with great longing to better times. The way things are going now cannot possibly continue in the long run – it will be too hard for us and also for you, dear siblings.

We are driven into deep anguish, and at times it seems as if the waves of affliction will collapse over our heads. And in such hours one despairs and doubts that God answers. It is wrong! But our own weakness and sin cling to us and impel us to ask, Why? Why? Should we have to spend the winter here, then the mantle of despair enfolds us and we no longer know in or out. It is almost disgraceful, dear siblings, to always and always cry to you in our affliction. But dear loved ones, to whom can we turn but to you? Who until now has helped us carry our burden? We know it and believe it that it has been hard for you because of us. I can believe you have had many sleepless nights because of us. But forgive me. When I see how helplessly my family stands there, how poor, how ragged, how skimpily clothed, how little bread, oh, then we weep and ask: Where to [*turn*]? Then we only know we must reach you! You have always helped us with advice and with deeds. We can thank you that many things have been sent to us. May God reward you according to His promises. Thank all those who have given towards our welfare, but you have touched those hearts on our behalf.

We just received your letter #5. Oh, how sad that your dear Peter had to have such a terrible experience. [*Young Peter Bargen in Canada has been kicked in the face by a colt, smashing his nose and cheekbones.*] He was such a lovely boy. Do you still remember how we both would wrestle at Grandma's? Now you, good Peter, would be able to throw me. Now your Uncle Jasch is very weak. I only eat bread and Pripps and not enough of that. But if we should come to your place, then we all want to be able to eat our fill. What do you think, little Peter, will that be possible? Do you still remember how much your Uncle Jasch used to eat when he came visiting to your place? Well, you good boy, may God grant you complete healing.

And you, dear busy little Lieschen, it is sad that you have to be sick and cannot help your dear Mama right now. We pray to God to grant you health again. And you, little Meka, what are you doing? You probably help your Mama make the meals. Now you, good boy Fritz, you are probably quite big already and are helping your Papa do the plowing and threshing. Always be very thankful to God that he brought you to America. You can be together at home and always eat until you are satisfied. Our children cannot do that every day. Miechi is standing beside her Mama saying, "Mama, I am hungry, for the noon meal I only received a very small piece of bread." And her Mama cannot give her anything. Many children have starved to death here. Such children as you are. Please pray to our Saviour that he will soon bring us home.

You, dear brother-in-law, write that there is unrest in the world. Write us how things are in Germany, maybe help will come from there – like J. Klassen mentioned to H. Friesen. We hope we can get help before the winter. We are very sorry that you do not get all our letters. We write often and we write lots. Today 8 of Marie Unger's boys came here – it is believed for the purpose of sending people even further. Oh, how afraid we are! If we are not being sent home, we would prefer to remain here. But as God wills it. We can only remain quiet and hold still. Today we received papers from Truda in [...] for 10 [...]. That is how God looks after us. We never received that parcel sent from [...]. We regret that very much. Please report it, perhaps it will make [...].

Dear siblings, we are delighted that God gave you a good harvest. Maybe you will send something of it across the ocean. We have had no news from home for a long while. We are not upset because of that dollar. If only Mama could enjoy her old age with Abram. We actually do not know where they are now. They are so afraid even to send their address to us. I do not think it would matter. We are happy that Abram is doing a bit better. We probably won't see our brother Hans again in this life. Today we have a new Kommandant, a very stern Boesewicht [*evil doer*]. He already ordered me to appear before him today. He asked me why I did not go to work. Until now no one had asked me. I suppose it will work out finally. God be with you.

Your humble J. and M. Regehr

*Although the family is still in Polowinka, this letter is posted in Tarabunka, the location of their former prison camp. The two prison camps must be fairly close, since Maria walks to Tarabunka for supplies up to four times a week. Freedom is always on their minds, and news from the home village raises both hope and terror. Apparently some have attempted to escape to the Middle East, but have failed.*

Tarabunka, 8/XII/1932

Dear beloved Franz and Liese and children,
May the almighty God protect you, and continue His work through you and in you. It is true, dear Geschwister, if we did not have our faith in God we would often have despaired. There are days and hours which I cannot describe today. Our thoughts dwell on the approaching season when so many people will be so happy and praise God that He came to bring peace. However, many thousands will celebrate no Christmas, and we are among them.

Then one remembers the days when we would all get together to celebrate the joys of the festive season – father, mother, and all siblings together. Those were blessed hours. Today father is dead, mama is being put to flight, we are here in exile where there is misery piled upon misery. Rivers of tears have flowed here. It is especially difficult for the poor children to go through such hard times. There are no joyful times for them. Then our hearts bleed. If only you could look into our home for 5 minutes at Christmas time. On the one hand, the joy would be great – throwing our arms about each other and feeling loved again! On the other hand, the grief would be so stark and raw!

A few days ago we had to use a whetstone again [*The intended meaning is unclear; a whetstone is used to sharpen a blade*]. Jakob is in [...] and will probably not come back again. He was hungry too long. Mrs. Joh. Regehr also died. We received a letter from Hein Goosen yesterday. He does not write anything good either. Meat is being confiscated there again. Every [...] is ordered to deliver 20 kilo meat per farm. People are giving up their last chickens, and still it is not enough. Consequently, they are judged as lawbreakers and turned over to the courts and everyone is promoted to the status of a labourer. Many had prepared themselves to move to the Middle East. When they were about ready, the authorities came in automobiles and arrested many of them and did not allow them to go. And this is a land of free citizens? How long can it continue? America probably won't help.

Three months have passed and things stay the same. This evil power is so powerful and harsh it destroys everything that does not obey its commands. If one observes the running and the striving and all the work, then one must say they are bankrupt. There are about 10 trucks working here. They drive day and night. They haul sand, cement, slag etc., etc. Last night no one was driving. There was a real crisis – no benzene [*fuel*]. The machines are standing. They had no reserves!

They are hard at work on the railway lines. The poor children have to work there day and night. Peter has a severe headache today. He really wanted to stay home today but immediately the Komsomol came and confiscated his bread ration card and [will] let him starve for days – a torment I just cannot describe. In Nero's days people were burned, or thrown to the lions – things were terrible. But at least a person would die in several minutes. Today it is taking years. and we perish slowly! There has never been such affliction as there is today – and the whole world is silent!

We just got the news from Modomzagia. All autos and horses are ordered to Kizel for 3 days. Could there be anything behind this? I am afraid it is only a trial mobilization. One becomes afraid to put one's thoughts on paper. If only we could be set free soon, that is our daily prayer to God. Outside there is a snowstorm. The children are all at work. Peter has especially hard work. From early morning until 6 at night he is engaged in backbreaking labour. For the third day he has a severe headache – but there is no mercy. As long as you can stand, you must work.

My dear little wife walks to Tarabunka to see if she can buy anything there. She walks there up to 4 times a week. Things are very hard for her too. She has become very thin and old. However, she is still courageous; she carefully portions our food for us, otherwise we would all have perished long ago. Our little Jasch often watches her with tears. Then her heart bleeds but she must be firm.

Dear Geschwister, you write that you are sending us a parcel via [...], Moscow. A thousand times thank you. There just are not enough words to thank you. We will immediately report when we have it in hand. At times it takes very long until we get it. Truda [*Marie's sister*] also sent us something in the month of June through [...] and it still has not arrived. We have received packages without return addresses; we thanked you for them and asked you to notify the people responsible. But that is not necessary, since Truda Goosen had sent both of them. She does so much for her siblings. God will reward her. To date nothing has arrived from Crebel and Isaac. We regret that a lot. Let them know. Have not had a letter from P.B. We do not know if they are angry with us. We love them. Give them warm greetings. Did they receive our letter? May God grant them and you a very blessed Christmas season and a happy New Year. Pray for us; we will think of you in these days.

Goodbye, your [...]

[1932/33]

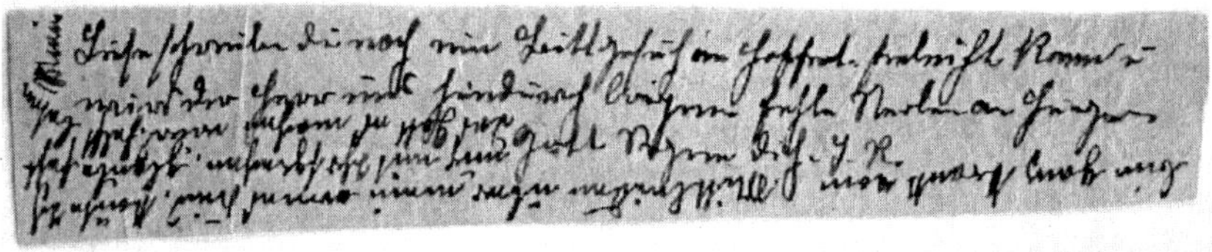

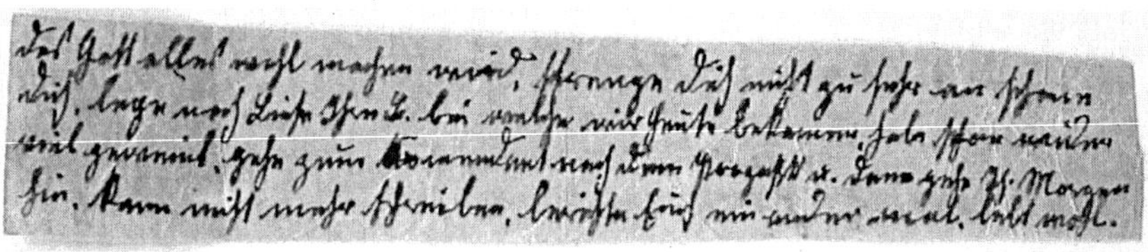

Dear Liese,

Please write a petition to Hoffert making a plea for help, maybe God can and will bring us through. Many die of starvation. God bless you, J.R.

I am actually ill with concern for my poor child [*Liese, who remains in prison*]. If only I could talk to her. I firmly believe God will make it possible. Help us to pray that God will make all things well. Do not work too hard, look after yourself. I am enclosing Liese's letter which we received today. I have again cried a great deal. I am going to the Kommandant and then I want to go to see her tomorrow. I just cannot write any more. I will report more the next time.

God be with you, Marie

## Jakob Who Hungers, Forgive Me

*Apologies for suffering and remorse for lamenting are difficult to understand. Yet Jasch is ashamed. His faith sustains him, but despair threatens to overwhelm him. He is sick, and he works only occasionally as a night watchman. He spends many hours alone in the bleak barrack space, with too much time to think. He thinks about Germany and this country's role in their freedom. Knowledge of Germany's anti-Semitic policies has not reached these prisoners. They have friends and family members in Germany who have sent parcels. Germany also provided a safe passage for Mennonites traveling to Canada in the 1920s. Hope for another wave of liberation lingers.*

Tarabunka, January 10, 1933

Dear siblings Frank and Liese and children,
If it would be possible to write all our days into a book under one title, it would certainly be called "Lamentations." There would be days that can never be forgotten and which must go to the grave with me, so to speak. The future is so very dark, only hunger and starvation, and again hunger.

Again we are left without bread. This for the 3rd day now. Still God can change it – it is all possible for the Almighty. He can feed us and care for us even here, and has done so until now. The only thing we often lack is the faith, and deep confidence and trust. The volunteers all try to escape from here – can't see anything good in the future. Still, we do not want to despair.

A few days ago my dear little wife said to the children, "With our God we can leap over high walls" [*a reference to Psalm 18:29*] and we should let Him carry our mantle of worry! Then we can be quite confident! And it is true, dear siblings: if God wants to sustain us even in these agonizing surroundings, He will do it! And you, dear siblings, and others who are our friends, God will reveal it to you: He saves only through people, and their prayers! This has happened so often. To you only do we unload our hearts and our sorrows. Yes, with what can we ever repay you for all your loving kindness to us? Truly, we cannot – but the Almighty can! When I think how wonderfully God brought you over to there, then you must exclaim, "The Lord alone did it!" Maybe he even brought you there to help us!

We just received a letter from Hans Regehr. He also writes that they are living only on [...], and through whom do they acquire it? Oh, my poor brother Hans, he is again supposed to pay a fine: 15 pud potatoes, 3 pud meat. He bought 3 pud potatoes for 105 rubles. He also believes that the authorities will confiscate and sell everything they own. Illness is no excuse for defaulting. Mama was at their place lately, but one night she had to flee for her life. They have persecuted her very severely and she has been very ill; she must be very skinny. Oh, our poor mother, she is being intensely pursued like a deer.

With Hans it is somewhat better, he hopes to get well again. What kind of business does your house guest have? And where is he? Is he hoping to get free and go to his family? How may things be going for him? How are things for those who went to Brazil and Paraguay at the same time as you left? We never get any news from those regions. The best bet will be America, don't you think? Oh, if only we could get where you are. We had hoped that our brothers would free us – as a nation. One seems to hear very little of this possibility today. How do things stand in Germany? Please write to little grandfather [*code for a political leader*] and tell him to help us.

Here things are going as usual. Today our Tina stood all day, from morning till late in the evening, in a queue for bread – and she was fortunate and got some! She got 2 loaves, so we now have bread for several days. But it is almost unbearable: the workers come home from work and there is no bread! Peter still works on the railroad lines. It is very hard work. He is outside the entire day. There have been 47 degrees of frost here, but they still must go to work. Now the weather is very nice. God has had mercy again.

Liese lost her good job and was replaced by members of the Komsomol who can take any job they wish. She got a different job, but one day the top machinist came to her and put her back into her old job. We see God's hand in this. She understands the machinery better than someone who has just finished the courses. She is very gifted. Mariechen has to stand watch for thieves today. Things are very uncertain with her. I continue to serve as watchman. Marie is always busy patching clothes. The clothes are so old and the footwear is worn out. We walk on wooden-soled sandals and look so gross that one is almost afraid of oneself. That is the way it looks when my dear Marie puts them on. Then my blood boils in my veins – but we want to be satisfied and believe that things will yet change and we can once more dress as human beings.

We have had no news of the package you sent. Joh. Goosen sent us one from August 7th. We have now received that. When yours arrives, we will let you know right away. Look up all your friends – and all please help. Please, please forgive our insistence, but we would rather not starve. May God bless you all.

Your humble Jakob who hungers, forgive me.

*It is almost unbearable for us to continue reading these letters. Day after day, the lament continues. How can we absorb so much anguish? When Jasch writes "Bread! Bread! Bread! ... Save us, save us!" how can we respond? Do we become numb, or stop reading? Is it too much?*

Polowinka, 3 March 1933

Dear Loved and Best Ones away in that great distance,
May God be with you in all your ways. It has cost us thousands of tears, and with a broken heart we report to you that we just read Mariechen's letter about the death of our dear brother Hans. Oh, we had such a great longing to see him again in this life! But God's [plans] were otherwise. Jakob Friesen also died. Mrs. Boschman writes that she found Jakob Dueck, minister in N. 5, dead near the shepherd's cottage on Feb. 22. In his last days he smoked and drank out of complete despair.

Yes, because of the lack of even poor food the people become so weak that it is beyond description. Pale, stooped over, lacking will-power, sick – but most have to work in spite of all that. Oh, my heart wants to burst when I see how people are being tormented. We are being robbed of our children when they are in their tender years. They have been made into slaves by these hordes. Our Peter must often work day and night. For weeks on end he does not get a day off. He is quite sick – and so thin. That poor Peter has to endure so very much. What has happened in this Red Paradise? It is a slave trade! It is slavery as it has never been before! The entire world keeps silent. Hundreds of thousands die of hunger! Oh, dear siblings, that we still survive is only thanks to you. If we had received no help, none of us would be here. That article you sent us about the rescue of the Germans has given us much hope. May it happen soon! We will sign anything, if only we are rescued at the same time. If we are not rescued, thousands of our people will perish.

Oh, dear Geschwister, what should we write to you? If you could only look into our house, we would not have to write anything – everything is missing. Bread! Bread! Bread! The future is getting ever more dismal. Today one loaf of bread at the bazaar costs 50 rubles. How can this continue? Besides, no bread is available. For 5 months the worker has not received any money. Could you send out a call for help? We are at an end and are looking for help as never before. Save us, save us! Do what you can. Maybe we can stay alive and even come to your place in time. We would work for you. May God make many hearts willing to send us bread across the water, and after many years they may find it again – according to God's word.

Dear siblings, our hearts bleed that we must always come to you as beggars. How much rather would we like to write other kinds of letters to you – and cheer you up! But our good days are gone – we have become a spoil of war, a victory wreath for the barbarians! We are nervous wrecks and old before our time. That package for 8 dollars from you has not yet arrived. Oh, how sad that makes us. Inquire where it has been lost? We did receive a package for 5 dollars. We already wrote you about that and described what was in it. Thank you very much for it. It cannot be long before we will be helped, for I am sure that everyone is working on behalf of our people.

Well, it would just be too tragic if we should perish as a people. Thousands have proven and presented themselves, on all fronts, as German [*Mennonite*] people. We are proud that we have overcome until this day! May God also grant us such strength for the future.

Often, when we have to struggle for survival without bread, our courage falters. Dear Geschwister, help us carry our burden so that we, with God's help, may represent the German [*Mennonite*] people as a people of honour. Help us pray, and help us carry the burden. I believe that our end will soon be here. Save us – only a few of us remain.

The article is correct: thousands of children of those sent into exile with us have died. And what happens here daily? If there is carrion anywhere, the starving people rush upon it and pick it clean. Goodbye, may God be with you. Rescue, dear siblings. My dear Marie will write too.

Your Jakob

*A new route of mail delivery through Finland appears to be functioning. Bread is still desperately needed, but suddenly men's trousers and suits are plentiful. Craving for food and freedom continues, and like worms, the prisoners "squirm to escape." Yet, astoundingly, "the world keeps silent!"*

[1933]

Will it happen as it says in Isaiah: Help may come, but too late? Whole regions and villages will die of hunger. Both the Dueckmanns, N. 8, Jakob and Mariechi, starved to death in jail in Kherson. Now the Government wants to free all who were sentenced to 3 years so that they are not responsible when all these people starve to death in the jails! And those in jails are mostly the farmers. And this is in Kherson, a small town – the national picture may be much worse. The world keeps silent! Should we, as people, really perish in these flames of hell? I sent you a petition for [*German President*] Hindenburg. Did you receive it? Send it off immediately. I signed my name on it because you asked for it. This night I dreamt he had sent us a nice package. When a package is sent, write us back immediately. Will he help us? Will he be able to come to deliver us and others?

We received your 5-dollar package sent via Finland. A thousand times thank you for the same. Did you receive the letter where we described the parcel? The 8-dollar package you mentioned has not arrived until this day – not [...] from there, it is just too bad, right? Lately many manufactured things have come here. Men's trousers, whole suits, we do not know where these are coming from. Do you know? Did Russia make a pact with another country? Please write. Now we could buy trousers if we had the money – and not even so expensive: 8 rubles 74k. a pair; one whole suit 25 rubles [...].Can they not provide bread as easily as they supply manufactured goods? Then we would all be helped.

Just now Tina came home after standing in line for bread. At 2 o'clock at night, in all sorts of weather, people stand in line-ups. Then around 11 o'clock in the morning they start to hand out the bread! Tina got some bread, but not today. She is very depressed – has to starve again today. Dear, dear siblings, have mercy! Send us something to eat. Oh, the poor children, they just cannot understand why they must suffer. Recently I fell very ill. I can hardly bear to see my dear Marie – she is just skin and bones. Dear sister Liese, you have accomplished many things in this life, try to keep us alive over here. Write more often to Jak. Janzen, maybe he will also get a warm heart – and the Regehrs boys, yes, yes –- at your place there are many good people!

Yes, we have experienced much, but we do not want to die of starvation – and then not in exile! We have not had a letter from home for a long time. The last one told us that Hans was dead. We do not know if they are still alive, or did they get typhus? Oh, that poor Susie. Where Mama is we just do not know. How is it, dear Geschwister, that you write so few letters? From 2 couples we have received no letters, only 2 cards. Are you tired of us poor beggars, dear siblings? Well, we want to believe – but every worm squirms to escape, how much more a human who has been created for life! We do not know whom we can go to with our sad lot, except to you. Please, know I mean this in a good way. The time may still come when we and our children could repay our debt to you. I do not know if my dear Marie will write too. Actually, she does not feel like writing letters today. Please take everything in love. It costs me a great deal to send a begging letter that lets you look into our hearts.

Your only Jakob

Polowinka, March 17, 1933

Dear Geschwister Liese and Franz,
I am hardly able to write. My feet are so swollen I can hardly walk on them. The doctor insists it is an infection from bad food and malnutrition. I really do not wish to get well – but God can determine that! My dear Marie, Liese, and Tina went to Kizel today. They wanted to get flour and barley at the store. Oh, how hard it is! The time is 3 P.M. and they left at 6 a.m! If the Kommandant meets them some place, he would definitely take everything away from them and most likely send them to the Schlansnoge [isolation cell]. I am really frantic and can hardly wait until they get back. But maybe the Lord Zebaoth is with them and will guide them unobserved through the enemy camp.

Dear Geschwister, will there be a Gideon for us? Oh, what if we do not receive word from our dear children? Here people are being sought and taken. When the worker comes from work, dead tired, he is still forced to take a spade and dig in the plot – and the Russians then scatter seed into the plot. Friends, you have no idea how cruel the guards are! The Kommandant just came in and wanted to confiscate our ration cards because we cannot go to work. Searches occur every day. I think they want to bury us alive. Dear friends, are there people like that where you live? He demands [...].
Polowinka, 25 March, 1933

Dear Geschwister Franz, Liese, and children,
I will try to write a few lines of love to you. My heart is broken today. It could be, dear Geschwister, that soon I will write my last

кулака, скупщика, лишенца, вредителя
ВОН из промкооперативной артели!
ПОЧТОВАЯ
ПОШТОВА
ПАШТОВАЯ
CARTE P
Куда
Кому
Canada.
Carlyle Sask.

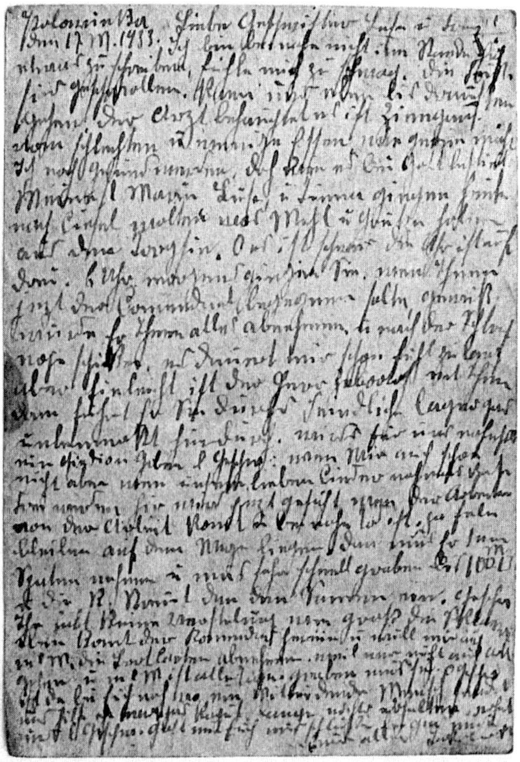

letter. In two days I have become so run down that it cannot be described.

I went to work as watchman. When I went home, my feet began to run back and forth and jerk as if I was a drunk. I ran into walls with my head. Somehow I could not control my feet. I went to the doctor and told him of my problem. They laughed about it and did nothing further. In the evening I again had to go to work – and in the dark. I was very concerned as to how I would go about it, for at night if I should fall down, I could miserably perish there. I went to work at 6 o'clock. Around 9 o'clock my dear wife came and looked me up. She was also very concerned. When she found me we had to walk 1 ½ km. We went into a hut that was heated. There we sat down and stayed for several hours, and then she went home – I had to stay until 1 o'clock at night. I walked with her a little bit of the way and then I walked back, and she walked home alone.

When I had finished my shift I went home. When I was half way home I began to stumble – but I could cope. I sat down on the path. When I was close to home, my feet ran off the path into the deep snow. But I summoned all my strength and finally got home. We have wept a lot. Today I must go to work again and I am afraid. A terrible blizzard is howling outside. How will I manage? God knows how heavy my cross is getting. Help me carry it, dear siblings all. God will reward you, as He has said in His Word. It is almost evening – the children are coming back from work. Mother is cooking soup, please come to us for supper.

On the 26th. Good morning, dear sister, I just now got back from my watchman's work and I have been busily eating my 200 gr. of bread which I dipped into mustard. Now I am finished. You remember, dear sister, that I was not a great gourmet. For lunch my dear Marie will get some provision from a package and cook us a rice soup. Oh, dear Geschwister, if we did not have those provisions, we would have perished. However, God has found ways and means to keep us alive.

I do not know how [*Russia*] will ever answer for all this unrighteousness. Hundreds, or rather thousands, have already died – and how many more will starve to death remains to be seen. The clipping that you sent to me is very interesting. If only it would happen that we as a people would be saved. Our [...] has not yet ceased the murdering and the sentencing. And it will never change unless a different [Russia] will rise up – and there is not even a hint of that. Are those with long pigtails and the yellow ones still fighting? Can this fire spread?

We received your letter of March 1st. You have been silent for so long. Since Jan 2 we have had no other letter except 2 cards and one letter from Tina – and a package from Lieschen. We received the 5-dollar package. I wrote you the list. That 8-dollar package is missing until today. We regret that very much. Well, make one enquiry after another, maybe it will be found. If not, then [...].

We have received nothing from Crebel. Where could it have stayed? Please enquire, dear brother-in-law. I also have written to him, but will he get the letter? It was a 10-dollar package. Well, we trust it will all work out in the future as well; and God will have ways and means to sustain us, if that is His will. Only be confident and do not be discouraged!

We have no word from home since Hans died. We do not know if they are still alive. I suppose they are also quite discouraged. We hear that they are out of bread there also. It would be a good thing if America would erect some good kitchens [in the famine of the 1920s, a Mennonite relief organization from the US set up soup kitchens in present-day Ukraine], otherwise it will not work in the long run. Many do not get any support and for them it is particularly difficult. In 1 ½ months it will be different there – then there will be Lodik [*an officially sanctioned document that gives prisoners a release from work*].

Oh God, make a way clear so our people can still be saved! I believe days will come over us as it was in Muensterburg [*a reference to the Mennonite village destroyed by the Makhno raids in November 1919*]. If these hungry people should arouse themselves, they would be reduced to devils. Liese and Peter are sleeping, they had to work all night. Peter had to put the [...] back on the tracks. It ran off the tracks. Liese must clean up the wood and debris from the mineshafts. She has to work very hard. It is work that a husky young Russian man should do. She has already experienced so much in her young life. Michi has to roof the barracks and work on the roof even in 20-30 degrees frost. Tina again stands in the lines for bread. At night I take a job as watchman. I got it in 31[...]. Lena and Jascha play.

Dear siblings, my page is full again. I have written of many things. May our God escort the letter and see it safely to your house. Please write more to us poor slaves. You have no idea how things are for us here – and how happy we are when we get letters from you.

Your humble Jakob

[1933]

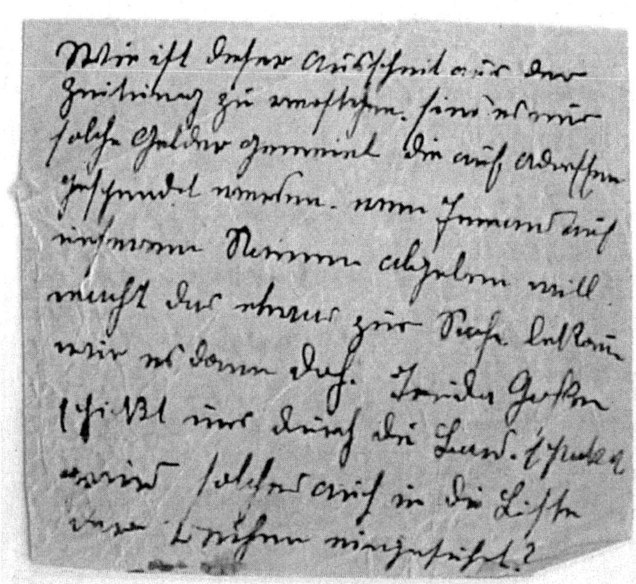

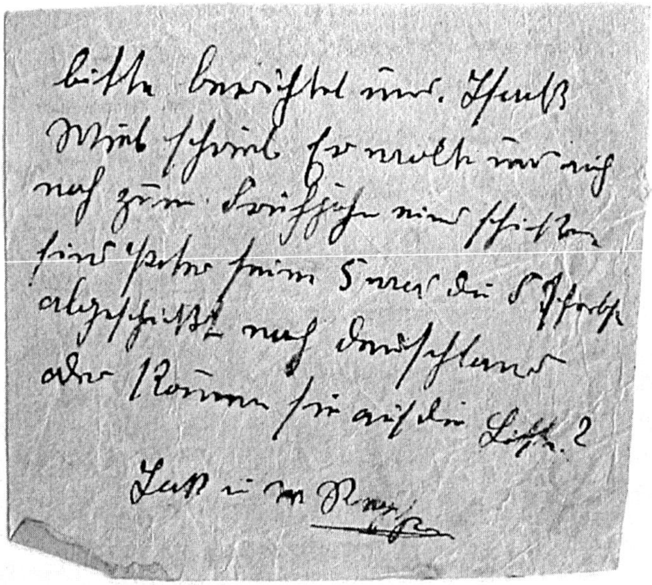

How is this clipping from the newspapers to be understood? Do they mean only such money as is sent to a specific address? If someone wishes to send something in our name, does that change things? Do we still receive it? Truda Goosen always sends a package through the bank. Is this then also entered into the list of the wealthy? Please report to us on this. Isaac Wiebe wrote that he also wanted to send something for spring. Are the 5 that you wrote were coming from Peter, sent off to Germany? Or do they get onto the list?

Jakob and M. Regehr

Dear Brother-in-Law!

If it is possible, try to send us, through Lieutenant Vogt, the address of Lieutenant Hoellig – you know, the one who was stationed at our home in those days [*a reference to the time during the Russian Civil War (1917-18) when German troops occupied parts of southern Russia*]. He said at the time that if we should ever get into difficulties we should write to him. We have lost his address and we do not know how to reach him. You, dear brother-in-law, are so busy working on our behalf. But do not grow weary – our need is great!

Jakob

[1933]

Dear Liese,

You ask if we received the letter with the receipt. Yes, I will send the receipt back to you because it is not to us but to J.B., and you may need it. We received the letter with writing paper and pictures. We wrote to you of it – also the letter with Is. Wiebe's letter enclosed.

The letters seem to be moving better in the last little while. Please write often. We have not yet received the products for the 5 dollars from Perm. It just takes too long. We have ordered 44 kilos of millet meal. That is how much it gives when they send it Tsoramom [*cash on delivery*], and then we can pay the delivery costs with our money. Therefore, send only the dollars here. I will enclose a card too. We receive one like this with every package or money order – then the name of the sender is on the notice. Sometimes the name is not on the notice, and we do not know who it is from.

What are your children doing? We are so happy, dear Liese, that you are so well. When is the good time coming for us when we will be able to bake and cook as we like? The children say, "If we ever get home, then we will cook a soup, only a thick hearty one." They are so sick of soup. If we ever come to your place, then you, dear Liese, shall treat us to Parishki [*a fruit-filled pastry*].

Polowinka, 18 March 1933

Dear Geschwister Franz and Liese and children,
May the almighty God protect you in all your ways. You, dear Geschwister, do not know what freedom is; we know what it is – we are so bound!

We cannot take one step without permission from the Kommandant, and even then we are relentlessly bathed in the glare of searchlights. At times it is almost unbearable. It gets worse day by day. Our portions of bread get smaller and we get it less often. Again we have been without bread for several days. Now the government is taking many off work, and those laid off get no bread – absolutely nothing. And such people, mostly the elderly, get no work. I am also one of them. I have already racked my brain to as to what one can do. It is unbearable. If only the news in the article could become reality; [*otherwise*] our people will not be rescued. If only the people of the world would have an inkling of what it means to be a slave and not have any bread, they would have devised more concrete plans and made greater efforts designed to free us.

Today is a terribly cold day. It has already been this way for a whole week – stormy weather like I have never seen before. A metre of fresh snow has fallen in these days. We all have to go to the forest to chop our own wood for fuel, and we must carry it back to our quarters. Think of it This chore is done mostly by my dear Marie and Tina.

Liese is also relieved of her old job. New volunteers, Tatars, have arrived. Now she has a very hard job, she has to work in the mineshafts, carrying sacks of coking coal and iron ore and things of that sort. It is the kind of work that could be done by a big burly Russian; that is, if he would get good food. One day her feet were so badly frostbitten that she could scarcely walk. But in spite of that she must report to work everyday – after all, she is an enemy of the State! What that poor child has already gone through is indescribable. They have sicced their dogs on her. For four months she only received 200 grams of bread. For 2 months in Nrofnog she had typhus. She was in the hospital for 1 ½ months. If she could only tell you herself. This child has had heart-rending experiences that should not happen to any human being.

The children go to work every day. Today I observed them when they started out. I wept! They staggered through snow up to their bellies – and so they must walk 5 km and then work a 10-hour shift without a break. Our greatest need is footwear. We need at least 2 pair of boots, 42n, and there is no money to buy them. And boots are not available even if we had the money. Besides, when they are available the boots cost over 100 rubles. At times one is almost driven to despair, dear Geschwister. How will it all end?

It is especially hard today. Today, together with all of you, we are in spirit at our dear dead Papa's birthday. We imagine we are before a table laden with food and are happy together. But what is reality? No bread! We do not know what we will eat today. The bit of Gruetze [*porridge*] we still have must be rationed. Dear Liese, I must tell you how such soup is cooked. Some people take 1 cup of water and 2 spoons millet meal, they cook it, salt it, and eat it. We dunk our bread in salt too – and drink Pripps. It almost tastes a bit better than with sugar. Most of the people are very pale and weak. We hear terrible things are happening at home. But at least those people are free! They have beds, pumpkins, cabbage, and even some potatoes – and some even have a cow. That is quite different. Yet it is deplorable how they are being treated.

It must be wretched in the prison in Kherson. The people are incarcerated and no longer have a free will or a free choice. Mrs. Regehr of N. 6 now lives in Kherson so as to be near her son who is [...]. She wrote a letter to H. Friesen that those in the Red Cross report that in June and July 870 persons died of starvation. Now up to 40 persons a day die of starvation. Every night up to 35 corpses are lying in the streets. They are loaded onto an auto, taken to a cemetery, unloaded with big hooks, piled onto a big heap and burned. No one wants to dig graves.

*Maria has no one to turn to but her readers in Canada, and her God who knows all her sorrows. Yet she does not write about "half the horrors" she has experienced. Her husband is very weak and now completely dependent on her. Maria now writes most of the letters. She must remain strong and go to work. Unfortunately, their Kommandant is merciless. Some are more humane than others, but this overseer has no compassion. As weak as he is, Jasch must walk almost one mile to the headquarters. Maria struggles to help him.*

*Prisoners are also forced into a Cydomnnkr, a "washing chamber" with a disinfectant bath that rids them of lice, bed bugs, and parasites. Crowding, swearing, fumigating, and stealing make these baths difficult to endure. Jasch is too weak. He resists.*

[Spring 1933]

Dear Geschwister Franz and Liese and children,
First let me wish you the best of health. May our dear God protect and sustain you in that land of freedom until we meet again, if not here then in glory. There will never be pain there, nor sorrow, nor hunger. And the way things look now, it will not be too long before we are there. Today is a very dark day. It is snowing as if in mid-winter, and it is a cold day. It is just as dark in our hearts. If you would see what is going on here, and how people are tortured and forcibly driven to work, you would weep with compassion. Oh, dear Liese, if I could just weep myself dry at your breast and tell you of my deep sorrow, then I too would feel a great stone roll from my heart. Things are so hard for me that I fear I will break down. Oh, how fortunate I count myself that I have a wonderful Saviour, who knows all my sorrow and to whom I can tell everything. He comforts us in all our distress so that we do not have to lose hope even in the darkest hours of our life.

Dear Geschwister, that is the way it is today – and it was so, especially yesterday. I will tell you if you wish. I am very tired and worried today. I just came from work. For lunch I had millet meal soup, and now I want to write a few lines of love to you. The people are literally being herded to the Cydomnnkr [*washing chamber*] by force. They have a very bad overseer as well as a member of the Komsomol as the Kommandant, and [...] they forcibly drive the people out of their houses. They told my dear Jasch that he should go too, but he always told them he could not. Then the Kommandant asked if he had a certificate from the doctor.

Liese, what do you think? The doctors do not give a certificate even if a person is near death. But they give one if there is a cut on the hand or the foot, even though the cut may not be as serious as other sicknesses. So yesterday morning those thugs were back again and forcibly chased everyone out. In the evening our overseer came and asked if Jasch had also been at work. He said no. Then the young man told him to get ready and go to the Kommandant. Jasch dressed and I did too, and we set out. You have to walk for 1 werst. I told him Jasch could not walk, and I really cried, but uselessly.

If you had seen how we walked, your heart would have bled for us. A picture of misery! Jasch had a stick in one hand, and I held him under his arm on the other side. That is how I dragged him to the Kommandant's office. His feet won't carry him anymore. At times his feet stop and he cannot move them; the next time they run so fast that he cannot control them. It was so hard I really did not think we would make it. But how much harder it was because the Kommandant's lackey walked behind us, but said nothing, not even that we should walk faster. When we had gone some distance, he asked us if Jasch's name had really been on the work list. He said that this just could not be right, because they would never send such a sick person to work. We walked and cried, and when we got there, the lackey immediately went into the Kommandant's office. We stood in the waiting room. Jasch was extremely tired, and we had to wait a long time until they finally called us. Jasch was dead tired when at last we got back to our quarters.

How often has our dear God heard and helped us! And it happened again yesterday. Forgive us, dear Geschwister, if we tell you of the things we have told you before. Our hearts are so heavy and we must tell someone of our misery and our woe – and to whom should we go but to you? We get no more letters from Mama. We do not know where she is, or where our other siblings are either. Are they still alive? Or our brother Abram – where can he be? If you know, then write it to us, please. Today we received 2 letters from you, one from Easter Sunday with the blank paper. Thank you so much for it, as well as for the picture. Compared to us here, how fortunate you are to be in such a nice home, and free! If only the time would ever come where we could talk to you verbally. Then you would listen and be shocked and astounded, and you would say, "Dear Geschwister, you have not written to us about half the horrors you have experienced."

We had to dig out these tree stumps, it was very hard and I am very tired. My body lets me know that I am no longer what I once was. Previously my dear Jasch always used to say: [...]. But he no longer says it. We still hope that better times will yet come to us. Ach, if only we could survive these evil days and again experience good times, then we could be refreshed and revitalized, right? You cannot imagine how happy we are when you write of hope. But it is taking too long. When will our great God finally intervene and put an end to this terrible tribulation?

Jasch, I, and Michi have no bread card, and we have no prospects for a new harvest or vegetables or fruit or such things. Then it is different at home, where they do have the prospect of having their own vegetables and fruit. That is a big help. There is just no comparison with us here. We have absolutely nothing else but a small piece of bread – and how long does that last? We do not want to perish here in exile! How we long to be back home, and together with our children be happy again. Jasch so often prays with the Psalmist, "Do not call me home after half my years, but let me dwell in the land of the living." If you would see him, dear Liese, you would weep and wail with compassion. The doctor says he should eat many vegetables; that would help him. And the climate is so much different than at home – in the land where things grow. Think of it, 2 years without milk or eggs. It seems that humans cannot live without those things; and so we slowly fade away. There already are fresh cucumbers here for 1 ½r. a piece, milk for 4r. a litre. Our earnings are just too small.

[April 1933]

Dear Geschwister,
I actually do not know just what I should write to you today. We write so often, but receive so few letters from you that we become discouraged. It is Sunday again today, and we again remember those wonderful days of the past. Those lovely Sundays, and Sunday dinners, and those blessed church services – and now? Oh, one could weep. When will God have mercy on [*Russia*]? Praise God, until now He has kept us in the faith and our anchor remains in Him. When we have overcome all the hardship here, we can then enter into His glory where all sorrow and misery will cease for all those who are washed in the blood of the Lamb. We wish you, dear Geschwister, the comfort of God in your sufferings as well.

We always thought that you, dear Liese, would completely recover from your illness. I would love to see you and Tina Klassen once more in this life. Papa and Hans are no longer here, and who knows how things are going with our dear Mama. She writes that she also lives in adversity. Things are far too hard for her in her old days. How nicely could she allow herself to be cared for by her children, if such evil times had not come upon us. When you left for America and we were all ready to go, who would have thought that this would happen to us? It never occurred to us that we would not see each other again in this life.

And my dear Jasch is also so poorly off. Even in previous days, during the good times, he did not have a particularly strong body. Now just think what he is like after having gone through so much. But his great desire still is to leave his family in better circumstances in the event of his death. How difficult it is to understand the ways of God when times are hard. But our dear deceased Papa always said: "The ways of the Lord are right." In fact, he wrote that to us in every letter – I have saved all his letters as well as the letters of dear Hans. He wrote a letter to us 10 days before his death. Such letters are so precious and interesting.

Dear Liese, please write us every time you send a letter. There are far too few to suit us. Do not think, dear sister, that your letters are not just as valuable to us – but both of you should write. How come P.B.'s sent Tina's letter to Kraebel? Could you not do so, if that is what you wanted? You do not trust him either, do you? It will be like with Truda's 10 dollars that she sent to him in order to send a parcel to us. He wrote that he would add another 5 dollars of his own. And we received a parcel valued at 3 dollars. Where did the rest stay? It will probably be like that with this one as well.

How did it happen that P.B.'s got Tina's letter? They never write letters to us anymore – and then he wants to be our intercessor? Well, I do not want to think wrongly of him. Have they again taken over such a big farm? And where does his GlassKorn [*hired help*] stay? If only we could now be your hired men and maids. Our Peter would be a very good and industrious hired man. Often he has to work day and night. It snowed yesterday and is snowing again today, but there is not much frost.

Soon it will be spring, but we are still in exile and there is no prospect that things will ever improve. H.F. are all still well – they get quite a bit from Germany. He is a strong Friesen just as all the F's were. Jasch's Liese [*both persons named were members of another Mennonite family in exile*] has also died – so many pass from time into eternity. I have written in love. We are anxiously awaiting the parcel from you. Liese is very inquisitive about her dress. If you also want to send us 5 dollars, may God be its escort.

[April 1933]

We do not want to grumble because our dear God is the one who has allowed it – it is to serve for our good. Often it is so hard for us. We remember the wonderful past, the nice times we had, the visits we made one to another – we were all together and happy. And now you are over there in such happiness, and we are here perishing in misery. Should that time ever come when we could come to you, you would be ashamed to speak with us. We are emaciated, dressed in rags. My desire would be to first stay in Germany long enough to fatten up a little; maybe each one of us would get a new set of clothes as you did. You will be thinking, "What useless thoughts they have." But a person cannot be indifferent to one's appearance as long as one is not completely depraved; and that is the way we feel as well.

A tragic accident occurred here in the mine yesterday. First thing in the morning, at 6 o'clock, the lift went down. They had just begun to work. They struck a spot where dynamite had been laid but which had not all exploded. Now the rest exploded and 9 men were wounded. The firemen with the fire engines are always ready when accidents happen in the mines. That is how it was now, and the wounded were taken to the hospital immediately. I went there too and saw as they brought the wounded out. Four could walk home, but 5 were taken to the hospital in Kizel by auto. Two were carried out on a stretcher. I thought they were dead, but they were alive and were treated and only bandaged up. But they did look terribly injured.

Previously I desired that Peter and Liese should continue to work in the mines, because the rations are almost double that for other work. But when things like this happen, I know it is better to work above ground and manage with less. Of course accidents can happen above ground too, but inherently the work is not as dangerous. God's hand must protect us everywhere. Liese's hands hurt so very much from loading the ore wagons and hauling stones that she feels she will never again be able to knit or do needle work. Bekommen alle den Rabass weg [*appears out of context; the meaning is uncertain*]. Oh, how fortunate your children are in contrast to this! Dear children, Franz, Liese, Peter, and Meka, consider yourselves fortunate.

It is raining here for the 14th day and then Jascha has to sit in our little hut and not jump around. Susie Born was visiting us for 3 days; she is as old as our Lensch [*Lena, who is now eleven years old*]. She came by herself. She must ride the train and then walk 25 werst. Yesterday morning Tina walked with her to Kizel, and from there she would go home by train. She told us she always went begging and would remain away from home up to 14 days. Often she would bring home 20 to 30 kilos which she would carry the 25 werst. It is sad that she is forced into that business. As a sideline she also learns to steal. The 4 boys are also knocking about in the world somewhere. I am so glad that we are still all together. At least our children come home every evening, all except Michi – but we hope that she will be able to come home for the winter.

## "No Night is so Dark that Day does not Come"

*Almost too weak to walk, Jasch writes of his need for food, which drives him to continue working as a night watchman. He reports that Liese is still working in the mines, cleaning debris left behind. It is wet and cold. The dirt not only wears out her clothes, but her lungs and her spirit.*

*There is no doubt that the Regehr family is suffering, but the fate of those in their home colony of Sagradowka is also very bleak. Reports of mass starvation and cannibalism are circulating. One letter to the Regehrs states that "190 people died of starvation in three days." Maria has not heard from her parents and siblings in her home village of Altonau for two months. She is very worried.*

Polowinka, 5 April 1933

All of you, our dearly beloved all!
May God bless you more and more. Who can thank you enough for all the kind deeds you do for us? God will reward you, for we

cannot. We received your card written on March 17, where you tell me you have sent 5 dollars to us. We have not received it yet.

Oh, you dear ones, do not forget us in the future either. I want to visit with you while I still can. I am extremely weak and walk with a cane. My feet refuse to obey me. The reason is the lack of nourishing food. But if it is true as you, dear brother-in-law, write, that America wants to help us get over there, it will be wonderful. Oh, how much I would desire to participate in that with my entire family. Well, as God wills it.

It is you, Fr. and Liese, you ravens [*a reference to the ravens that fed the prophet Elijah in the Old Testament*] who provide us with bread here in the land of darkness. With what shall we ever repay you? If we could only come to you, then we would demonstrate our thanks to you. Yes, dear sister, I believe I am no longer of any use in this world. Because of the very poor and meagre diet, I have come to the point where I can only walk with a stick and even then not as far as I want to go. However, in spite of this, I have to be a night watchman for 8 hours every night and walk 1 ½ werst to work. It is so hard for me, dear sister, that I cannot begin to tell you how hard! But if I want to earn a small piece of bread, then I have to do it. Dear Geschwister, pray that our deliverance may come soon, otherwise we all perish.

The children also have it terribly hard. Liese came home from work at 1 A.M. and had to again leave for work at 5 A.M. She works in the mines. Tunnels are being built with wood, iron and stone, and she must clear and clean them out. This is terribly hard on clothes, since everything is always wet. We are almost out of clothes. But I do not want to complain about clothes, rather, our bodies "thirst" for bread. The 5 dollars, when we receive it, shall provide us with millet meal, and if the Schmelzung [*literally "thawing," but the meaning is unclear*] is with it, then we will think we are the most honoured of wedding guests!

We have thin soup twice a day – that is, if we have anything at all. Our Peter wishes he could have it 3 times a day. And even then my dear Marie measures out each meal and portions it out, otherwise it would never provide for all of us. We never eat as much as we would like. Just as it begins to taste good we often must stop. Well, we are used to it, may it continue like this until we are delivered from here. Well, we believe you will help and entrust our future to you, dearly beloved. Do not forget about us.

How is it, dear Liese, that you do not write at all any more? How we long to get more news of you. We have not had any news from home for 2 months now. We do not know, are they still all alive? I wonder if dear brother Hans died of starvation? For several months he had had no bread in the house, and lived only on what he got from the Torgsin – and that was little enough. There should be bread for a meal. He has earned his rest; he has joyfully gone home. I wonder if Mama is still alive? We have no news. In the last letter she wrote how unwell she was. She had already walked to Koselsk 12 times. She is not safe at home and has often hidden herself somewhere in the villages to escape from her tormentors. An unprecedented persecution! And the world is silent. If only we as a nation could be rescued. Thousands of our loved ones are perishing. The Dueckmanns, N. 8, are both dead in Kherson – starved to death. Goodbye, it is night, I have to go to work.

The 6th.

Good morning, you loved ones! The cold night has passed again. No night is so dark that the day does not come; and we so much want to believe that our deliverance will also come. Marie and Tina have gone to do the laundry. Lena is standing in a line-up since early morning – 200 gr. of sugar are to be available. Lena can hardly wait until she is able to taste it, so great is the joy. The children do not get to know what good times are. At home the children had nice clothes and my dear Marie used to dress them very neatly. Today they go in coats made from the sacks out of the packages. No shoes! I could weep when I think of the past.

We really regret that the parcel in which you, Liese, remembered our Liese, has gone lost. A search is being made as to where two other parcels have stayed: N. 661, 22/IX/32, insured for 115 rubles, and N. 473 of the XI/32, insured for 230 rubles. Could it be one of yours? What does that money help, and who will get it?

It is the 8th. I am alone at home. My dear Marie and Jascha are in line for bread. Lena went to stand in line for sugar again since she got none before. Tina got up at 3 A.M. and walked for 1 ½ Werst to sign up to get bread. When will we be free and be able to eat our own bread again? Today I opened the Bible to Psalm 37:4-5. I just cannot grasp it! We, and so many others, have already prayed for this for so many years. I read further and pleaded to God to convince me that He was leading us. Then I got to Verse 19. There I stopped, and had to pray "Yes, Lord, it is true, you have known how to preserve us until this day, and we will continue to put our confidence in you."

My dear Marie and Jascha came back and said they could not get bread. They stand there depressed. But verse 19 comforts us. Yesterday we got 1k. meat – pork, weighing about 1 nyg. Very skinny pig. It had been skinned and looked like only bones. In the government store it costs 4r. 62k. per kilo. They call that cheap, right? At your place one could buy a whole pig for such a price, is that not right? You, dear Liese, write in your letter of March 10th that you hope to see us again, and that I and my dear Marie will rest and eat the very best of food. Oh, dear sister, your love to us has made us weep. But still I said, "If only we could eat the crumbs that fall from the Lord's table." It is too much, little sister. Yes, dear Liese, see to it that you support us here until the hour of our deliverance strikes. Call on others to help too, dear Liese. We will not send letters without stamps again. Do not redeem the letters again. It is terribly expensive to have to pay more than 2d. postage due. God will reward you a 100-fold. I will write immediately when we have it in our hands.

I have written a small article to Hoffert and all who take pity on us about my kidney trouble. The package through Crebel from Pet.

Bargens, from the month of August 1932, has not been received to date. We regret that very much. I wonder where it could have got to. Dear Geschwister, one question: You give so much, P.B. nothing. Are you better off than they? Psalm 112:5 and 6 is a word for you. [*"Good will come to those who are generous and lend freely, who conduct their affairs with justice. Surely they will never be shaken; the righteous one will be remembered forever."*] The sheet is full, but my heart is still full too. Could we talk face to face today, we would speak of many things. Children all send greetings.

Jak.

Polowinka, 16 April 1933

You dear, dearest ones, and children,

We wish you a happy Easter! Our thoughts were often with you today as we recalled the good times of the past. Yes, where are those times? We feel like crying, like weeping and wailing when we consider the pain of our sorrow. God, give us different times – but as You will – that is the best for us. But give us strength that in the darkest hours we stand firm even when this terrible hunger strikes. Send us help in time – at the right time.

Hunger tolerates no resistance. It hurts; in fact it hurts so much that mothers take their children and slaughter them. Yesterday H.S. received a letter from Wilh. Klas., N. 1, who writes that in Sagradowka 190 people died of starvation in three days. Women took dead bodies, cooked them and ate them. In N. 7 J. Barg, H. Bold – in N. 9 Ab Wiens, Isak Braun, Peter Koop are all dead. In N. 7, as far as we know, of all the old landowners only Jasch Martens still remains. The others are all dead. It is reported that it is 10 times worse than in the Urals; then a person could still borrow something from another. We have not received any news from N. 9 for over two months; we have no idea why. Are they still alive? Are they [...] where our mother sometimes stays? Help her as much as you can, dear Geschwister, for she is old, has no home and is chased and pursued like a deer. And then that terrible hunger!

Oh, how great is our distress! This morning I opened my New Testament and was given 1 Peter 5:6-11. And so we do want to humble ourselves under the mighty hand of God, and cast all our burdens on Him. Then we shall not want. God will soften many hearts and send us bread. We are completely at the end of our rope and, humanly speaking, tremble when we think of what will happen in the future. We do not want to despair but continue to lean on God's Word. The ways of the Lord are right, even though today we do not understand the deeply woeful ways He is leading us.

Just like our Liese, who now must work down in the coal shafts, many of which are 100 metres deep. She too cannot understand the way she must go – and then only for that small piece of bread. Please pray for her too, that she does not despair of her life. No Sunday, no holiday is celebrated. We never hear the word of God. Without any freedom, we cannot go one step from home. Dear Geschwister, every day we are cursed and sworn at and live our life in slavery. You have no inkling, no idea, of how it is. It is like slowly being murdered. Nero's tortures were predictable and lasted only for minutes. Here it takes years.

Liese told us that one worker with whom she worked in the coal shafts crawled out of the shaft and, while walking home, fell down on the road and died. Such events occur often here – always so evil, and so very little to eat. I too am so very weak and so Blutarm [*anemic*] that I cannot walk without a cane. I get so dizzy in the head that I have to be careful that I do not fall. Oh, how strangely are our bodies organized. You cannot even imagine. We do not weep for ourselves but for our dear children. One cannot bear to see how they are hassled and abused; if they do not fill their quota at work they get no bread at all!

Yesterday – Easter Sunday – our dear Peter was forcibly driven into the shaft to work. He was always deathly afraid of the mines, but no one took that into account. He is still not well, and now into the shafts! Many, many accidents occur there. Who in his life would ever have thought that we would be robbed of everything, driven out of our home and sent 4000 km away, there to work in coal shafts for one-half a piece of bread! In all this swamp and mud our Mariechen must now dig out big tree stumps to clear the land. It is so hard on our footwear! We cannot earn as much as it costs us. My dear Marie was also driven to work yesterday and forced to dig out tree stumps – can you imagine? But she gets only one [...] of black bread a day – it is supposed to be that much but it is never that much. They still keep robbing us!

By the month of May I will be forced to beg. It is impossible for me to go to work, so it may come to that. I do not want to die yet, dear Geschwister; I still want the opportunity to square our account with you. Tina just came from the post office and brought a letter from you dated 22 March, with a receipt for 4.50. A thousand thanks, dear Geschwister. We will cash it right away for we are at an end. Oh, the good Lord provides! Now we can get millet meal. It does not quite give three pud meal – we still need half a ruble. That is, if they allow us to use our own money, then it will be enough. If not, then it gives as much as possible.

What is this news that you bring us? That there is hope for us? Please write more of this. You, dear Liese, have you forgotten us entirely? You do not write anymore. Yes, it is so, dear little sister, if you should see us in our rags and clothes I wonder if you would admit that we are your relatives. Yes, we often feel forsaken by God and people. When we get a letter, we are often lifted up and encouraged. Well, dear Liese, we leave our future in God's and your hand. If you will provide for us, then we may survive. Please, please save our lives! God bless you and your whole house. Yes, Liese, you too be encouraged. Well enough, as God wills. God bless your acres. Do you own the entire farm? How much we would like to help you. What have Bargens undertaken for themselves? Do they still live in such a grand style? We did help him. They have forgotten us. Well, Aufwiedersehen [...].

J. and M. Regehr

*Mothers are normally concerned with making dinner for their families and buying clothes for their children. Mothers are also known to worry about their children. But this mother's daily concerns exceed normal anxiety.*

[April 1933]

Dear Geschwister Frank and Liese,
Today is the 2nd day of Easter, the day when we, all our dear, dear parents' children, were happily and joyfully together in the family circle praising God who had blessed us and had given each one his daily bread – and much more. Oh, what a glorious time that was, a time we can never forget. Yes, dearly beloved, yesterday and today we have remembered and spoken so much about you. Oh, how different it is today, everyone is scattered, Papa and Hans are dead, the home of our dear parents is wrecked. God has allowed it, but it is not His will! But our trespasses and sins are the reason! So we fall down into the dust and cry for mercy, and believe that God will hear us and not leave us forever in this tribulation.

Today we received your letter of 22 March with the order. Thank God that we have the letter in hand. Dear Geschwister, what have we done to deserve such love from you? Yes, dear Liese, you still have the same compassionate heart you had then. We always knew it. We have no news from home about the whereabouts of Mama and all the Geschwister. Our family is still together, but from the other German [*Mennonite*] folk we know nothing.

It seems that Geschwister grow apart from one another, just as you and Tina. We get no letters from her, and that is not enough for us. They should at least show us that much love. We know they are poor and cannot send us anything, but we do not ask for that either. But in spite of that they should write us a letter. And, dear Liese, in the last while you have not written often enough. Do not write so much to friends and more to us. I am almost jealous. Please, dear Liese, do not misunderstand me. Should the time really come that we should see one another face to face, both of us will hardly be able to bear the Wiedersehen [*greeting*]! What a moment that would be, is that not true, Geschwister? May God grant that it happen soon!

We get a new lease on life when we receive news from you, or we hear that something good will happen here. Too bad that they are groundless rumours. Today I stood in line until 1 P.M. to purchase a pair of white underpants. They had 4 pair in the [...]. We needed them very badly but they cost 4r. 18k. There are also many tailored dresses in the shops, but they are terribly expensive. But bread is unobtainable and the quota is so small. I too am tempted to go to work, not for the joy of working but to obtain the necessary bread. As soon as school closes Tina will go to work again as well.

Dear Liese, let me describe to you the way I make soup twice a day. I take one pail of water, 2 cups of millet meal and 2 cups flour – remember the blue cup we all had? – and if we have grease or oil, one tablespoon full. Then once a day we have Pripps, but seldom a piece of bread with it. Liese and Peter are working in the mineshafts. It was a hard decision to allow them to work there, but we do not have our own will in this matter. They are constantly in great danger. It appears that all of Russia is slated to starve to death. Terrible things are happening here, things one can hardly believe; but they are true!

Jasch has briefly written us that it takes too long until help comes. The parcel of 8 Dec. has not been received. Please investigate this, dear Geschwister, and if the parcel is lost and you get money for insuring it and have a choice, then please send it to us as you have sent this order. It would buy us so much here. Please forgive me for telling you what to do, but we do not want to continue to starve, or perhaps to die of malnutrition. My dear Jasch is in bad condition. He can no longer tolerate even the skimpy diet we have. But we do not yet want to die apart. May God sustain us and you and give us a Wedersehen [*a reunion*].

Mrs. P.B. is still as [...] as before; thinks she is the fairest – and again taking on such a big farm! They have completely forgotten us. We were not allowed to have a church service on Easter day.

To your dear children, a hearty greeting from your Uncle Jasch and Aunt Marie

[1933]

Dear Geschwister Frank and Liese and children,
May the almighty God be with you and give you health, and whatever you need for this life, but much more for eternal life. Our dear brother Hans has proven that our sojourn is not here on earth. Oh, that good Hans had to leave this world in his early years and leave his family in such misery.

I am fraught with fear when I see how ill my dear Jasch is. He has lost weight just unbelievably in the last days. He also has great pains and mostly lies in bed. Maybe we will all have to perish. Today I went to Polowinka, I got nothing but mustard for 1r. a glass – something to put on our bread. Dear Geschwister, you just cannot imagine how sad it is: the father of the house sick and we live in exile! The children just came home from work. It is a nice sunny day today, and warm. We always believed that the time would come when we too would be set free, but it has been a futile hope.

How is it that we get no letters from you? Have you forgotten us? Or do the letters go lost? We have not had a letter from you since January 2nd. How do things look with your health? Are you free from your great illness? Dear Liese, we have not had a letter from home for a long time. When will the time come when we can see each other face to face and be happy together once again? May God in His compassion have mercy on us in this great tribulation here in Russia. I will close for today for I am utterly discouraged. What is yet to come? We trust only in God.

Your humble Geschwister, Jasch and M.

*The next day, Jasch writes on the same paper.*

Dear Geschwister,
Since the letter was not ready to be mailed yesterday, I will add a few more words today. How quickly does man's life vanish. I am very ill; have a big boil in front and down below. I also have great difficulty in passing water. Well, I must lie in bed all day. I take it very easy, maybe it will pass. But it does not look good. Today the weather is rather nice. My dear little wife went to Polowinka; she wanted to see if she could buy mustard for the bread. Our salt is almost all gone. You cannot get salt here anywhere. So now we have eaten our black bread that way for 2 years. If you eat the bread with salt or mustard, it tastes very nice. In this way, we daily half satisfy our hunger when things are available.

For 2 days our Tina stood in line all day in order to get some bread. We were without bread for 6 days. On the last day she brought home enough for 3 days. Then there is such a crush, the Russians fight and hit each other, for every one wants to be first to get the bread. There are many here who live only from their belt down. Their violence comes from their despair. May God have compassion on us in all this misery. Many horses here die of starvation – and they search through the carrion for food. If a horse is overworked, they quickly slaughter it before death and the meat is sold for 3 rubles a kilo. And the people take it immediately.

Dear Geschwister, your help has kept us alive until today. If we could buy a little millet meal and 2 pud flour per month, then our rations would be enough. We do need your help for this. Here it costs up to 7 ½ d. per kilo. According to the article you sent us, we believe our deliverance will come. Is it time for congratulations? Write to us. How are things in the world? Has grandmother seen that article? It probably won't help, but it won't hurt either. If it is God's will, we will stay faithful until the end, even if it means death by starvation. Pray that we have strength, for we are at our wit's end. Many times the depths into which we are led are too deep. Write more, dear Geschwister. We have not had a letter from [...] except the 2 cards. We cannot afford to put on stamps, or even buy paper.

Your loving Jasch

*Events in Europe and United States offer hope to the Regehr family. With Hitler becoming Chancellor of Germany, Jasch believes the country is strengthening its position. However, it is not clear how this will affect the beleaguered prisoners. Will the "Moses" – the Deliverer whom Jasch awaits – emerge from a stronger Germany or from the United States? Considering the isolation of the prisoners in Russia, their confusion about the prospects is certainly understandable.*

*The joy of drinking milk – the first in two years – is also understandable. But not the horror of cannibalism. Small wonder that Maria considers the days of Nero to have been less dreadful.*

Polowinka, 1st May 1933

To you, our Geschwister who save us, Franz and Liese and children!

Luke 18:8. The first 10 words are now in our hands. [*"I tell you, he will see that they get justice, and quickly."*] We thank you that you write to us of hope. Could it happen soon? Oh, how happy Jakob would be to rejoice in Israel – and if they would free us German people from exile, and allow us to go home, and bread would be sent there – then we would soon be happy again, gain new courage, and work so that we could acquire a cow. Oh, the milk – how we appreciated it – and now we have not had any for 2 years.

We believe that if events really develop that far, then the US would lead, right? He is also too big [*a masked message that seems to refer to someone from the United States*]. Whoever will now come with bread will be accepted and followed by the people! Dear sister Liese, you write we should not thank you too much for that 5-dollar package. Yes, to a small degree we still understand, but do not be surprised by it. Hunger is so painful – oh, so painful – that in many places widows have slit the throats of their loved ones, have cooked and eaten them. Others again have dismembered corpses and fried them. That is what starvation can do. This has often occurred among the children of this land. Please do not think that they did not love their little children – no, never, but the great pain drives a person to this insanity.

With a thousand tongues we would like to thank you and all those who give. Every crumb we get is worthy of thanks. Lazarus is still lying before the doors of the rich man and begs for crumbs that drop from the rich man's table [*an allegory in the New Testament*]. We know that you cannot help everyone, but if you could manage that we get 1 dollar per soul in our family each month, then maybe we could barely get by together with what we get here. We need such help. Dear sister, you write that you have written to Switzerland for help. Dear Liese, their addresses, send us addresses also from Switzerland, as well as Holland, as well as America – addresses of affluent people. If the time of our deliverance should soon be here, as you write, then we want to take courage again.

Longingly we await a "Deliverer." Moses, come out! And you believe he is here? I am almost 50 years old, and I will not make it many more years – have been too often in the clutches of these devils. However, I would yet like to greet Moses. Dear siblings, I am so weak on my feet I can hardly walk. I fall down – too anemic because of the poor diet. There is no meat, no butter, no milk, only and always Pripps, soup, and a tiny piece of black bread per person for each day. The young seem to cope better than the old ones.

I am really surprised about P.B. We stand at their door and knock, but they do not acknowledge our entreaty. How much did we help them with grain – how often did we invite them to our place for meals when they did not have anything. When they were not allowed to eat their own produce, then they would come to us. And we always did it gladly too. Well, we will never be sorry for it – only sorry that it cannot be so again. If they lock the door to us, leave it be, God does not need them for it. And we will get by otherwise too.

Oh, dear brother-in-law Fritz, you are so inventive, would you not be able to get the [...] and Rosa's address to us, as well as Majund's? Do try it, send us those addresses. We received your 4 ½ dollars – I wrote you that immediately. To date there is no sign nor trace of the 8 dollars. Demand the money back and send it here in Opgepr [*a money order*]. That would be so much help to us. In Kizel, 12 km from here, there is now a Torgsin. Now my dearest Mitsche wants to get everything from there by foot. And we can go that far even if it will be hard, if only we can get something for our deprived stomachs. My dear Marie is only skin and bones, and I am so weak that I can hardly walk. Actually, I can only walk to the outside door. So often we ask ourselves, "Will we ever be able to return home, or even somehow get to you?"

You, dear siblings, just cannot imagine how long the time seems to us here in exile. It is like being a dying person in the darkness of the night. One continually asks, "Is the night soon past?"

Today it is the 1st of May [*International Worker's Day in the former Soviet Union*]. However, it is just like any other day, only our officials are vigorously boozing it up. In general, the people here drink wine like it was water. The cheapest wine here costs about 25 rubles a litre – previously this wine cost about 15 - 20 rubles. Butter at the bazaar costs 30 rubles per pound. There are no potatoes to be had – from the month of October until now we have not seen any. Sunflower oil also costs 30 rubles per litre. Our wages are steadily decreasing: we get 1 ruble, 90 kopecks per day. Then you can figure out how much we can buy. It steadily gets worse.

If we do not get help soon, we perish. They have manipulated things in such way that in future we will fare even worse than today. The whole Christian world sees what is going on here, how many thousands of their brothers are perishing here, and remains silent. Where is the League of Nations? We thought we would be set free as a nation! Such acts of horror do not even occur among the heathens. This martyrdom is going on too long. We can endure it no longer. Nero was a Menschenfresser [*people-eater*]. He condemned thousands. Today we say he was a wild man, but at least he did not continue to torture his victims. Here, when a person is already totally kaput, yes, he is so weak he can no longer walk, then he is cursed up and down and ordered to work. The poor victim slowly makes his way to work, falls down in the mud and gives up his ghost, and miserably expires in the mud. And such things are the order of the day.

And the League of Nations is silent! Thousands of the best men perish – die of hunger. The children get nothing, no milk, no butter, no meat, only 400 gr. of sour bread. Actually 85% of the children between the ages of 1 to 10 years who were sent here have died. And from what did the children die? They died of starvation! And so we are all slowly sinking to our death. We call to Nero: "Come, dear man, and end our suffering; it only took you an hour and the agony of your victims was over, but now there is torment without end!" Never has there been a persecution so great and terrible as today. We do not want to bring shame upon our German [*Mennonite*] people – we will bear it as long as possible. But send us bread that we do not die of starvation! Only with your assistance and God's support can we emerge as the victors!

Our papers report that a "World Commission" is to meet in America these days, but ours [*possibly a Russian representative*] is not allowed to enter. Our son just received news that he will be removed from the coal mine. He has almost worked himself to death in order to complete the plan there. Now the railway building plan must be completed, so now he is sent there. And so they torment and harass them back and forth. It is especially hard with the children – they are beginning to doubt God's Word because for so long there is no answer to prayer. Pray much for us, dear Geschwister.

We received your letter of May 25. Report on the current political situation. [....] What will grandfather say? [*reference to a political leader.*] Has he improved a little bit? Would God that He inspire the leaders in D [*Deutschland, i.e., Germany*] to eradicate all this evil. Report our situation to Crebel and tell him that to date we have not received the parcel. Ask also to which address it has been sent. Maybe he will still send us a little help to Kizel. Please beg him for us. We believe he will do it. God be with you, in love.

*Jasch is losing control of his limbs, a symptom that his disease has attacked his muscles. Maria must now work longer hours and is brutalized by the guards. Jasch longs for a liberator. Again he wonders about world events, specifically Russia's role with England and Germany. With the lack of an intelligent news service, confusion and rumours prevail. Jasch wonders if Hitler could defeat Russia and establish order in this land of chaos where "grandfathers are forced to work."*

Polowinka, May 5, 1933

Dearly beloved Franz and Liese,
May God bless you greatly, since it seems that you alone are bearing our load. How is it possible with Peter Bargens – do they betray all people? They have forgotten us completely. We have received nothing from them except when Truda sent us her 10 dollars. There P.B. had also enclosed 3 dollars. It was a package worth 13 dollars. But when it arrived here it was only 3 dollars' worth. We just do not know where the mistake was made. What Liese wrote about the Corbel [*a Russian store through which goods could be sent to recipients in Russia*] – the $10 – did not arrive either. Who knows to which address it may have been sent? Please inquire! The package from Isaac Wiebes did not arrive either. The money order of 5 dollars sent by you did arrive. Many thanks, dear siblings.

Oh, if you could come to see how great our misery is, then you would say, "We did not even know the half of it." That package for 8 dollars is still missing. It is important to know where it was sent from so that you can find out where it is stuck. The sender is responsible for inquiring, right? We are very sorry not to get it. Oh, what this starvation is doing to us! I am still very weak. I only walk when I must. I just can hardly use my legs, they will not carry my body any longer. I do not want to die yet, dear siblings – but if it is God's plan to let me die, it may happen soon! Yes, dear siblings, beg for us, very, very much.

Today it is again a very hard day. It is snowing and raining heavily. Everyone is sent out to work for the Commune. And when you come home from the regular work, you must still do this extra work. There never is rest! My dear Marie has been at work since early morning. We know it must be Easter Sunday sometime during this time. Yet people come in and order her out to work, grab her, and shove her out of the door. There was an incident here yesterday, and the Kommandant actually screamed at the prisoners: "You will stay here and work for 50 more years."

We notice they may be trapped by their own politics. Until today there has been great unrest. Will Papa R. [*Papa Russia*] come into a conflict? And England? Write back soon! I suppose Hitler is a stern disciplinarian. Would he establish order here where grandfathers are forced to work? Is he still living? May God grant him courage and fortitude. Well, everything is really in God's hands.

We have not had a letter from home for 3 months. We do not even know if they are still alive. Where may our dear Abram be? He has to live his youthful years as a slave here in this exile. Just now our dear Jascha came in from the Banja [*bath house*]. Is he ever a smart little boy. Often he goes out to see the workers working. He even walks to the store all alone. If only he could go to school to learn. They have taken this possibility away from the other children. That is just so sad. Our Peter is already grown to manhood and has had very little schooling. He was not allowed to go to central school because he was the son of a kulak. It is an important time in his life. That discourages our children so much. Our children always loved to learn.

Tina and Lena still go to school. But what are they taught? Always and only the justice of the sentence that has been passed on us! Should we, and can we, really forgive these people everything, considering everything they have done to us? Of all those from home, David and Jakob Koehn are the worst off. We hear nothing from Hans. He is even more innocent.

Just now Marie came in from the store, very worried. She said the Kommandant grabbed her arm, flung her into the mud, and chased her back to work. Now it will be that it gets worse from day to day. For the third month we have not received a bread ration card. Oh, what will happen? Yes, dear loved ones, we are looking for deliverance by your hand. Have mercy as much as you can. Yesterday we received your letter of the 9th of April. May God grant you luck and blessing on your farm. May God bless your work. My Marie is just too sad to write today. She sends warmest greetings. Please pray for us and send us help, especially for the children.

Jakob

Polowinka, 9 May 1933

Dear Geschwister F. and Liese and children,
We hardly know what to write. But we received your very welcome letter of April 16th, with picture. Many thanks. We will send it to Mama. We are happy that things are going well for you, and you are happy with your big farm.

We have no joy left in this world; rather, we are gradually becoming a sacrificial offering. There has never been a persecution so brutal. I was deathly ill when the supervisor came and said I should go to work immediately at the Cyodomnm [*a place of added work; the same word has variant spellings here and elsewhere*]. I said I could not walk. Then he started screaming at me, vociferously. The next day he came again, threatening and screaming, making the same face. Then he went into a big act – that was yesterday – and sent me to the Kommandant. Then I took my stick in my hand, and my dear Marie with her arm in mine on the other side, and with a heavy heart we began to walk. When we had walked 200 metres, the Kommandant's assistant came and sent the supervisor away. He would guide us to the Kommandant. So we continued with many moans. However, he was very careful and let us walk as we could.

When we finally got there it was 10 at night. Then he said we should just stand there. He personally went to the F.M.T. [*a person in authority*]. In a while the F.M.T. came and asked why we had come. I said, "Because of the supervisor." Then he told us to remain standing there a while and soon he would hear us. And so we stood for several hours. Finally he called all the supervisors for a conference. Ach, I thought, will I have to die like this? I began to tremble. Suddenly I heard the F.M.T. scream at the supervisors, why they had sent such a sick person here? Did they want to listen to a [...] from him? Then the supervisor came out and said we were free to go, but Peter should come there immediately. So we started back.

God had helped us again. During the night we arrived home. Oh, what we experienced on that trip! My dear Marie practically had to carry me. She was completely exhausted. When we got home, I told Peter that he had been ordered to appear. But he just rolled over on his other side and continued to sleep. It is good he did not go. And so they continue to brutalize us.

My dear Marie is just home from the Cydomnmer 5 km away. They set a quota for digging out tree stumps, and if you fall short you get no bread. It has never been as bad as it is today. Will the distress soon be at its greatest? Please let us know. According to my estimates, about 75% of all people here will soon be dead of starvation. Dear Liese, you write I should write to J. Warkentin; I have done that twice. When they send you dollars to distribute among the Regehrs, am I not also a Regehr? Ach, how will we get by? Dear Geschwister, we fall at your feet and beg you not to forget us.

Today we received some bread; we had not received any for 8 days. Then you can figure out how well we live here. Your 8-dollar parcel does not come; could it have stayed in Tober? If you could send dollars to the Torgsin in Kizel which is the closest to us, 12 km, Mama and Tina will carry it all home. Hunger yields to no obstacles. Oh, how much I would love to look into your eyes once more, but we do not know if it is so determined by God. Let us trust Him. Pray for us that our deliverance may be soon.

We have not had a letter from home for over 3 months, do not know why. Here everything is as before. Everyone is well, except me. We will see what the future brings. Let us trust God. Send us help when you can. We need 7 dollars every month so that we, 8 souls, can satisfy our hunger once a day – no more.

May God bless you. Your Jakob

*The cost of food is extremely inflated in the northern prison camps. Since little can grow in the northern climate, most food products need to be imported. Exploitation of the desperate prisoners also increases the prices. Jasch asks for seven dollars to feed his family for one month; by comparison the recipients of the letters in Canada (Franz and Liese Bargen) earn ten dollars a month with which they feed and support a family of two adults and four children.*

[May 1933]

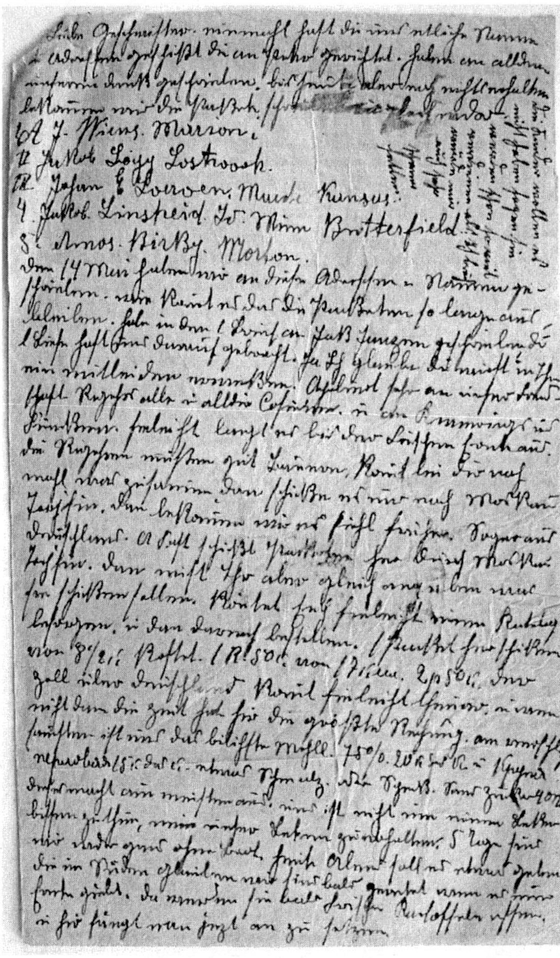
A. J. Wiens. Marion.
III Johann E. Loewen, Meade Kansas.
4. Jakob Linscheid ... Butterfield.
5. Amos. Kirby. Morton.

Dear Geschwister,
Once you sent us some names and addresses of those who would send things to our Peter. I have written a thank you to all of them but have not received anything yet. Should we get the parcels, then I will write immediately. These are the addresses.

1. A.J. Wiens – Marion
2. Jakob Lepp – Saskatoon
3. Johan E. Loewen – Kansas
4. Jakob Linsheid – Id. Minn Butterfield
5. Amos Birby – Morton

[*Written on the side of the paper*] The children do not want it; they say they will earn enough for my needs too. It would be very hard for me too.

On May 14 we wrote to these names and addresses. How is it possible that those packages do not arrive? In the letter to Jakob Janzen we wrote that you, dear Liese, gave us the idea. Yes, I believe you will awaken compassion in him. Appeal to our friendship, all the Regehrs and all the cousins, and to Reimers and Friesens, maybe it will last until the next harvest. The Regehrs are all good farmers, maybe they could gather something for us and send it to the Torgsin in Moscow. Then we receive it much sooner – even from Germany. A. Fast sent packages here through Moscow's Torgsin. You have to notify them right away what they should send to us. Maybe you could get a catalogue from them, and order from that? To send a parcel of 8 ½ kilos costs 1r. 50k. A package of 17 kilos costs 2 rubles 50 k! The duty to send through Germany may cost a bit more, but time is saved and here that is the greatest consideration. The cheapest flour, 75%, lasts the longest here, 20k.per [...]. 15k per kilo for a bit of lard or bacon. Granulated sugar goes the furthest.

We are not concerned with obtaining fancy tidbits, no, we just want to survive. For 5 days we have again been without bread. We are to get a little this evening. Those in the south believe we will soon be helped if there is a good crop. There they will soon eat fresh potatoes while here we are just beginning to plant. Here we must wait 3 full months for a new harvest. It is still very cold here and people are still walking in felt boots. Well, dear brother-in-law, please thank Hoffert for me. I enclose a thank-you letter – send it to him, maybe our good God will encourage him to help again. God be with you, M.R.

Dear siblings away in that great great distance,
I have such a great longing to speak with you and look into your faces. However, since that possibility does not exist, I will do it by letter. I thank you, dear siblings, for the letter and especially for the birthday present which you sent to me. The way I understand your letter, the children sent it to me in sympathy. Many thanks dear children, P. and L. and F. and Meka [*Jasch and Maria's nieces and nephews in Canada*]. May the dear Lord bless you and make your mama completely well, so that she can remain with you until you are all grown up.

It is true, dear siblings, you do more for us than you actually can afford. I wanted to write yesterday but I went to work in the afternoon. I had to plant cabbage plants for the Commune. For that I received, or said more correctly, I was promised 100 g. of bread and a ½ litre of milk. Then they sell it to us for 35 k. per litre. The work is not too hard – it is much harder to run around in this primeval forest. I went to see the doctor in the morning; I am not very well. I guess many of us will find our final rest here, if it continues to take so long before we are rescued.

If only our Liese would soon be set free – this grief is the hardest on me. Sometimes we just cannot understand the ways God leads us. However, some day we will understand. If God would only deliver us soon and finally bring us all to glory. I have such a great longing to escape this misery and be free again. If I thought that I must end my life here like this, then I would rather not live very long. I am so glad that your health problems are easing and that you hope to get well again.

Dear Liese, let me tell you how fat my arms are. Above the elbow I can easily encircle my arm with the middle finger of my other hand. Only skin and bones are left – would be happy if I could regain what I lost. We have received all your letters except the 2 with thread enclosed and the one with Peter's address. We did receive the one with the cucumber seeds enclosed. Also the one to us and to Mrs. J. R. I sent her the letter but she will not send it back. I am very sorry. Today I cooked rice for lunch, using the 1.5 litres of milk which we earned at the Commune. Oh, that tasted delicious. Those packages save us from death, dear siblings. I thank you, dear Liese, for that lovely comfort from the letter of James [*in the New Testament*], and the poem. Yes, I believe I will not go to work. Will write again in a few days.

[May 1933]

[...] we would tell you, if we were there with you. We would tell you of all our misery and sob out our grief. The joy of being with you will probably not be ours in this life. How beautiful it will be in Heaven, where there will be no tears or sorrow. We are so thankful for this yearning for Heaven!!

Greetings to B. Kl. [*Benjamin Klassens*] and give them this letter to read. They do not write to us, not even once. We would love to read a letter from them. I wonder what keeps you busy? Have you finished with the harvest? Did our dear God give grace in all things? We would so much like to know these things. I believe I wrote you that the products in the Torgsin have all become cheaper. Rye flour used to cost 16k. per kilo, now it is 10k. per kilo. Schlicht flour also 10k. Flour that is 85% pure is 12k. Before, rice cost 50k. and is now 45k. Millet flour was 23k., now is 16k. Cream of wheat was 50k., now 20k. In the same way also the dry goods, but they are not important to us. But how much more we get with the money that is sent to us! The notice for those dollars from you we received a long time ago. It was sent to Camkanen, but now we want it transferred to Kizel, because then we can get the products ourselves – and we get more for it. 75% flour used to cost 28k. and now it costs 15k.– half price. Today we got a card for 14 Marks 60 c, we do not know from whom. The dear Lord cares for us and does not forsake us. Dear Geschwister, another hearty greeting from your suffering Geschwister,

Jasch, Marie and children. Pray for us.

*Since the following red postcard was found in the Campbell Soup box in Canada, it likely never reached the intended recipient: David Boese in Oklahoma. Perhaps it was returned to the sender with the forwarding address unknown. Once again, we – along with the survivors interviewed for this project – may wonder how a letter from a Soviet prison camp could be sent to the West with an address to the United States blatantly written on the outside. How would this bypass a wary censor or prison guard? Was the subversive mail delivery network so successful that this postcard could travel unheeded? Or was the US address added only once the postcard was safely out of the USSR?*

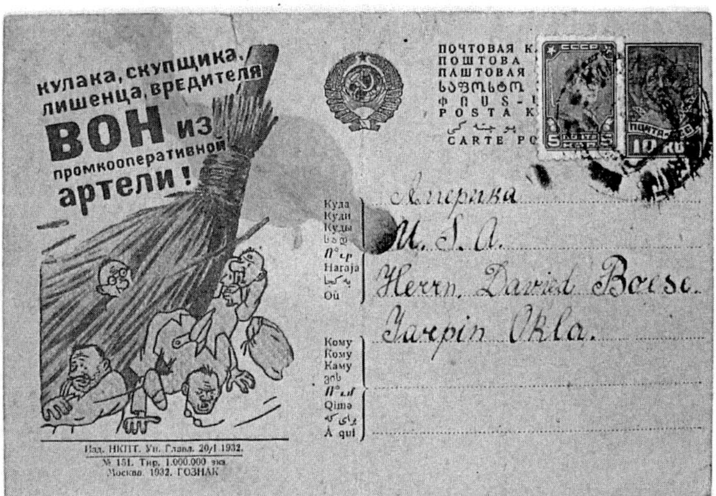

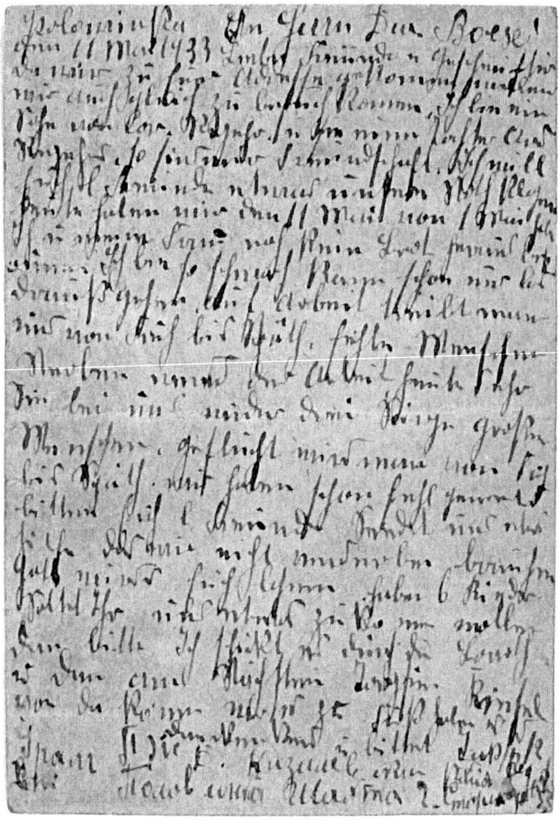

Polowinka An Herrn Dav. Boese!
den 11 Mai 1933

Polowinka, 11 May 1933

To Mr. David Boese!
Since we have received your address, we immediately want to come visiting. I am a son of Kornelius Regehr and am a cousin of Aron Regehr – that is how we are related. Dear friends, let me picture to you our distress. Today is the 11th of May, and since May 1st neither I nor my wife have had any bread issued to us. I am so weak that I am only able to walk as far as the door. But I am forced to work from early until late. Many people are dying from being overworked. Three coffins containing grown men drove by here today. One is cursed at from early until late. We have already wept so much. We

ask you, dear friends, send us some help so that we do not have to perish! God will reward you. We have 6 children. Should you want to send something, then I ask you to send it through the Board to the nearest Torgsin at Kizel. We would walk there to fetch it. Thanking and pleading,

Jakob Regehr [*an address in Russian follows the signature*]

*Jasch becomes too tired to write, and Maria narrates their activities – digging out tree stumps in wet marshland.*

[May 1933]

Dear beloved and precious Geschwister Franz, Liese and children! First, let me wish you the best of health, which you also need and which is the greatest treasure in this world. God's protection and blessing on all your ways.

Today I hardly have the courage to write, since the future is lying in thick darkness before our eyes. If we will be able to survive these hard days of testing is known to God alone. He could change everything, even our sad situation. How long we have waited for our deliverance and, until today, still quite uselessly. Such hopeful stories came from overseas that it could not be otherwise than that our deliverance would assuredly come this spring. And how is it? May is soon past and no help has come to us.

Today we received your letter of 30 April in which only you, dear Liese, had written – and you enclosed 2 sheets of white paper. Many thanks. We are so happy when we receive letters. We received 2 letters from home [*Altonau*], 1 from Mama and 1 from Susie. They rejoice that the vegetables are already there and are a great help. On the 13th May we quite unexpectedly got a letter from Tina Klassen in America. I have already written back to her. Tina writes that they too are very poor and that the R. [*Regierung, or Government Authority*] has sold their farm because they could not pay for it. It is difficult to remain a farmer when one has only small children. And yet they should be so happy that they fled and escaped this hellish [*Russia*]. At least you do not have to live through these hard times – hunger, frost, cold, and then taken into forced labour, working from early until late. It often occurs that Peter and Michi have to work day and night.

Here at this mine they want to clear a part of the forest and convert it to agricultural uses for seeding and planting. But that is so terribly much work. Dear Franz, you will be familiar with such a virgin forest. Then imagine digging out those roots and turning the sod with a spade. And so they have dug up thousands of dessiatines – and this only by sick, emaciated people who are already tired when they arrive on location. They have to walk 3 to 5 Werst into the forest, and then over roots and through water, through swamp and muskeg. When they dig, there is water everywhere. I have caught a terrible cold, and now I have a severe cough and feel that I have overexerted myself doing this. And this work has been done literally with skeletons and sick people. It is exactly like it says in the news clipping which you sent me, dear Liese. They are sent here and there, everywhere, no mercy or compassion, and without food.

How long we have already prayed! Should there not be one righteous person among all these exiles so that the dear Lord would save them for his sake? I believe there is. The time will come and will not be delayed, for so it says in the Word of God. Yes, dear brother Toews [*their "house friend" Johann Toews*] also had to give up his life here in exile. He will also have prayed and believed that God would grant him a reunion with his loved ones, but the dear Lord in His wisdom has determined otherwise. How difficult it is to understand the ways of God! We too cannot understand why my dear Jasch has to be so ill, with such terrible pains in his legs – and such pains in his head that he thinks it will split. If at least we would be free people so that we could go somewhere to seek help, but no: Stay in one place and perish!

It is, as Liese writes, no comparison with those who are at home where everything seems to be available again, vegetables and nice fruit, the harvest. And here there is nothing available the year around, only that chunk of bread that we are given for our work. The doctor says that Jasch should eat more nourishing food, there is no alternative that will help – no medicine. He should have lots of vegetables, milk, butter, and eggs, but where can one get them? One cucumber costs 1r. 50k., milk 5r. per litre, an egg 1r. 50k., butter 20r. – and so everything goes. And these are the very things he should eat or he will not pull through, and we want so much to do all things possible.

Dear Liese, I could scream for help! If at all possible, send us something so that he could have better food, maybe he could survive. We do not want to die here but want to go back home. He can no longer walk alone. When you send letters asking for help for us, then mention us separately and not just on a list with others. We think that would be better since those in exile should have the priority. H.F. are being sent a lot, and always in money, since it is more economical. When packages are sent, then shipping costs absorb half the value of the parcel. That Mr. Kl. from the United States wrote to Fries. that he had always submitted the names together on a list, but he has since learned that it is better to separate those in exile since they are then placed on a priority list. We are now being sent very little; we only get that from you and think that that may be the reason. We do so much want to stay alive and not starve to death. Please do not be angry with us because of this, dear Geschwister.

Dear Liese, you write that we should send our thanks to Wark. and Boesen. Jasch has written 3 letters to W., but we do not know if they have sent us anything – no message from them. We would do it so willingly, even bow deeply into the dust, to those who send us help. How did you designate that 1 dollar which you sent to the Board? Were they to send it in money? That is better than a package. We also got the 5 dollars sent to Tina by Hoffer and believe that is from him personally, because he had included his photograph. There was no letter, only the money order. Have you tried to trace the package for 8.30 dollars? Do everything possible to see that it does not stay lost.

Why do exactly our parcels have to go lost – and then so many? How much it would mean to us if we would receive it in money! 2r. 56k. is what rye flour costs, 3r. 20k. for millet meal. Things are so difficult that we can hardly endure it. Also, they have promised Truda 10 dollars from there – they will send it sometime. Jasch says that I should ask you how you sent the letter to H. Barg, whether just to our address or to the other Geschwister M. and Barg. as well? Jasch had high hopes. Please do not misunderstand me, dear Geschwister. We so much want to be helped – and there is no comparison between us here and the free people at home. They can cook something else; they live much better even when that is finished. But here everything must come out of our purse. And then imagine how far we can stretch it – we are 8 souls.

Often I am so anxious and afraid. I always cook a thin soup but it is never enough. Have mercy on us and do not forget us. If you ask only for us, perhaps more will come than if there are so many. A very warm greeting to Miss Ema from us, and thank her for us for the dollar. [*Miss Ema is the sister of Margaret Clark. Margaret and her husband Charlie hired and housed the Bargen family when they arrived in Canada.*]

Am closing because I am so tired. Jasch sends hearty greetings. He lies here and cries because he cannot write.

*Liese, now twenty-one years old, knows that all the letters from her family are an endless litany of gloom, but she does not shield her readers from her own cruel conditions.*

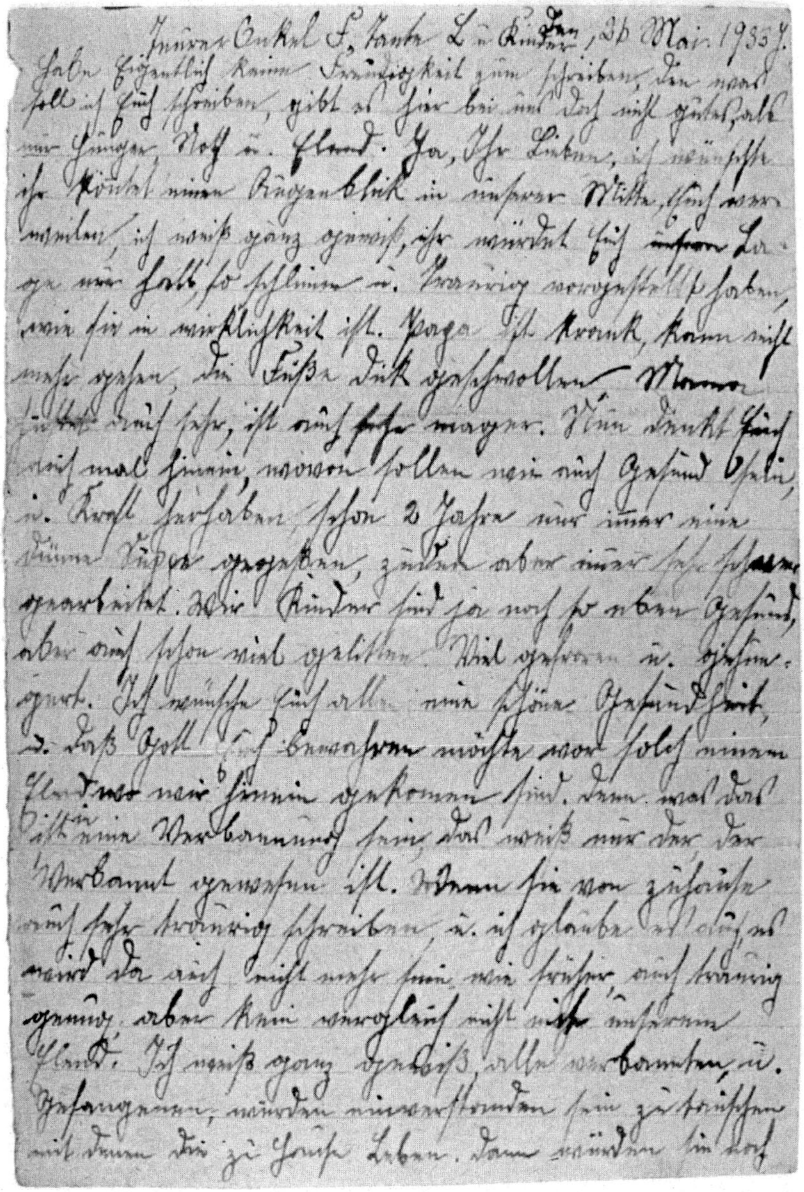
Innere Onkel F., Tante L. u. Kinder, 26 Mai 1933.
Habe eigentlich keine Freudigkeit zum schreiben, denn was
soll ich Euch schreiben, gibt es hier bei uns doch nichts als
nur Hunger, Not u. Elend. Ja, Ihr Lieben, ich wünschte
ihr könntet einen Augenblick in unserer Mitte, Euch wei-
weilen, ich weiß ganz gewiß, ihr würdet Euch unsere La-
ge nie halb so schlimm u. traurig vorgestellt haben,
wie sie in wirklichkeit ist. Papa ist krank, kann nicht
mehr gehen, die Füße dick geschwollen. Mama
leidet auch sehr, ist auch sehr mager. Nun denkt Euch
doch mal hinein, woran sollen wir auch Gesund bleiben,
u. Kraft herhaben, schon 2 Jahre nur immer eine
dünne Suppe gegessen, zudem aber immer sehr schwer
gearbeitet. Wir Kinder sind ja noch so eben Gesund,
aber auch schon viel gelitten. Viel gefroren u. gehun-
gert. Ich wünsche Euch alle eine schöne Gesundheit,
u. daß Gott Euch bewahren möchte vor solch einem
Elend wo wir hinein gekommen sind. Denn was das
ist eine Verbannung sein, das weiß nur der der
Verbannt gewesen ist. Wenn sie von zuhause
auch sehr traurig schreiben, u. ich glaube es auch, es
wird da auch nicht mehr sein wie früher, auch traurig
genug, aber kein vergleich nicht mit unserem
Elend. Ich weiß ganz gewiß, alle verbannten, u.
Gefangenen, würden einverstanden sein zu tauschen
mit denen die zu Hause leben. Dann würden sie doch

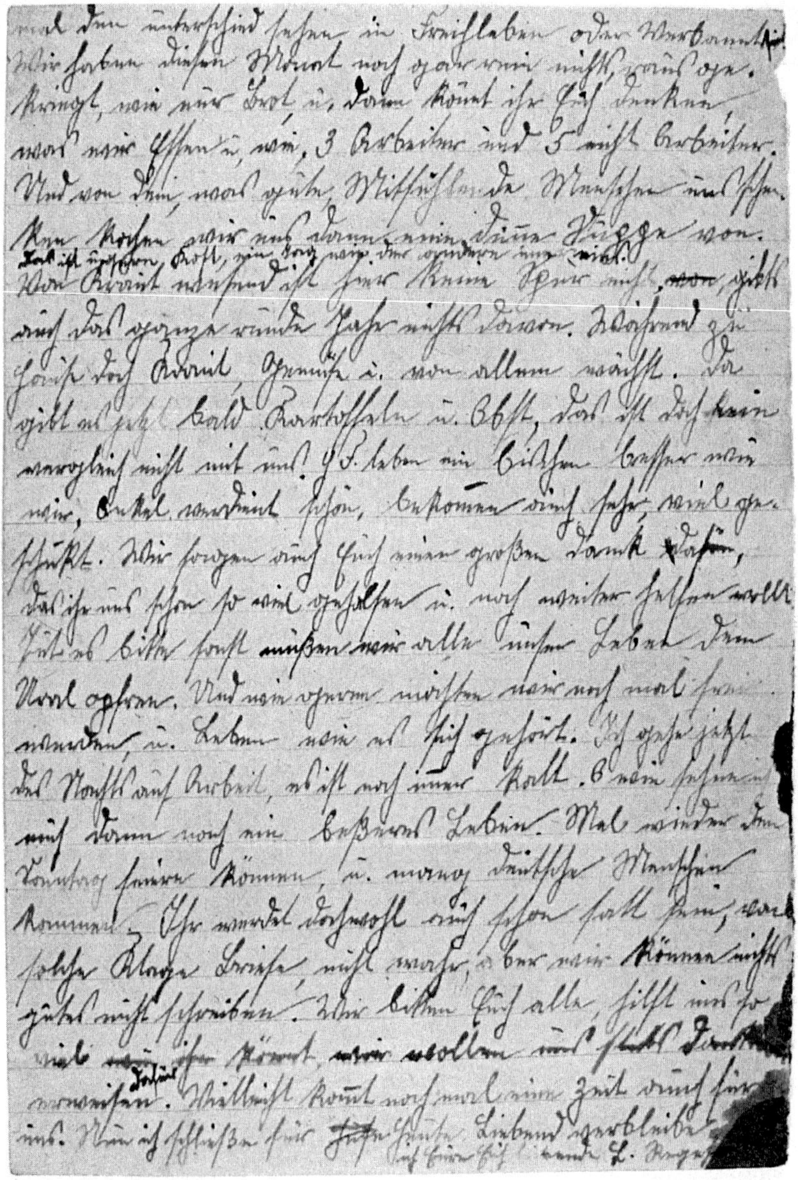

26 May 1933

Dear Uncle Franz and Aunt L. and children,
Actually, I have no joy in writing – for what shall I write to you? Here there is no good news, only hunger, distress, affliction and grief. Dear loved ones, I wish you could be in our midst for a second; I know you would have imagined our situation only half as bad as it really is. Papa is sick, he cannot walk anymore. His feet are extremely swollen. Mama coughs a great deal and is terribly skinny.

Well, just put yourselves into our situation: From where can we draw our health and our strength? For 2 years we have eaten only a thin soup but still have had to work very hard in spite of that. We children are reasonably well but have also suffered very much. We have frozen and starved.

I wish you all the best of health. May God protect you from the misery which has overtaken us. Only he who has been in exile can know what it means to be exiled. Even when they write of very depressing things from home – and I believe that they do not have as much as previously and things are depressing enough – there is no comparison with our misery here. I am absolutely certain that all exiles and prisoners would agree to trade places with those who are living at home. Then they would see the difference between living in freedom or in living exile.

This month we have received nothing except a little bread. Then you can imagine what and how we eat, 3 workers and 5 non-workers. We cook a thin soup from those things which kind and compassionate people send us. That is our diet. From one day to the next it is always the same. The year around there is no trace of cabbage or herbs, while at home they do grow cabbage, vegetables and everything. Soon they will have potatoes and fruit – that cannot be equated with our situation.

H.F. are living a bit better than we are. Mr. earns quite well and they get a lot sent to them. We also thank you that you have helped us so much and want to help us still more. Please continue to do so, or the Urals will claim our lives as a sacrifice. Oh, how gladly we would like to be free again and live as one should live.

I go to work at night now. It is still always cold. Oh, how I then long for a better life – to celebrate the Sabbath once again, and to be among German [*Mennonite*] people again. You will probably be fed up with these letters of complaint, right? But we can write about nothing good. We ask you all, please help us as much as you can, we always want to express our thankfulness. Maybe a time is coming for us yet. Well, I will close for now.

In love I remain your loving L. Regehr

*Pain and weakness consume Jasch, and every word he writes requires immense effort. Can we imagine being without bread for six days? He pleads for anyone to help.*

Polowinka, 6 June 1933

Dear Geschwister Bargens,
I will gather all my strength and visit you once more. I have already been bedridden for the second week. I cannot walk anymore, my feet are all crooked and I have great pains in them. The reason, of course, is lack of nourishing food. Today, for the 6th day, we are without even a small piece of bread. There is no flour. The end result, dear siblings, will be that we and our family will die of starvation if no more help comes.

In the past months we have received nothing. What is the reason, dear siblings? If you send us something send an order to Kizel, it helps us a lot. When one is ill, one needs nourishing food. Save my very weak life, dear siblings. Write to Regehrs. Let Crebel know, and then send us what is gathered. Received your [...], dear siblings. You write of great hopes, but how? Do not forget us, your thankful Jakob.

Will they then be humbled? Oh, how our heart yearns for release. You cannot imagine how we have suffered – and our family also. The children work very hard. I just do not know what I can write to you. The nerves are so taut that they have snapped. We have been without bread for 6 days now. This has already happened several times. Well, we will try to have courage, as it pleases God. Send us more addresses. Write us more of Rome [*an allusion to the centre of political power, wherever it may be*].

*Five days later, Maria carefully measures their portion of food received in packages. Although the soup is still thin, the package saves them from starvation. Mail delivery is now more efficient and letters "go quite well lately." Is this a sign that their situation might improve, that they might be set free? Despite the ache in her heart and belly, Maria is grateful. Her children and husband are still with her.*

Polowinka, June 11, 1933

Dearly beloved Geschwister Franz and Liese and children,
Today is Sunday, the day that God himself set aside at creation and on which He commanded all people to rest from their labours. All the peoples kept this command, and we were also allowed to keep it holy – until we were disenfranchised and resettled. I can clearly remember when I gave my testimonial in church and that rule was read to us. We were told never to break this commandment and, if possible, to attend church services where the Word of God was preached and where we could sing songs of praise to honor God! How happy we were – and today we are not allowed to celebrate Sunday. We have to work as usual.

Dear siblings, believe me – we often do not even know when it is Sunday! It is a disgrace to confide this to you, but it is a fact. No one has calendars here, and you must work every day alike. Often when there are things in the store, we also go to buy. The R. [*governing authority*] is like that, if they can regularly arrange for buying on Sunday, they do! What do you think, dear Geschwister F. and Liese, will God mark it down as our sin? [*Sunday was a day of rest and a sacred ritual for these practicing Mennonites.*] How will we ever stand before God? We have so often spoken of this. But grace will be greater than our sin! We will be saved only by grace!

I cannot put into words the deep desire we often have to go to the House of the Lord with other children of God, and be joyous. I often think of past times, how nice things were – we could live as humans, eat and clothes ourselves – and where have we ended up? Alas! I would like to weep and weep! When will the hour of our deliverance strike? Or will we have to perish here? We would so like to be free again, and be able to eat our fill. That is our daily, heartfelt plea to God. If we must continue to live here, our time here may not be very long. God knows!

Yesterday we received 3 letters, one from sister Truta, one from Isaac Wiebes and one from you. It is always such a joy to read letters. And the nicest part is if we read you are well and have your daily bread. We received a very nice letter from Wiebes. They both wrote. The dear sister writes so comfortingly. She wrote that they had sent 3 dollars to the Board and had really begged the Board to increase that amount. They think that the Board would do so. When it arrives, we will immediately write a thank-you letter to them. Now we wait to see if they have succeeded.

Dear Liese, you have written us such a letter of hope that we are greatly encouraged. If only it would really be true that our exile would finally end. We firmly believe that if the foreign countries only knew what is happening here, and that it is exactly those Schaedlinge [*those convicted of harming the motherland*] who are foreign nationals who are perishing – those whom the home countries are trying to save – they would finally and vigorously intervene! After all, Russia is so poor that it could not really resist such intervention.

Your letters in the last few months have all been received. Also the one with a picture of your farm. Write often and do not fear. The letters go quite well lately. How happy we would be if ever we could escape this exile. You know, happier than you were when you separated with P.B. P.B. always wants the honour even if he does nothing to deserve it. You have already sent so much to N. 9, and then to be unthankful! How can that possibly be? But the proverb is true: "Thanklessness is the coin of the world."

I am quite convinced that no one from home would change places with us. They would say, "Rather get no parcels than to be resettled." Imagine, they have already grown things in gardens – green beans, vegetables, potatoes – and then that lovely fruit. And here there is nothing – only forest, and more forest. Can you even compare their place with ours?The future looms so dark. Our family is large, our earnings get ever smaller and are not sufficient to buy products. Jasch is sick and has been bedridden for 3 months. The doctor says his sickness can only be cured by better nourishment. And where can I get that? Imagine, dear siblings, I go to the package twice a day and always measure carefully with a cup, and it is soon all gone – and so fast. We do not even permit ourselves to cook a solid substantial soup, always only a thin soup.

*How will the Regehr family cope? Will Jasch receive food in time to survive? Will the children survive? In the summer of 1933, the"Holodomor"(enforced famine) is still wreaking havoc throughout Ukraine and Russia. In Canada, the Great Depression is in its peak with twenty-seven percent unemployment, and the Prairie provinces, with their dependence on wheat, are suffering greatly. Franz and Liese Bargen now own a small farm in Canada with increasing financial obligations. Yet somehow they find ways to save money and to send letters and parcels to the prison camp in Russia. But are these poor Canadian farmers the only people who can help? Where are the voices of those in political power? Where are the dominant nations? And where is "Rome"?*

# Chapter Three

## The World is Silent
## 1933 - 34

Jasch becomes aware that America is making a business deal with Russia. Could America be the new Rome? Could this nation rescue them? Chaos and contradictions are everywhere. Crops are abundant in the countryside, yet Jasch sees "hundreds of thousands perishing." He and his family struggle to stay warm, but Jasch sees piles of coal near the prison camp.

In this land where "tears are our food day and night," winter leaves late and arrives early. Even in June, the forests and rivers are cold. In surprising eloquence and despite his weakening state, Jasch describes his family's ongoing saga both to readers in his former home village of Altonau and to multiple readers in the forbidden West. Armed guards stand outside his barrack door, and dogs hover around the perimeter. His children mine coal and build railway lines to transport products to "America."

Bread remains scarce, and promised quotas are delayed. When bread is distributed, it is wet and heavy. During times of bread shortages, camp kitchen workers soaked bread rations in water to fulfill the allotted weight (usually 700 grams).[1]

## Will We Ever be Free?

Polowinka, June 26, 1933

Dear Geschwister Franz, Liese and children Bargens,
Today I remember the days gone by. Where are they? As a smoke or a vapor, they have gone. Yes, dear siblings, in those days we could often get together whenever we wanted to, and where we wanted to. And today – where are we today? In this hellish exile where we and our children must suffer so much! Our tears are our food both day and night, and our sap dries up as a plant dries up in the summer heat. Will we ever again have good days?

The future looks ever darker. Every night there is a watchman at our door. We are not allowed to take one step in freedom. The workload is being doubled. Peter goes to work at 6 A.M. and comes back at 6 P.M. Then he must go for another 3 hours to work at the Cyddomen [*a place of additional work*]. But wages have been reduced. It is not possible to describe how the children are tormented. Liese has to work in the mines; she must work every night. They have sent Miechi 10 miles away from us, and she must remain there day and night. She has it hard there; she must work on the railway line – day and night.

There is a great deal of work being done. Much coal is lying around here, millions [...], as it appears in the articles. Then America and Russia make a business deal. Too bad they do not bankrupt that devil, then this misery would finally be brought to an end. We are astounded that the whole world keeps silent while hundreds of thousands of people perish. This is not during a crop failure but during a time of excellent crops.

Yesterday our Tina went to [...] to the bazaar, that is 15 km away to buy something to eat. However, she got nothing. She cried when she got home. We have not received any bread for a couple of days. But when we do get some, it is always so wet and heavy that the little piece we receive is extremely small. When will we be able to eat our own bread? Or when will we stop begging? I could cry, cry bitterly, when I think of the future and that we must live on alms – alms, dear siblings.

Every worm squirms before it dies; how much more a person who has been created for life. Every day we must think,"What will we eat? With what will we clothe ourselves?"There is no possibility to get clothes or shoes here. And even to fix old shoes here costs up to 10 rubles, and then they only last a few days. Our little Jascha is standing and crying and begging his mother for a piece of bread. And the dear mother cannot give him any, since we do not have even a biscuit in our house. This is very hard for the dear mother. He finally falls asleep. Especially the children must suffer.

We received your letters of June 2 and June 4. Thank you. Your landlords have heard, am I right? Oh, it touches me that people who do not know us think of us. We received a parcel, but whether it is from them we do not know since there are no names included. We are so sorry that we do not even know whom to thank. I would write them a thank-you letter. Will you please thank them for us? If only the petition that America is submitting to Germany would help us! Marie believes it will not work without names. But God can even make it work in such ways. Oh, how eager we would be to go that way and live free once again – if only we could satisfy our hunger. In our house a Jak. Nietstein is dying of hunger and we cannot help him – we have to silently watch! With my health it is somewhat better. Dear siblings, we plead, Send help or we perish! We get very little food! Well, whatever comes, as it pleases God!

Your brother Jakob

*As Maria thinks of her sister-in-law in Canada performing simple domestic chores, she is filled with pleasant thoughts. Cleaning a house would be heavenly for Maria, but she has little time to spend in the barrack quarters. Industrial work consumes her days and nights now, especially since her husband can no longer work and earn his bread ration. However, the petty concerns of life also invade this dark place. Rumours and innuendo from the home village travel with the letters. A woman has apparently been accused of committing an improper act. Several letters have referred to an incident, but Maria takes the moral high road. She knows that "words can be poison."*

[1933]

Dear Liese,
You write how busy you were cleaning your home on Saturday. How you must enjoy it! You also mention how busy our dear Franz is with the farm. We are happy that he took time to write to us, and tries to encourage us! It certainly is necessary. We are often in such a dilemma. The future is so dark for us, we wonder what will finally happen. If only the Ausland [*foreign land*] would quickly intervene so that we could have a future. We would so much like to leave here.

Here Nietstein [*a fellow prisoner*] is starved – lies in bed, does not know anything anymore, completely dumb. They had tied him down securely on the bunk, and in this state he calls out and screams, groans, moans, laughs and makes a [...]. It is hard to listen to. One almost becomes a nervous wreck oneself. Here misery is everywhere, and the doctors do not concern themselves. Today the Kommandant was here, observed the scene, and wrote out a paper that the doctor should admit him to the hospital because things could not go on like this. Now, we will see what the doctor will do.

Oh, how longingly we look for deliverance. We would be happier than you were when P.B. moved away from you. Lately we have received all your letters, except the one sent to Lena and the one in which you wrote about Susie. How could something like that be possible? Who could have done that? Mrs. Woelk did not – she has a completely different handwriting. We had a letter from her, but absolutely no similarity to this one. Susie looked after Hans and loved him with all her heart. No neighbor's wife wrote that letter either! [...] we refuse to send that letter there. That is the better way, since the misery is already great enough. That is only envy, dear Geschwister, just as you say.

We got a letter from Mariechen with exactly the same information. I could send them to you but I do not want to yet. The proverb is true when it says: Words can be poison. It hurts me so much! But promise me, dear Liese, for God's sake keep silent about this. Do not write one word of this to N. 9! I just do not want them to know anything of this, or that I have even written to you of this. If we ever come to see you, then you shall read!

Anna wrote that Lusa came to her and begged for a piece of bread. Ab. is serving in X. and sends bread home, otherwise they would not have any either. How much we would have to talk about. Please do not let anyone guess about this affair. After all, you are my Jonathan [*a reference to the loyalty of two legendary friends in the Old Testament, David and Jonathan*].

*Jasch now has long empty days to think, reflect, and write letters. A petition has been circulating. He wants his name added, but he is afraid. During his days alone in the barrack, Jasch attempts to gather firewood and help Maria make breakfast, but he is increasingly disabled. In the next four letters, he describes their daily routines and reports on the state of parcels and letters.*

*A common practice among Canadian Mennonites was to send letters from Russia to the national church papers such as Rundshau, Bundesbote, and Der Bote. Readers were eager to maintain connections with their scattered families and friends. Tina's letter with her sketch of the smelter has evidently been published. A generous donor has responded.*

[Early 1933]

[....] Since Wiebes had asked and you enclosed something also, the Board will have sent it altogether. Write to us if what you had ordered was sent as a parcel or as money. When you ask for us, tell them that money goes further and the Torgsin is close by. We can get things personally – and we don't lose half of it to pay the shipping costs. I can also tell you, dear Geschwister, that the card we enclosed in the letter has been received, and the Uzbenyerric [*postal notice*] is already here – it is already in Kizel. When we received the card, we did not know from whom it was. Jasch always said it is from no one else than Pet. Dueck N. 3, for he had written to him. Otherwise he knew of no one, and it could not be from a stranger.

However, it seems to have turned out differently and it seems you, dear Geschwister, are again our saviours. It humbles us into the dust. May our God reward you, for we cannot. When the packages came from Germany, the name was often on the paper. Now, however, the names are sometimes on the cards. Most times, however, the cards arrive in the Torgsin without indicating the name of the sender. Also, the Torgsin did not know who the sender was, so that we could not thank anyone. Now it almost happened like that again. We almost thanked Peter Dueck. Maybe that would not have been a mistake either, for then he might have also sent a 5-dollar note. Or do you think not?

Where are B. Klassens? We do not get any news from them. It seems so uncaring – she is our sister and we get so much from you, Liese. Then again, Tina does not write at all. We have not received anything from J. Martens. Who said that they had sent us anything? Give them a hearty greeting from us. Perhaps they would send my dear sick Jasch something with which to buy confections in the Torgsin. He has such a great hunger for it. If they could just see him lying there, I do not doubt they would have compassion and definitely send something.

I wonder if Pet. D and Pet. Penners received our letter. Have you heard? Our Tina got a letter from Maria Siebert to whom you once sent a parcel. She also sent a picture of her and a Mariechen Wiebe. She wrote that she had seen Tina's letter which she had written to her cousin Lieschen B. in the church paper, the Bundesbote. She had felt such compassion but also thought that she had read many such letters and she could not help everyone. However, she could not shake the letter which she had read in the paper and so she finally had to send something. She wrote that they had already given much, but they never had relatives or friends to whom they could give a personal gift. She had never expected to get any acknowledgement, and now she got a letter from Tina. She was so touched that she wrote a long 2 ½ sheet letter back. She wrote all about her heritage. She is a 40-year-old lady. She washes clothes in a hospital, in fact has done so for 10 years. We will send you her address.

I did not fill my letter yesterday so I will finish it today. Today it is Sunday, and raining again as it has during the week. The children are all at work. Tina and Lena walked to Polowinka; we hear that there may be stockings there. We need them so desperately and they are so hard to get. They are available at the bazaar but cost over 5r. a pair. Jasch is in bed and often says, "I would love to see my sister once more. I no longer have Papa and Hans." He cries so often that he must be so ill. Compare that to H.F., who works all the time and is never sick as if he is made of iron.

Yes, people pass through this world differently; not everyone needs to be thrust into the Schmelzofen [furnace] of suffering and tribulation. "Teach us to hold still, dear God, for it is so hard." Pray for us that we do not despair, even if our way is through the Jordan of death. Your Geschwister who love you and will never forget you,

Jasch, Marie and children

[July 1933]

It is too bad that the dollar is continually falling. Now it is worth 1.28r. and before 1.33 – and in spring it was 1.96. That helped so much in getting products more cheaply. Then the millet grain cost 12r. per kilo, today it costs 23r. How can this be happening? How can the Russian ruble be rising so much? It is so sad for those of us who get help from our friends. We have not had news from home for a long time. They wrote that the harvest is good. People are being mobilized in the regions and ordered to go threshing. At certain places entire Russian villages have been starved out. Your brother Wilhelm has died of hunger and typhus. The time is 8 P.M. My little wife is not here.

Will close. J.R.

*Jasch continues to try to "do my share," but even writing is becoming difficult. Love and concern motivate him. Some of daughter Liese's experiences are horrific. Her anguished father describes her struggle in the mud, dogs forcing her further and guards molesting her: "That is our picture ... and the world is silent."*

Polowinka, July 22, 1933

Dearly beloved Geschwister Liese, Franz, and children,
Soon the clock will strike 12. Oh, why must I have such a miserable existence? I cannot walk. I wanted to do my share and carry some wood, since I was home alone. But I just could not. I fell down 3 times. The second time I fell it was on the stairs at a sharp corner. I hurt my left side. It is really painful. The kidneys with which I have been suffering for a long time entitle me to 1 kilo of sour black bread per day. That has to be enough for me!

We never imagined how long we would have to endure this "Paradise." Millions and millions of people are sacrificed in a weaponless and peaceful way. As one observes what is happening here, one can only cry. My dear Maria has been ordered to cut 250 sq. meters of hay with a scythe, and if she fails to do this they take away her bread ration card. She has never had a scythe in her hands before, and now in her older, starved, years she has to cope with this. And this they do to us. Maybe many will die in the forest. To live in exile, dear loved ones, is just indescribable. How hard it is! We are chased and yanked to and fro, and one is never asked, Can you or not? Never – only "Ckopeu!" [*scurry! hasten!*] And so my dear Maria takes a bite of bread and a gulp of Pripps and goes to work scything hay. When she gets there, her quota is no longer 250 sq. m. but has been raised to 500 sq. m.! Such corrupt pigs!

It gets more tragic from day to day! But the hardest is that we have to see how they are destroying our dear children. Liese was a proud young girl, with some education. In 5 months they had practically killed her. Poor children. In the spring during the high water time they were forced to walk the muddiest streets of the village. Mud up to the belly. Then they got stuck in the mud. Liese was almost dead already, since she had received only 200 grams of bread up to this time. Then they released several dogs which got her on the move again. Then the guard, or I should say the murderer without a gun, chased her – and when she got here we were not allowed to defend or help her. Then add to that the horrible typhus. She was not given a bread-ration card. So we had to feed her from our extremely meagre supply. She was far from being well when she was ordered back to work in the mines. There she, as a young girl, suffered too much.

Oh, those murderers, look what has happened to our Peter! He is all stooped, has a bad leg which is all crooked. Yesterday he visited the doctor who chased him back to work. And so we see it every day. My nerves are so weak I can hardly hold the pen to write. May you excuse my writing. I do not write because it gives me pleasure. I write because of pure love for you. If only we could sing songs of jubilation instead of writing letters of lamentation.

We received a letter from Lena yesterday. She is in Perm and boarded in a kindergarten. She wrote, "I am here 2 days and get 4 meals a day so that I have enough to eat." That poor child, she is so anemic and pale – she is so lonesome for us – but all the food she gets there induces her to stay. Tina must hoe potato fields 10 miles away from here. Yesterday she came home to get 1 cup of Gruetze [millet], and with a heavy heart she went back. She is a good worker but her health has suffered from her forced labour. Michi still works at her old place. She is also tired of this slavery. She actually wanted to come home today but has not arrived yet. The time is already 6 o'clock, maybe she will come tomorrow.

My dear Marie still is not home – has been gone since early morning. How is that petition coming? Will they be able to help? Oh, how gladly we would like to be delivered before we perish. Now I alone of all the Ubak [*"average Joes"*] am the worst off in health. Today I wanted to dare and carry in a bit of wood – I fell backwards, as big as I am, and there was no person anywhere to help me. Then I roused myself and wanted to go into the house. I was able to get upon my feet but then I again fell down sharply on the barrack steps, and I believe I have knocked some kidney stones loose.

Let me say it a second time so that you can understand how we are brutalized and murdered daily. We should still be considered human beings, and that is why it amazes us that no one intervenes for us! Shall all the noble sons and daughters of our Reich be murdered? No one asks, "What do you need, you German [*Mennonite*] brothers?" Oh, then we would have to say, Freiheit [*freedom*]. We are being bound like a lion in a cage, and they give him only enough so that he can stand up and be led where they will. That is our picture. It has never happened before, and today the world is silent even if it sees thousands and millions dying. Fewer of the Germans are dying since they have received much help from America. May God reward you, for without your help we would no longer be here!

But this constant begging also pains us. God's Word is true: It is more blessed to give than to receive. We have had the experience; my dear little wife has given away much. One evening she had invited poor people over. She led them to the cow pen. Then she said, "You can take the best cow, it now belongs to you." I wanted to reason with her, but the deed was done. I have often cried about that. But I also have loaned over one thousand pud wheat to others like them – to those who cannot repay. Why do Peter Bargens not write to us at all? How we helped him during the famine [*the famine in the early 1920s*]! Where are they today when they have the opportunity to help us? It pains us very much. I would never have thought that they would respond like this. Mrs. Wiens' 4 dollars cannot be traced either. Remember our tribulation. Maybe the Lord will come soon.[2] The letter with the 10 dollars – not yet. If it comes, then we shall eat.

August 19, 1933

Dearly beloved Geschwister Franz and Liese and children,
Wishing you God's richest blessing in all your ways. At your place there will probably be harvest time, right? And how did it turn out? Dear Geschwister, your harvest becomes our life. We wish you the best of health in body and soul. Everyone here is well and alive, except for me. I am so unwell that I cannot even walk. I am so weak I can hardly write a letter. But my love for you is driving me to send you another token of my love.

Oh, how hard it is for me to think that I must die in exile. Then I think of my dear family, and especially of my little Jascha. Oh, how has that boy grown into my heart – of course he is still so small. Oh, how I would want him always to walk in God's ways. Yesterday our Lena came home from Perm from her Verein [*society or union*]. She had been there for 32 days and she had enjoyed it. They provided meals for them 4 times a day. She got 600 gr. bread, also porridge and soup. But too bad they cut her hair off with a machine. She had nice hair. Two of the children were drowned. They had to bathe often and then lie in the sun 11 minutes. Each morning when they got up they had to perform gymnastics. In the evening before they went to sleep, the supervisors asked them if there were any among them who prayed. Everywhere they agitate against God. Our little Lena told us she had prayed every evening underneath the blanket.

What do you hear of the petition? Report to us about everything. A few days ago a Komsomol came into our house and recorded us all as foreigners who had immigrated from somewhere [...]. Only H.F. protested against this. He said, "I am a Russian citizen." Now you do not hear anymore of this. We wanted to believe that maybe Grandfather [*code for a political leader, possibly from Germany*] was demanding his children be returned home. We are ready to go.

You loved ones just cannot imagine what a hard life we lead here. Grey is my head since my incarceration. In the month of August it has rained here every day. Then the children come home wet, and also all other workers. Then they change clothes and get dry ones.

Then the air inside gets so foul that it is hard to breathe. Our house is 6 metres wide and 8 metres long, and 22 people live in it. Then you can imagine how we live. Will there be deliverance for us? Are people working on helping us?

Peter still works on the railroad tracks; he has to parallel the rails after the water has damaged the bed. He works from 5 A.M. to 6 P.M. He must go to work every day. Liese still works at her old place, but she only has to work 8 hours a day. Miechi told us she had seen Truda Loewen in a punishment cell. They live about 100 km away from here and provide for themselves mainly by begging. A few days ago little Susie was here for 3 days and told us that Truda is a servant for some Jews. Now they eat. Now she is here. The little one told us that she begged for 14 days and had walked 25 km to the station. [...]. She is so happy with our Lena.

If the weather turns nice, my dear Marie will go to Kizel. We still have a little left from your dollar. I regret very much that we cannot get any more pork to eat. We buy only flour and Gruetze with money. Will your thanksgiving celebrations remember us too? Will something be left for Russia? Oh, if only the time was here that we could write letters of jubilation! I guess we will not live to see that day. No, such times can come only if it is the right way of the Lord – as our dear departed Papa used to say. So this must really be our way. Yes, pray that our adversity may not cause us to despair.

The winter is coming – few clothes and no footwear. The winter approaches with its horrors. Many will again despair and perish. We have not had a letter from home for a long time.

The harvest is supposed to be very good – up to 25 pud barley per dessiatine, but they cannot harvest it with machines because the rye and wheat break and shed so much. The grains that are threshed are immediately hauled away. Again, very little will stay for the workers. At places large Russian villages have completely died out from starvation. We just do not know where our dear Mama is now located. She has a very hard life. My dear Marie is making our evening nourishment. She has a very hard lot, from early morning until late at night. She must get up at 5 A.M. and cook breakfast for

Peter, then Liese goes to work at night, and she must always get up and prepare food for them. Yes, the days are indescribably hard.

It is especially hard that we are not allowed church services – and no Sundays. The poor children forget everything in time. For almost 3 years they have not heard the Word of God. I must close – my hand is so shaky – you'll have to be satisfied with this. My nerves are in a very bad state. [....] Please write if there is something happening [...]. Oh, how we wait for deliverance! [....]

The clock is 7 and Peter is still at work [...]. In our mine we pay [...] and [...] 36 hundred are to arrive here [...].

[August 1933]

Dearly beloved Geschwister Franz, Liese, and children,
May the almighty God be with you and give you what you need. We are so happy to read that you are all well again. Also that God has kept the devastating grasshoppers from your fields. We hope you will be able to harvest your crops without any more bad luck. How terrible that grasshoppers have ruined so many crops there and that that terrible drought is burning up the grain.

We always pray that the people overseas may not get tired of helping the helpless ones here in Russia. However, it may be as you write, dear Liese, when human efforts have come to an end, then maybe God will step in with divine help. Then things will move much more quickly; I am sure that then it will be done the best way. The great God has known how to care for us so marvelously until now, has provided for us through your gifts and those of other people. He will reward you richly even here – and how much more in eternity. And how wonderful it will be when you hear the words as given in Matthew 25:34-40. Your reward will surely come over there!

I thank you, dear Liese, for those very comforting verses that you enclosed in your letter of July 19th, and which we received on August 19th. Through the night to the light! Through the cross to a crown! Through suffering to glory! That is the way of Christians here in this world. However, it seems so difficult, and our desires are to live in good days. But it is so comforting to know that these momentary afflictions are not worth the eternal weight of glory that awaits us. It is true, over there all our suffering will be at an end.

There is no change with my dear Jasch. He is very weak. He often says he will probably not see our homeland again. Dear siblings, it is so extremely difficult to be sick here that I cannot even begin tell you of how great a trial it is. We would love to lean on your sympathetic shoulders and weep and weep until we could cry no more. And in spirit we often do so. If we had no Saviour, how unbearably sad it would then be. Where, oh where, could we go with our deep distress? Whom could we tell?

Today it is Sunday, a very rainy day, dreary enough to make one despair. Jasch is sick. Michi had to leave yesterday in pouring rain and walk 7 Werst. By the time she got there, she was soaked through and through. Peter had to leave early in the morning and go to work in all that rain. Liese came home this morning all soaking wet – she had worked all night. She is sleeping now but she was frozen. Peter just came back again and put on another jacket underneath – he was also freezing. Just imagine working at the railway tracks all day in that freezing rain. It has been raining here for over a week and is very cold, very much like it used to be in autumn when we stooked corn sheaves. I am still hoping for a few nice days, but we are in the high north and it may well stay cold until winter comes?!

You will probably be happily in church today. I am sure that many prayers will rise to God's throne on our behalf. Those prayers nourish us, and carry us, and sustain us, so that we do not despair. Dear siblings, how great is our desire and longing to be together with other children of God and together partake of Holy Communion. May God grant it to us again in this life.

[Fall 1933]

Dear Brother-in-Law,
Please send the petition to Germany in my name and on my address. How it will turn out we'll see, but it should all go through you because I am afraid to do it from here. If God has shown us the way, He will also help. Keep these things to yourself. If you could only direct us to Hoellig and send us his address. He was from Saxony. I believe you will be able to gather more for us at your place. I wrote to Peter's nephew in the belief he would send it to us through you.

My dear sister, how is it you do not write anymore. Are you tired of us? Are you sick? Please report lots of news to us. We cannot write decent letters any more, only letters that beg! But it is true, dear sister, I speak to you openly. If a nice parcel is now opened and mother must cook 2 meals a day for 8 people, then it empties fast – right? My dear Marie deals very frugally with what we receive! There is no day in which we can we satisfy our hunger. Little Jascha and Lena, as soon as they have finished eating, ask for some more. But everything is rationed here.

Dear Liese, do not leave Jak. Janzen in peace. If my legs do not carry me, it is from the lack of nourishment. To be completely without fat or pork may be possible for a young person, but for an old weak person it becomes too hard. Pray and help us carry our load. If only we had a bit of [...] it might be easier. Well, dear siblings, I have shown you my heart. Do what you want. I close. My Marie is making noodles.

8 September 1933

Dear Geschwister Franz, Liese, and children!
May the God of peace give you the best of health, your daily bread, and spare your land from this terrible Communism which has broken out in our land and is now in full tempo. And no one seems to be able to tell them: "Thus far and no farther!" But the time will

come when God will judge these Communists! They have thousands of deaths on their conscience.

Dear Geschwister, I just do not know what I should write to you today. In fact I did not want to write today, because I cannot possibly put my inner mood on paper. My heart wants to break to see my dear Jasch lying here – and our living quarters packed with so many people; and then the Fusslumpen [*foot rags*] and clothes lying around and drying generate such foul air in the room. It rained every day in the month of August, and again in September. We thought it would be nice in September because it is surely too early to become winter now. But to all appearances we have had our nice days.

We do not wish to think of winter. We had a small hope that by winter we would be free. How often you sent us such nice clippings from the newspapers that really bolstered our spirits, gave us fresh courage, and allowed us to discuss and comfort one another: Just a little longer, and then we will be free! But again disappointment! All our hopes again shattered! We stay right where we are, and no one seems to care or be concerned about us poor, miserable, and unfortunate ones. How earnestly have we already cried to God – and no response! Is it really God's will that thousands die of starvation or are tortured to death? No, that I do not believe! But our great God does permit it, and we are to be drawn nearer to our Saviour who sacrificed and accomplished everything for us.

Often we cannot understand why my dear Jasch has to be so sick and suffer so much. Oh, it is so incomprehensible, so difficult! I did not want to write today but he does not leave me in peace. For several days now he has urged me: Write a letter to F. B. while I am still alive. His hope is to go home to his Saviour soon, where he will see that which he has believed. If you could only see how pitifully he lies there! Perhaps it is just as well that you cannot see how those you love must so mercilessly perish here. My dear Jasch has been in bed since 10 March – 180 days – very hard days. I just cannot describe them to you, but I will tell you about them if God should ever allow us to meet again in this life.

On September 1st I went to do my washing; it was Liese's day off and she stayed with him. Then he had to do his business [*euphemism for using the toilet*], so Liese helped him up until he was seated on the pail. At that time he could still sit alone. Liese went to get a drink of Pripps and when she got back he was lying on the floor. When I got home, she told me what had happened. On September 2nd he told me he was very ill and felt so very tired and exhausted. Then until noon he was completely confused, had a little to eat and fell asleep. When he awoke, he talked of how confused he had been but he knew just what he had said. I was so afraid that it would again happen as it had once before at the whetstone! But thank God he has remained quite clear and lucid until today.

He is just waiting for the hour when he can leave this old world! Oh, how I weep for him; he has not slept for 4 nights – says that sleep has been taken away from him. He has often said to me: "Pray that I may sleep." It is so sad – he is so helpless, his body without strength. He falls backwards or sideways or forwards, and barely endures sitting up until his bed is made. He must be completely cared for as a helpless child. Often he cannot even control his bowels; then he cries and says it is such a humiliation to him. He knows full well what is happening but can do nothing about it. On the night of Aug. 19 he woke me and told me what had happened to him during the night. He had been so depressed that he had asked his Saviour for his passport to heaven. Then he received the answer: Isaiah 54:10 [*"Though the mountains be shaken and the hills be removed, yet my unfailing love for you will not be shaken and my covenant of peace will not be removed."*] He asked me if that was sufficient, I said yes – absolutely.

He said that he would die on September 24! That I did not want to hear, for what would I do alone with 6 children here in exile? The future lies before us dark and foreboding. I always said if only we could get across the border, even though he was already very sick – if only he could experience it! Then, in the care of good doctors in a proper hospital and with a nourishing diet, he could again regain his health. But there is just no possibility of escape from here. We will have to perish here, and no man is concerned about us. But we have a God who keeps a watchful eye on those who are His and does not abandon us even in our darkest hours. Psalm 73 has often been such a comfort to us, especially verse 23: "Yet I am always with you; you hold me by my right hand." Yes, I find so many words of comfort and encouragement in the precious Bible.

I really thought that there would be a letter from you or from home at the post office today – but nothing. Jasch is impatiently waiting; he still wants to hear one letter from you all. In the previous letter he still wrote to you and to home. He could hardly do it but it was a sign of love to you, dear siblings, whom he loves so very much!

On Aug. 20 we mailed a letter to you, and I think another one later but I did not write it down. Formerly Jasch used to write those things down – when letters were received and when answered. Nothing further is written down. Since Aug. 11, no letter from you. We have received very few letters in the last month. We have just finished our noon meal. We had rice. Yesterday Tina went to work after school, cutting oats with a scythe. She earned herself one-half litre of milk. The previous day she had also earned herself one-half litre of milk. Today we took the milk all at once and were able to cook a nice rice soup. Ach, how nice that milk tastes, much nicer than it did when we had rice with whole milk at home.

The oats is all green and very sparse and certainly will give no seed. In fact it will not be threshed. We already had frost in July. Only potatoes grow here and they are quite good ones. The forest is still being cleared here and the sod turned by spade in preparation for seeding rye. This is all being done after a day's work with the Cydomenki [*free labour pool*]. Those poor people are almost tortured to death for that one small piece of bread. At first it cost 15k. per kilo, but now it costs 1r. 25k., and that is the way it will stay. And then there must be a Cepabku from the Commune certifying that he has been on the Cydom, or it gives no bread. And so those poor people are tortured every day.

Our children are still working at their former jobs. Mariechen hopes that she can come home on the 15th of this month. She often feels like she has been orphaned. Jasch says that only little Jascha still keeps him alive, for when he sees him he cannot allow himself to die. He says he would be happy if he and little Jascha would be allowed to die together. Dear Liese and Frank, how much we would [...]. H.F. went to Kizel today to get something from the Torgsin. They send their greetings. He is still reasonably well, can dig as hard as he likes and often works 2 shifts a day. How fortunate that he is well and is able to work.

M.R.

[1933]

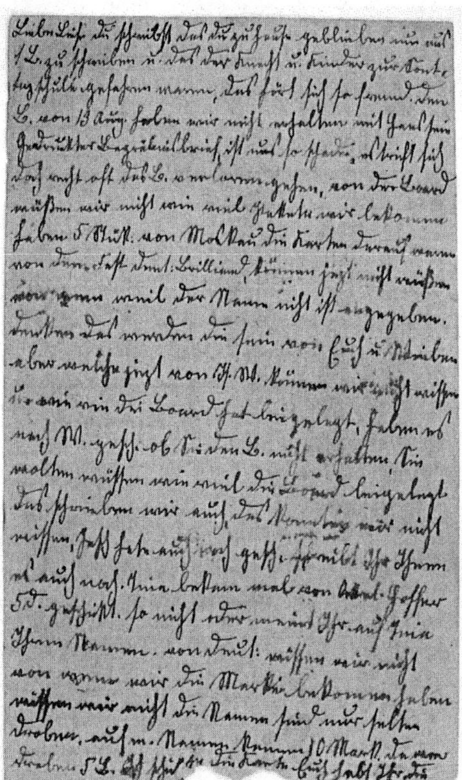

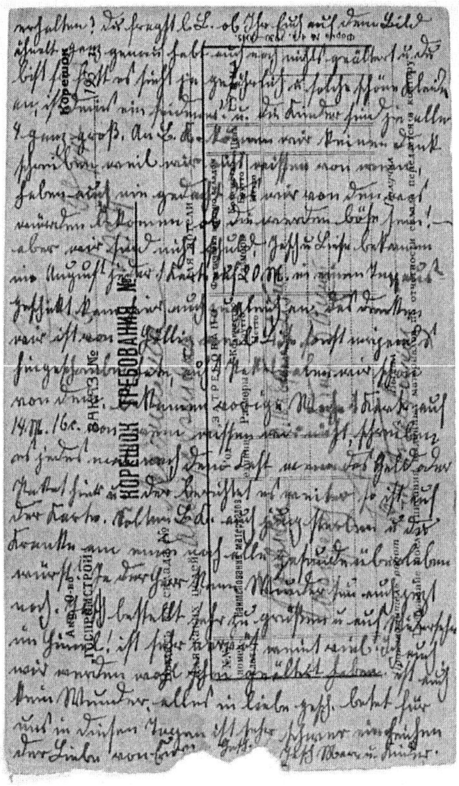

Sept. 14
Precious Geschwister Franz, Liese, and children,
May the great God who can do everything, comfort and strengthen your hearts and give joy to your soul. I report to you that on September 12th we received the letter you wrote on August 20th. We also received one from home from Hans Kruger, written on August 27th – it went only 7 days faster than yours and the way to America is more than twice as far. Yesterday I wrote to Mariechi, and today I write to you, loved ones. I already had written a letter previously so I just did not know what to write. Today it is not much different, except that we received a letter from you. I really was only going to write cards because I and Liese both wrote on September 11th. But you had included writing paper so we could write back.

Yes, we are all well except that our dear Jasch is sick. These will probably be his last days. I only sit at his bed. He cannot even sit alone – cannot button his pants. He just has no strength to keep his head erect while he is eating. If I do not hold him, his head drops down to his plate. It is so that I can't even describe it, dear siblings. But those living in these barracks see how sad it is. It is not so long ago when H.F. said, "Jasch does not want to work. Even if not hard work, surely he could do light work. That man should not get so used to lying around!" Everyone could see how sick he was, but H.F. thought everyone is as strong as the Friesens. That hurt me so much.

We already had the misfortune to have a sick husband and father who just could not earn anything, a condition that is very serious here! Friesen earns up to 318r. per month. Often he works 2 shifts and then he does a lot. He always has money. He even buys brandy and earns 10-fold – and for a bottle of brandy the overseer credits him with double time. And then he claims he starves more than others. He writes to all the countries that he has the poorest family and they are the most needy. Well, leave him! If only he would leave the rest of us alone.

I have cried so much – and now that I see death approach my dear Jasch with great strides, it even hurts more! I cannot forget it. By today H.F. also believes that Jasch is sick and cannot work. He has often said to Jasch, "You are so lucky. If you do not have to work, you do not tear your clothes or shoes." That used to hurt Jasch so! He said to him, "I would rather work and earn something! But if that is luck, then I wish you my luck too!" Galatians 6:7: "Do not be deceived, God is not mocked." He will not escape out of God's hands.

Dear siblings, do not think I want to besmirch the character of H.F. No – I just find it so very hard to bear and then I unload my heart to you. Then it becomes a little easier. Allow me to do this. Think of my situation if my dear Jasch should really die! What shall I then do? I just do not know! My mind just stops. Our happiness, at least on this earth, has been completely destroyed! But my great comfort is that in Heaven we will again be happy – and no parting ever! I also believe as you do, dear Liese, that these are the end times and the Saviour will soon return to gather His own. Even if we have no special hope for better things in this world, we would not like to live long in the misery in which we now find ourselves!

It must have looked terrifying to have so many grasshoppers that they even ate the curtains in the windows. One pail of cucumbers is very little for your family. We, of course, have none but we just cannot compare our situations. Do you get enough potatoes? How rich you are to be in that country where you can get everything and have peace and security as well. May God preserve it for you. We will, no doubt, have to perish here! We were sent to this place for that purpose and the Communists will, no doubt, achieve their ends.

My foot has healed up completely. There was this thing about Tina which you did not understand. It was like this: Tina was at work in the potato field heaping and cleaning the potatoes. She was always sent further and further away, in fact so far that she was to be sent by train. One mine gets workers from another, and that is how this was too. But that time several stayed behind because they were so young. However, they had said goodbye and were at the station 5 Werst away from here. It was so perilous that we again cried about our serious adversity! Yes, when will things change?

I read your letter to Jasch, dear Liese. Then he cried so very much! Then he said, "In this life I will not see my sister Liese again." If you were here, dear Liese, many things would be easier for me. Oh, no – ! Who would then fight for us and plead for us? It is better like it is! Many a penny has come into our hands through your pleading! And you, dear siblings, have given your last for us. God has led us all correctly, and has made no mistakes, even though we are here!

M.R.

[1933]

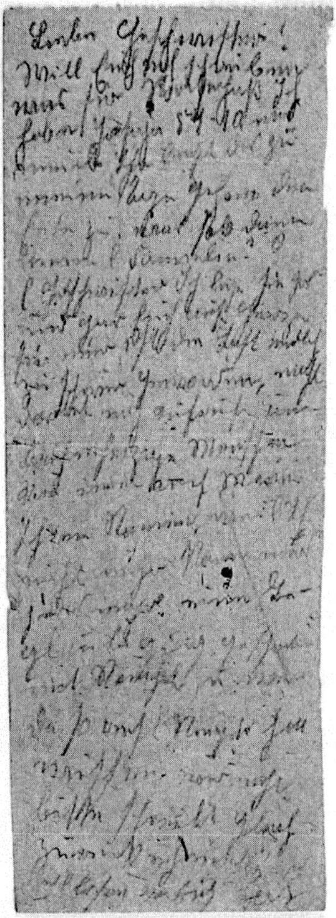

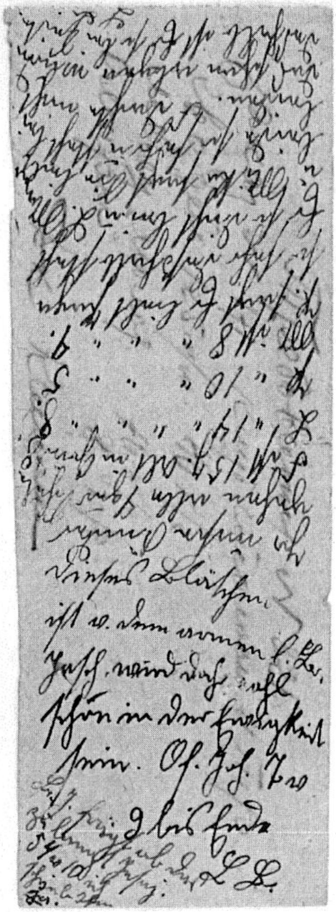

Dear Liese,

You write you have stayed home just to be able to write us a letter. You say the hired man and the children went to Sunday School. That sounds so strange. We did not get the letter of Aug. 13 which contained Hans' printed funeral letter! Oh, we are so sorry. It happens so often that letters go lost.

We do not know how many packages we shall receive from the Board. [*It appears that a charitable relief organization with a governing board is receiving donations from North Americans and forwarding them to the Regehr family in Russia. This organization could very well be the Mennonite Central Committee, but the writers do not identify it as such.*]

We have received 5 which were sent through Moscow. The card on it said from that party in Germany, Brilliand. We cannot know from whom, since the name is not given. We tend to think it is from you and Wiebes. Now we will not know which parcel will arrive from Is. W. We do not know if the Board has added to these parcels. We wrote to W. to see if they had not received the letter! They wanted to know how much the Board had included, and we wrote that to them. We just could not know. Jasch wrote to them too. Will you also write to them? Once Tina received 5 dollars from a Mr. Hoffer, or do you think it only came in Tina's name? If things come from Germany, we do not know who sends us those Marks. Names of senders are only rarely included. Ten Marks were sent to us in my name, and on it was F.B. I sent the card to you. Did you receive it?

Dear Liese, you ask if you still can be recognized in the picture. Oh, yes. You have not changed a bit, and you are so fat it looks dangerous. And such lovely clothes! Is your dress silk? And the children, all 4 of them are so grown up. We cannot write a thank you to B.K. because we do not know from whom. We never thought we would get anything from them! Could they be angry with us? It certainly is not our fault. Jasch and Liese each received a card for 20 Marks this August and it arrived here on the same day it was sent. We think it is from Hoellig. Dear Liese, nothing else was written on it. We did have a package but it was from December. Last week we had 1 card for 14 M. 16 c.– we have no idea from whom.

We write to the company every time that money or packages arrive, and they notify the responsible parties! It says that on the cards. Should B.K. also die young and you, the sick one, outlive them all? But we all know that God can do miracles. Jasch sends hearty greetings and says: See you in Heaven! He is very nervous. Cries a lot. I too. We will have aged a lot – and it is no wonder. Everything is written in love. Pray for us in these days. It is very difficult.

In love, your siblings,
Jasch and Maria and children

*Since Jasch's demise, Maria has been writing more frequently. However, Jasch rallies his remaining strength to write one last letter. His words are sparse and heart-rending.*

[1933]

Dear Geschwister,
I just want to write to you of my health problem. Isaiah 54:10. ["*'Though the mountains be shaken and the hills removed, yet my unfailing kindness will not be shaken, nor my coveriant of peace be removed,' says the Lord who has compassion on you.*"] My days are nearing the end. What will my dear family do then? Oh, dear Geschwister, I put them totally on your heart. The burden is finally becoming too great for me. Use this letter as a call for help to many hearts. People should send things on Marie's name, since I cannot carry on any longer. [...] died in the faith. [...] with [...] and who has the [...] we do not know. Please write back soon. [....] Jasch

Tarabunka, Oct. 29 [1933]

Dear siblings Frank and Liese and children,
With a heavy heart, I take pen in hand, and will send you a sign of life and of love. Today it is 3 weeks since I had to bury my deeply beloved Jasch in that frightful, gloomy primeval forest. I shudder as I think of it. Think of it, dear siblings, I can never weep over his grave again. Now it is winter and everything is under snow.

Every day some dead bodies are carted off! And everyone must bury their own loved ones. Then, because of the deep snow, people do not bury them very deep – or they may dig up an old grave and put someone else into it as well. So in spring, when it thaws, many bodies appear above ground. It could be that some Russian is put on top of my dear Jasch because the snow-covered grave mounds are not even visible.

Yes, our dear God helps to carry the sorrow. We experienced that so often when my dear Jasch was still alive. We have experienced so much – but God helped carry it too! This which you, dear Liese, have written on this paper with your own hand is proof that we have received it. It was a real comfort to us even while my dear Jasch was still alive. The letter in which you had enclosed 1 dollar got to us a week before his death. Then he said, "Write back right away and greet Liese with Psalm 23, and write that December 8 is my birthday." How intensely he longed to go back – or even see you again in this life! Our great God has determined otherwise, and he had to die before his time!

Or how shall I understand it? Why could we not be with him there too? No, we have to stay here and continue to go through all these hardships? And that may not even be enough – we may have to pay with our lives. How many years now have we asked, Why? – and no answer! Dear siblings, how hard it has been for me in the 3 weeks since my dear Jasch died is known only to my dear Saviour and no one else. But He will not abandon us, no matter how hard things get. He promises to be a father to the widows and orphans!

Psalm 73 is exactly our life! That is how we feel when we see the godless: as if they succeed in everything and no misfortune befalls them. They walk through this life on roses. But then comes verse 12 – and after this life comes eternal damnation. Praise God for our great privilege, for the living hope we have in verses 26 to 28! May God grant me this assurance at all times! I long to be there too, but my dear children still need me so. Oh, if only we could all be there already – there where there is no parting at all.

Today is Sunday. You probably will be happy in God's house, hearing the Word of God Pray that we too can get to such a situation again. Such times of reawakening! We too would love to be in God's house and be happy. We often ask, Will we ever experience that again? Oh, these hard times of exile, when will it ever end??? We speak every day of the time when we will be set free! Or how things will be when our situation will change! Should we give up all hope, and succumb here? If we have no hope – then life ends.

I am reporting to you, dear siblings, that we received the card sent on Oct. 5th, on which you, dear Liese, write of Jasch's death.

I sent a card to you on Oct. 8th. I am sure you will have cried with me. On Oct. 11th I sent a letter to you, in which I described everything – how he died and was buried. Did you receive them? Our tears are our food day and night. Actually, my eyes hurt from crying so much. I have to stop now and make lunch – I am boiling potatoes. Then I have to go to the store and sign for the potatoes; that is how we pass away a Sunday here. Just imagine what a painful day!

Monday morning. Things are as usual. Where are my thoughts? With my dear Jasch! And he will never again return, will never again say a word to us, will never again give us wise counsel! Oh, what a deep wound my heart has received! Dear siblings, I will write you how I passed my Sunday. At 12 noon I went to the store to sign for the potatoes for my family. I stood in line until 3 o'clock! The workers get 30 kilo potatoes, and the workers in the mines get 100 kilos! Then from there I walked to the place where they distribute the potatoes. There were so many people there that I still have not received any potatoes. There is so very much confusion and mismanagement everywhere. Everyone is hoping that this will soon end – but it drags on, and for many it is too late.

Today they brought 10 wagonloads of potatoes here. When the train comes, there is only 1 person to receive, weigh, and distribute them to all those people. Then very little is achieved. Even in the winter the potatoes are piled high under the clear sky – and they freeze. Well, for night they do cover them with straw. But it snowed last night! First they rot and freeze – then they sell them.

In the evening Liese came home. She can come home for 2 hours each Sunday evening. The lady is very nervous and particular. Every morning Liese must wash all the floors and sweep the floor in the kitchen 3 times a day. But there is absolutely no broom in the house. She works from 5 A.M. to 12 midnight – not hard work, but she must be there punctually. The lady of the house touches nothing.

M.R.

*The family has reached its nadir. But Maria has little time to mourn. Now that she is the only parent, the management of the family, the daily routines of waiting in line, working, and surviving dominate. Letters from Canada and some from her former home village continue their same precarious route. Maria reports that daughter Liese's lot has improved somewhat. She no longer toils in the forest or mine but works indoors. Could better days soon begin? It is already late fall. In Canada, the economy slowly improves after 1933; in Russia, Stalin's Five-Year Plan has been completed well ahead of time. New policies might usher in a gentler age.*

## We Can Live More Easily Now

*From the letters written at the end of 1933, it appears that camp administrators have eased up in the intensity of industrializing the country and persecuting the people. Perhaps Stalin believes that most "enemies of the people" have been dealt with. Relief is evident in Maria's words. Her life becomes more bearable. Particularly in 1934, the letters change in substance; there are fewer cries for help and less emphasis on survival. Some of the children are in school, where they receive three meals a day, albeit still meagre portions. The older children continue to work. Liese's job as a maid restores some of her dignity. Maria, now a forty-three-year-old widow, mends, cooks, cleans, and waits for her children to come home on Saturdays.*

*Although she mourns the death of her husband, Maria reports that "we can live more easily now and have it a bit better too, since we now get some potatoes and cabbage." The money and parcels from overseas also help. Yet she worries that something is wrong. Some packages have been opened and items are missing. But, more seriously, letters from her home village have stopped. Is Stalin's paranoia affecting the southern villages? Is there an uprising?*

[November 1933]

[. . .] real lady, at least she doesn't have to work outside in this terrible winter. Peter and Mariechen have to work outside on the railroad line. Tina and Lena go to school. Jascha, that poor orphan, is with me. He isn't well. He looks so pale and is very ill. Jasch could hardly part with him. Oh, that tormented evening! I sit here dejectedly with the children! Oh, what we have lost!

I report to you, dear siblings, that we received your most interesting letter in which you alone, dear Liese, on the 5th of October had enclosed an envelope! Should it really happen that they stop all correspondence between us? That would be so deplorable! Is there really something wrong? In September we received 4 letters from you – also the letter with the 1 dollar. We received no letters from home. Could there possibly be an uprising?

We received a letter from Mariechen on July 26. Only one letter, that is all. Jasch Friesen from here got one letter from Jasch Voth. He only wrote about the youth – someone had died [...] Jasch Boschmann with Justina Wiens! Hans Warkentin married Lena Kasdorf. They got enough products out of the Commune so they did not have to starve. If you let them read this, do not mention anything of our family and how things may be going for them, or where Mama has to hide out. We are so interested; if only things would be better for them. I guess it is easier for you too, if everyone isn't starving at once.

We have no harvest here. We only live here by charity, and the alms which good people are kind enough to give us. Dear siblings, I thank you that you have again begged for us. Yes, you do a lot for us. May God reward you a thousandfold. Dear Liese, you write, "If we only could have sent more," maybe Jasch would not have died. But you could not. If only he had not gone to work, he would not have caught that awful cold and would not have died.

Was our way ordered by God before we were born or not? Why could we not have gone to America when it was still possible – before this tragedy? We wanted to so badly, but no, we had to stay. It was God's way!! Our Tina got a package on October 28. In it were 10 kilo flour, 3 kilo cream of wheat, 2 kilo sugar/butter, oil – and 100 ip. tea had been removed. It had been repacked and filled so as to appear nice! Well, we won't fuss. Too bad we do not know who sent the parcel. In spring Tina got a parcel from a Maria Siebert.

Could it be from her again – or from Mr. Hoffer? I'll send you the addresses. Sometimes this constant begging is very hard for us. But as long as we are here in this Siberian slave labour camp, we have no other recourse.

For me the great pillar and comfort of my life has passed from this world. My heart just bleeds and aches! Why this way, why??? Where are B.K.? Are they already with you? Are they well? Are you, dear Liese, completely free of your health problem? Why couldn't my dear Jasch get well too? Could God not hear our prayer and grant him health? I cried so hard when I saw the address on the card – and also on the letter. Jasch's name will never be written again. It hurts so much, dear Liese. Oh, if only I could sob out my grief at your breast! Whom have I got here who sorrows with me? May God reward you for your help. I have received all packages. Too bad that often there is no return address. J.J. did not see my dear Jasch as a corpse. It seems so inhuman.

Your deeply sorrowing sister and children – without my lovely Jasch

*We can only speculate why so many packages do not have return addresses. But during this time of momentary reprieve, Maria offers to forward her mother's letters to Canada. She evidently feels it is safe to do so.*

22 Nov. [1933]

Dear Geschwister Frank and Liese and children,
May the God of peace be with you and give you what you dear ones need for this life, and even more for your eternal life. We too are all alive and well.

But how abandoned I am without my dear Jasch! I always keep asking: Why did he have to die while another can be well and live together with his loved ones? Michi went to the post office today and only brought a letter for Fuensten, but again for us there was nothing. Then H.F. came from work and brought me a letter from you – a card and a package. You had enclosed 4 sheets of paper,

11 pictures, and a Kalenderblatt [*calendar page*] on which you, dear Liese, had written on around the edges and sent to comfort us – and that it did!

It is really true, God's children are not spared the tribulation. However, they learn to speak in faith when they are in tribulation. If God be for us, who can be against us? No evil can strike us without His will – but my dear Jasch did have to die! How can I understand that? Jasch was so diligent in writing letters, and now I alone am left. Dear Liese, you do not mention receiving the card or the letter in which I described everything. But I understand from your letter that you already knew that Jasch was dead! And you write only to me and the children. Oh, it always hurts me every time Jasch's name is not mentioned anymore.

We received 2 letters lately, one from Hans Koops and one from our dear Mama. I have forgotten when I received the letter from Mama, but it was not too long ago. I will send the letters to you because you write that you have not received a letter from her for a long while. It has been very cold here for a whole week. Then I am always so happy when the children get home from work and get indoors and no one is frost-bitten. How good it is to know that wherever we are, we are secure in God's hand.

Liese is at least in a warm place. She always comes here Sunday evenings. She is always so busy – no time to write letters. She has received 2 dresses, a woolen jacket, 2 pairs of stockings, and completely new felt boots. She gets 25r. a month. I will write to you how much we earned in the Coz. We got 42 Trudodnie, and per Trudodnie we get 2 kilo cabbage (but not nice heads like we used to have at home, only green leaves), 2 kilo potatoes, 250 ip. turnips, 4 ip. radishes, 4 ip. table beets, 3 ip. carrots, 1-½ ip. onions – these were of every sort, 60 kilos potatoes, 40 kilos cabbage. Per worker we get 25 kilos cabbage, 16 kilos potatoes, so that now we can save a bit on the flour and millet.

Dear Liese, you again write that we will still be able to come over there. Could that really happen? In the Ukraine it seems to be peaceful. The Fleischbeschaffung [*literally "meat business," but it could be understood as "slave trade"*] is again beginning, so that they are faced with the same things as in the past year. No end is in sight. We would so much like to be free and away from here. But my dear Jasch will have to stay in this huge forest, and I will never be able to see his Grabhuegel [*grave mound*] again!

Your very loving and deeply sorrowing sister-in-law,

Marie and children

In heaven we will see Jasch, Papa, and Hans again. Pray for us.

*Suspicions of an uprising in southern Russia and Ukraine continue. The route of mail delivery has altered. Maria has received only one letter from her home village this autumn season, and the Bargens in Canada have not received any since summer. Other events signal a change. The family's prison camp is expanding. Twelve new barracks are under construction. Are more arrests and more prisoners expected?*

December 8 [1933]

Dearly beloved Franz and Liese and children!
God's grace be with you and give you what you need, for this life and for eternity – that is the most important thing. As you write, dear brother-in-law, maybe our life here is almost at an end and soon we can be away from this earth. I long to go home [*a metaphor for heaven*] – if I did not have the children. When I think that we must continue to live as we do, then I do not wish for a long life. But it is, as you write, it is a small thing for God to save us. But for us it is taking too long!

All our leading men are passing from the scene – just like Mr. Toews. He was a man who gave his entire life to God, and he had to perish so miserably in exile too. I have lately been thinking of that Word of God which was read at your father B's funeral by Jak. B., your uncle: Isaiah 57: 1 and 2. With this I comfort myself as well, and should this really be the end times, then we have no more good to hope for in this life.

We did receive your valued letter which you had written on Nov. 5th. I received it Dec. 5th. Liese had been at the mail and got the letter. She brought it to us yesterday. I am happy that you, dear brother-in-law, also finally wrote. Also Lieschen. Write more L., you can still write German very well. Liese, I thank you for that lovely poem which you composed yourself – it affected me deeply and brought me many tears. It hurts me so much when I think of the last days of my Jasch. How wretchedly and unmercifully he had to perish. Never in this life can that wound be healed. I believe you, dear Liese, that you wrote that poem with many tears. He just could not leave little Jascha. Why does it have to be like this?

You write that the sleigh stands ready to take you to Sunday School. That reminded me so strongly of the past. At one time we too could go to church – and soon it is 3 years that we have not been allowed to hear God's word. What a difference between you and us! Is that not true, dear loved ones? To take everything as being out of the hand of God requires much strength from above. I am so sinful and so afraid, but it is God's grace that has carried and sustained me and my loved ones. In my mind's eye I can still see and hear how my dear Jasch would cry. When I asked him why he was crying, he said, "The love of God has become so great and overwhelming to me." It is as you write: Only grace will get us to heaven!

Are you completely free from your ailment, Liese? You write that it is so very expensive to have a funeral there. Is it so only among the English [*a term for those not of Mennonite ethnicity*]? Are there also Christians among them? Or is it that way everywhere in America? Also by Uncle Hans? I did not mean you should celebrate a funeral in the church, I only meant you should sorrow with me, dear L. You have made such efforts on our behalf. Did they, out of love for Jasch, really preach a funeral sermon for him? He is worth it! How gladly I too would have heard that sermon. But it is impossible. Here we even have to bury our own dead. Oh, how terrible to have do that – but no one is given a greater burden than he can carry. We have experienced that so often and you, dear ones, have experienced it with us, right? Even though not in identical tribulations.

H. Friesens were all here, even their Jasch, but they did not even help carry out my dear Jasch's coffin. He had business elsewhere and walked away. They are people without compassion. Later I told her that her husband had not even seen my dear Jasch after he had died. That is how far things have gone here! There is no love of neighbour here. It was even a bit too much for his wife. When he came home from work that night, she asked him if it was really true that he had not seen Regehr dead. At first he started to deny it, but he finally had to admit it. He is the only person who works, but he accomplishes much with Brantwein [*brandy*]. I only write this because you asked why they had not been at the funeral.

We received the letter with the 1 dollar. We also received all the letters from October – the ones with all those printed poems. I still have not received the letter from Joh. R. We received one letter, written on Nov. 24, from home [*Altonau*]. I will enclose it here because you write you do not get any letters from home. I sent you a letter on Nov. 23rd and also enclosed the letters from home. We also received a card which I will also enclose (from Koop and Ab.). We hear nothing here of any uprising. It is horribly cold here – has been for 3 weeks – in fact so bad that the windows never defrost. We sit as if we are in a cage.

There is building going on here day and night. They say that 12 houses will be ready again by Jan. 1st. There is no thought that we will ever go home again. Rather, many more will be sent here! Bosch. wrote that Jasch B. was in Ekatarineslav. Jasch Bosch. and Sara Wark. are getting married on Dec. 9th. I wrote everything in love.

From your sorrowing Marie – without Jasch. How sad!

A heavy lot has become mine! Greet B. Klassens and Hans Martens.

Jan. 13 [1934]

Loved ones and siblings Frank and Liese and children,

May the almighty God give you what you need in this life, and give you peace in the land and good health, which is the greatest treasure in this life. The great God has led us in very unusual ways. Dear Liese, when you were so sick even here in Russia, we often said, "Liese will not reach old age." And now Papa, Hans, and Jasch are all in eternity before you, dear Liese, and they are waiting for you as for us all. That is how God's ways are. We just cannot understand it in this life.

I submit myself to God, but I cannot describe to you the mood I am in. How my heart aches never again to see Jasch in this life! I long to die too, but my dear children need me here! How hard our life is! When will we ever be free? Do you have any hope? Previously you wrote so much about hope, and enclosed paper clippings from the foreign countries – how they were working in our behalf – and now all is silent. No one can help us; do we all have to perish? Exactly those whom the foreign countries were trying to save are perishing here, as well as in our home region.

Well, today is the last day of the Old Style calendar [*Julian calendar*]. It is New Year and brother Peter's birthday if he was still living! He had to perish shamefully. Oh, how many innocent ones have had to lay down their lives because of this great unholy calamity which has descended upon us here. And no person can order the architects of our disaster to call a halt. But it is like you write, dear sister, "When the hour has come, help will break forth with great power." That is how it will be – then all will be rectified! Neither can we know if these are our last days, or if we will continue to live longer yet. It is hidden from us! That is why the Saviour himself says, "Watch."

How is it at your place? Are you allowed to attend Bible conferences, like it used to be in Russia? Oh, how happy and blessed we were in such hours! Remember the time Mr. Toews [*their house friend, Johann Toews*] was at your place – those were blessed and happy times – and they will never return! Where are all those loved ones with whom we were together then? Longing! Oh, the longing ache of grief! How you weigh my heart with sorrow!

I wrote you a letter at Christmas, and on Jan. 6th I sent another. Did you receive them? I do not receive any letters from home either. They do not write; if they did, surely one letter would get through. Mariechen owes me 2 letters already; she has not answered. I have sent you 3 letters I received from home. I have no letter from Ab. Regehr since May 22. I do not know, do they not write? Or do the letters not get here? I have written so often. He who has never experienced our situation just cannot sympathize with us. We live in exiled isolation, and how often do we look for letters – and uselessly!

I have received all the letters from you, and also the cards which you, dear Liese, have written. But I have not received the letter you mention, the one written by Jasch and me and which you had typed up and then sent back to me as a remembrance. I regret that so much. I have received the letter where I described Jasch's death and which you copied for me by pencil! Neither did I receive the one in which you said you enclosed some Christmas verses. It is so sad when even one letter goes lost, especially if you know of it.

You ask how things are going for the J Reg. children [orphaned children in a nearby prison camp]. I was in Kizel last week and I met Lutheran Germans who live together with Regehr's children. They said the children were doing well. They had enough to eat and even got a parcel. And Nesa, Michi, and Jasch were looking well. Lena's husband wants to go and get the children but didn't have permission from the Soviet Comm.! When he wrote the letter, he was asked if he was a Mennonite – because he has such a funny name, right? H. Voth and H. Wiebes' daughters are also in Kizel and live in the Odnyin barracks. There are many rooms, and the girls as well as 2 boys live in one room. That cannot be good in the long run. Michi and Tina went to visit there yesterday and they told us many things about them – things of which they disapproved. The previous evening they had been in the club until 2 A.M. with those boys and had much to do with them. Michi said the fellowship was too intimate.

Yes, truly the devil does not rest even here in exile. Wiebes' daughters are basically on the wild side – and then the opportunity is there. Much happens in these sad times. So much is also written of what goes on at home. Many people believe these are the end times and we should prepare ourselves for eternity. And preachers whom we deemed to be true children of God smoke and live in sin. Remember how strict S. Wiens of N. 3 was? He would immediately notify everyone when anyone was being disciplined. He has never been converted! And where is he now? When we were living in N. 7 and S. W. , Andrea's P. and Franz Kl. drove through the village, all three on their two wheelers. Jasch often said, "Something will yet come to light about this trio." I always said, "Keep silent."

When T. Kl. (who was married to Graensen's daughter of N. 3 and lived in Pet. Goosens' house – that was then when we were all being resettled, that spring) [*said*] that Klassen was so mixed up in his faith and could not believe anymore that he would be saved, Ar. R. and Ab. F. often spoke to him. Wiens and Pankratz, with whom Jasch often drove to Ar. R., didn't say much. And it often caused me much sorrow when my dear Jasch would speak about the preachers – you know about what – and now these things are becoming confirmed and clear! But what will the unconverted be saying now?

May we all be sustained and ready for eternity. And even if we must walk even deeper paths, I never want to leave my Saviour – only hold Him nearer until I see Him with all the saints who are already there! That is my greatest desire. In deepest love and great longing, never forgetting you, I remain your loving sister,

Maria and children

[*Written in the margins*] I thank you so much for your help and for your prayers. It will not remain unrewarded. Is Ar. R. not home yet? What of Jasch Bargen? No letter from Mama in a long time. I wonder if Isaak Wiebe is still alive. America? J.R'.s Lena has a 4-month-old little one.

[1934]

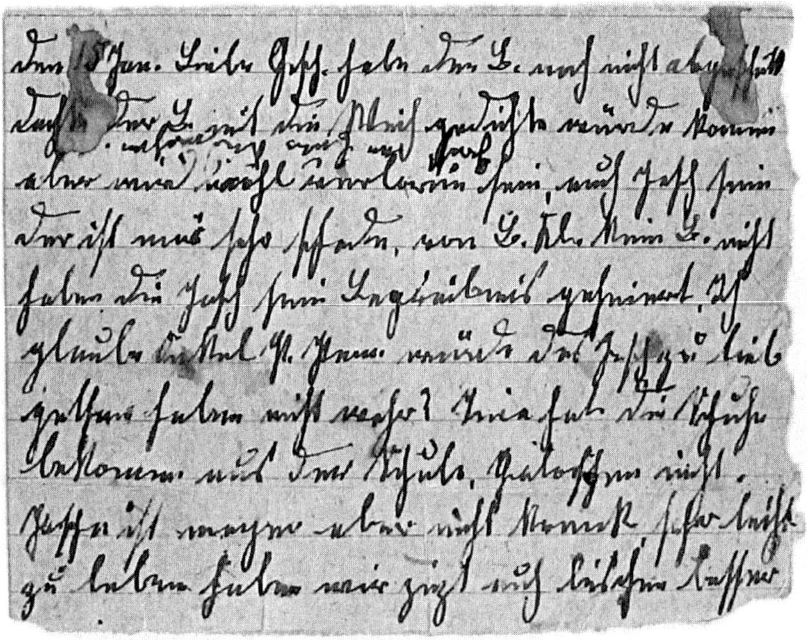

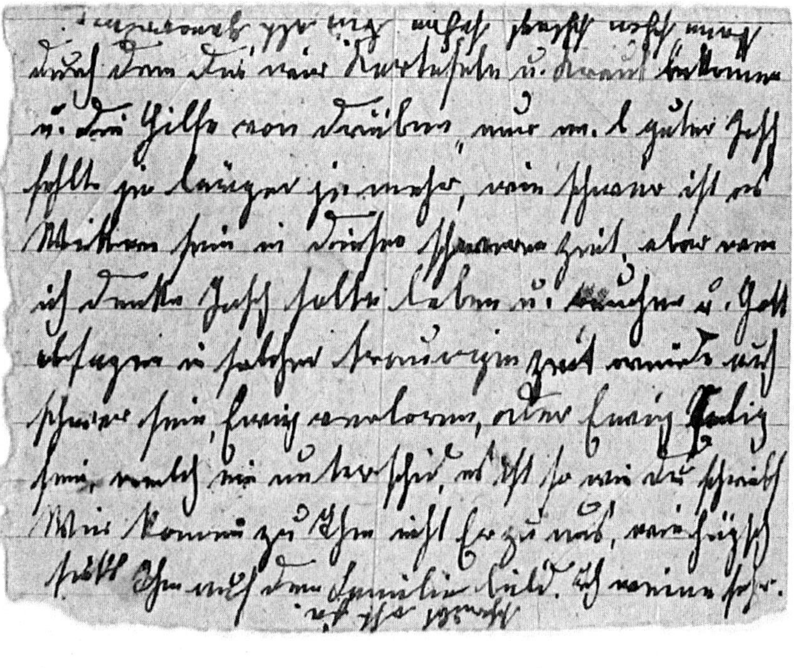

15 Jan.

Dear Geschwister,
I still have not sent the letter. I was hoping the letter with the many poems would come, but it probably has gone lost. Also the letter Jasch had written – I regret that a lot. Have received no letter from B. Klassens. Did they celebrate Jasch's funeral? I believe Mr. P. Penner would have done so because he loved Jasch, right? Tina has received shoes from the school, but no galoshes. Our son Jascha is very thin, but he is not sick. We can live more easily now and have it a bit better too, since we now get some potatoes and cabbage. The continued help from overseas helps too.

Only I miss my dear, good Jasch. The longer he is gone, the more I miss him! How very hard it is to be a widow in these terrible times. But when I think that if Jasch had lived, suffered, and then denied God in these sad times, that would be even harder to bear. To be eternally lost or to be eternally in glory – what a difference! It is as you write, we are going to him, and not he to us. How handsome he looks on the family picture. I am crying so much. Write often, please. I can see very poorly, have gotten old. Greet all your children.

*Finally, communication between Maria and her home village resumes. Maria is homesick and describes her domestic life to her mother in Altonau. Like other letters, this one circulates until it finds its way to the Campbell's Soup box in Canada.*

*Food is more plentiful, and together with Maria we breathe a sigh of relief. The family has fresh pork and enough bread to share. Rumours circulate that by the first of February their lives will improve again. Life in the home villages has also resumed a normalcy that allows for canning plums and baking pastries. But a census has also been taken, and Maria is troubled about the registration process.*

January 25 [1934]

Dearly beloved Mama in that distant homeland,
Today is Monday again, and again I am alone and so lonesome that I do not know how I will endure the time. Liese and Miechi left early as usual and little Jascha is in school – and then I am all alone. Of course there is enough work to keep me busy fixing and mending. The children bring their clothes and laundry home, and I mend and wash them during the week. When they come again, they take it along and leave their dirty clothes and laundry. In this way one is not busy the entire Sunday.

I am always happy when Saturday rolls around because then the children come home. Then I have the food prepared, the water is ready for washing, and the clean clothes are mended and laid out for them to change into. I get impatient and can hardly wait until they get home. Last week it was so horribly cold that I had no inner peace and could not sleep well at night, worrying about those poor people who had to work in such frigid weather. No, some day we want to get away from the Urals which have robbed us of the father of our family. [....]

Dear Mama, I have also received the lovely picture of F. and L. I could not contain the tears when I received the picture (the 10th of January). Could we not have been as fortunate? Mama, why does it have to be this way? That is what we ask time and time again! I have the picture before me even now. Oh, those dear siblings! How we loved each other so much! I can still hear the words of my dear Jasch. When I wrote the last letter to them when he was still alive and I asked him,"What shall I write to Liese?,"he said, "Greet Liese heartily with Psalm 23, and tell her my birthday is Dec. 8th."That was exactly 2 days before he died. I have cried so very, very much here in exile! [....]

When will the time come when we again will be free people? Here we hear nothing. Many believe that we will be able to go where we please, even though it will be very expensive. But we only want to get away to a warmer region where life could be better. Mama, you write that you are canning plums and baking pie-by-the-yard [a long narrow fruit pastry] for the New Year. How I, with my dear children, would love to be your guests. Life in your area must be much different. Mama, you also write about a census that was taken. Are there those who have allowed their name to be registered? Are they believers? There are very few believers here. Has someone told you that they now were enfranchised?

I just cannot comprehend the fact that our preachers do not have a firmer foundation. Remember Mama, how often Joh. B. said that Christendom would be decimated and scattered. Many did not believe this, but what is happening today? Should there not be at least 1 righteous one? Mama, where are [...]Kroekers N. 6? H. Voth is still in [...] in the hospital. The toes on his left foot have been removed – one joint on each toe. He wants to take up work there and have his family join him, if that is possible. But our C. believes that he can still keep us confined here. He is no friend of the German people.

We are happy that you, dear Mama, can live a little more easily and also get some help from overseas. For a short time we also had it a little easier. The children earned quite good wages, and we even slaughtered 2 little piglets but could render no lard. The meat remains fresh here the entire winter so that we did not even have to salt it down. It stays frozen hard as a rock. The children can buy things at the Basa [base camp] where they work, and I keep this until Sunday when they are home so that I then can provide for them properly. If only you could see, Mama, how we then eat, like in the old time manner. But it would be nice to eat white bread without a quota.

The bread situation is quite meagre here. Saturday I got only 2 kilo white for 2r. 30k. They gave only 1 c., but one woman who was in the lineup ahead of me considered it too expensive and took the 1 c. for me. This we apportioned so that we would have two meals for 5 people. There was enough. I still have 1 c. black bread left, and that I want to send by mail to Tina and L. They will also be without bread again. It is rumoured that by the 1st of February our situation should improve again. Wishing you, dear Mama, very good days to come and much happiness for your birthday. How glad I would be to be a guest at your house. Continue to remember us!

Maria

[1934]

Have received the 2 dollars you sent. Was in Kizel and took the money for the 13.90 dollars. The dollar costs 1r. 21k. They are both of equal value, the Russian and the Canadian. Before the Russian was more expensive by 20 to 30 kopeks compared to the Canadian. I just couldn't believe it. So I personally checked it in the paper, that is where they chart the cost of the money.

You write, dear Liese, that you have sent us two money orders from Germany. We received 2 cards announcing that they had sent marks to our address. One card in my name for 13M, 49c. and sent 16/12/33. And the other card in Jasch's name for 9 Marks, 40c., sent 19/12/33. Are these the ones? Too bad the sender's name is not on them. The only thing on my card is "Thiessen," the one who mailed it is not the giver. Too bad that we cannot thank the giver.

Dear siblings, how can we ever thank you enough for what you do for us in our distress? If that should stop, I do not know how we would cope. You do so much for us. We have written that to you so often. So often Jasch said, "What a difference in those two sisters, Liese and Tina." Tina doesn't even write a letter, and Liese writes so many letters – and begs for us and sends her own money too to help us here. Dear siblings, I would like to hug you around the neck and to see you face to face. May God protect those things you send to help us in our sufferings. Remember us in the future. Liese, our daughter, just does not want to work in the mines anymore.

M.R.

# Notes

1 Interview, Lena Regehr Dirksen (October 2005).

2 This statement expresses Maria's belief that an event often referred to as the "Rapture" or "the Second Coming" will occur in which Jesus Christ will return to earth and take believers to heaven to join him in the afterlife. Clearly, optimism marks Maria's statement and her belief.

# Chapter Four

## Do Not Forget Us
## 1934 - 37

Like ocean tides, hope rises and falls. Optimism increases when Stalin's second Five-Year Plan (1933-37) is less aggressive than his first. The general tone of his political speeches is calmer.[1] Rationing of food is actually abolished in some areas, and supplies flow more freely.

But Maria continues to hear rumours of an uprising in southern Ukraine. She fears for her mother and siblings in her home village, and wonders if she and her children will ever be free. Hope rises again when food is more accessible. They now have corn bread and homegrown potatoes. The older children are given galoshes and rubber boots to work in the mine. But Maria is tentative in her trust. Her belief in a better life has been eroded, and she still feels vulnerable. She knows that many people will die this spring from disease and lack of food. Her recurring plea – "Do not forget us" – reaches her family in her southern home village and in Canada. The flow of letters continues for a time.

## Yearning for Liberty

*On this red and white Soviet postcard, liberated women operate an armoured tank in a show of solidarity for the State. On the reverse, Maria writes about her longing, her anguish for Liese's plight, and her dependence on a gift of one dollar.*

[1934]

Dear siblings F. and Liese and children,
Reporting to you that we received your card of the 22 of October. Also the [...] you, dear Liese, as well as a letter with 4 empty pages for writing – and pictures. There was another letter with 1 dollar enclosed. God brought the letter with the gift into our hands. May God bless you as He promised in His Word.

Yesterday it was Sunday, and my longing for all those loved ones scattered across the surface of the globe is so great! How we miss you and all our loved ones. Oh, if only I could once more enter the House of God with all my children and rejoice with all the other children of God! All those that enter the house of God are happy there – with their children. I wonder if such a lovely time will come for us too?! How thankful you should be, to be over there.

If only we could be there too, and my dear Jasch had not died before his time. Now I have to be alone with my children! It is so hard to understand. It is as you say, dear Liese,"It is God that has done it – and no man." I need strength and grace to understand and believe! Dear siblings, Liese was here yesterday evening and on through Sunday evening. She is very busy from early morning until late at night. I helped her rinse the washing in the wash-house. They have very nice laundry, which Liese must rinse by hand at least 3 times. Her lady is very particular. I sent you a letter a few days ago and enclosed a letter from Mama and M. from home. One hears nothing about that uprising here. Will we ever be rescued? I had a letter from Truda yesterday. Write often and do not forget us in the future.

Your deeply despondent Maria Regehr

*The following red Soviet postcard depicts the glory of the "Artels" – the national system of cooperatives (Kolkhoz) that signify a socialist collective of productive people joining to bring success to fishing, mining, and logging enterprises.*

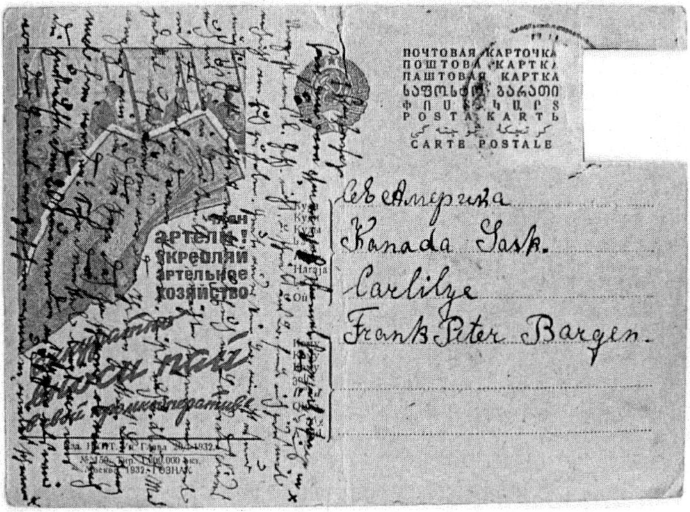

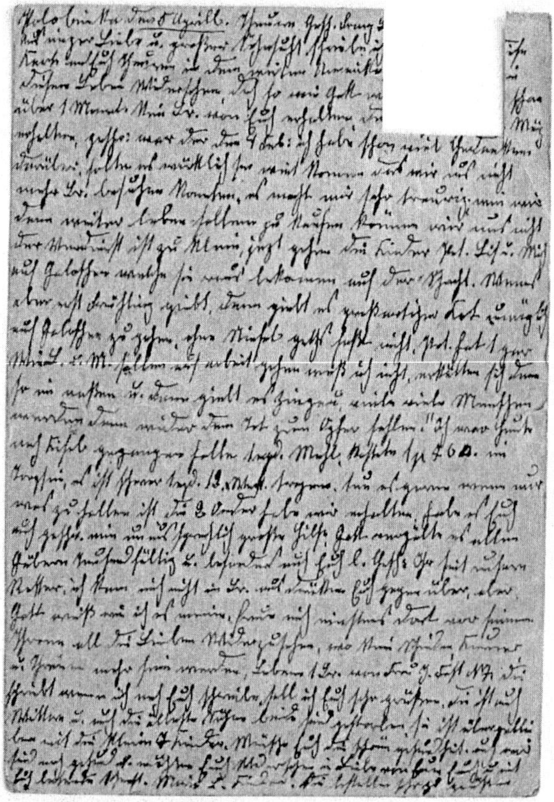

Polowinka, the 5 April [1934]

Dear Geschwister Franz [. . .]
In deep love and longing I write [. . .] card to that far away America [. . .] in this not to see each other again, but as God wills [. . .]. Have not received a letter from you in over a month. The [. . .] received [. . .] March. It was dated Feb. 4.

I have depressing thoughts about the possibility that it should ever come to the point where we could not even visit by letter any more. It just saddens me so much. How will we ever live through the winter? Our wages are far too low to enable us to buy anything. On their feet our children Peter, Liese, and Mariechen are now wearing only galoshes which were issued at the mine. When spring comes, the thawing creates unbelievable mud here and it is impossible to wear only galoshes then. If you do not have rubber boots, walking becomes almost impossible. Peter has a pair, but how Liese and Mariechen will go to work I do not know. They catch such severe colds in these damp, wet, and cold conditions. But if they do not go to work, they are denied all food and bread.

Many, many people will again be death's victims. Today I went to Kizel to get 1 [...] flour. It costs 1r. 76k. in the Torgsin. It is hard to walk those 12 km, but one does it gladly if only it is possible to buy something there. In our previous letter we mentioned the 2 orders we received. Many thanks. A true gift from God. May He reward a thousandfold all who participated in giving, especially you, dear Geschwister. You are our salvation! I just cannot express it in written words, but God can see our grateful hearts! I am looking forward to seeing all our loved ones before His throne of Grace, where there will be no more parting, no more tears, and no more grief ever again!

We got a letter from Mrs. J. Fast, N. 7. She writes that I should send greetings to you when I write, and tell you that she is now a widow and that her oldest 2 sons have also died. She has survived with her two youngest children. Wish you the best of health. We are also well at the moment and would love to see you again. Prayerfully and in love, from your sister and children who pray for and with you,

Maria R. and children

The children send hearty greetings.

Do not forget us, dear Geschwister, and write to us often. We are happy every time we get a letter from you. Today, again there is no letter. How is that possible? May God keep and comfort you there in the land of peace, as well as us here in this land of tribulation. We would so much like to escape from here with our life. Please greet B. Klassens, and remember our suffering before the throne of God.

I am so depressed. The days are so unendurable. Will we ever be free again! The future before us is very dark and dismal. On June 20 it will be 3 years since we were driven from our home, and we have suffered much hardship and deprivation during this time. Only God knows what still lies before us!

*Mail delivery has again resumed the former route; Maria sends her letter to her mother in Altonau, who sends it via a safe corridor to Canada. But this letter contains perilous information. Liese is planning another escape. Maria is consumed with fear for her daughter.*

[1934]

Dear Geschwister,
I cannot and will not ever forget what you have done for us. You have brought us through by providing life's necessities so that we did not starve. And God cleared the way and gave His blessing so that we could nourish our emaciated bodies. God has now changed our situation somewhat; we can live better now, even if not as well as you over there or as we had it before. But we now have enough cornbread and potatoes. Of course it would be very tasty to have other things to go with that. H.F. received several parcels from overseas with lard, soap, and cocoa. But we are satisfied and thankful that we not starving any longer.

I received a card from P.B. written on April 7, where he writes that he wants to send us and Mrs. Pet. Loewen something. Well, tell them that the card was sent to H.F. and we finally received it. Hearty greetings to them. Do you live far apart? Or even Ben. Klassens? Greet all the relatives heartily from me – and Uncle John and Aunt Agatha. We would love to see you all again in this life. How very privileged you all are in this life compared to me. If only Jasch was still alive I would be completely satisfied, even if I was condemned to lifelong poverty. Can God not draw me to Him in a different way? Therefore – I must need it, God. Forge on!

Liese wants to go home now. You will probably know the whole story – Mama will have written it to you. I just cannot allow myself to think that she is going. We always wanted to go together, and that is why she has postponed it several times. I do not want to keep her tied to me for life either. She cannot stay with me forever, and I have fears that she will be mistreated. To get away from here must be done secretly and stealthily, and then to travel 100 km on foot – and the way is swampy. She must have some clothes to take along – and then some bread – to get to the station. And it is again so very risky for anyone who tries to escape: they are sentenced for 3 to 5 years for trying to run. And then if she should again be so unfortunate as to be caught?

She tried to get back once before. And how was it the first time? No one cares or is concerned for her, and she is also terribly afraid. P.K. [*Peter Koehn, whom she later marries*] writes that nothing will happen to her. He tells her to come. But to go by train without proper papers is dangerous. I am very disturbed and my heart is very harried. Pet. and M. also encourage her to go, for then she can at least escape this tribulation. How would you advise me? What do you think about this, F. and L.? Rather let her go to her homeland and marry one of our people than stay here and marry a Russian? I will be so very lonesome for her, since she always was with me. Even though the others all went to the club, she would stay with me! She says she is already very lonesome even at the thought of separation.

Peter is visiting with a Lutheran girl called Alma Keller. She is a good, pretty girl. But when I ask him, he says he is not thinking of marriage yet. Maybe our situation will change someday, and if we must stay here he can take leave and marry one of our own people in the homeland. That would be better, right, F. and L.? I will send this letter to Mama and she can send it to you. Then I hope to get a nice letter from you through Mama. God be with you, dear siblings, until we meet again.

Your sister, Marie Regehr and children

*Liese's escape plan is now more certain. Maria writes to her mother (Liese Regehr in Altonau) of the plan and informs her that a package will precede her. Such a letter raises many questions: Do the prison guards not read outgoing mail? Is the censor asleep? Can they not read the German Gothic script? Perhaps the subversive system of mail delivery to southern villages is so secure that Maria can dare to write openly about an escape plan. Or perhaps her attitude toward risk is similar to that of Victor Serge's. In* Memoirs of a Revolutionary, *he recounts his experience in 1933. He has been arrested and is being interrogated. During a brief respite, he writes to a friend in Paris. He knows that "Persons corresponding abroad were often charged with espionage (a capital offence)." Yet he takes the risk because "we are bound to be murdered one way or another in the end, for there are plenty of ways of going about the job . . ."(288). Perhaps Maria is weary of caution. She has already lost so much: her freedom, her youth, her health, and her husband. How much more can the regime take away from her?*

[1934]

Mama, this is for you alone,
Mama, you say it is being rumoured that Peter has been married and you wonder if that is so. No, he often jokes about it, but he said to me he did not want to marry here in the Urals. I would also not want one of the Lutherans either. Maybe the time will come when we will be able to be home among our people.

Liese will probably come home – I no longer want to resist her going. She is no longer young, and that Peter really loves her is quite evident, or else he would already have taken a different one over there. I have nothing against this match. I love him, and I know that if Jasch were still alive he would gladly accept him as son-in-law. I am so afraid and anxious when I think of Liese going on that long trip – to steal away without an official permit – if that will not jeopardize our situation here? She thinks she will wait until May 1st. We will see what is being said, and then she will definitely leave.

We will send off a package addressed to Ab. R.. Do not open it until Liese gets there. P.K. has written she shall come to Ab. R. It is extremely hard for me to let her go. But I believe that after a while I will also be able to come with the 2 little ones, but I would not like to leave the others here either. I have prayed so often that God be my counselor in our planning. So, she will leave here in the beginning of May. You, Mama, represent her there, yes?

Auf Wiedersehen [*farewell*]

*Possessing any books, never mind a Bible, is forbidden in the camps. Children like Lena and Tina are questioned about their parents' religious practices in school. Having a Bible in the barracks is hazardous. With twenty-two people sharing a small hut, it would be difficult to conceal such a book. Perhaps prison guards overlook this harmless text read by an old weary woman with little left to lose.*

*Rumours of freedom continue to circulate, and Maria is hopeful once more. On May 1st thirty young men are released from their prison terms. Although the implications of this release are not certain, Maria wonders how it will affect her family. But another scenario challenges any notion of freedom. Two young women escape on April 18th: news of their arrest travels quickly, and their punishment is harsh.*

Polowinka, 10 May 1934!

Dearly beloved Geschwister Franz, Liese, and children,

For you loved ones so away in the great distance, I wish God's comfort and presence, good health and well-being. We also are alive and well. We owe God a great deal of thanks. Even if He leads me through much suffering, I know God loves me, and He is only preparing me for that glorious heaven.

We are still in this brutal place of exile, and there is still no end in sight. Today the entire world is celebrating Ascension Day [*formerly a religious holiday*]. Only we here in exile are not allowed to celebrate this. What a great longing and desire one has to listen to God's word and rejoice together with other children of God. It would then again be such a different life. We keep asking ourselves, "Will we ever experience such a time again?" God alone knows. We think of you, dear Geschwister. Will you be in church? Pray for us, that our shackles may be loosed and we do not despair. God puts burdens on us, but He always helps us carry them as well. We have so often experienced this.

I now have a Testament with large print; my Bible is in such small print and my eyesight is so poor. That beautiful poem or song which you, dear Liese, sent me – or was it Mrs. Joh. Goosen? – was a real comfort. The title reads: "Do you too want to leave me?" This has comforted me this morning. The poem says: "Hear Jesus' words: Do you, oh child, want to leave me too? Would you not want to reach the goal together with me, even through tribulation? Do you desire the full blessing now, even though you are touched by sorrow? Thank God that he has led his dear child into the wilderness, for here in this deep, sincere silence He is alone with you, and His Word and His nearness will be everything to you." That is also my comfort in the lonely and difficult hours I have endured here.

God knows what else we must face in the future, and the future looms forebodingly before us. We would so much like to leave here. I had placed great hopes on May 1st. Much was rumoured of setting us free. Actually, 30 men did receive notice – they are the ones that work in offices and do not have hard work. They are the young ones up to 25 years. Whether they can go anywhere they like or only in the region of Kizel here, I do not know. Many escape at night to their homes; it seems that no one asks for papers or who they are. They are welcomed in their homes – that is what the Russians write.

We have not had a letter from home for a long time. I do not know what the reason can be. Had one letter from brother Heindrich, March 15, and one from sister Susie on March 18th, and one from Mariechen and Hans Koop on April 9th. I sent that one to you. Those are the last letters from home. Have not had a letter from our dear Mama or Abram for a very long time. Mariechen wrote in the last letter that Mama had applied for her right to be enfranchised. If she receives it, she could occasionally be in the village again. I still do not know if she was enfranchised. I received your last letter on

March 2nd. Also received one February 20th, one on January 26th, and one January 4th. The letters seem too few. I suppose many go lost. I wrote to you on March 13th, and March 27th, April 5th, April 12th, and May 3rd. Did you receive them all? I am waiting very much for a letter – I can hardly endure the waiting.

There is still snow here. Almost every day we have rain mixed with snow. We have had only very few nice days. There are still big snowdrifts in front of our doors and windows. But in other places the snow is almost gone. This place is going in full tempo, digging out tree stumps. When that is done, the entire field must be dug and turned over. This the workers must do after their day's work is completed. Each worker is responsible for 300 sq. metres, digging out the stumps and turning over the soil. It is extremely hard. Every day after work the poor souls must walk deep into the forest and do their quota and bring back proof that they were there; otherwise they are considered absent and their bread card is taken away. I go to work in the Commune every day for 5 to 6 hours. My work is carrying manure and dirt in the [...] with the Nasilka [*meaning unknown*]. It is very difficult. Where the snow is gone and the earth is not frozen anymore, it is muskeg. We have no proper waterproof footwear, and our feet are wet and freeze very quickly. It is an unhealthy region. All of May and June it stays cold. We have nice weather only in July and part of August, then the rains begin again.

How lovely it was in our homeland. There the children will all be running barefoot, and here they must wear shoes and stockings the entire year. It is very expensive to clothe ourselves here. If we had not received so much from you, dear Geschwister, conditions for us here would be very sad indeed. We have been able to buy some things we need very badly. I have patched so much here, more than I have in all the years at home. My daily prayer is that our dear God reward you a thousandfold.

It is evening. The children are all asleep. I am still up waiting for our Liese. She was called to work today. She really did not want to go because it was Ascension Day, but we are fettered and compelled. Maybe a time will come for us when we too can keep the Sunday holy. All things are possible with God, even if things loom so dismally before us. We are in a time when we no longer are our own masters. We are slaves and sold!! When will our shackles be loosed?

I and Mrs. Fast walked to Kizel, there we met both the Doerksen boys, Mrs. Born as well as Mrs. Pet. Loewen. You probably know that Pet. Loewen is dead. All their 4 children are in the project [the cooperative]. She is alone and does not enjoy it. Both of Mrs. Born's girls escaped to home on April 18th. But they got only as far as Perm, where they were arrested, and now they must work under guard. These things happen if you try to leave without permission. We will try to endure until our sentence is over. If only my dear Jasch was still alive, it would be different; he would know what to do and what was best. Well, we have our God as guide. He will know what is best – and then no one can stop us in our pilgrimage. Many believe we will be set free this summer. It is also said that we are free already – as of the 17th Crezd. [*a reference to a date on the Julian calendar, still in use in the USSR at this time*]. I get so afraid when I think of staying here another winter – that long, cold winter. No kind of weather is taken into account; the children must go to work. I do not even want to think of it.

This year we too want to plant a few potatoes. We must dig out the stumps and make a small garden. We want to buy one pail of potatoes for planting. They cost 11 rubles per pail and are hard to get. How nice potatoes taste. At home we had an excess of them. What nice times we used to have. We did not cherish those times enough. We will treasure such times much more if God should grant them to us again. You will probably have planted everything and again have hope for bread if the great God blesses your fields. For the 6th year we are without a harvest, are knocked from pillar to post, and have no permanent place to be, never knowing whether we will be here tomorrow.

May 11th. I wish to report, dear Geschwister, that after much waiting I received a letter from you today which you, dear Liese [*Maria's sister-in-law in Canada*], had written on April 13th. Liese

[*Maria's daughter*] brought it to me last night. I can't describe how happy I was when Liese handed me the letter. Imagine, I had not had a letter from you in over 2 months. What can be the reason for the letters being so slow? By what you write I understand that you have not had any mail from us for a long time either. How can that be possible? I already had very strange thoughts. And C. is not as you write; no one can help us. We had always kept alive the hope to get to your place, but now we have given it up. We will have to end our lives here. However, as God sees fit. I have not received the letter you mentioned.

Our loneliness and longing to see you and all the others again, dear Geschwister, is indescribably great. If we do not see each other on earth again, we will all meet before God's throne in glory – with Jesus in His light, and there nothing will disturb our joy. No more parting ever again. Oh, my Saviour, bring us there soon! What do we have here on earth? Only misery and affliction. B. Kl. have a hard life too – they have no cow. Such days as we once had here, days when we were all together, will probably never come again. We have received the picture where you are standing in the garden. Mama also got one.

H. Friesens got a letter from Bosch. describing how May 1st is celebrated in N. 8 [*the neighbouring village to Altonau*]. Three pigs were slaughtered, a variety of baking was done. Bosch. was the official host. She had not even gone or attended because she did not fit in. There was freedom and equality [*underlining in original*]. At Loewens and Joh. Voths in N. 9 there has been an outbreak of typhus; some people from the old colony [*the Chortiza Colony was referred to as "Old Colony" by Russian Mennonites*] had been night guests and the outbreak started there – Flecken typhus. J.V.'s Mariechen has died from typhus. Tina is still in the hospital in N. 8, as are Jasch Loew., old Mrs. Berh. P. and Jasch Koehn's daughter Lena. The grim reaper is harvesting everywhere; happy is he who is prepared.

Aron Rempel is marrying Neta Isaak. Mrs. Wilh. B. is very sickly and their Willie is flat in bed, so Mrs. Bosch writes. Their Heinrich is a big strong man, but Pet. is somewhat simple-minded. In N. 9

they cooked 30 pails of Moos [*fruit soup*] for the May 1st festivities, and baked Katletten [*meatballs*]. It seems just like the times of Noah: The people do not allow themselves to be drawn to God. Only last year there was such a great famine and so much starvation, and now they live without restraint or control. She writes that there is no rain again this year – it is very dry and much wind. She writes that her onions aren't even up. Imagine, it was May 1st and they should have been big already. I wonder if next year they will live as they live now. I often feel it does not pay to go back home, for God will come soon. If only we would all be ready at His coming!!

Dear Geschwister, what else can I write to you? I thank you and your children so much for what you have done for us. I thank you in tears. You write in this letter that Boese's son again gave you 1 dollar to send to us. May God bless him. That dollar costs 1r. 12k. here. In February we received a card of 8 Marks from a Mrs. M. Woelke of Arlington, California, America. May God, according to His promise, reward all those who have given. As of April 1st Liese is again working at those Germans' where she worked during the winter. They are going to their homeland on 15 of May. Liese has received much from that lady. She always comes home each night. She goes there at 6 in the morning and comes home at 10 P.M. She gets 40 rubles a month. He always says to her that she should go home and not work in the mines anymore. We do not know how it can be any better. We would all like to stay together. I believe we will get a letter from Mariechen shortly. Mrs. Bosch. wrote they had received my letter and they will write back to you. I will send it to you again. What do you all do? And you, dear brother-in-law, do not work so hard that you too become ill. If you have nourishment and clothes, be satisfied. I remain your loving and praying Marie and children, God be with you.

H. Voth is also very poor. He gets very little from overseas. He is the only worker in the family. Michi is sick; she has T.B. Their Hein. eats alone at the project. Their Liesbeth has registered herself in marriage with a Russian. Both H. Wiebe's girls were here Sunday for a visit. They are also considering heading out for the homeland. They sold and ate up everything. And so it goes with all of us, and in the end it costs our lives as well.

So it is, and our great God is silent!

*Although the letters, parcels, and money from Canada continue, the Prairie provinces, particularly Saskatchewan, are still striving to recover from the Great Depression of the early 1930s. Wheat prices are still low, and farmers are still lining up for aid. Then the winds sweep across mismanaged and impoverished fields, creating a colossal Dust Bowl. The year 1934 is the worst. From her brother-in-law Franz Bargen, Maria receives news of the lack of rain and dry conditions. Paradoxically, she and her children are drenched with rain, and constantly wet from the marshy roads and fields.*

*An encounter with bandits exposes another threat. It is not only the prison guards and militia that the Regehr family fears. Wandering rogue gangs are also menacing and threaten their safety.*

*Letters and packages are still arriving, but their pace is slowing. For two months, Maria and the children have received nothing. Is this just the result of a shoddy system, or is it an intentional action? Do letters get lost, or are they intercepted?*

Polowinka, 30 May 1934

Dear Geschwister Franz and Liese and children,
I wish to let you know, dear Geschwister, that on May 6th we received the card which you, dear brother-in-law, wrote on the 28th of March. Thank you, dear Geschwister, every letter is a sign of love from you. It is too bad that so few letters have arrived in the last while; judging from what you write in your letters, they probably have gone lost. I regret that very much. I received a letter from you on March 2nd and also on May 18th. But for 2 months there were no letters at all. You can imagine how lonesome we were for you and for some news about you. And now we have received the card from you, which is always a sign of life.

I am so sorry that you, dear brother-in-law, are not very well. I wish you a speedy recovery, and that you can be the family provider again. I never could have imagined that it would be so hard to live in widowhood. I have always had compassion for poor widows, but I had not experienced it myself and now realize that I could not really understand their situation. I often feel that my dear Jasch will come again; but then I come to my senses and realize: He is really dead and will never come again! Why does it have to be this way? Our dear dead Papa used to write in every letter to us,"Dear children, the ways of the Lord are right!" To be able to believe that requires the answer to much prayer! God leads us through very deep valleys; He gives us burdens, but not more than we are able to bear. This is also our experience every day.

In the forenoon, when I received your card, I was washing clothes in the [...]. Mrs. Trekemna, who also lost her husband, was also there. We decided to go to the cemetery in the afternoon, and we did. I took Tina, Lena, and Jasch along and Mrs. Trekemna also took her small children – three boys. Mrs. Nietstein, whose husband had also died, also came (her grown children were all at work.) We went there at 2 o'clock [...]. When we got there, our hearts were again wounded and shattered.

I found the grave mound immediately. I had noted the shade trees carefully and had driven a large tree trunk into the ground at the head of his grave. It was just as I had left it; even the pegs driven into the ground at each corner to mark the outline of the grave were still there. The peg at the head of the grave, on the left side, is even growing. Our dear God will allow a large tree to grow there as a sign! Also, in this sign I recognize God's great goodness and love to us, even though here on earth I cannot understand the paths in which He is leading me, I still know that He loves me, that He wants to bring us eternal joy, that a Wiedersehen [*a reunion*] is coming! Here on earth we have no joy anymore and very little hope of meeting friends again; but in the great beyond we will all see each other and never be separated again! Oh, if only we would all be ready to meet God! How my heart aches, and how we cried as we were there and fixed up the grave. When we were finished, we knelt down and prayed and cried to God. Oh, dear Geschwister, if only you could have been there to see the grave mound of our dear father!

Many coffins were just scattered around – a little dirt thrown onto their lids. It was a gruesome sight to behold. When will the great God put an end to such incredible misery and save us from this savage generation?

On our way home we stopped by Voths and Mrs. Loewens (the road goes right by there). At Voths we found only the small children at home. Both of the Voths were digging in the forest. They had received orders to dig 400 metres to plant potatoes. We went there and visited them. They are both incredibly thin – and she still with a baby at her breast. He has great hopes that we will be set free. Mrs. Loewen had gone for some bread but could not get any. Her children are still in Leugenka in Prigut. An hour ago her Nicolai came home for a one-day visit. He looks much better.

Now I will tell you what happened to me today. I wrote to this point yesterday. Yesterday we decided to go to Kizel early this morning. Many wanted to go. Because it is so dangerous to walk through the forest here because of the bandits, we decided to go as a group. During the night it rained very hard and this morning still threatened rain. But we decided that since H. Fr. had a rest day and was going with us, we would go anyway. After we had gone some distance, 12 men came towards us. Men and women ran. We asked what the problem was. They said: "Bandits!" We definitely heard someone screaming, "Pamysmi, pamysmi" [*bandits, bandits*]. H.F. was courageous and said we should continue on our way and not be afraid. A man and 2 women came along, but the others turned back out of fear. After we had again gone a short distance, we saw many were already standing beside the road. As we came nearer, we saw what the trouble was: they were being stopped by our Activisten [*activists*], seeking to force them to the Cydomeins [*free labour farms*]. There was no chance to flee.

We were caught and we stood there about 1 ½ hours, until all those who were going to Kizel were there. Then we were taken far into the forest to dig and turn the sod. The spades were brought to us and 30 square metres were measured out for each of us – it should have been 50, but because of the rain the norm was reduced. We came home soaked to the skin. I immediately changed my clothes and lay down to sleep a little. And now I am writing this letter to you out of love and longing.

I wanted to get some flour but now will have to go some other time. It is raining and has rained hard all day. Friesen went to Kizel because Mrs. P. Loewen in Kizel was expecting him. (She came to H.F.'s at 11 o'clock yesterday night with a Russian woman, stayed the night, and left again this morning at 4 o'clock. Lucky for her, or she also would not have gotten away.) H.F. had described her situation and sent it to Mr. J. Kl. Am., and they sent her 12 Marks to H.F.'s address. But she could not get possession of it without H.F.

This is the 3rd letter I have written to you in the month of May – and 1 card – the 3rd May, the 11th, a card on the 28th, and this one. I wonder if you have received them. I sincerely hope so! I received one from the 5 May from home, from Mariechen. I had written you everything, also that our dear Mama has been operated on again. It is still very dry there – no rain. But now letters have arrived stating that recently it has rained much and a late harvest is a possibility. It is a sign of the last times, is that not so? Even you, dear brother-in-law, write that it is extremely dry in your region.

We had not heard that P. Dueck has again been exiled. What could be the reason! I do not understand if P. Duecks have separated! Have not had a letter from sister Truda since 18 Feb. No letter from J. Goos. since December. I do not understand it. Do they not write? I beg all of you there, dear Geschwister, endure yet for a little while, maybe our situation will soon change. After all, our time and our destination have been determined – as you, dear Liese, often write us, not one hour longer than God allows! That thought has comforted me so often. Do not forget us in the future either. Our situation with the R. [*ruling authorities*] is the still same as it was;

we have been able to live better through the help you sent us. God reward you for it, dear Geschwister – and all those others who have given – according to His promises! That is also our daily prayer.

It is impossible to live from that which we get here. When will we again be able to eat our own bread? How will it ever end? Dear Liese, how much would I have liked to accompany you to Sunday School with your children. May God bless your acres and maintain your health, and also give us a Wiedersehen with you dear ones, if not here then in our heavenly home.

In love I remain, never forgetting you,

Maria and children

Write more. Greet B. Kl., also J.M. How are things with them?

How are things going with P. Koop and Jak Mart. Pet. B are already "auf dem gruenen Zweig" [*the metaphor, "on the green branch or green way," describes improved living conditions*]. The J.R. children are living and still have enough from the Torgsin to live on. Miechi writes that she drove to […] in […]. for 1 month. She wrote you about it in her previous letter. Maybe she did not get there. Will write about it again.

Sunday, 3rd June [1934]

Dear Geschwister Bargens,

Let me tell you that yesterday your much and long desired letter, written on April 29th, arrived. The card that you mention in the letter, and sent at the same time, still has not arrived. The card from May 5th has arrived. You cannot imagine how happy we are that finally, after 2 months, we are again receiving mail. The letters of the 10th of May, the 28th of Feb. and the 2nd of June, have gone through many hands.

Everything seems to be quiet here. We would so much like to see you face to face; I hope God will grant us that joy. Yesterday we were in Kyderca at J.R.'s children [*orphaned children*]. Things are not going well there. They still had 2r. 75k. left, otherwise nothing else – no products either. Their Agnes was alone at home with little Jascha. His glands are very swollen, and Rg. has T.B. He will not be long for this world. Did not see Hans, he was at work, but I am told he too is very skinny.

Joh. Peters live in one barrack with them and keep an eye on the children. They have 2 children, 10 and 8 years. They are from Gruenfeld. They said things looked very sad with those children. I wonder if not all the people realize that this is all that is left of the whole family. I feel so sorry for the little children. I remember former days, our younger years, how happy we were together with J.R.'s; and now both of them, and my dear Jasch too, are in eternity. And we are here in this great tribulation, away from everyone. I too cry bitterly.

I was in the store and they had shirts and finished trousers, but I did not get any. [....] Oh, if we could only be delivered! That is, instead of going into the house and praying, "Oh God, intercede!" My heart cries – and there is no response! I wrote to M. M. on May 3rd and 11th, and a card on the 28th and again on 30th. Did you receive them all? I will write another card. I have just written a letter, but you mention that cards seem to go more securely. Is our dear God going to allow the people to perish by starvation? You wrote of seeding time; the letters from home say there is still no rain. H.F. got a letter from Bosch. Yesterday, May 23rd, J.B. and A.R. are 90 Werst away from Wengada. Ar. R. gets food and clothing. J.B. lives out of his own pocket there. W. Bargen had been at Bosch. and had cried and said, "Why didn't I die of starvation last year? So much misery in this great nation!" May God reward your landlords for the 1 dollar, and you also, dear Geschwister. Yesterday I wrote a letter to Liese's landlords. I wrote in love.

Your loving M. and children

Went with the children to the graveyard. I wrote about it in the letter. Tina went to Kizel to get ½ nyd. flour.

*Letters from Maria's mother in Altonau are also decreasing. Is their safe passage at risk? Or, as Maria wonders, are these letters simply lost? She also wonders if her mother and others are just weary of writing. She pleads with her readers to "Endure with us a little longer."*

Polowinka, 17th June 1934

Dear Geschwister Franz and Liese and the dear children,
What shall I write to you this Sunday morning? It is 7 o'clock, the children are at work, Lena went to line up for bread, and I'll go later to change places with her. Jascha is still asleep. It is raining very hard. Truly a sleepy Sunday for those who can sleep. Jasch is no more, I miss him so much.

Oh, how lonesome my life is and how hard. How slowly time goes! I only write this letter because I love you so much, dear Liese. We would love to see you again face to face, and speak to you. Who can know if this joy will be granted to us in this life! Until now I have always firmly believed that our deliverance would come only if we could come to you. But this belief has been shattered lately. We received a letter from Mariechen, June 9th, and she enclosed a letter from you. I will do this also and trust you will receive it. Boldts do not write to us at all, only one letter after our things were taken from them. Mariechen writes that that is the reason. I am sorry about that. After all a letter is always a sign of love – at least that is how I perceive it. I get very few letters from Mama after the death of my dear Jasch. I still believe M. loves me. Maybe such thoughts are only temptations. Or are the letters going lost? I am so anxious to know how things are going for everyone.

I would love to be in a church today, together with all the dear children of God whom I have known. In these hard times I have learned to understand Psalm 42: ["*As the deer longs for fresh water, so longs my soul for you, oh God.*"] That is my deepest desire. When will the time come, dear siblings? How will you be celebrating this Sunday? I would love to be in your midst.

How is it that B. Klassens do not write at all any more? Are they so poor that they do not even have money for stamps? I received a letter from them on January 23rd and I wrote back promptly. Then I wrote again March 22nd, and I also enclosed a letter from Mariechen. I wonder, didn't they receive them? They do not write at all. Ask them, will you, and let me know. We do not owe them a letter now, nor when Jasch was still alive. I would really like to know the reason. Brother-in-law B. has never written a letter – is that not too little? They once wrote that they could not send us much and did not like to write. Write or tell them even if they couldn't send us anything, maybe they could speak to others of our misery. It could be that one or another could spare a widow's mite for us! Just like you, dear Geschwister, are doing, and our great God would recognize this. Also, maybe many times I would be encouraged by their letters. Maybe our situation will change. So endure with us a little longer, dear siblings. We would so much like to experience better times. The end is not in sight yet.

The [...] was completed by May 25th, at least that was the plan. Everyone went to get a reward. They promised that it would happen on June 1. However, now our quota has been increased by 13 hectares of thick green virgin forest. The sawing and the digging are very hard. And all this must be done after our daily work, when the worker is already tired and exhausted, but the extra work must be done. Today it is already the 17th and it is hopeless! The blind man is led and knows not where!

I have not had a letter from Truda and Joh. Goosen for a long time. Do you hear anything of them? Truda once wrote me that she had fallen in love with that [...] Epp. She postponed it so that nothing would interfere with the support she was giving us. May God reward her too, according to His promises. Dear Liese, do not write to her of this, please. You know I have no one I trust on this earth. I received a letter yesterday from home, Kronau. Many are again being thrust into much tribulation! And we thought He would deliver Israel! This is the second letter to you in June. If only you would receive them all. From you we received the last letter on April 13th. We received one letter with 3 empty sheets of paper where only you, dear Liese, wrote half a page and left the other half empty. On April 29 you had both written. Then we also received 1 card, written by Franz on March 5th. We are anxiously waiting for some more news. May God at least preserve this one thing for us, that we get news of each other through letters. I am deeply humbled, dear siblings, that you want to undertake for us in the future. We need it in order to survive. You will receive the reward.

In deep love I remain your sister-in-law, who loves you deeply,

Marie and children, goodbye

## Our Own Fresh Potatoes

*It is summer, and the sun warms even this cold place in the north. The prisoners still work hard in the communal fields, the forests, and construction sites, but now they have rights to their own small garden plot. The first potatoes are an unrivaled feast for Marie and her children. But how long can these summer days and their small garden plot feed them?*

Aug. 19, 1934

Dearly beloved siblings Franz and Liese and children,
I would like to send you some lines of love and of our well-being, across the water. Our Peter and Jascha have had terrible stomach cramps and diarrhea for 5 days. This illness is making its rounds here. The doctors have no medicine for this. How are things with you and your health, dear brother-in-law? You, dear Liese, are about like our dear Mama was when we got married.

I would just love to see you, yes all of you, face to face. We would have so much to talk about – about the things that happened in the times since you left here. We have only had a few good days since then, and in the end we may have to pay with our lives. To believe, at all times, that these ways are the right ways is very hard and can only be the product of much prayer! Today it is again Sunday

– a beautiful day. The sun is smiling so friendly into the window.

Driven by this great longing and love, in spirit and thought I visited all my loved ones, also you dear siblings. So I write this letter to you, dear siblings. I wonder if you are attending a church service. I also have this great desire to experience such a time again, those days when you were still living in N. 8 and dear brother Toews lived at your place. How happy we were then! He also had to end his life here in exile, as did so many of our leading brethren whom the Ausland [*foreign country*] wanted to save. They have perished – and we could and can do nothing.

H.V. and Mrs. Loewen of N. 7 were here for a visit last Sunday and spoke of many things, also of brother Toews. H.V. said that Toews' wife, when she was a widow, had been run over and that is why the Ausland could not do anything and demand his release, since she had no man [*the meaning is unclear*]. It was clearly evident, even then, that V. did not care for him too much. I think it was because Toews was so far above him. Voth also feels that if we ever get back, then the little group of believers will again gather into a church, and he will be the Elder! I think not! He handles his family differently than most. His children, Hein, and Liesbeth, cook on their own and eat on their own. Their Michi was sick but now has entered the work force – and she takes her bread and the wages she earns, alone. He has all the little children registered to him. If they would pool all the earning power of 4 workers (all the products are given only to wage earners), the money would go farther and he would have it so much easier. From our former home we remember him as a very strict man, and yet it appears that in his family he has nothing to say.

Once, when I met him for the first time coming from milking we talked of so many things – how much we had experienced, deprivations, hunger, cold, and how much distress we were experiencing. Then he said to me, "This quota on bread is the deliberate thought and work of the devil. Many fights and divisions in families are created by it." And that is the truth too! It is very hard if you do not get enough food to satisfy your hunger. To live in affluence is definitely easier. But what is this affliction compared to the glory that awaits us if we remain faithful! May our God lead us in His right ways – that is my prayer!

Wednesday, 22! I was interrupted in writing my letter. Mrs. Trakman, who has also buried a husband, sent a message to ask if I did not also want to come to the cemetery with her. In her barracks a child had died (4 years old.). They are Catholic. The entire mourning group consisted of 5 souls, Mrs. Trakman, myself, the driver of the team, and the parents (it was their only child). Here people are so emotionless. No one is allowed to go along to show compassion. I and Mrs. Trakman could go along to visit our own husbands' graves – to cry at their graves. The wound tears open each time we go there. How lonesome and forsaken I feel here in this exile. Still, our great God has never discarded us or I would have despaired long ago.

Every day when the workers come from the bureau they are driven to the Cgdomems [free labour farms]. Sixty hectares are to be prepared for seeding. The plan has been filled many times over, but new burdens are constantly added. The people are being tortured without end and without mercy. I wrote a card to you on the 15th, in which I told you that this month all the [...] Rozanika [*meaning unknown*] are not to receive a ration card for bread – must go to work. All the mothers who [...] are without a card, except those that have a certificate from the doctor saying they are incapable of work. And there are very few of those. The R [governing authority] does not take people into account at all. I share my food, which you have sent to me, with these poor people. May God bless you and all others who helped send things here. And He will do it, too.

We are already able to eat fresh potatoes – and our own. I am happier to get these few potatoes than I was to get the thousands of pud of grain we used to harvest. Then we used to take it for granted that the harvest would be big and the granaries would be full every year. We never thought then that such a time of tribulation lay before us. Our loving God has let us experience that we are completely dependent upon Him and we cannot just take anything we want.

We must pray for it. I already wrote to you that I had received a letter from M. Welke, Arlington, Calif., who has since winter, on 4 occasions, sent us 8 Marks. She wrote she wanted to keep her promise to God and send a tenth which belongs to Him. That letter humbled me deeply. I do not even know the people, or if she is a widow. The letter was beautifully written. You can tell they are educated people. I have no idea how they came to do this or get our address. Maybe through your efforts, dear siblings.

Peter is very sick. He has no appetite. He looks as if he has been in bed for a month. I am beginning to be afraid, but we have a God who has life and death in His hand. We pray to Him, for He answers if we pray in His will. Sometimes that is so hard for us to understand. I truly believe he will get well.

*As another political holiday approaches, speculation about the release of prisoners again circulates in the camp. One holiday must have just passed, and the October celebrations are on the horizon. Hopes are rising once more.*

[August 1934]

I have not had a letter from home for a long time. The last one from Hans K. on June 30th, from Ab. Reg and Susie on July 10th. I do not know what the reason can be for this lengthy silence. I can hardly wait until I hear from them again. I also do not know where our dear Mama is. Mariechen only wrote that after her operation Mama intended to visit Ab., but I have no word yet that she arrived safely. Why must we all be scattered to the winds like we are, so that no one knows anything of the other! We can get news only through letters and they travel so slowly.

I received a card from you on August 4th. Dear Liese, the letter which you wrote immediately after the card, but sent at the same time, has gone lost. How is it possible? H.F.'s do not get any letters from Bosch. either. I guess they have no time to write during harvest. I would love to know how the harvest is there. Will they have bread, or will they starve again? This year they probably will not eat as much white Bulkje [*bread*] as they ate last year. In the future they will probably not drink as much Brantwein [*brandy*] at the weddings. W. Kl. of N. 1 and J. Bosch. write that for their weddings they bought brandy for 100 rubles. The way things look to me, people are not getting any better. It is as in the times of Noah, people do not want to be corrected by God's Word. I would so gladly speak with you face to face, but it is impossible; so we must be satisfied like this – and be thankful we can still correspond.

There is no sign of our release; it has been postponed until the October celebrations. That is how they comfort us from time to time. Now I have a burning desire to be set free! How are things at B. Kl. and with Tina's health? I and Lena are very busy carrying in the wood for winter fuel. We need a lot of fuel and must carry it on our backs. It is very hard work. I get afraid when I think of winter. The woolen stockings are in shreds, and I have nothing to mend them with. I regret the letter went lost. From whence will we be saved? Do you hear of anything? [...] is supposed to have died, that is what we read in the papers. What will happen now? Well, stay in God's care until we meet again. All the children send regards.

[October 1934]

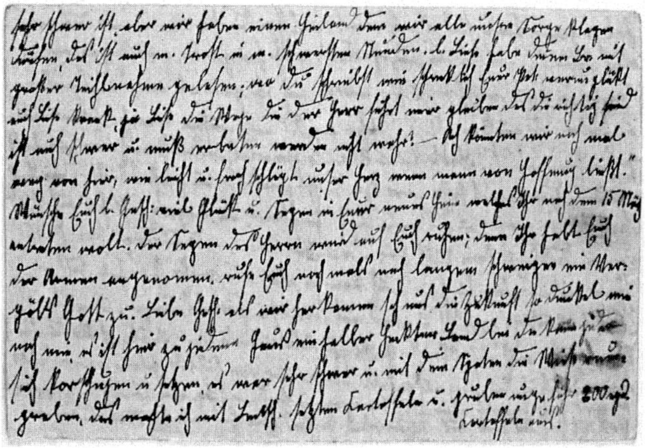

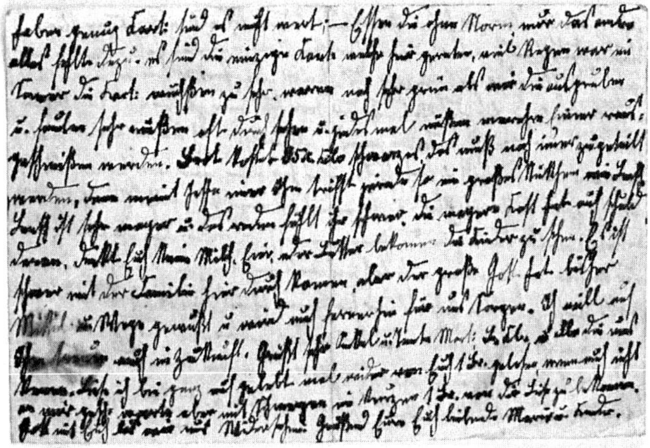

[. . .] even if it is very hard, we have a Saviour to whom we can tell all our troubles. That is my strength and comfort in hours of my greatest need.

Dear Liese, it is with deepest sympathy that I read about the terrible accident your Peter had [*while harvesting, twelve-year-old Peter caught his leg in the combine, and he narrowly escaped the machine's whirling blades*]– and Liese being sick as well. It is true, Liese, the ways of God are often hard to understand. But they are always right. Is that not so? Oh, if only we could get away from here! How our heart leaps with joy when we read that there may be hope. I wish you much joy and blessing in your new home which you plan to move into after March 15th. The blessing of God will rest upon you, because you have cared for the poor. Let me again say, May God reward you richly.

Dear Geschwister, when we were sent here, the future looked as dark and foreboding as never before. Here there is a ½ hectare of land for every house. Now everyone can cultivate a garden. It was extremely hard to turn over the sod with a spade, but Lena and I did it. We planted potatoes and now we dug out about 200 ydá. potatoes. We have enough potatoes! We are not worthy. We eat them without observing norms – but we lack everything else that goes with them. These are the only kind of potatoes that prosper here. There was very much rain in summer and the potatoes grew too fast. They were still green when we dug them out, so they rot rather fast too. We must sort them often and have to throw out several pailfuls each time.

Bread costs 95k. per kilo, that is, black bread, and is still rationed. Then our little Jascha thinks he should have just as large a piece as Liese. Our Lena is very thin. She speaks very slowly and with difficulty. The poor diet certainly plays a big part in this. Imagine, no milk, eggs, or butter can be bought. It is hard to get by with the family. But our great God has found ways and means for us until now, and He will continue to do so. I will trust Him for the future.

Give warm greetings to Uncle and Aunt Martens, Benjamin Klassens, and all those that still know us. Liese, I was so cheered again to read a letter from you, even though it was not written to me. I am anxiously waiting to get a letter from you in the near future. May God be with you until we meet again.

Your loving Marie and children

*Lining up for bread or supplies is a dreadful experience. Desperation drives the hungry to grab, push, and stampede. To her horror, Maria is robbed of her food certificate in the crush of people reaching for their food rations. Yet even in this dark place, a miracle occurs.*

4th December [1934]

My dearest Geschwister Franz and Liese and children, far away in the great distance,

I wish you God's blessings in all your ways, and that this letter may find you in the best of health. We too are well and alive. We owe God a great deal of thanks, even if the ways He leads seem dark to us and we cannot understand why.

Sunday, December 2, I and Mrs. Faust and Mrs. Wetstein walked to Kizel to buy bread. Early in the morning I went to see the Kommandant to get permission. No one is allowed to go out of the camp without a pass. I had no thought of misfortune. When we got to Kizel, there already were three lineups waiting to buy bread. I was going to pull out my money purse, but it was not there. What a shock! You cannot imagine how I felt. There was no other way; I had to leave, and stay without bread.

You would not believe what happens here when we go into the store to buy. The strongest gets to the counter first – it is terrible to see. It is a matter of life and death. One must exert all the strength one has. I had taken all our money along. The children had just been paid and wanted bread, since we get so little as our ration. Every month we take the 3 children's ration cards to get flour so that we can stretch our food supply a little further. I had 50r. with me – and the great misfortune to also have the Iklada [*food stamps*] of 60r., which we had for Abangi (potatoes and cabbage). Even that is gone as well. I do not know why I kept it in my money purse.

I am almost at the point of despair, everything gone, all our assets. I almost preferred to stay in the big forest. I sobbed and inwardly shouted to God, "Why this yet as well?" Could He not have protected me from this? We needed it so desperately to live on, and now all is gone! The Iklada was 30r. from last year and 30r. from this year. And so far we had received nothing on it. It was promised, and that is the way it stays. What a heavy heart I had on the way home – and then to have to tell the children of my misfortune. After all, I do not earn anything. I told them what had happened, and that it could not have happened except for the stampeding and the pressing of the people.

There are some Ckyenri [*outlaws*] who do that full time. The children did not blame me. They only said that the money was gone but they would earn more. Maybe the Iklada would still give us something for it anyway. How long we had already waited for those potatoes – and now everything is gone! It overwhelms me! Why did I have to have that misfortune! Mrs. H. Friesen was already here and waited until I came. But I was not happy to see her. She is just like she used to be at home. She always wants to know what her neighbour had for lunch. However, often I am happy when she comes. I was very tired, so when Lena finally came home from school we went to sleep.

We had just lain down when Lena said, "Oh yes, we have 3 letters." Our daughter Tina had been in the post office to mail a letter and the postmaster had given them to her, and she had given them to Lena in school. The mail is always delivered to our house; how Tina happened to get it I just do not know. One letter was from you, dear Liese, where you write that you had knelt down and prayed that God should deliver the letter into our hands. He has done it. Then there was a letter from Nov. 6 from J. Goosens with 2 dollars enclosed, and another letter with another 5 dollars from B. Kl. I got up, opened the letters, and read them all. Then Peter said, "See, Mama, now God has immediately given it back to us." I also said, "What great fortune, what a happy day, if only that misfortune had not been sent to me."

We received the notice card about the 5 dollars last Sunday (Nov. 25). Mrs. P. Loewen, N. 7, was visiting here at the time. She is bitterly poor. She wears only mules and her feet are wrapped in rags. The card was sent on November 7 and arrived here on Nov. 25; and the other also on Nov. 7 and got here on December 2.

*The October holiday celebrations have passed. Daughter Liese (now twenty-two years old) believes they might be released during the next May holiday. But her tone is cynical; she has lost her confidence in people and politicians. Her betrothed, Peter Koehn, begs her to attempt escape one more time, and implores her to return to her home village and marry him. But she is afraid.*

*Her fear is not unfounded. Although Liese would not be aware of the greater political sphere, drastic changes are occurring. In 1934, letters destined for the Campbell's Soup box diminish significantly. Only two are written in 1935, one in 1936, and three in 1937. Political tension has risen, and fear controls both the writing and the delivery of letters.*

*On December 1, 1934, Sergey Kirov, Stalin's right-hand man, is murdered. His death ignites nationwide fear. Stalin becomes paranoid and claims that a larger conspiracy led by Trotsky against the entire Soviet regime is looming. The crescendo of tension results in another purge, worse than the first. Everyone is suspect.*[2] *As yet the effects of Stalin's paranoia are not felt across the whole nation, and in the massive system of prison camps, changes evolve slowly. But storm clouds are gathering. For now, Liese thinks about her clothes, her home village, her young Uncle Abram, and her brother Peter.*

5 Dec. 1934

Dear Aunt Liese and Uncle Franz and children,
I will try to write a letter even though I am in a great hurry. I want to send you a sign of love. We are still quite well, which I also wish for you with all my heart. Actually I do not know what to write to you. If I would write good things, they would be lies. There is just no good here in the Urals, and by now you certainly know all the bad there is here.

We have had a nice winter until now. If it stays this way, we will have enough wood for fuel and we will not freeze. We had real hopes for the October celebration but it has passed, so now our hopes are for the month of May. In October rights were restored to 6 men. I guess our situation is like the proverb says: "Von Hoffen und Harren wird mancher zum Narren" [*From hoping and waiting many are made into fools*]. I wish I knew how things are at home [*in Altonau*]. Here it is terribly lonesome. There is only one other Mennonite couple here, only H.F. Then there are two families of Lutherans and a few Catholics. But I can't feel at home with them.

We get no letters from our relatives anymore. Grandmama wrote a month ago that Abram [*the young uncle who was arrested with the family, escaped, and is living in Altonau*] could not get by on forged papers any longer. He will be sent back here. On October 30th he had been in jail in Kherson. But whether they will send him here, I do not know. P. Dueckmann, N. 8, is in Kizel. Mama spoke to him recently. His wife is in Kherson. Grandma writes that Abram's clothes are all very old and worn; we should give him what he needs! But where shall we get it from? The clothes I took with me when I ran away all stayed at H.R's. They wrote to me several times about sending them to me: a blouse which they probably wore all summer, a pair of over- washed pants, and an apron made of sack cloth which I had made for myself here in the Urals for sawing wood. Mostly things which I had never worn here. Everything else stayed there. Even if it wasn't much, I need it. Also an overcoat and 10 metres of cloth material I had received for my work here. I could fill many pages with how cheated I feel. But it is far better to keep quiet. When I was at home, they fled from me as from a fire. I would not have to be here today if [...]. But if I ever find myself in a better situation than now, I will tell everything.

Abram has not sent us an address, and in two years sent us only 2 little pages which he enclosed with Mariechen's letters. He does not need us. But if he should return here, we would not let him know how we felt, since I too know what it is to be a prisoner. Well, enough of this.

Yesterday was my birthday (the 7th Dec., new style) [*The new Gregorian calendar has replaced the Julian*]. I guess no one thought of it. I am already 22 years old. All my friends from N. 7 have already married. I always get letters that I should come home, but I never wanted to. When I was there, they did not know it; when they found out and came, I was already gone. Dear Aunt Liese, you ask if I've grown taller. I do not know. I am now 69 kwo, that is 4 nyg, 12 ½ w. When you moved away I was 4 nyg, 20 w. That is enough for me. I do not want to get any fatter. I have short hair, but it is only wavy if I make it so – but that happens very seldom. I have no desire for it.

I would love to go home again. If we ask, the Kommandant can give us a pass to go home for a holiday for 2 weeks to 1 month, but it is just too expensive for us. From what they write, things are not going too well at home either. Aunt S. wrote that P.K. [*Peter Koehn, the man she eventually marries*] is waiting. That is so. He writes letters to me and wants me to come home. But I just can't make up my mind. And I do not think at all of running away. Only time will tell if I will ever get home again. Our relatives from home urge me to come and say that I will never regret it. But I still do not know. I also get other letters.

Be heartily greeted from Liese Regehr

Next time I'll write more.

[December 1935]

[...] abundance, no, in sympathy for the children, because they have no papa. I thought the children would suffer the most, and they were sent nothing. I still am not sorry but regret that they do not write at all how things are going for them. I feel so sorry for all loved ones there in our homeland. They do not have bread either. We have experienced so often how hard it is not to have anything. Even you loved ones have had to experience that it is more blessed to give than to receive, right?

Dear Liese, you ask for a picture, but I only have one and wanted to keep it as a memory for the children. I sent one to Mama, so I will send this one to you in love. I have a grey dress and kerchief on. It is a good thing that my dear Jasch bought me such a good dress when we still could. Michi is wearing a woolen jacket and a cotton blouse underneath. Tina is wearing a green overcoat which I made for her to go to America. Do you know that Lenchen had received a green suit from us? Jasch and P.B. drove to Kherson once and brought it along from there. J. Barg. also had one like it, as well as W. B., but it is already very worn. Lensch and Jascha are also wearing [...] received from the Germans. Lensch's skirt is made from a black dress which was so torn so that I could barely get a small skirt for her. I would need a bit more to sheer the waist. Michi works with a young Tatar girl and they stood around and joked about it. M. laughed so much.

I have a lot of grey hair and I very much need a pair of glasses. I can see very poorly. After Jasch's death it got worse; I never noticed it before. It certainly is a sign that I am getting old. Oh, but I would rather not be old yet! Even if we are in exile, we still resemble ourselves. You have learned of the brutal nature of this exile not only from us but from reports in the foreign newspapers as well. Our condition is a bit easier than in the beginning. We have better quarters, and also the difference between you and us is no longer so great. Even without writing it to you, you know that this exile has devoured many sacrificial victims. No one will have said: We, too, want to be exiled! But he who has not been in exile cannot imagine what it is like. The children of Israel were also taken into exile and slavery, but when they called to their God in their tribulation, He delivered them out of all of their terrors. And so I believe our time of deliverance is coming as well. We will live to see it!

The 5th of December, evening: I just want to tell you that we received another money order of 5 dollars from Kor. Loewens, Kansas, sent through J. Harms of Hillsboro, Kansas. It cannot possibly be the letter of which you, dear Liese, write, because they had promised to send each of us two such letters. I believe it will yet arrive as a package.

Again and again I see that God is looking after us. Do you know those Loewens? They have sent us something several times. J. Goosens write that sister Truta is intending to get married to a Ewert. She is no longer working for English people. She is now in British Columbia, where there are more Germans. I guess then she won't be sending us so much anymore. She has done so much for us. May God bless her for it, and [may] she will still have enough to give in the future. He is supposed to be an unbeliever, and that is not too acceptable to the Gossens. Goosens do not write why she did not accept that Benj. Epp.

I am happy for Benjamin Klassens that things are going easier for them. Would gladly have been their guest sometime, or visit you and Uncle and Aunt Martens. I guess they are doing very well. Greet them from us. I was at H. Voth, there I saw a picture of Uncle Hans, and then in my mind's eye I can see you all as you were when I last saw you. Where is Uncle Jasch? How many children do they have? I am so happy for the letter, dear Liese. You wrote so much, and of so many acquaintances whom I know so well. Greet them all from me – old Penners and all their children, P.D. of N. 3. They are not unsympathetic people. Maybe they could also spare a penny for the poor, if God has blessed them with a good harvest? Jacob M. have 7 children already? And Mrs. Martin Dueck has also died? I will tell Wilhelm – she was his aunt. Do you ever hear anything of sister Toews, your house friend? What about Abr. R. and the old Toewses: what do you know of them? Write all you can about each Russlaender [*Russian Mennonite*].

Your M.R.

Auf Wiedersehen

*Life appears to be improving for this family. While they are certainly not living in luxury, and Maria requests a coat and blanket to be sent from Canada, they have received clothes from the "Germans" (ethnic Germans who had previously settled in the Volga region of Russia). In fact, the Regehr children are now able to extend some charity to another family. But the morality in the camps worries this mother.*

[December 1935]

It is now a week later. On November 25 I sent a card to Ben. Kl. and to you. In it I reported that we had received it. I think they will also write a letter to me. In fact, I am eagerly awaiting it, and then I'll write a letter to them. On November 2nd, I again wrote a card to you. Actually we write to no one as often as to you. There is also no one who sympathizes with us as you do, dear Geschwister – and support us so. Our dear God will reward you a thousandfold, this is my daily prayer.

Oh, I thank you many times, dear Geschwister, and also you, dear children, F. and L. and P. and Meka, that you continue to care for us and sympathize with us. At times I feel so alone and forsaken. I certainly do not wish or pray for a long life, but then when I think of leaving my children alone here in exile – among only Russians and godforsaken people – it hurts so much that I can hardly sleep at night because of it. There is no seeking or asking after God here.

Even our children – they all want to go to heaven and they certainly are not godless, but they are not believers.

The life of the worker on the Proiswotswo [place of production] is no life at all. There is confusion; all work together, old and young, men and women. Age is not respected as it was at home. Do not think, dear Geschwister, that this is against the parents! No, this is at work. Everyone is yelled at there! Our children often say to me, "Mama, if you would hear what those old men talk about, you would be shocked!" Depraved Russian people! And then they have the Club, where every evening there is Cobrpanic [*meaning unknown*] and dancing.

My children make me very happy, since they never go anywhere after work. They stay with me. Again and again my prayer is "God protect our children from sin!" Where there is the occasion to sin, there the danger is also greater. There is one thing: We are so oppressed and can barely eke out our living, otherwise it would be very sad. I often think of old Mr. J. Janz, who once said, "In Serjenwka the devil had no more work to do. He just lay down at the end of the village and rejoiced – for all the people were already serving him!" There are many Russians here who have been married up to 10 times; they divorce (their children have all starved to death), they swap mates. Many a father and mother, when they get old and can't work anymore, go begging. (They get very little because everyone is looking after themselves.) The grown children do not want to support the parents and younger siblings. It is a very sad picture. It is very hard when there are many little children.

In our family there are 3 workers and 4 non-workers, and it is hard too. If we did not receive the help from overseas, we could not possibly get by. We see time and time again how God cares for us! I will also continue to trust Him for the future; He will make hearts and hands willing to send us a "mite" from over there in order to make our situation somewhat easier. I have not had any mail from home for a long time. I had a letter of November 14th from Mama and sent it to you on November 20th. Have you received it? All the others do not write; they probably have forgotten us. I once wrote to Ab. R. that they should send me a blanket and Tina's overcoat. With that request I think I spoiled everything, since now they do not write anymore. We have no more claims on anything. At times it hurts so much. Is it not enough that we lost all our goods and property; Jasch had to die here in exile; and who feels for us? No one as you faithful ones do! It has to be experienced! Our children sent a parcel to Susie's children: 1 kilo sugar, grits, 2 pairs stockings for Liese and Hans and Sonja, a small woolen jacket which Liese received from the Germans for Jascha but which was too small for him. It weighed 6 kilo, not from our [...].

*More than a year of silence sounds an ominous note. Marie is relieved that letters are again arriving. But she can no longer send letters from her location. Others in more distant places post her correspondence. The three older children (Liese, Mariechen, and Peter) have been sent further north to a remote forestry camp and rarely see their mother.*

Feb. 1, 1936

Dearly beloved Geschwister Franz and Liese and children away in that great distance!!!
May God's grace, and mercy, and patience keep you until we meet again. Most beloved siblings, I must report to you at the very beginning of this letter that after 11 months of silence I was again able to hold this letter from you, dear ones, in my hands! Dear Geschwister, I am just unable to describe the feelings that overwhelmed me when I saw your letter. On January 28th I received a letter from our dear Mama, in which she enclosed your very precious letters of October 17th and December 2nd. It is the 2nd letter from Mama since we arrived here.

We have gone through very hard times since we have been in this region. But God granted grace to carry us and has helped us wonderfully, so that we are still all alive. In the beginning we wrote many letters but got no responses until now – and no one else got any answers either – so that we did not know if any letter even reached you. We were just cut off from everything. Then you can imagine what we went through. Should God lead us so that we should meet again, then we will have much to talk about.

H.F. got a letter on December 28th from brother Jakob and a letter from J. Peters, where he writes that he read in the big newspaper that we are here. And from that I gather that you must know our address as well. Many deep sighs have risen to God: Please send us word of our loved ones! Well, now we heard. Praise God! Should we see each other again in this life, dear Liese, may God grant that it be soon. Many, many hoped and believed they would experience a time of reunion – but they are no longer with us!! Oh, I weep so much!!

Dear Liese – I do not know if this letter will reach you. May this letter get into your hands. That is my plea. I wrote to Ab. and will enclose this letter and ask him to mail it from there. Sending something from here is useless. Yesterday a girl came here – from those girls where Tina is (Tina couldn't come; her shoes were ripped apart) – and she is going back tomorrow, Sunday. I will give this letter along to mail it from there, Bep Izba. I also wrote to Mama.

Right now it is terribly cold here, down to 55 degrees. Liese came home on the 27th February during a severe snowstorm and heavy frost! I never even thought that one of our own could be on the road. I was shocked and could not say a word when she walked in. She had felt boots on, but they were torn and frozen together with stockings and foot rags. It was almost impossible to remove them. She was home for 2 days and then she had to go back. Our poor children have already cried so much – must spend their young lives here in exile. And no deliverance. L. and P. and M. are working 25 kilometres from here. They must load wood, which is very hard and dangerous work, and many have had accidents. Jasch F. broke his left leg and is now in bed in the Tsvirnmya [*a place of convalescence*]. There is no electric light here, but you must work even at night when no one can see anything.

Here at this Tlocinor are only the old mothers with the little children. The workers are over there. There is a rumour that this Tlocinor will be terminated. Many have already been removed this way; build up and tear down seems to be the plan. Peter had not been here on the Lenab [*meaning unknown*] for 6 months. Then he came home for 5 days, but had to leave and went to where he is now. So the children are never with me. The conditions here and the thoughts and worries for my children burden me so much that it often [...].

Should Ab. be freed sooner than we? Our time here has no end – that is why we get so discouraged. We have been here for 5 years already. Who would ever have believed it? Greet all your children.

It also encourages me for the future, dear Geschwister, to know that if it becomes necessary to do something for us, you will make representations on our behalf. Liese, you know what I mean.

*Thirteen months later we finally have another letter from Maria. Were letters written but not delivered? Or was their journey interrupted? And what happened to Liese's plan to escape? In spring 1937, a letter from Maria to her mother in Altonau finds its way out of the Soviet Union to Canada. Instability is increasing. Clues to mail delivery are shrouded, but they do reveal that letters are sent to one person and posted by another. Maria informs her reader that letters "are never sent from here." She also wonders if "that is the only reason we are here."*

March 9, 1937

Dearest, faithful and loving Mama, far away in our homeland!!

May the almighty God comfort and protect you in all your ways, give you the best of health and supply all your needs. We also are still alive and well, for which we have great reason to be thankful. I really wanted to finish writing letters yesterday but I was hindered: Mrs. H.F. and Mrs. Michel came here for a visit. Her husband is home [*back in his home village*]. He fled from here, so now she is here all alone. Her first husband was a Harwoht, from those Harwohts near Wladimivbka. He was murdered at the time the forester and his sister in the Forstei [*forestry service*] were murdered in the stone quarry by a band, of which a Harder of N. 10 was also a part. Remember, they also wanted to kill my Jasch at that time. Mama, you will of course know that whole story, right? What terribly hard times we have already experienced, and it looks like the times are getting constantly worse. If only God could accomplish His purpose in us and we be saved!

Here there is no inquiring after salvation. H.V. told us that harsh judgments seldom improved a person. Should that be true? My striving is to get to heaven. Dear Mama, you write that in one way you are happy that Abram is not there. But even here there is enough opportunity to be carried along with the stream. How wonderful and pleasant it used to be when each family was alone – the parents with their children could be occupied with farming. The elderly were respected and honoured by the younger ones. But now everyone just shouts "Hey, you" at us. That is the result of communal togetherness, and I am sure it is the same where you are.

When P. Dueck came from there, he told us that the youth have become quite degenerate. When we get together, we often speak of how things will be, should other times ever come when the church of God will arise in strength. But no church listens; everyone follows what is in their own heads. Does Mr. Block still preach? The blessing is still spoken over the young people. The time seems to have come of which Joh. B. often spoke: All of Christendom will crumble. It will require a very wise Solomon to bring order out of chaos. Well, our great God will know how to protect His own, even in affliction. That I believe completely!

Dear Mama, you have again written me such a nice, comforting letter. I was waiting so much for a letter from you. I was so happy to get some news of home. Mama, you have written so many things to me, of my aunts and uncles. Greet them all heartily from me – Mrs. F. Kl. with her children, and Mrs. Joh. M. Many a night I lie awake and think. Many thousands of thoughts march through my head – and one can do nothing. We are just helpless here. It already has been 5 years and there is no end in sight for us! Mama, I have received that letter with 3 of Liese's enclosed, which you mention in this letter. I have written to them already. Liese can comfort you so very much. It is too bad that I received no letter from them. Do they know our address?

I received a letter from brother J., Am., who writes that he read in the "Rundschau" [*a Mennonite periodical distributed in Canada*] that we are here, so he writes here. I received the letter. I even wrote back. I also wrote to Liese and sent the letters to Abram. He was supposed to post them out there, since they are never sent from here. Can that be the only reason we are here? In September I received 75 Francs through the Red Cross in Moscow; from whom it came I do not know, but it came to this address. It is so strange. No one in any foreign country knew where we were sent. [...] wrote several times from [...]. We were ordered to make [...] and we tried to do this [...]. We sent letters there and were able to delay it until we could pay for it in R. [*Russian*] money. But I still have not done it. Now I have to write there again. One stamp costs 33k.

It is regrettable that the Torgsin has been closed. The dollar is far too cheap. We still have a bit of the help left. Where would we be if other people had not helped us from overseas, Mama? Well, our great God will know how to look after us in the future too. The children's wages go so fast too. Until now I have received no picture from J. Martens. J.F. of N. 8 is still alive. We cannot buy any thread here.

*The danger of writing and sending letters increases. Maria is being watched more closely now. She cautions her reader in Canada that letters traveling to her in Russia are also being watched, so "it is better for us to write less." But the family's food supply is improving. They have a cow and a pig. Their sheep and goat have died, but the garden is planted, and potatoes, cabbage, and beets are growing.*

3 June 1937

My dearly beloved Geschwister Franz and Liese and children,
May God be your greeting and joy, and give you what you need for this life and much more for your eternal life. It is only God's mercy that we too are well and alive. Thousands have had to forfeit their lives in these hard times. God only knows who will live through it. I want to be quiet, and submit myself to God's will. He can and will help, even though it may seem too long to us. But it does not last a minute longer than God allows! I believe you, Liese, as you have often written: not one minute longer than God allows!

We are now waiting for June 15th. Then, if things do not change we must remain here. All those who were tried and sentenced in court got a specific time, but no time was set for us. We are now dealt with as strictly as we were in the first years. No one is allowed to leave the [...] without permission of the Kommandant. Because the wages here are so low, many of the workers agreed that when the Necocbanka was finished and the Cerab started *[exact meanings unknown]*, they would leave for Bumep and from there per ship to Kepmr. The wages are much better there. However, they were all chased back and have to work here.

Peter and Michi were among them. Now all three – L., P., and M – work at Cerab, always in the water. They are 20 km away from TTocenok. Liese wrote me a letter on June 1st that I should send Lena, and the clothes which she had made for herself to take along to our old home, to Bep:oz ba, since they would have to move further with the logs on the water by the 2nd or 3rd. They may only get back by winter time. Yesterday morning Lena and Jascha went to Bep:oz ba to Tina, and from there Liese wanted to take the clothes. They go past there with the logs. It is about 27 km away. Jascha will be very tired. They are supposed to come home today.

Poor children, from early childhood on they have had to go with those packs on their back. Jascha has finished 2 grades and will start the third next year. Lena finished the 5th. She was let out of school sooner than the other students. All those that were sick and stuttered did not have to take part in the [...] because it would be too strenuous for them. She came home on May 25th. The others had to study until June 1st. But Lena did pass to the 6th grade for next year. She learns very easily – only too bad that she has a speech difficulty. She also grew so rapidly; she is long and thin. Tina has to study until June 15 in the 7th g., then she has to go to work for 2 months. She must saw wood in the forest to earn something to make it a bit easier for her siblings. The children often get despondent that they must work for the little ones. And it is hard for them. They have remained in exile and must do the heavy work, and must continue to survive in the freezing wind and cold – in the dark forest.

If my husband Jasch was still alive, many things would be different – and how much easier for me. But every one of my days is counted, and no hair shall fall from our head without His will. If that were not so, I would despair. Even if the children often grumble, they do bring all their wages home. I keep it hidden and buy what is necessary.

At H. Voths it is now different. There the father is still alive, and the children from the first wife look only after themselves and give nothing to the parents. His feet got frozen this winter – he got lost when he went to get hay out of the forest. Well, you probably will have heard of it. He was in the hospital for 5 months. They had to remove all his toes on his left foot but left one joint on each toe. He can walk quite well in spite of it. He is now in the Commune and is night watchman in the barn with the cattle. However, he would like to get a job in the Kontor [*counting house*]. He even got a paper from the commission stating that he can do only work in which he would not have to walk too much. Together they have 3 children who are still alive. Their youngest, Peter, is as old as our Jascha – 9 years!

Heindrich F. are also all alive and have enough to live on. They have a cow and 2 goats that they milk, and 3 smaller goats and 1 pig. Their son Jasch just got married to a Russian – none of the German girls would have him. We have also bought a cow for 453r. and she had a calf in January. She now gives us 5 L. milk. The meadow is quite nice already. Because of the poor fodder, she was down to giving only 2 L. We also bought a young piglet. Also had a sheep with a little lamb. The old one has died. Last year we bought a goat for 300r.; it also died. We just do not have any luck. Then our children said they did not want me to buy anything anymore – the money was so hard to earn and no luck.

But we would love to live in a different manner and eat differently – not only eat bread and potatoes. Ach, the milk helps so much, and the piglet will provide some meat for us for the winter. On June 20th it will be six years since we had to leave our native home. We have not eaten an egg or any fruit since then. How different it is in our native home. Our little Jascha cannot remember anything of our home. We would just love to move away from here.

Dear siblings, our situation has greatly changed since the early years. When we were first brought here, we all thought we would have to perish here – it appeared so sad. Now it is already quite different. Everyone has his own quarters and a garden plot. Our yard is 75 long and 50 wide [*most likely metric measurement*]. We planted the whole area with potatoes on June 1 and 2nd. Then in late August or the beginning of September we can dig them up. We even planted a few carrots and beets – other things do not grow very well here, the summer is just too short – and some cabbage. The plants look quite nice already. My 7 pepper plants I keep in the house on the window; they just do not ripen outside.

It hardly pays, but then we are still those who cannot be without work! That is why we have fallen into this misfortune, isn't that right, Franz and Liese? If only we could see each other once again in this life. How often I long for that time. I have not written a letter to you for a long time, dear Geschwister, but not because I have forgotten you or do not love you as before, no, no. Dear Liese, you know me and know that we always loved each other – I just cannot put my thoughts on paper. It is like you wrote in the letter of May 18th to Mama. She sent it to me. How happy I was to be able to read a letter from you again, dear Liese. How your letter humbled me! What am I in God's eyes? There is nothing good in me – only grace carries me and will see me through to glory with my loved ones. There is no searching after God, and we never hear God's word. What a time we once enjoyed – we were allowed to attend Sunday school, church services, prayer, bible, and choir practice. And for our children here there is nothing. However, God will know how to prepare them for eternity too. My duty is to show the way to them – to pray.

I believe that they will not forget how their father, in his last days, called each of them by name and told them that his deceased mother wanted to see all her grandchildren again. And so we must come with all our children, protect them, and He will not allow them to be lost! Liese, I am greatly troubled that you will think that I do not write so often because we do not get any more parcels – no. I wrote to you often before, but now, seemingly, no letters reach you and we receive none either. So I just stop writing. We are also being watched so very much here, and it is better for us to write less. And the same is true for you, dear Liese – from there to Mama.

F.R's friend is boarding with us the whole time we have been living here. We eat together; he is like our child. He is often at home (like now too). Because of the great rheumatism pains in his feet, he can hardly walk. He is almost like M.B.'s brother Hein. A very nice young man, orderly, doesn't smoke. But Peter does – yet never in my presence, he respects me too much. Hans's sister Marichi and that Jascha are also in the project and do not know any German. They are 100 k. away from here. Hans has visited her twice in winter when circumstances allowed. I thank you again for all the deeds of love you have done for us, and call to God from this great distance that He may reward you a hundredfold. What of P.B. and Germany!! Or, sister Liese, do you know anything of J. Goosen and Truta? We get no news of them. I would like to know how things are going for them. Is Truta married? Mrs. P. Loew is very poor, the poorest of all our Germans. Does her brother live far from you? You can tell him. She has Nickolai with her. The 3 girls are in the project.

*Liese's escape has been successful. She has reached her home village and has re-united with her grandmother, a few uncles and aunts, and her betrothed, Peter Koehn. But for many months, Maria had not heard any news confirming Liese's safety. Her relief now is palpable. The risks of writing remain, but this letter to Liese and new husband Peter in Altonau somehow finds its way to Canada. However, some words appear odd and the meaning is not clear in places.*

Dec. 19, 1937

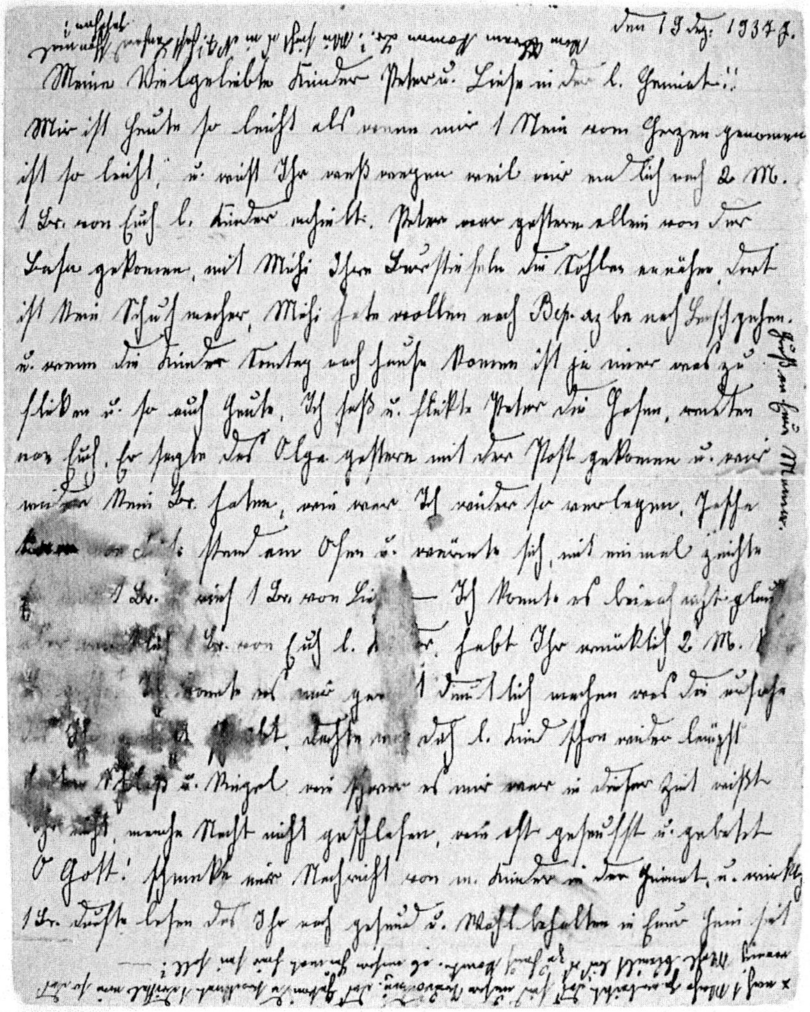
Den 19 Dez. 1937 J.
Meine Vielgeliebten Kinder Peter u. Liese in der l. Heimat!!

My dearly beloved children Peter and Liese in our beloved homeland,
My heart is so light today, as if a stone has been removed from my heart. And do you know why? Because after waiting for 2 months we finally got a letter from you, dear children. Peter came alone from the Basa [*base camp*] with Michi, to have her felt boots re-sewn. There is no shoemaker there any longer. Michi had wanted to walk to Bepaz to Lena's. When the children come home on Sunday, there is always some mending that must be done. That is the way it was today too.

I sat mending Peter's pants and we spoke of you. He said that Olga came from the post office yesterday and again we had no letter from you. It really depressed me. Jascha came by foot, stood by the stove warming himself, and suddenly turned and showed a letter from you – a letter from Liese. I could hardly believe it! Was there really a letter from you, dear children? Did you really write a letter 2 months ago? I could not understand why you did not write. But I had thought that you, dear child, were again under lock and key. You just cannot imagine how hard that was for me during that time. Many a night I did not sleep; I just sighed and I prayed, "Oh God, send me word of my children in the homeland!" And now, really, a letter! I could read that you were well and comfortable in your home. My prayer is that God will protect you and uphold you and bless you a lot in your entire life. Yes, your letter brought me so much joy and removed a big burden from my heart. Do not wait so long before writing again. Peter already went to the Basa at 2 P.M. Then Jascha and I took the hide from the goat and sheep away; there was a man here who gave cloth material for them. The 2 hides cost 3r. 43k., and for that I got 1 ½ cotton material and 46k. in money. The hides were both shorn! And now, this evening, I intend to answer your precious and important letter.

It is just horribly cold outside, and together with the wind it is very bad! I am pleased that Peter went today, since it will be much colder early tomorrow. This year the weather is completely different than in previous years. Those who have lived here longer cannot remember a year like this. There is no snow to speak of, but there is extreme frost. Many have looked into the pits to check on their potatoes – they are frozen, the frost has gone so deep. But it has now snowed for 2 days and there is a snow cover of half a metre. We have not checked on our potatoes yet; after all, the cow will eat them in March as well. The workers in the forest are happy that there is not so much snow, because then they can produce their quotas more easily.

Peter works with the horse; it is an extremely lazy one. He wants to have a different one. (The horses are from the Commune.) He and Steiger work together. Schurka has promised him a different one. Many had to do threshing in the Ilonscoz on the Flonana [*meanings unknown*]. Peter also had to work for a week, from the 5th to the 12th of December. He really was very sorry because at the Basa they still had the summer quotas and he could earn good wages. In 14 [...] he had earned 201 r. and now earns 5 to 6 r.

Michi is at Leamna. Liese, did you get the letter where I wrote that Michi married Rufe Otto? She stayed with him from Sunday until Friday. Then she left him. She regretted the marriage the next day. She said to me, "Mama, do to me as you wish. I just cannot live with him." He still has hopes that she will. I really did not want her to marry him, but I did not want to forbid her either so she would not blame me later. There was such a marriage fever around here that she felt there would be no marriageable German left. I had received no letter from you, and here Michi caused me such heartache that it was very hard to endure. I am so sorry for Michi, that that Rufe [...] her! I really don't know – if only nothing comes of it [*a reference to pregnancy*]! That is my only worry! Most people tell me not to force her to return to Rufe.

Liese, I found it very difficult that you had to leave here in a similar manner, but I knew you were getting a good Peter who would support you and any future family well. But this one! I feel so sorry for Michi. Peter, as well as Heinz, thinks things will improve in time. The whole thing happened on the Basa. When they came home the other Saturday, they had already separated.

Liese, you write that Aunt Liese was visiting there. Does she still look like herself? How many children do they have? And where is Uncle John – or are they all sent here? You mention nothing of this? You only mention that Grandmama is home from the hospital. I know nothing of this. I have received no letters from the homeland since October 5th. Liese, on your birthday I thought and remembered you a lot. What a lovely birthday present you received from your dear Peter! When is your birthday, dear Peter? Please write it to me so that I may especially think of you that day and be with you in spirit.

Were there great preparations for the election at your place too? There were here, we were all allowed to vote – great privileges! Our [...] was also there again! We are still in his hands. Jeufanus Jasch came yesterday. He submitted an appeal that he was not guilty and now he is completely free. Martha gets no information of Otto. The old Neugabauer was at L., wanted to go home because Martha could not feed him (she still has 3 m. [*meaning unknown*]). Then the L. said that was not allowed, but to resettle the son here is a possibility.

From what disease did Ab. Baergen's Mariechi die? And why was she in Schoenau? Mr. H. Voth is in the office in the Basa. His wounds have opened up and are putrefying. They probably did not take it off far enough. She is very unwell as well. H.S. wants to have one cow in the Commune for Jasch, but Mgpra [*the boss*] does not give him one. He whines, as before. Never has any money. He wanted to borrow money from Peter to pay for potatoes – in spite of there being 4 workers in that family and only 2 in ours. We were ordered to pay 53r. 90k. Naloge [*taxes*]. May this letter find you in health. We also are in the best of health.

I remain your loving and never forgetting,

Mama Regehr

Peter sends warm greetings.

Greet your Mama. Is there no letter from Abram? How are things in N. 7? Have you run across [...]? Greetings to Grandmama and siblings. How much did you get per Trudoden [*ration points*]?

Per day we got ½ kilo barley and ½ kilo rye and 1 kilo potatoes, 300 p. carrots and 200 p. cabbage and 100 p. Pena for 62 days, until Sept 1st. Reported are 156 days. Then Peter had to work another week. Those are our Trudoden. The grain shrinks by 1/3 and so little flour remains by the time we get home. I wonder if this will be our homeland always. Please write often and do not wait too long. Liese, have you received the letter from Michi and Hartweg's Truda and from Hans, where he enclosed a sketch of our house?

*Despite the familiar reporting of previous correspondence, and despite the plea to "write often," this is the last letter. Dated December 19, 1937, it ushers in an impenetrable silence – an eerie, ominous absence. Terror in the Soviet Union escalates to an unprecedented intensity. These voices from the Gulag cease.*

*A neurotic and paranoid Josef Stalin executes his final "Great Terror." The purge of the Red Army and the Party itself is accompanied by a purge of the entire society. A new edict in the winter of 1937 expands Stalin's list of "undesirables" to include "ordinary criminals, returning* kulaks, *churchmen and sectarians."[3] Mass arrests, exiles, and executions inaugurate an unparalleled period of repression and tyranny.*

*Over seven million people are arrested during this second wave of Stalin's purges. Of those arrested, "we can hardly allow 10 per cent to have survived; in fact a Soviet historian tells us that 90 per cent of those who went to the camps ... perished."[4]*

*The gentle and weary Maria Regehr is one of those arrested. Her teenaged daughter Tina and her son Peter are also accused of heinous crimes and arrested for treason against the state. The other children are scattered and tormented. Miraculously, some Regehr children survive long enough to tell us about the years of silence. But not until much later – more than fifty years later – when the threat has subsided, and they are safe in another country.*

## Notes

1 Robert Thurston, *Life and Terror in Stalin's Russia 1934-1941* (New Haven and London: Yale University Press, 1996), 2.

2 Ibid., 19ff.

3 Ibid., 59.

4 Robert Conquest, *The Great Terror: Stalin's Purge of the Thirties* (London: Macmillan, 1968), 495.

# Chapter Five

## Silence and Survival 1989-93

After five decades of silence, Lena, the little girl who knelt to compose a letter on a crude wooden trunk in her Gulag barrack, writes to her cousin Peter in Canada. In 1987, Peter hears that some of his relatives have finally been able to leave Russia and emigrate to Europe. He wonders about the many years' silence. He wonders what happened after the letters stopped. Through the family network he finds Lena and Mariechen in Cologne, Germany, and asks them to "put their experiences on paper." Now free from a hostile reader's gaze, the two Regehr sisters describe their survival in Stalin's prison camps.

Although they apologize for the "great waves of sorrow" that sometimes erase their memories, Lena and Mariechen can remember a surprising amount of detail. They share a longing to assemble the scattered pieces of their lives and to try to make sense of their experiences.

### "Great Waves of Sorrow": Lena's Memories

*Lena was only nine years old when the family was arrested. The youngest of four sisters, she loved her three-year-old baby brother Jascha. Of all the children, Lena received the most education in the Soviet system. However, her education was random and chaotic; she sometimes had to walk 120 kilometres just to reach her school. Lena's letter is briefer and her memory is sparser than her sister Mariechen's, but her recollection of events is valuable. Lena apologizes for her "many mistakes." She cannot write well in German, having been immersed only in Russian at school. But she enlarges our perspective, and she fills in some of the gaps left by the silence.*

23 November 1989

On October 1st, 1930 in the night, 2 high officials of the NKVD came and drove us out of our home. Our family consisted of 8 people: Papa, Mama, and 6 children. There was no mercy. We had to leave everything in our house, just as it was. Horses, cattle, sheep, pigs, all were confiscated; our parents were not even allowed to take along some warm clothes for the children, or even any food. First Papa and Mama prayed that God should not forsake them and their small children. Then Papa went to friends to ask them if, maybe, they would take in Mama and the small children. But it was such a time of fear that people were afraid to accept us. And so we lived with some acquaintances in one small room.

But not for long. There was a typhus epidemic and even those people who had sheltered us caught it, and we had to leave. So we left for another village. We were pushed hither and yon. Our dear Papa was sent to jail. But our dear God did not forsake him even there. On June 6, 1931, the bandits came and loaded us all, Mama and the 6 children, into a wagon and off they galloped. They drove the horses very hard. There was very little to eat. Mama constantly cried loudly, "My children, my children," for the wagon bounced so violently she was afraid we would all fall out. All this happened at night. Then finally we got to the station of Belaja-Kranitza, where many, many people were being held in an elevator or big barns, and we were also driven into them. The door was left open a crack but locked with huge locks! Also, guards were posted at the doors, just as if we were horrid criminals. It was extremely hot and there was no air circulation, which was particularly bad for the little children.

The next day a very long truck load of tired, sick people arrived. These were the men out of the prisons, and our Papa was there too. Each man was ordered to his family. They then brought train box cars alongside, and we were all ordered into them. The cars were then locked and the train headed for the Urals. We drove for 9 days, and it was intolerable. The cars were packed with too many people.

It was hot with poor or no ventilation. Many of the children were ill. Once a day we were allowed out of the train for 15 minutes. We were ordered to go to the toilet out on the steppes but they would scream, "Don't go far away" or "Hurry, Hurry." All the people were very sickly and weak.

When we arrived at our destination in the Urals, we were ordered to disembark. There were many people there already. There were very large barracks. The village was called Lunowoka. It was rumoured that in the days of the Czars prisoners were kept here. There were 2 or 3 storey barracks. We, Papa and Mama and 6 children, got one corner 1 ½ meters long and the same width. The workers had to go far away to work, over 100 km. That village was called Ustupil. My sister Liese, 19 years old, was there as well as my brother Peter, age 16. Our Papa was quite ill and stayed with Mama and us. The rest of us children could stay with the parents because we were very young. The road to Ustupil was muddy and mostly muskeg. You could not drive there with wagons; you could only walk. You received a little bundle of 400 grams frozen bread, tied it to your back, and set off on foot. It was a very hard road to walk. But when you arrived there, it was even sadder. The barracks were cold, no beds, nothing warm to put on your feet and no warm clothing to put on your body. People were hungry but there was no food, and the cold was terrible. You just felt you could not live, much less work, there in the forest.

Then several people decided they would try to escape, and among them was my sister Liese and my brother Peter. They would escape back to our grandparents in Lunowoka. They left at night, but they were being watched. Liese and several others made it, but they caught Peter and made him walk back to Ustupil. Then he was treated very cruelly, whipped, hit, and for 5 days he received no food. After a time he risked it again – but they caught him again. After that, they were even more cruel to him. They hung 10 pairs of work boots with wooden soles around his neck and a rider drove him back (on foot) to the place from which he had escaped. All he got was 400 grams of frozen bread, hard as a rock, and was ordered into the forest to work. He was very hungry, and ate the frozen bread and got very sick.

There was a Kazap [*literally "goat"; usually an insulting name for Russians*] who brought supplies to the camp (everywhere there are good people too). Papa talked it over with this Kazap that on one of his trips he should bring back his son Peter. Then several days passed; and then this Kazap did bring back our brother Peter. He was very weak and sick and hungry. We lived in these barracks at Lunowoka for 11 months. Then we were driven to Kapitalnaja to Mine No. 2. There we got a little house. In the middle had been a big oven. Four families were ordered into one little house. There were also barracks but otherwise there were no living quarters. There was not much to cook with, so one stove for four families seemed to be ample. We were 4 German families in this house. In one corner were we, the Jasch Regehrs, with 8 people; in another corner were Heinrich Friesens from N. 9 with 6 people; and then 2 other families with 5 people each, and each in their corner. These 2 families were from Kronau from near our region at home. Then we had to go to work. Our brother Peter had to work in the lower mines. Liese and Mariechen had to work in the upper mines. Then in 1933 our dear Papa died. It was very hard for him to leave his family in these circumstances. But he had such a strong faith in God.

In 1935 Kirov was killed, or maybe he was shot in Moscow by the government – but we poor people were blamed. I can remember it. We were at work when a man came and called us out, and said we should go home and get ready to leave in 24 hours. Then we were driven to the Polowinka station and loaded into a train. Off we went to Solikamsk, which was the end of the line – the railway tracks go no further. When we arrived, they shuttled our cars to a side track, and there we stayed for 3 days and nights in cold cars. We were hungry, and it was February. On the third day many horse-drawn sleighs arrived and drove up to our cars. Then they told us, "We have come for you. We are the NKVD." We and all our goods were loaded into the sleighs. Of course we had very little – 4 pillows and

2 blankets for 8 people. The very old and the little children were on the sleighs, and off they went. We bigger ones had to walk 120 km into a dense forest. There was very much snow and the going was extremely difficult.

The people were weak, hungry, and cold. There was 40 degrees of frost. Several of the small children died on the way. We were underway for 2 days and 2 nights. We would each get 200 grams of frozen bread for food. There was no water. Our Mama took a pot, put some snow into it, and thawed it until we could drink. When we arrived at our predetermined destination, things were even sadder. It was a large village where they had kept prisoners like us before, but they had all died out or starved to death. We were the third party to be unloaded here, as well as some others from different villages who still remained alive. In short, that village was restocked with people again.

We were unloaded at the school. The school was unheated and very cold, so that even the walls were frosted up. Then the authorities, or the NKVD, whichever it was, delivered a speech and said, "You must stay here, you must live here." Then they showed each family to a house and told us to fix it so that it could be lived in. Each of us got one axe, one saw, and one hammer. It was sad to see. The windows were without window panes! The brick oven had collapsed. But what could we do? We had to make do! Then the oldest – Liese, Peter, and Mariechen – started to repair the house. Then they worked and worked. First they closed up the windows – not with glass but with boards. Then they put together a stove. Peter, our brother, did this. Liese and Mariechen went into the forest and broke branches for fuel. There certainly was enough wood in the forest. Then they built a fire in the stove and it burned nicely. When the room was nice and warm, they went to get Mama, who was with the younger siblings, Tina, Lena, and Jascha. The next day the three oldest had to go to work. The work was in the forest.

We lived there like that until 1940. The workers would get 400 grams of bread a day and the others 200 grams of bread a day. When summer came, we planted potatoes and bought a cow. We younger ones had to cut grass in the forest and bring it to the house, dry it, and store it for the winter as feed for the cow. It was a red cow, and her name was Tagilcka. Then things were beginning to be much easier for us; it was not so hard to live. We were even given a small amount of sugar – 200 grams per person in a month, and one piece of soap per family. But suddenly on January 7, 1938, at night, 186 working men were sent to jail. They were all people like us, and included was our brother Peter. He was still young. He was born in 1914. He never came back! Then in the same year women were also sent to jail. Our Mama was one. She was forcefully driven on foot, walking in wooden mules, 120 km to Solikamsk, and then sent further by train to a prison in Swerdlowsk. There our Mama was for 1 year and 6 months until August 1939, when she was allowed to return to us.

Then we lived in Kolschim until the war. Mariechen and I were taken into the work camp. Our sister Tina was also taken into the work camp in 1938, but she returned in 1 year. Mama stayed alone with our brother Jakob. When the war was over, we came back again to Kolschim, where our Mama was. In 1948 we were moved to Krasnovischersk. We left the house and all our things, and were paid nothing for it. We only took what we could carry. We walked more than 100 km. In Krasnovischersk we lived until 1954. Then we moved to Solikamsk. Our brother Peter and Jakob died. Peter died in jail in 1938 and Jakob died in 1962. We 4 sisters are still alive. I, Lena, and Mariechen live in Germany. Liese and Tina are still in Russia.

If you want to know something special, please write and ask. We will gladly answer and tell of what we can remember. Such great waves of sorrow have swept over us that at times we cannot even remember it all. One forgets in time. Dear Peter and Anni, you wrote that you found a box of letters. That is good. Many letters will be from our dear Mama. She always enjoyed and loved Peter's parents so. We had to burn all our letters and pictures. We were not allowed to take any over the border. We were 6 siblings: Liese,

b. [born] 1912; Peter, b. 1914; Mariechen, b. 1916; Tina, b. 1919; Lena, b. 1922; Jakob, b. 1928.

– Lena Regehr

## Meeting Lena

*It is October 8, 2005. I have flown to Europe to find Lena. After many phone calls and conversations, I see a woman on her deck in Cologne, Germany. She is waving. Fair-haired thick braids circle her head in a ring of grey and gold. Her clear blue eyes do not reflect the horror and the suffering. Her smile confirms our instant love, and her generous warm body embraces mine. Our hug tells me we have known this love before, an affinity that transcends words.*

*Lena Regehr Dirksen at age 83 in Cologne, Germany in October, 2005.*

*Lena briefly describes her current family. While still in Russia, she married Jacob Dirksen in 1966 in Solikamsk. Both Lena and Jacob (with daughter Ludmilla, born in prison camp in 1947) emigrated to Cologne in 1989. Today, Lena finally lives in peace and takes pleasure in her daughter and two granddaughters.*

*We talk for days, interrupted only occasionally by a discreet tape recorder and camera. For the first time, Lena sees the letter she wrote from her prison barrack at nine years of age. Tears flow. The narrative continues, and many questions are answered. But this is difficult. Lena does not like to remember; she has packed the memories in a remote place. Yet for her daughter and granddaughters, she does remember as she recounts the stories of survival in the bleakest era in modern history.*

## "So Life Went on": Mariechen's Memories

*In July 1993 (almost four years after Lena's recollections), Mariechen sent her memoirs to Peter and Anne Bargen in Canada. She was fourteen when the Regehr family was arrested in their home village, and her memories are much more detailed and expansive. Her insight into activities in the camps, attitudes of the Kommandant, and actions of fellow prisoners give us a more comprehensive account of the family's sufferings. In the spirit of a survivor, she accepts that "life went on."*

*Mariechen had attended school in her home village before the family's arrest, but unlike her younger sisters Tina and Lena, she was too old to attend the school offered to young prisoners in the camp. She was expected to work like an adult in the forests, mines, and construction sites. Along with her sisters, Mariechen applied for an exit visa to leave Russia in 1978. After ten years of waiting and applying over and over, she was granted permission to leave in 1988. Finally, she could leave the country that had held her hostage for so long and join her younger sister Lena in Cologne. Mariechen had eleven peaceful years living in the freedom so generously extended to her by the German government. She died on November 5, 2001 at age eighty-five.*

20 July 1993

It was 1937. We were in our fifth year of exile in the Ural Mountains. We were living in the village of Kolschim. We had been relocated there from the village of Polowinka. By 1935 our family had been decimated, and our life had sadly and steadily deteriorated in Polowinka. We were the third group to be resettled to Kolschim. The first two groups had died of starvation and now we had been moved to live there. We were a family of 7. Our dear father was no longer alive and he rested in his grave in the Polowinka forest. Father died on October 7, 1933. He is resting in the arms of our Saviour and now beholds Him in whom he believed. Mama was left with 6 children.

Life went on. Liese, Peter, and I had to work in the forest. Mama and the 3 little ones were at home. To heat our small place Tina and Lena had to carry chopped firewood to our house. When we came from work, we were soaking wet from working in the deep snow, and our clothes were actually frozen stiff. We had no warm covering for our feet, either – we had only sandals which had been given to us. The sandals had to last for 10 days, but they never lasted that long. Along with these we were given a few rags to wind about our feet. Mama would weep when we came back from work, wet and frozen. But we had to get by and stay alive. It was really sad.

Then a school was opened there, and Tina and Lena could go. The following year Jascha could also attend. We older ones had to continue to work in the forest, felling trees, sawing and splitting them into 75 centimetre sizes. Then we had to put them into piles for drying. In summer these piles were then hauled into the village, for it was impossible to do it in winter – far too much snow.

We were organized into workers' "brigades": Peter, Liese, and I; Jasch Friesen (son of Heinrich Friesen); Peter Dueckmann; and Mr. Heinrich Voth. We were all very weak, but we had to make our quota or we would not receive our small piece of bread at the end of the day. Splitting those logs was extremely hard. When evening came we were exhausted, but we still had to drag back the huge saws and axes. Those axes used to split the logs were very heavy. In the evening we had to turn in all that equipment, and in the morning we had to drag it all back. This went on until all the forest around us was chopped down, and the workers were then posted to a different section. We worked 10 kilometres away from our families who remained in Kolschim.

From this new posting we could not get home for the night and had to stay in barracks in a village called Denascher for the entire week. Here we had to fell trees which were hauled together. In spring, when the river thawed, the logs were rolled into the river and floated 200 kilometres to Kertsch. The level of the river rose and fell, and the logs had to be rolled into the water by our brigade. One brigade would be on one shore and another on the other side.

The school in Kolschim only went to the fourth grade. Whoever wanted to study further had to go to school in Werch-Jaswa, which was 27 kilometres away. Tina went there, and a year later so did Lena. Little Jascha was still with Mama.

In 1937, Liese left this place of exile and logging and went to the Ukraine. About 200 kilometres from Kolschim there was a railway. Peter and I stayed at Kertch on the Splaw, where we continued to roll logs into the river. Then Mama wrote us that one of us should come to her – either Peter or I. We discussed it and decided that I would go and Peter would stay. When winter came, we all had to go back into the forest and fell trees. So that is what we did.

When I got back to Mama, the Kommandant knew everything – that Liese was no longer at work. There were always bad people who would inform on anyone. The Kommandant was very bad to us, he cursed Mama and harassed her with questions of every sort. That winter Peter came back home – all workers were allowed to come home. Then the older children were ordered back into the forest, 10 kilometres away from home and Mama. So life went on.

On Saturday, January 6, 1938, all of us workers went home to our families in Kolschim. It was now a somewhat larger village. Beside our small house was a small piece of land which we had dug and cultivated with a spade. We had planted potatoes there; the harvest was good because the black earth was so rich. When we came home, we fetched a few potatoes to supplement our rations for that week. And so life continued.

In the winter we had to work in the forest. In summer we three siblings (Peter, Liese, and I) did not always work in the same place. Mama was in the village with the 3 youngest (Tina, Lena, and Jascha). It was in 1936 that my sister Liese escaped to the Ukraine. In January of 1937 Peter and I walked back to Mama. But the time to go back was soon at hand. I picked up our shoulder yoke on which 2 pails were hung – we carried our water from the river in this fashion. It was a small river called Tulimka from which we carried our water. When I came to the bank of the river, there stood the Kommandant with his dog beside him. The dog raised his muzzle and howled gruesomely. He said to me, "Mariechen, this is a sign: Either someone will die or a great accident will happen." I filled my pails with water and left.

When I got home, Peter and I each put a pail of potatoes in a sack, strapped them to our back, and said goodbye to Mama and Jascha. Little Jascha cried so bitterly and begged Mama to let him go with Peter. He must have had a premonition that he would never see Peter again. Mama just could not understand and said, "Peter and Mariechen have to go to work in the forest. Where can you stay then?" But Peter urged her to let him take Jascha. My, was Jascha ever happy! With the sacks strapped on our backs we three walked off to work, while Mama stood and looked and looked until she vanished from our sight in the distance.

The school was out and the students were on holidays. Walking on, we met Mr. Heinrich Friesen with his son Jakob. With them was little Willie, who had gone along with his father. We met many others who were also accompanied by their little school children. There were mothers with sacks on their backs, and their little ones running and skipping beside them. Maybe the children had discussed it in school and all had decided to go? This happened on January 6, 1937.

We arrived at our place of work. Peter and I were housed in separate barracks about 200 metres apart. My little brother Jascha, Willie Friesen, and several other children dropped off at the men's barracks, but I walked on to my barrack. The next day, January 7, was the Russian Christmas day. That evening we sat late into the night and talked of how things used to be at home in the peaceful Sagradowka villages. Slowly the conversation diminished and died out; we gradually drifted to our bunks – for we all faced a day of hard labour in the forest tomorrow. There were 35 women in my room. Through a small hallway (maybe 1 metre wide), there were about 100 men. However, my brother Peter was in a different barrack.

We had just crawled into bed and had not yet fallen asleep when there was a loud, powerful knocking on the door. A woman opened the door and there was the night watchman. He said, "The Mess Hall is filled with NKVD and the atmosphere is very tense. Something is sure to happen!" The night watchman had barely left when there was a loud, urgent knocking on the door. So another woman got up and opened the door. There stood 3 men from the NKVD, armed to the teeth. We were terrified and shocked, and started to get up until one of the men shouted, "Everyone stay where you are!" All of us were trembling with fear. The three men then walked to every woman, flung back the blankets, and searched the bed for any man who might be hiding with us. When no men were found, they left our quarters but locked the door from the outside. They then crossed the hall to the quarters where the 100 men were housed. We could hear everything clearly, "Get up! You are all under arrest!" Finally silence came, and all the 100 men were gone.

We rushed to the door to get out, but it was fastened from the outside. We knocked and shouted but to no avail. Eventually our shouting got the attention of the night watchman, who came and opened our door. The watchman told us what was happening: All the men had been rounded up – even those in the barracks where my brother Peter was quartered. Now we feared for the small school children. Where would they be? We dashed for the barracks, calling the children's names, "Jascha, Willie…." There was no answer; only silence greeted us. Our imaginations ran wild and played host to our frazzled nerves. Surely they would not have taken the little ones as well! During that night 186 men had been arrested, everyone from the village of Kolschim.

Then we hurried back to my brother Peter's barrack, where Jascha, Willie Friesen, and several other children had been kept with their fathers and brothers when we had last seen them. The fathers had all been arrested and taken away. Hidden in a corner behind the bed were several small boys rolled up together in a blanket. The boys were too afraid and fearful even to respond to their names when we called. Then Alma Keller and I returned to the place where the men had been arrested. There we saw several rows of NKVD with their weapons leveled at the bunched-up men as if they were guarding the most dangerous criminals on earth. The men held their heads up high as if they were quite contented.

From the rear, Alma and I got quite close to them. Of course we were very quiet. Once more I could see my brother Peter, and Alma saw her 2 brothers who had been arrested with this group. As we got closer one of the NKVD turned and shouted harshly, "Uchodi!" which means "Go way! Beat it!" and he knocked us over so forcefully that we were pitched into the snow. When we finally crawled out of the snow and regained our feet, everything was quiet – the place was empty. That night 186 men had been arrested, all from the village of Kolschim.

We finally walked back to the barracks where Peter had been quartered. There we found my little brother Jascha, Willie Friesen, and many other school children who had come here with their fathers or brothers. The adult men had all been carted off. We then went to the women's barracks where I was quartered. All the women and children gathered here to decide what was to be done now. Somehow we had to get a message to our village of Kolschim and inform them of what had happened to the men – and what to do with the children. But how could we send a message? It was -39C and the village was 10 kilometres away. No, it could not be done. After some discussion the women decided that we *all* would refuse to work and, as a group, take all the children and bring them to their mothers. With this plan in mind, we set out for the village.

The parade was led by a few women, then a group of children followed by another group of women followed by more children – a long line of misery and sadness. The path we followed was deep with snow – 2 metre drifts were often encountered – and it was so narrow that most of the time we had to stumble along in single file. We had to be constantly alert that the children did not get frostbite on their face and hands. It was morning before we reached our village of Kolschim.

First we came to the house of Mrs. Neubauer, whose son was with the children. Her husband was one of the men arrested. The neighbours soon gathered with fear and terror shining in their eyes. Everyone asked what had happened. While we were explaining, the children were crying and wailing. Soon the women from the village joined in the wails and cries of lamentation. It was a heart-rending scene. Slowly we walked on to our house, which was at the end of the village. Someone came running out of every home we passed, and we had to tell the story again and again. Our house was two houses away from Henry Friesen's. Our little Jascha and little Willie Friesen ran ahead and told our Mama everything that had happened. When I finally entered our home, everyone was crying and I soon joined them.

Jascha told us how rough the NKVD men had been with the men of the village. They struck them with rifle butts, bellowed and swore at them, saying, "Hurry and get dressed." The small children were witnesses to this brutality. Then Mrs. Friesen came in with little Willie, followed by several neighbours. Everyone was extremely upset. What to do now? Such a futile question! Our life was not our own – but goes on and on. Lena, my younger sister, was in school in the village of Werch-Jaswa, 27 kilometres away. The following Sunday she was able to come home. Tina had already finished school and had been sent 200 kilometres away, and was teaching in the village of Bondjuck. Tuesday I walked back to my work in the forest, and Lena went back to school. Mama and Jascha stayed home. Our dear Mama was very uneasy and kept saying, "Something else will still happen." Yet her great faith in God helped her face the future with the prayer, "As God wills. He gives us burdens but He helps us carry them as well." But no one had an inkling of what was coming. And then it happened!

After Peter's arrest I worked for 3 weeks and became so ill that I walked home to Mama and Jascha. It was February 15, 1938. I had lain down on the bed. Mama had visitors – Mrs. Keller, whose 2 sons had also been arrested. They sat and talked. Suddenly there was a loud knocking on the window. Mama opened it. It was Mrs. Keller's daughter-in-law. She was extremely upset. She said that the Club was filled with NKVD men and something was happening again. The Keller women went home, but Mama did not go to bed. Our little Jascha began to cry, for the one terrible word "NKVD" brought forth the greatest fear in his young heart.

It did not take long before there was a loud knocking on the door. Mama opened up. Two armed men entered. Little Jascha wept and screamed, for he had seen this scene before when they took his brother Peter. One of the men turned to Mama, and told her she was under arrest and she should get dressed. I was in bed, and he came to my bed and said I was under arrest. I said I could not walk because I was sick. The men conferred quietly with each other and one of them went out. In a short while he came back with our neighbour, who was the doctor in our village of Kolschim. The doctor was a German named Goerter. He took my temperature (40 degrees C.). The doctor said I was very sick and could not walk. Then the NKVD indicated that they would come again in 3 days. Our little Jascha threw has arms around Mama's neck and both wept bitterly. One roughly told Mama, "You are crying about your daughter. She will join you in a few days." Little Jascha was screaming as they led Mama away. The doctor and his wife were also arrested.

What now?? What should we do? An extremely agonizing question. Outdoors it was very cold. Because of all the excitement and fear Mama had been dressed very lightly. We did not have many clothes, but we did have some warmer ones Mama could have put on. Jascha and I searched for and found some warmer clothes – a warm pair of socks, a kerchief, a warm vest that Peter had worn at times. We tied all these up in a bundle and went in search of Mama. We thought that in all probability they would be at the Club with the rest of the prisoners. Little Jascha was very upset: "If the NKVD see you, they will arrest you too – and what will I do then?"

We set out to find Mama. I fell down often but Jascha helped me up; the snow was quite deep and the road was narrow. Suddenly we realized that someone was approaching us. Jascha, trembling like a leaf, turned and took my hand. But as the man approached we realized that he was not NKVD but one of us, although he had often helped the NKVD. We had always known he was of that kind. When he came up to us he stopped, looked closely at me and said, "Mapyes (Maria), they did not arrest you and left you home, and now of your own free will you are walking into their hands?" Then I told him my mother had been taken dressed only in very light clothing. Little Jascha tearfully pleaded with him not to report us. It must have touched the fellow, for his 2 brothers had also been arrested with our Peter. He said to Jascha that the NKVD top brass had driven off and only 2 men were left to guard the women – but they were not in the Club. They were being held in the government offices – Mama as well. To Jascha he said, "Now go. You know where it is, and do not tell anyone that you met me. Two men are guarding the door. Just knock on the door, and when they ask what you want, tell them that you are bringing a small bundle of clothing for your Mama. It is cold and Mama is only dressed very lightly." Then he turned to me and said, "But you, Maria, you go to that little house which is close to the office, and be sure that no one sees you."

With our hearts beating wildly, Jascha and I went on. I went behind the little house and sat down on a piece of wood which lay there. From there I could see and hear everything. My little brother Jascha, nine years old, went to where the prisoners were being held. I heard him knock, and the door was opened. There stood a NKVD, who roughly asked, "What do you want here, little one?" Jascha said, "I want to give this to my Mama. It is cold and I do not want her to freeze." Jascha had a clear voice, and Mama recognized it immediately and began to cry bitterly. The package was taken from him and he was sternly told to quickly go home at once. Then Jascha came to me and said the man had been very angry and would not let him kiss Mama good-bye.

Then Jascha carefully looked to see if anyone was around. He could see no one. And so we began the trek homeward and met no one on the way. To this day I do not remember how we got home. I was finished – exhausted – and Jascha was chilled to the bone. We had some wood in the house. Jascha said, "I will start a fire in the stove because I am freezing." Both of us were shivering with cold and trembling with fear – very upset. What else could come upon us? No doubt nothing good.

For a long time we just sat there and wept, with our arms thrown around each other. The fire in the stove was burning and the room got nicely warm. As I watched, my little brother Jascha fell asleep. Very carefully I tried to put him into his bed, but he awoke and began to cry again, "Mama! Mama, where are you?" But Mama had already been taken far away. Then I said to him that Mama will come home again. "No," he said, "The NKVD has taken her far way – our brother Peter as well – and soon they will come for you. Where can I go then?" Yes, where? I had to comfort and calm him. Then we lay down to sleep, but he said, "I want to sleep with you," and so we went to bed. He held on to me so very tightly – but not for long. He awoke and screamed, "They are coming again. Now they will take you." He hung onto me so tightly that I could hardly breathe. He fell asleep again, but again not for long.

In the distance a dog was barking. I was wide awake but nothing more happened. That is how we spent the first night after Mama was taken. Dawn slowly came and another day began. Around noon our sister Lena came running home from school (school was in Werch-Jaswa, 27 kilometres away). Then we all wept and lamented together, and tried to comfort each other. It was a heart-rending scene. I asked Lena how she knew about Mama so quickly. I wondered if someone had told her. She said that no one had told her but she had seen Mama sitting on a sleigh. They had whipped the horses hard and dashed by, but she had recognized our Mama.

This is the way it was: All the men were arrested and taken away, Russians, Germans, Tartars – everyone who was a male was taken. But only the German women were taken, including our dear Mama. As I said, the school was 27 kilometres away in Werch-Jaswa. In our school in Kolschim, the classes ended in grade 4; in Werch-Jaswa the grades 5-6-7 were taught. On February 16, 1938, the women were arrested and the next day, on February 17 at 8 A.M., just after the children had gone to school, the sleighs with the women dashed through the village past the school. The poor horses were whipped again and again to make them run faster. And so the pupils recognized their own loved ones, and Lena also recognized our Mama. And so the children headed home (the 27 kilometre distance) and came running up to us.

It was bitterly cold with much snow. The road was drifted and heavy. Lena was chilled through and through. Little Jascha immediately lit a fire in the stove. Then we ate our lunch and considered: What now? Tearfully Lena said, "I just won't go back to school. They will come again and arrest you too. Where can Jascha and I go then? We want to go with you." I felt so burdened, so harried. I said to my two siblings, "It is not possible for you to come with me. Lena, you stay here for a few days and then you go back to study in school. Life must go on. You can see how hard I have to work in the forest – with the axe and saw." But she did not want to study. Always "No, no, I will not go. How are we going to live? You are sick and we have no money." I said to her, "I will get well and go to work again." Also we still had a few dollars which our uncle and aunt, Liese and Franz Bargen, had sent us from Canada. To Lena I said, "You will get the little money which I will earn, and Jascha and I will live on potatoes and milk." Then she was in agreement. At that time we already owned a cow and did have some potatoes. So everything had been discussed and agreed upon.

Now let me tell you how we got the cow. It was the year 1935-36. About 20 kilometres away from our village the government had a small animal farm at which horses, cows, and sheep were kept. The farm went bankrupt and everything had to be sold. But the animals belonged to the government; there was no private ownership. The farm was a government business operated by the town of Krasnovischersk, 100 kilometres away. Our village Kommandant had seen how undernourished and weak the people of the village were, yet they had to work so hard in the forest. So he drove into Krasnovischersk and discussed it with the authorities: Why not give every family a cow and a sheep, and garnishee the earnings of the family workers to pay for the animals? And thus everything was discussed there.

When the Kommandant returned to Kolschim, he called together all the workers. We were filled with fear. What is coming now? What dark cloud was again descending upon us? When the workers had gathered, the Kommandant reported on all that had been agreed upon. There was a general grumbling and no one was in agreement with what was being done. We just did not have the money to pay for the animals. The Kommandant then told us, "Your earnings will be garnisheed. Tomorrow morning at 7 A.M. I want one or two members of each family to meet me here and we will go to Pult." Pult was the name of the village where the farm was located. Early the next morning Peter and Mama went, and towards evening they came home with a cow and a lamb. Mama milked the cow but there was very little milk. The cow was tired, had walked 20 kilometres, and everything around her was new and unfamiliar.

So now we had a cow and a sheep. We were so happy about it all, especially our little brother Jascha. He said, "Every morning when Mama has milked the cow, I will now drink a cup of warm milk." But soon the people became very uneasy: We would now have to pay a tax – that is, we would have to deliver a quota of butter to the authorities. Yet the Kommandant maintained that we would not have to pay anything. But that was not the case. In short order we received written notice that we must deliver 3.8 kilograms of pasteurized butter. We then bought the butter and delivered it as demanded. We also had to deliver 60 eggs and we did not have a single hen! This was at the end of 1936.

We butchered the lamb in the beginning of 1937, but we kept the cow and life continued. After a short time an uneasiness settled on our village. Two men had been arrested and sent to prison. The entire village was very disturbed. Then things settled down until 1938. It was on the Russian Christmas day, January 7, 1938, that the disaster struck us. During that gruesome night 186 men were arrested, among them our brother Peter. The turmoil was horrendous – terrible howling of the dogs – and fear possessed us. Then, on February 16, 1938 our Mama was arrested. Our sister Tina had studied as a teacher of the German language and in September 1937 had been sent to the village of Landueck. The village was about 200 kilometres from our home. Tina taught there until March 1, 1938, and then was also arrested. We received a letter from a woman who had worked with Tina telling us the news. This was a terrible blow to us – the third one in our family was taken. But life for us had to continue. I continued to go to work, Lena went on with her studies, and Jascha went to school. Ten months later Tina was released from prison and came home. Now we 4 siblings were together again.

Then Tina told us she had been arrested, and sent to Solikamsk and pushed into the same cell with Mama. Mama had been terribly shocked and frightened. Tina was a young girl, 18 years old. She had been charged with burning down a Butterfabrik (butter factory). In the village where she taught there was a building to which the surrounding villages brought their quota of milk levied against all those who owned a cow. I have forgotten how many litres had to be delivered. Tina had to sign a paper confessing that she had set fire to the building. Everything had been burned. Tina signed: Yes, she had set the fire. This was in 1938.

In 1989, the year I received permission to emigrate to Germany, that same building was still standing, and the villages had always continued to deliver their quota of milk there. Where I lived in

Solikamsk, there was a woman who was from the village of Landueck – it was her home. I was still interested and asked her whether the building was still standing. The woman had traveled to Landueck 3 weeks previously. When she returned, I asked her whether the building was still there. She answered that it was still standing the same as always. And poor Tina had been tortured in prison for 10 months for burning a building that was still standing and in use.

During that time we had a very wicked Kommandant who was especially brutal to the Germans. One week after Tina returned, he sent for her. We were all very upset: What is happening now? What tragedy are we facing now? (And thus we lived in a constant state of fear.) There was no teacher in our village and the Kommandant wanted to employ Tina as teacher. Tina flatly refused. "I will not teach in this school. The children will yell and taunt me because of my prison record. No, that I will not do even if you imprison me again."The Kommandant shouted, fumed, and banged the desk. "Go home for now – but the time will come when you will think about me again."

Tina came home terribly upset and excited – as was I. I suggested to her that maybe she should accept the position as teacher. "No, no," she said, "That I will not do! They can do what they want with me! The children will just holler at me that I have been in prison." Tina was with us for 2 weeks, and a young man was sent to our village to be the teacher. The Kommandant again sent for Tina and told her, "Now you will go to work on the water" (Splaw River). The workplace was 130 kilometres away from where Liese, Peter, and I had previously worked, and from where Liese returned to the Ukraine. And so Tina worked there. We three siblings stayed in Kolschim and life, though wretched and sad, went on. We had no choice.

Often when I came from work, my little brother Jascha would be standing on the street waiting for me. He would say, "I was so afraid you would not come." Then he would cry bitterly and ask, "When is our Mama coming home? Where is she?" I could not answer him, because I knew nothing of what had happened to Mama nor where she was. So one day passed as another. Tina was working on the river Splaw, I was working in the village, Lena was in school in Werch-Jaswa, and Jascha went to school here in our village. Winter passed and summer came. We heard nothing about Mama. One day a young Russian man returned from prison and told usPeter would never come home again: he was dead, tortured to death in the town of Irbit near the city of Sverdlovsk. Life went on, no matter how wretched. We had no choice.

School was finally out and all the students came home. About 9 kilometres away there was a small Kolkhos [*collective*]. Every day the older students had to go there to hoe the grain, pull out weeds, work hard all day, and in the evening walk back to their homes. My sister Lena had to do this too. So everyday they had to walk 18 kilometres and work hard. At noon they would get a thin aermliche [*poverty*] soup and a small piece of bread. Jascha was at home, and his work was to drive the cow into the shed when it was returned from the pasture and to clean the shed of manure. Lena and I always came home late, and often Jascha would make supper for us. The potatoes were cooking, and with kernels of grain and milk it always tasted good. Then came autumn and the children had to go back to school. Lena now had to attend the seventh grade and went back to Werch-Jaswa. Jascha and I stayed together in Kolschim. And so the second winter passed without our dear Mama.

I was working with the horses. We were four women and each had 2 horses and a sleigh. We had to get hay for the livestock. It was a small Kolchos and we had some livestock. We started in the morning very early and came home late in the evening – sometimes in the middle of the night. We lived in the far north and sometimes experienced extremely stormy weather so that the roads were closed with snow – the horses could not get through. Then one of us women had to go in the lead to find the road, while the others forced the horses ahead. And so we often came home late, half frozen. When we got near the village, we saw someone standing on the road. It was my little brother Jascha. Then I asked him, "Did something happen?" "No," he said, "I was just afraid that you would never come back."

Then Jascha would help me unload the hay, unhitch the horses, unharness them, put them into their stall, and give them feed. Then together we would go home, warm ourselves, eat our supper and go to bed. Jascha always kept the room warm, since we had scrounged enough wood during the summer. I said to him, "You should not always stand out there in the road – it is cold and you are half frozen." But he just said, "I was afraid you were not coming back again." He cried and asked, "Where is Mama? When is she coming home?" What could I tell him? Nothing. So we both cried ourselves to sleep. Often in his sleep he would call, "Mama, Mama!"

On one occasion we came home very late. The chairman of the Commune was standing in the road with Jascha, waiting for us. After we had unloaded and cared for the horses, we all went to our homes. The chairman patted Jascha on the shoulder and said, "You little one, do not stand on the road again. One of these days you will freeze to death." Jascha began to cry and said, "I am afraid my sister Mariechen won't come back again. Mama is gone." Tears filled the eyes of the chairman. "See here, my father and 3 brothers are also in prison." And so we parted.

Early the next morning I milked the cow, went inside, strained the milk, and put it away. Jascha also got out of bed and then we ate. Before I left I begged him to stay at home and not go out to stand on the road. It was very cold. He promised that he would not stand on the road again – but he still went to the barn with me. It was not cold in the barn since some cows were being kept there. And so the winter passed. Summer came. The livestock was driven into the pasture. and I continued to work with the horses.

Lena had finished the seventh grade and was now at home. Everyday she and Jascha went into the forest to cut grass and hay and carry it home to feed our cow. They each had a sack and a sickle. They would fill the sacks, carry them home, and spread the grass out to dry to provide feed for the cow in winter. I praised them for their work, for they had gathered quite a stack. Then they set their own quotas: so many sacks before noon and so many sacks in the afternoon, and then they would rest. The dried hay was removed and stacked, and a new load was spread out to dry. And so we brought together a large stack of hay. Time went by and we lived on.

Having finished the seventh grade, Lena now should continue her studies. Several of the girls who had studied together agreed that they should study and become nurses. To qualify for nursing school, they had to take an entrance exam in the city of Krasnovischersk. They applied, wrote the exams, and passed. Soon they were on their way. Each had a bundle of food on her back; the city was 100 kilometres from us. In those days there were no autos in our region – we had never seen an auto – and everyone walked. And so these girls left home to walk to their school. Now I and little brother Jascha were alone again.

Haying time came. Enough hay had to be put up to feed the livestock during the winter. But there were no workers, since the men were all languishing in prisons. The hay field was 15-18 kilometres away from the village. I have told you where I worked: it was a small Kolchos. The chairman was a Russian, also exiled as we were. Haying time was coming closer and the weather was very nice.

One day in mid-July I was called to the office. When I got there, the chairman was alone. I said, "Good day." Of course we spoke only Russian. He looked at me a while and then said, "Sit down, Maria." I sat down, and he said, "I wanted to spare you but I cannot. You know that we have livestock and it is now haying time. The weather is very nice. But whom shall I send? There is no one I can send away for a month to harvest the hay." Now I really became uneasy. What is descending upon me now? Then he said, "I have thought about this a long time. There is no other way. You have to go there to work for a month – there are no other workers left." When he said that, nausea began in the pit of my stomach. I sprang out of my chair and wept so loudly – with cries of anguish – but I could speak no words.

Finally I said, "What shall I do with my little brother Jascha? He has no father, his mother has been taken from him, his brother Peter has also been taken and is dead, and now I am to go away from him. This just cannot be! Besides, I also have a cow to care for." I wept so bitterly. He had tears in his eyes as well. Then he said, "Just calm down, things will work out." Then he asked me, "Maria, if you were in my place, what would you do? You know very well that if any of the livestock dies I will be shot – and in this case you too. You know very well whose hands we all are in. My father and 3 brothers are also in prison. You know that."

Slowly I calmed down a little, and he said, "Let me explain it clearly to you. Your little brother will be cared for and you must take the cow with you." The chairman then said, "I will find an elderly woman who is responsible and can be trusted to care for your little brother. But you must take the cow with you, because the butter is the tax you owe and must deliver. Every day you must record how much milk the cow has given, and when you get back we will balance the account. Here your Jascha can have all the milk and cottage cheese he wants."

Mrs. Heinrich Voth was then employed to look after Jascha. She also had a little boy named Peter. My little brother was not very eager for this arrangement, because he feared that another calamity was engulfing him. I had some trouble in calming his fears. The next day we left: 15 persons and one man, "Uncle Willi," who had just come home from prison. The trail was very narrow, allowing only single-file walking, and it was very swampy. Willi led the way, followed by 4 horses loaded with supplies. The sacks with the supplies were divided in the middle and slung over the backs of the horses so that the load was balanced, one on either side, and the whole was firmly strapped onto the horse. And so we went!

The trail was not fit for any wagons. There was much swamp and quagmire. The workers walked behind the horses and each had to carry a load: scythes and sickles for mowing the hay, saws, axes, hammers, nails, ropes, and other items which we would need or find useful. I was in the rear with the cow on a rope. On my back I had strapped a bundle of hay on which the cow occasionally nibbled as an incentive to move along. Another woman walked behind the cow and drove the cow when she lagged. When we came to larger swampy ground, the horses would often fall down with their burden of supplies. The same thing happened to my cow. We had to work hard to get all the animals back on their feet and moving again. Each of us also carried a sheet and a blanket. We arrived at our destination just before evening.

Now we quickly had to build some sort of shelter, a hut or lean-to. We had to have a place were we could get some rest. We were all very tired but the job had to be done. So, forward!? One woman volunteered as cook. Quickly we pounded 2 heavy logs into the ground, fastened a pole across, fastened a pail on it, kindled a fire, and cooked a soup. There was plenty of wood lying around. The cook milked the cow, and Uncle Willi and several 15 or 16-year-old boys went into the forest to cut down some slim birch trees. There were plenty of birch trees in the forest. We cut off the branches, gathered the cut trees in one place, and began to build. We trimmed the trees on two sides so we could make a roof, then we laid the branches on top of this so it would hold the hay without it falling through. The women had already cut some hay and piled it close by. (My thoughts were constantly with little Jascha – but the dear Lord protected him.)

Finally our little abode was covered, and grass had been carried inside to serve as sleeping mats. When we had finished, the cook called us to supper: "Come and eat!" We were as hungry as wolves. After we had eaten, everyone took their sheets and blankets into the lean-to, spread out the sheets on the grass, and went to sleep under the blanket. Uncle Willi announced, "Tomorrow I will awaken you very early. It looks like it will be a nice day and we have to take advantage of it. We have much work ahead of us." During the summer the area where we lived enjoyed only daylight – no night there. The sun set and rose again almost immediately.

We had only slept very little and then the call came to get up, to eat and get on with our work. Our orders were to fill the 5 year plan in 2 years – and so it had to be. Every week one of the boys had to ride to Kolschim for more supplies. I always gave them a letter for my little brother Jascha. He always wrote back, and indicated that he was comfortable and satisfied but very lonesome for me. And in this way 4 weeks passed.

One nice day after we had worked until noon and had our lunch, our overseer said, "It is very hot and we are all tired. Let us go into our shelter for half an hour and rest." I fell asleep immediately, and then I had a dream. I had washed my head and hair, and was hanging my head down so the water could run down from my hair. The water was very dirty – actually black. Then Mama came with a dipper of water and poured it over my head. The water ran down through my hair and came out clean and clear as crystal. That was my dream and then the wake-up call came. Uncle Willi hollered for us to get up.

I got up and turned to the Russian neighbour who slept next to me. She had 2 girls, 12-14 years old, who were home in Kolschim like my brother. Her husband was also in prison. I told her the details of my dream. I said, "Traeume sind Schaeume" [*"Dreams are frothy bubbles"*]. "No," she said, "Everything before you now seems very dark, the future is black dark. Your Mama is coming and will dispel the blackness, and everything will become bright and clear. And she is coming soon, real soon." I started to cry and said, "We know nothing of her, we don't even know if she is still alive." Then she said, "You will remember my words. She is coming soon, real soon." The two of us were always together. We then each took a hand rake and began to rake together the hay which had dried by now. We worked about two hours. I was immersed in my own thoughts, and was upset and crying quietly.

It was in August 1939 – I have forgotten the exact day. Suddenly I heard, "Mieche!" – that is how I was called. Then I thought, "Am

I no longer normal? Is everything whirling in my head? Am I still dreaming?"The woman then called me and said, "Your little brother Jascha is running towards us, waving a piece of paper high in the air and loudly shouting, 'Mieche, Mama has come home!'" He shouted in Low German. He ran up to me, (he was 11 years old), threw his arms around me, and we both wept for joy. Several times Jascha said, "Mama is home!" All the workers came running together, very excited to learn what had gone wrong again. I recall that out of every family that worked there, at least 1 or 2 were in prison – from some families there were even more. They all rejoiced with us. The woman then said, "Maria, this is your dream! Things looked black, but now your Mama will rinse everything clean."

Jascha took a rake and helped us rake the hay into piles. Uncle Willi came and greeted Jascha, and asked him, "Boy, how did you get here by yourself? Were you not afraid?" Jascha had come 15-17 kilometres through a dense, dark primeval forest – very dangerous and frightening. Jascha responded, "Yes, I was somewhat afraid when I heard noises and rustling and everything was dark. But then I ran very fast, and when I got tired I looked around and could see nothing. And so I went on following the path I was told would lead to you. As it became lighter and the forest became less dense, I thought, 'Soon there must be some people here.' Then I began to run, and sure enough I found you! At times when it was so dark in the forest I thought I was lost. But no, I just stuck to the path, believing that I had to get out of the forest some place. And now I am here with you!" Then I read the paper which Jascha had been waving. Mama had written that she was home and I should come to her.

We continued to work. Somctimes I wept, feeling so alone in this primeval wilderness. We worked until the sun set, but it was always light and the sun soon rose again. The cook called for us to come and eat. I then went to Uncle Willi and asked him to set me free for 2 days. He said, "No, I cannot give you free time. First we will go and eat, and then I will give you a horse to go to the village for fresh supplies. After all, someone has to ride to them, and it might as well be you. So you can get the supplies and regulate things at home while you are there." I would have liked to stay home for 2 days, but I also realized that under the circumstances that was not possible.

The weather was nice and warm. We finished eating and the boys brought out the horse. The sacks were strapped onto its back, and Jascha sat on top and I got on behind him. And so we headed into the dark and dense virgin forest. We had not gone very far before we ran into a large muskeg. I said to Jascha, "Hold fast to the reins or the horse will fall." I had no sooner said that and the horse sank down and fell, sending us toppling into the swamp. We struggled to the side and waited until the horse regained its feet. I said to Jascha, "We will let the horse walk alone – it will find the way. Horses never get lost. You walk behind the horse and I will walk behind you." That is what we did, and things seemed to go a bit better.

Often we would hear rustling and noises beside the path but did not know what animals were lurking in the dark. We had gone too far to turn back, so we just kept going, but fear clouded our spirits. When we got within 3 kilometres of our village, the forest became less dense since some of the area had been cleared, and it was not as dark as it had been in the virgin forest. The horse seemed to sense that we were close to home, whinnied loudly several times and began to run, leaving us behind. Mama heard the whinnies and soon saw the horse with empty sacks on its back come running up. Then she knew we could not be far behind. Mama ran to meet us. We threw our arms around each other and wept until we had no more tears left. Then she said, "I have come home, and Tina is home too, but Peter is not coming again, he has been tortured to death."

We then went to the barn on the yard of the Kolkhoz [*collective farm*] to see if the horse had arrived. The watchman assured us that the animal was in the barn and everything was in order. Mama suggested we go home, eat something, and then have a sleep. But our attempts at sleep were futile. We talked and talked; there was so much to say, but little that was good. Towards morning I did sleep a little. Then I had to go and report, and prepare the supplies for the return journey. And so life went on.

Mama and Jascha stayed home, and I went to the office to see the chairman. Of course he already knew everything. We discussed the whole situation. He said the cow should stay with me at the workplace; it did not pay to bring her back and then drive another one all that way. I had to stay at the hay field until the work was finished. "The weather is nice and I have no one else to send. Besides it does not pay, since the work will be finished in less than 2 weeks and then everyone will come home." He said he would give Mama and Jascha everything they would need to live. So I rode back, the horse laden with sacks of supplies. Within 2 weeks I also returned with my cow. Mama came to us [in the week of] 20-25 August, 1939, and I returned home 2 weeks later.

Lena had been home during that time. She had passed her examinations and could continue her studies as a nurse in Krasnovischersk, about 100-120 kilometres from our village. Tina had finished her work on the river and came home for the winter. Tina then got work in the office, and life went on. Now we were all together again, our dear Mama with 4 children: Maria, Tina, Lena, and Jascha.

Now I want to relate how our Mama was punished in prison. Mama told us that when they left our village here it was very cold. They were taken to Solikamsk, and on arrival were imprisoned in a Kloster [*cloister*]. The cell was already fully packed, but they were shoved and pressed into the room anyway. They were all freezing, chilled to the bone, but inside there was such heat that they were soon dripping with sweat. It was almost impossible to endure. The next day they were taken out into the fresh air for 5 minutes.

The cell was divided in the middle by a board wall. On one side were the women and on the other side were the men. As the women went out, the men were herded back inside. As they passed each other, they noticed that the boards in the dividing wall were uneven and not very flush, and they could see and talk through the cracks. Among the men was a Heinrich Friesen from N. 9, Altonau, from our village. He recognized Mama and said, "Mrs. Regehr, sign everything that is required of you." One of the guards had seen that something had been said, and Friesen was thrown into the cellar (dungeon) – where he died.

And so the people languished in prison and never knew why they were being punished and tortured. After 2 weeks sister Tina was also thrown into the same cell with Mama. Mama asked her if she knew anything about the rest of the family. But Tina knew nothing, since she had been arrested at her place of work. After a time Mama was taken to the office to be interrogated. Of course this always happened during the night. A large pile of papers was read to Mama, and she was ordered to sign a confession. She then said, "I did not do such things." The judge became furious and shouted, "Take her away!" Mama was again thrown into the overcrowded, hot, stinking prison cell.

In a few days Mama was again dragged before the judge, asked the same questions, and ordered to sign a confession. She then remembered the words Heinrich Friesen had spoken through the wall: "Sign everything, everything you are told to sign." Mama then signed a paper saying she had poisoned 200 cows in our village of Kolschim and had set fire to 70 hectares of forest which then burned to the ground. In the whole village of Kolschim there were only 20 cows! Mama was taken back and again stuffed into that overcrowded, stinking cell. The prison contained no toilets, only a 15-20 litre pail with a lid. Often the pail was full and overflowed onto the floor. Often an especially sadistic guard, too lazy to remove and empty the pail, would come in, curse loudly, turn the pail upside down – and finished! The poor prisoners then had to breathe such stinking air. And so things went on.

After a time Mama was taken from Solikamsk to the prison in the city of Sverdlovsk. I do not recall how long she stayed there – I believe about 2 or 3 months. From Sverdlovsk she was sent to the city of Scherden and then back again to Solikamsk. By that time Tina had been released and was no longer in Solikamsk. They continued to interrogate Mama, always at night when the Russians do their dirty work. So, for a time she was in Solikamsk in prison. Then she was again taken to Scherden where she had been before. She was thrown into solitary confinement for 2 weeks. Her cell was so narrow she could only sit. She was alone. Every night she was taken out, interrogated, and put back into her cell. It was terrible – being questioned all night and thrown back into the small cell. During such treatment people became very mixed up and confused, and were thrown into solitary where there was no one to talk to, all alone in the dark with the vermin and the mice. Mama said she could not have survived it one more night, she was so confused and mixed up in her mind.

One day Mama was again taken to Solikamsk and thrown into prison there. There it was also crowded but she was not alone. One of the prisoners was a Mrs. Margarete Neufeld, who also was an "exile" like we were, and who had lived in the village of Danilov-Lug about 120 kilometres from our village of Kolschim. Danilov-Lug was close to the river Wischere, and the ships from Solikamsk passed there on their way to Krasnovischersk. There was a work camp about 2 kilometres from this village, where workers from Danilov-Lug, as well as some from our village of Kolschim, worked on the construction of a canal. Tina had worked there. Liese, Peter and I had also worked there in summer. In winter we worked in the forest. (The logs were transported to this point by log rafts on the water, and here it was sorted and then continued on.)

But let me continue my story. Mama and Mrs. Neufeld agreed that whoever would get out of prison first would go to the other's family and inform them of what had happened to them – if either one of them would ever leave prison alive.

Some time has passed and now it is winter. Mama was called out and ordered to bring all her belongings. Mrs. Neufeld immediately said, "Mrs. Regehr, you will be set free." Then Mama was again taken before the interrogator. This time the interrogator was an NKVD officer, a huge pile of papers lay before him, and he began to read everything that Mama had confessed doing: poisoned 200 cows, set fire to 70 hectares of forest, and other things. He turned to Mama and asked, "Did you really do all that?" Mama looked at him and answered truthfully, "No, I have never done anything like that." Then he said, "Why then did you sign such a confession?" Mama said, "I had to sign it." Then the officer said, "Now you sign this paper, stating that you did not do these things." When Mama had signed, he said, "So, now you are free. Now go!" He then touched three fingers to his mouth as if to say, "Keep your mouth shut and don't say a word." Then a guard came and took Mama to the gate, unlocked it, and said, "Grandmother, now get out of here, follow the direction of the four winds and go where you will." He locked the gate behind her.

Mama said she sat down right on the ground before the gate and wept bitterly. Where to now? No bread, no Kopek [*money*] and no sense of where she was. She had received no news from us. Where to? Yes, where to? At this point Mama said she wished she had stayed inside – at least she would have a roof over her head. But she could not stay sitting there, nor stay there over night. The cloister prison was located on the bank of the Usolka River, and ships passed by on their way to Krasnovischersk. Mama then recalled that Mrs. Neufeld had given her the address in her village. She decided to find a way to get on board the ship and go to that village. Maybe someone there would know where her children were.

With a heavy heart, and without a ticket, Mama went to the ship and managed to hide herself in a dark corner on the lowest level of the vessel. The ship got underway. Sitting near nearby was another woman who continually glanced at her. Mama became very uneasy, thinking that the woman might report her because she had no ticket. Mama said she then quietly began to sing the song, "No never alone, no never alone. God promised never to leave me, never to leave me alone."

But things were not as they seemed. The woman had seen Mama [come aboard], emaciated and dirty. After the ship had been underway for a while, the woman came to Mama and asked her where she was going and where she had come from. Mama was frightened and said, "Now you want to report me because I have no ticket!" "No, no," said the woman, "I can see from where you have come. I just want to help you. My man is also in prison." She was a good woman and gave Mama a piece of bread and a ticket. So, on this ship Mama came to Danilovka-Lug, the village where Mrs. Neufeld's relatives lived.

Mama disembarked and searched for the Neufelds. These people received her with great hospitality, especially when she told them of having been together in prison with Margarete. It did not take long and the room was full. The word spread rapidly through the village that someone had arrived who had come out of prison. It was a fact that every family had members who were incarcerated. Mama was asked where she was going, and told them she was from Kolschim, but she did not know if any of her children were still there. She asked if there were any workers from Kolschim in Danilovka-Lug. Mama knew that every summer some workers from Kolschim were sent to work here on the canal.

One man spoke up and said, "Yes, there are some workers here from Kolschim. There is a young girl here named Tina Regehr." Mama said she jumped up and cried out repeatedly, "That is my daughter Tina! That is my daughter Tina! Now I will find the rest of my children!" The people all got very excited. Mama said to the man, "Where is she? Take me to her." The man said, "No, Oma, I will get Tina, who is not very far away. But you are very tired. I can see that."

The Neufelds (Margarete's family) lived about 2 kilometres from the village. In a short time the man came back with Tina. He said, "I had a hard time keeping up with Tina, she ran so fast." Mama and Tina threw their arms around each other and wept bitterly – but with joy. Everyone present wept with them. Everyone thought of their own loved ones who were languishing in some prison. Mama asked Tina if she knew where her siblings were. Tina said, "Yes, I know. I have been with them. Mariechen, Lena, and Jascha are still living in the village of Kolschim where we all used to live." Mama announced: "Our Peter is no longer alive. God has brought me to this point, and I hope that I will be able to get to my children."

Kolschim was still 150 kilometres distant. Tina said to Mama, "Come with me. I have a little room where you can rest up for a few days, and then we will see what we can do." Then old Mrs. Neufeld said, "No, Tina, You go to your place, since you must go to work very early. Your Mama is coming to our place for the night." This Mrs. Neufeld was the mother-in-law of Margarete Neufeld, who had been in prison with Mama. Old Mrs. Neufeld wanted to hear everything, because they had not known where Margarete was. (Later we heard that Margarete was tried and sentenced to 10 years. She served the entire 10 years and came back crippled and ill.)

But to continue the story. After work the next day Tina came to the Neufelds and took Mama to her own room. Mama rested a few days, for she was tired, very tired, and had little energy and no strength. Then she said to Tina, "I have found you, and now I want to go on to my other children." Yes, but how? Tina took Mama to her workplace where there were others from the village of Kolschim who knew Mama. They all greeted her warmly, and everyone asked about their own loved ones.

Tina took a day off and went to the Neufelds with Mama. The ship Mama had come on passed near their place on its way to Krasnovischersk, which was 30 kilometres away. Tina bought a ticket for Mama and put her on the ship to continue her journey. Tina gave her some money, some bread, and a few other things for her trip. The ship departed, and Tina went back to her work. Tina also gave Mama an address in Krasnovischersk – the address of acquaintances, Russians but good people, who were exiles like us and who had been with us in Kolschim but then were transferred to Krasnovischersk. These people often received transports of goods from Kolschim, and the drivers stayed there overnight. Our village was 120 kilometres away – quite far – but in those days there were no buses or trucks, and horse-drawn transport was used.

So Mama arrived in the city of Krasnovischersk, disembarked, and then wanted to look for the people. Another lady disembarked at the same time. Mama showed her the address and asked her if she knew where that was. "Yes," said the woman, "Come with me, I know those people since they are our neighbours. I will take you there." When they got there, Mama asked if any transports from Kolschim had arrived. The proprietress informed her that there were no transports there now but some should arrive the next day. She told Mama to come again the next day. It seemed clear that they did not want to keep Mama over night. The woman who had brought Mama said Mama could stay with her over night and that she would bring her back here the next day.

The woman showed Mama very friendly hospitality and gave her comfortable quarters. The next day they again went to the other people and asked if transports had arrived from Kolschim. Yes, two transports had arrived and were now loading products, and would start their return journey this day in order to reach Kolschim the next day. In a short time the heavily loaded transports arrived, and Mama asked if she could go along with them. There were two men but they were not from Kolschim. They did not know Mama. One of the men then said they could not take Mama with them, since they were so heavily loaded and they themselves would have to follow the transports on foot. Mama then begged them to allow her to come, and she would not ride but walk as well. She did not want to go all that way by herself. The men agreed to this and she was allowed to come with them.

And so the journey continued, always at a slow pace. When the horses got tired, they were unhitched, fed, allowed to rest a while, and then continued their journey. The next day they came to the village of Werch-Jasva where Tina and Lena had studied. Kolschim was still 27 kilometres away, so they stopped, fed the horses, and rested for a while. Suddenly a young man from Kolschim came by and recognized Mama. He said, "I am here and do not have a heavy load. I am leaving for our village immediately. Come with me and I will take you along." Mama was very happy to do so and, after warmly thanking the two men, went with the young man. From there she could ride the 27 kilometres and did not have to walk.

She was very tired and the young man brought her directly to our house in Kolschim.

Lena and Jascha had just come from the forest, where they had cut and sacked hay and grass, carried it home, and spread it out to dry as winter feed for the cow. The young man shouted, "Jascha, Lena, look who I have brought you!" Jascha and Lena both looked up, ran to the wagon, shouted and cried, and called again and again, "Mama, Mama has come!" The joy was indescribable. The neighbours came running, greeted, and kissed Mama and rejoiced with the children!

(The father of the young man who had brought Mama was also in prison, sentenced for 10 years. No one knew how he had been tried or judged. In those days there were no judges: the NKVD condemned whom they pleased, sentenced them to 10-15-20 years, and transported them to camps in the most miserable places they could find in the "North." The people were all innocent and yet were abused and tortured – for what?)

Finally the people dispersed to their homes, and Mama, Lena, and Jascha went to our house and made themselves something to eat. Our mother was very tired and lay down on the bed to rest a while, while Lena and Jascha sat at the foot of the bed and talked. Jascha said to Mama, "Now I won't always be alone. Mariechen is always at work, and Lena has been studying and must go away again. But now, Mama, I will be with you, yes?" Mama said she now hoped that we could stay together.

Two days later Lena had to leave to go for her studies. She had passed her exams very well, and it was time to start the next semester. Since there were no autos she had to walk the 120 kilometres on foot. A whole group left for school, small packs strapped to their backs and off they went. It was a tragic picture, but if these children ever wanted a better life they had to go this way. And so little Jascha did not remain alone, because Mama was now home. At this time he was 10 years old, and Mama called him "my big boy." This made him very proud. Mama was home and life took on a new meaning. The time was the end of August 1939. Mama had been in prison for 1 year and 6 months. When she was seized, eleven other German women were arrested in our village of Kolschim. Only two of these women ever came back, our Mama and Tina Peters, who was alone and had no children. The others were all sentenced to ten years! For what???

Autumn came, and Tina came home since the work on the water had come to an end. I also came home with my cow. Lena continued her studies as a nurse. And so life went on. Tina then worked in the village office, Jascha went to school, and I also worked in the village. I had to get and stack the hay we had cut during the summer. Our constant hope was that we would yet be set free and be able to return to our home in the Ukraine. But nothing happened, and our hopes were never realized. We had to stay where we were.

We were comforted that at least we were together again with Mama. And we had some food: potatoes, and milk; in summer we picked and dried roots, berries, and mushrooms for the winter. And so life went on. We shredded the raw potatoes and baked patties – we had no flour, but the patties tasted so good, excellent. This was at the end of 1939. Then came 1940 and we slowly continued our life, cut off from the rest of the world – no radio, no nothing.

It was 1941. Lena had finished her studies. She came home and said to Mama, "I have finished my studies, and before I go to work I want to go to our homeland, the Ukraine, and visit my sister Liese." That was okay with all of us. No one was opposed, so we all agreed.

Two days later Lena received written notice to come to the city of Krasnovischersk and report to the military recruiting office. She was to come with all her belongings. There was war; the German had fallen on Russia. Well, yes, Lena had to go. The whole village was terribly aroused, disturbed, and agitated. Everyone had hoped that in time we would get out of here. But now this! Well, yes, Lena had to go, and with her several others who had studied with her. Again our family was separated.

At the beginning of the war Lena worked in a hospital, caring for the wounded. In time the authorities learned that she was German and she was conscripted into the Trudarme [*army of slave labourers*]. I stayed at home until September, and then I too had to go away. Again there was a separation in our family. Jascha was studying in the school (27 kilometres away) where Tina and Lena had also studied. He then dropped out of school and stayed home with Mama – it was too hard for her alone. It was a very difficult time for all the people. Mama and Jascha stayed in Kolschim. No one else was sent farther. Yes, where could they have sent us? We were in the far north already. It was wartime, a very difficult time for all of us. But that is all behind us now. Some have survived, but many have not.

In brief outline I have written where and how we lived. Many years have passed since then, and I have difficulty in recalling many things. If certain things are not clear to you, then please ask and I will gladly answer. I am no literary author and you will have to put the pieces together yourselves. I have forgotten much, but when I make the effort I can recall many things.

And now we are in Germany! We would never have thought – or planned it – or believed that such a thing could happen in our life. We are so content! We have everything we need. We are living better than we have ever lived in our life. Only it is so sad that our loved ones could not have lived through this time – Papa, Mama, Liese, Peter, and Jascha.

Now they see that which they have believed!

– Maria Regehr

# EPILOGUE

## WHAT THEN MUST WE DO?

*– Leo Tolstoy, 1886*

When we have read the letters, sensed the suffering of the victims, and felt the numbness of despair, what can we do?

Attempting to make meaning out of the absurdity of the Soviet system in the 1930s is a complex venture and likely a futile one for us in the 21st century. Wrestling with the monstrosity of Stalin and the injustice of the Soviet system feels hopeless. Even Jasch Regehr is confused, though he grasps that he and his family are living in an unprecedented horror: "What has happened in this Red Paradise?" he asks. "It is a slave trade! It is slavery as it has never been before!" Yet "the entire world keeps silent."

We can address the silence. We can expose the injustice. We can begin with ourselves and our families. Others must also come to know what has happened, not only to the Russian Mennonites but to the Russian Jews, the Polish Catholics, the Black Sea Germans, the ethnic Ukrainians and others who perished during Stalin's Reign of Terror. Their bodies died, but some of their voices live on in these letters. They must not have died in vain.

To forget is to erase, to expunge, to obliterate. It is to become "a-historical": separated from history; unconnected and unconcerned. It is to assume that our lives are concerned only with ourselves and the present moment.

If we forget, we are only vacant shells:

> We are the hollow men
> We are the stuffed men
> Leaning together
> Headpiece filled with straw. Alas!
> Our dried voices, when
> We whisper together
> Are quiet and meaningless
> As wind in dry grass
> Or rats' feet over broken glass
> In our dry cellar.
>
> —T.S. Eliot, *The Hollow Men*

"Remember us as we remember you" is the plea from a father for his family in a prison camp in Stalin's vast Gulag. The world does not know this story. The silence is unfathomable. The Gulag and the millions who died must enter our public moral consciousness. We can transcend the chronological limits of time and link past, present, and future. We can remember. The act of remembering allows us to encounter the world more realistically; it shapes our attitudes and, we may hope, it fosters tolerance.

If we remember, we can respond.

# Appendix A

## Number of Deaths in the Gulag

D.M.Thomas, in *Alexander Solzhenitsyn: A Century in His Life* (1998), cites the following:

> It is worth reminding ourselves of the extent, in brutal round numbers of deaths, of the horrors he set himself to evoke. Professor I. A. Kurganov, an émigré statistician, analyzed official statistics and came up with a total of some sixty-six million deaths in the war of the state against the people. Dmitri Panin, in *The Notebooks of Sologdin,* on the basis of his own and friends' research, arrived at the following estimations, which bear out Kurganov's figures:

This gives, at the lowest estimates, almost sixty million. No one, Solzhenitsyn asserts, has seriously disputed Kurganov's figures; the most cautious estimates say that at least forty-five million died.

| *Years* | *Cause of Death* | *Victims (in millions)* |
|---|---|---|
| 1917-21 | Shootings, tortures | 6-12 |
| 1922-23 | Famine in the Volga region and other areas | 7.5-1.3 |
| 1922-28 | Destruction of the old social classes, the clergy, and believers | 2-3 |
| 1929-33 | Liquidation of *kulaks*; organized famine | 16 |
| 1934-41 | Mass executions in prisons and camps; starvation in camps; artificially created epidemics | 7 |
| 1941-42 | Destruction of *zeks* through hunger and overwork | 7.5 |
| 1943-45 | Death in Stalin's wartime camps | 5 |
| 1946-53 | Death in Stalin's camps after the war | 6 |

Add the thirty-one million now officially admitted to have been lost in the Great Patriotic War: a fifth of the population! (When and where, Solzhenitsyn asked, had a people ever laid down so many in a war?). Add the living dead, who somehow survived with breath still in their bodies, but with lives and family relationships shattered; add the grief-stricken relatives of victims, and the millions of young women who never had the chance to become wives and mothers. It becomes clear that when [Anna] Akhmatova spoke in *Requiem* [1973] of 'a hundred million of my people' crying through her 'tormented mouth,' she was not using hyperbole.

Easy to understand how Shostakovich, seeing mountains of corpses, was overwhelmed by a sense of the unbearable gray despair of his life, in which 'there were no particular happy moments.' What is astounding is the absolute vitality of Solzhenitsyn that allowed him to begin his 'threnody for sixty million with a piece of savage black humor and startling poetic metaphors'" (442-43).

## Further Data on Deaths in the Gulag

While the vast geographical area and scope of the camps is formidable, the numbers of prisoners incarcerated, exiled, or executed is no less overwhelming. Robert Conquest reports that, of those arrested during the second wave of Stalin's purges in 1938, "we can hardly allow 10 per cent to have survived; in fact a Soviet historian tells us that 90 per cent of those who went to the camps before [World War II] perished" (1990: 495).

More recent publications report that the improved accessibility of Soviet archives has provided further data on numbers of prisoners. In their introduction to a collection of Soviet diaries from the 1930s, Veronique Garros, Natalia Korenevskaya, and Thomas Lahusen supply figures on political prisoners from 1935 to1939. In 1935 they record 965,742; in 1936 they note that 1,296,494 prisoners were sentenced for "counterrevolutionary crimes"; in 1937 they report 1,196,369 prisoners; in 1938 they report 1,881,570 prisoners;

and in 1939 they note that 1,672,438 prisoners were incarcerated (1995: xiii). While these authors remind the reader that "the whole is of course not explainable by the addition – or subtraction – of its parts," recent researchers continue to try to account for the number of arrests during the "Terror."

Robert Thurston investigates the purge of 1937-38. He notes that although the local NKVD could manipulate the numbers of exiles and executions, final accounting and validation required the permission of state officials. Under state direction, people were divided into two categories: one for execution and one for exile. Notably, Thurston reports that "In Moscow oblast' ... five thousand were to be shot and thirty thousand exiled; in Leningrad oblast', the numbers were four thousand and ten thousand. There were wide variations in Central Asia. Ten thousand were to be executed in the labour camps" (1996: 59). These numbers include only those who were sent to the labour camps. They do not include prisoners in common jails, deported prisoners, prisoners killed or deported. Thurston says these numbers may be pessimistic rather than hyperbolic because "police in various areas bombarded [the head of the state agency] with requests to boost the permitted totals.... Siberia asked to be allowed to raise the limit ... to *eight times* his assigned figure"(1996: 60).

Referring to a report by Merle Fainsod, Nicholas Riasanovsky (2000) notes the following:

> The arrests mounted into the millions; the testimony of the survivors is unanimous regarding crowded prison cells and teeming forced labor camps. Most of the prisoners were utterly bewildered by the fate which had befallen them. The vast resources of the NKVD were concentrated on one objective – to document the existence of a huge conspiracy to undermine Soviet power. The extraction of real confession to imaginary crimes became a major industry. Under the zealous and ruthless ministrations of NKVD examiners, million of

innocents were transformed into traitors, terrorists, and enemies of the people" (505).

Despite the plethora of reports and variation in numbers of prisoners, it is evident that cataclysmic events occurred in the Gulag during the decade of 1930s in which thousands of Russian citizens' lives were disrupted and destroyed. Solzhenitsyn names this mass migration of *kulaks* to the Gulag as "The Prison Industry" which, during the first wave of Stalin's purges (1929-30), "drove fifteen million peasants, maybe even more, out into the taiga and the tundra" (1973: 24).

Robert Conquest places the number of Gulag inmates in 1938 at 8 million (1990: 485-86). Antonov Ovseenko estimates the 1938 camp population to be 16 million in his documentation of *The Times of Stalin: Portrait of a Tyranny* (1980: 212), while Roy Medvedev in *Let History Judge: The Origins and Consequences of Stalinism* claims that between five and seven million people were arrested during the 1937-38 purges (1989: 455). A further consideration is the number of deaths resulting from malnutrition and scarcity of food in the camps. An analysis of archival data by R.W.Davies on victims of famine notes that, although the newly released Soviet data on birth and death registrations places the famine deaths of the 1930s at 4-5 million, other scholars, in the belief that many births and deaths occurred outside the official recognition system, contend that the toll was as high as 8 million (1996: 142-44). One of the most recent estimates, including all forms of death resulting from the mass exile of people to the Gulags is that more than 20 million people were victims of Stalin's penal empire (J. Otto Pohl, 1997: 5).

The exile, displacement, and death of millions of the Soviet people caused even Stalin to respond. In a *Pravda* article of March 2, 1930 titled "Dizziness with Success," Stalin acknowledged that the devastation of collectivization had reached cataclysmic proportions, and he held over-ardent, fanatic officials responsible.[1] Although abuses and deviations are inevitable in any political system, recently available archival documents (Politburo Special files and NKVD documents) confirm that in "not a single case did the NKVD decide on important issues without Stalin's approval" (Oleg Khlevniuk 2004: 331).

## Notes

1 John. B. Toews, in *Journeys* (1998), expands on Stalin's role and comments on the Pravda article.

# APPENDIX B

## Percentage of Letters in the Bargen Corpus by Year

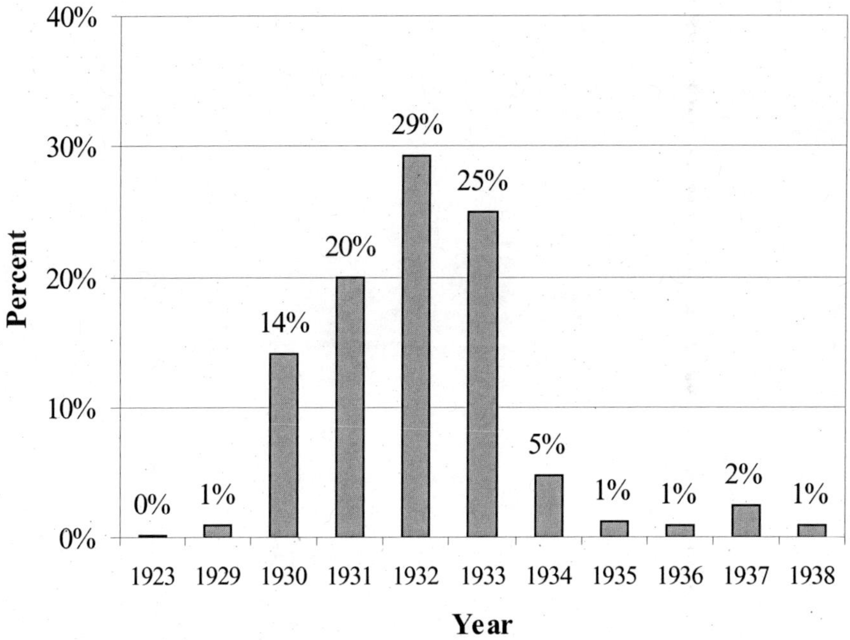

# APPENDIX C

## MAPS

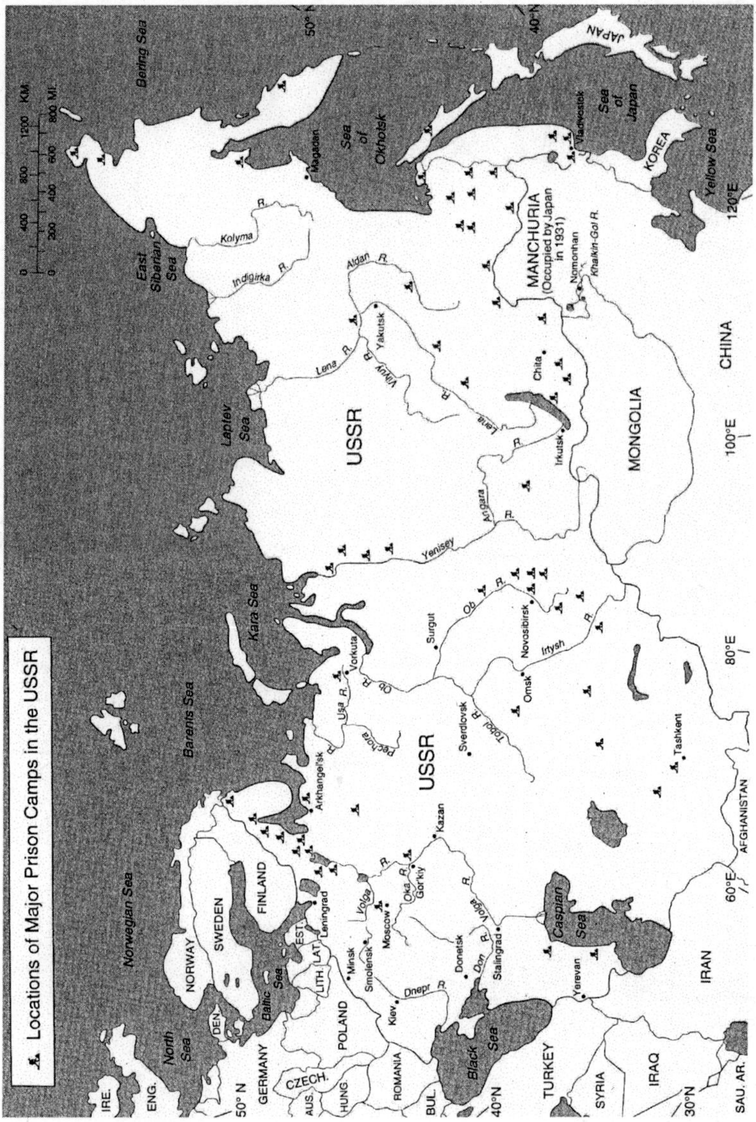


*Location of Major Prison Camps in the Former USSR in 1939 (Thurston 64).*

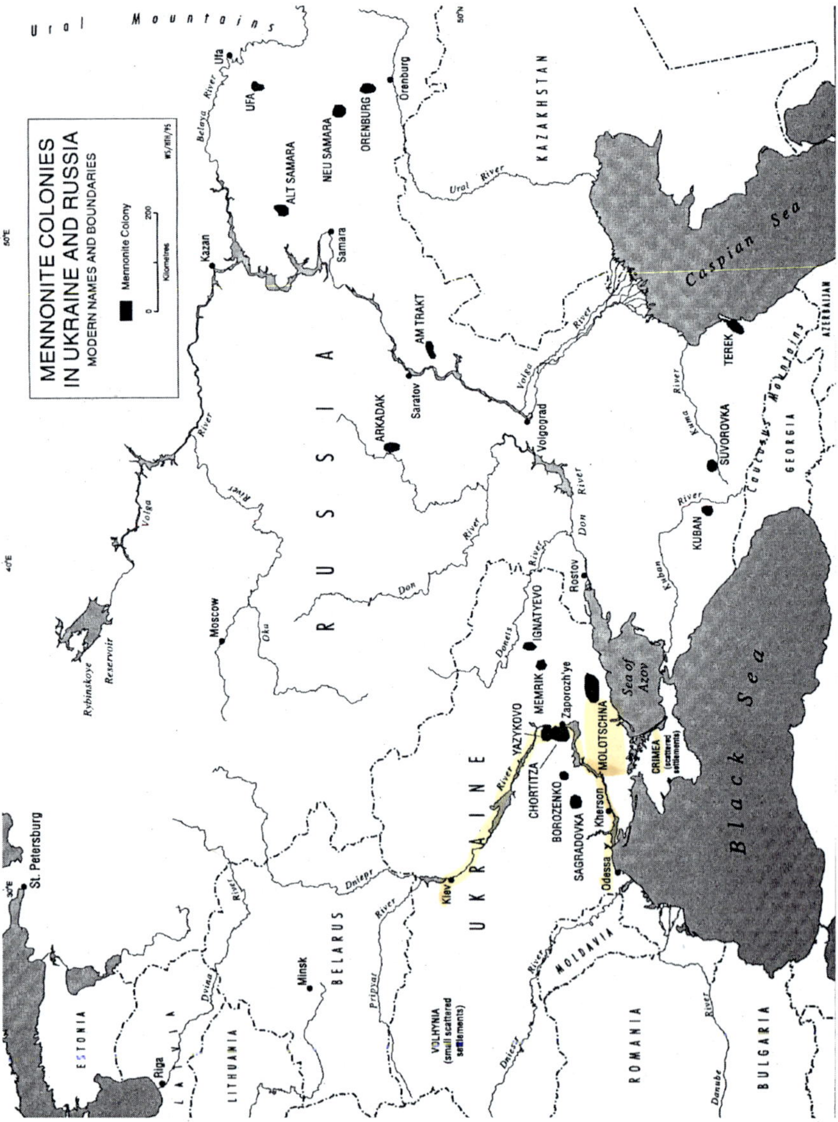


*Map of Former Mennonite Colonies and Villages (Schroeder and Huebert 14).*

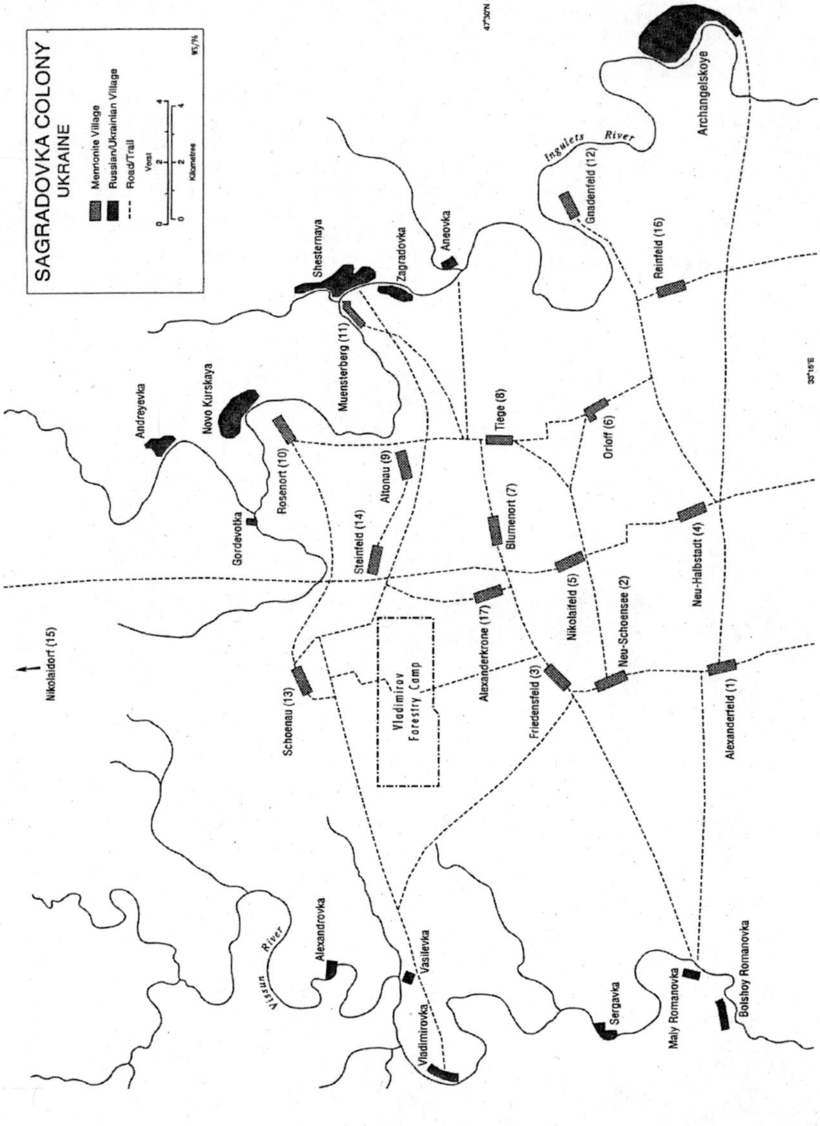


*Map of the Former Mennonite Colony of Sagradowka (Schroeder and Huebert 46).*

# Sources

## Works Cited


Applebaum, Anne. *Gulag: A History*. New York and London: Doubleday, 2003.

Bargen, Anne and Peter Bargen. *From Russia with Tears*. Kelowna, BC: Private Publication, 1991.

Barth, Fredrik. *Ethnic Groups and Boundaries.* Boston: Little Brown, 1969.

Bentley, G.C. "Ethnicity and Practice." *Comparative Studies in Society and History.* (1987) 29:24-55.

Conquest, Robert. *The Great Terror: A Reassessment*. New York: Macmillan, 1990.

Conquest, Robert. *The Great Terror: Stalin's Purge of the Thirties.* London: Macmillan, 1968.

Fleischhauer, Ingeborg and Benjamin Pinkus. *The Soviet Germans: Past and Present*. London: C. Hurst, 1986.

Friesen, P.M. *The Mennonite Brotherhood in Russia (1789-1910)*. Fresno, CA: General Conference of Mennonite Brethren Churches, 1978.

Friesen, Rudy, P. and Sergey Shmakin. *Into the Past: Buildings of the Mennonite Commonwealth*. Winnipeg: C. Press, 1996.

Garros, Veronique, Natalia Korenevskaya and Thomas Lahusen. *Intimacy and Terror: Soviet Diaries of the 1930s.* New York: New Press, 1995.

Huebert, Helmut T. *Events and People: Events in Russian Mennonite History and the People That Made Them Happen*. Winnipeg: Springfield, 1999.

Khlevniuk, Oleg V. *The History of the Gulag: From Collectivization to the Great Terror.* London: Yale University Press, 2004.

Klippenstein, L. "The Mennonite Migration to Russia 1786-1806." *Mennonites in Russia: Essays in Honour of Gerhard Lorenz*. Ed. J. Friesen. Winnipeg: CMBC Publications, 1989. 13-42.

Medvedev, Roy. *Let History Judge: The Origins and Consequences of Stalinism*. New York: Columbia University Press, 1989.

*Mennonite Encyclopedia*. Scottdale, PA: Mennonite Publishing House, 1955.

Ovseenko, Antonov. *The Time of Stalin: Portrait of a Tyranny*. New York: Macmillan, 1980.

Pohl, J. Otto. *The Stalinist Penal System: A Statistical History of Soviet Repression and Terror, 1930-1953*. Jefferson, NC: McFarland Publishers, 1997.

Redekop, John. *A People Apart: Ethnicity and the Mennonite Brethren*. Winnipeg: Kindred Press, 1987.

Riasanovsky, Nicholas V. *A History of Russia*. 6th ed. Oxford: Oxford University Press, 2000.

Schroeder, William and Helmut T. Huebert. *Mennonite Historical Atlas*. 2nd ed. Winnipeg: Springfield Publishers, 1996.

Serge, Victor. *Memoirs of a Revolutionary (1901-1941)*. Trans. Peter Sedgwick. London: Oxford University Press, 1963.

Shifrin, Avraham. *The First Guidebook to Prisons and Concentration Camps of the Soviet Union*. New York: Bantam, 1980.

Smith, Henry. *The Story of the Mennonites*. 4th ed. Newton, KS: Mennonite Publications, 1957.

Solzhenitsyn, Aleksandr. *The Gulag Archipelago 1918-1956: An Experiment in Literary Investigation*. New York: Harper & Row, 1973.

Thernstrom, Stephen (ed). *Harvard Encyclopedia of American Ethnic Groups*. Cambridge: Harvard University Press, 1980. 1076.

Thomas, D.M. *Alexander Solzhenitsyn: A Century in His Life*. New York: St. Martin's, 1998.

Thompson, John M. *Russia and the Soviet Union: An Historical Introduction from the Kievan State to the Present*. 5th ed. Boulder: Westview Press, 2004.

Thurston, Robert. *Life and Terror in Stalin's Russia 1934-1941*. New Haven and London: Yale University Press, 1996.

Toews, John B. *Czars, Soviets and Mennonites.* Newton, KS: Faith and Life Press, 1982.

_____ *Letters From Susan*. North Newton, KS: Bethel College Press, 1988.

_____ "Cultural and Intellectual Aspects of the Mennonite Experience in Russia" *Mennonite Quarterly Review* 53 (April 1979): 150.

_____ "Early Communism and Russian Mennonite Peoplehood." *Mennonites in Russia: Essays in Honour of Gerhard Lorenz*. Ed. J. Friesen. Winnipeg: CMBC Publications, 1989. 265ff.

_____ "Abram," *Mennonite Stories of Faith and Survival in Stalin's Russia*. Ed. John B. Toews. Hillsboro, KS and Winnipeg, MB: Kindred Productions, 1998. 97-136.

Urry, James. *None But Saints: The Transformation of Mennonite Life in Russia, 1789-1889*. Winnipeg: Hyperion Press, 1989.

_____. "The Closed and the Open: Social and Religious Change amongst the Mennonites in Russia (1789-1889)." D. Phil. Dissertation, Oxford University, 1978.

## Works Consulted

Barth, Fredrik. *Ethnic Groups and Boundaries.* Boston: Little Brown, 1969.

Bentley, G.C. "Ethnicity and Practice." *Comparative Studies in Society and History.* (1987) 29:24-55.

Bourdieu, Pierre. *In Other Words. Essays Toward a Reflexive Sociology.* Trans. Mathew Adamson. Cambridge: Polity Press, 1990.

Brucks, Jakob H. and Henry P. Hooge. *Neu-Samara: A Mennonite Settlement East of the Volga.* Trans. John Isaak. Ed. Tena Wiebe. Edmonton, AB: Jackpine House, 2002.

Burke, Kenneth. *On Symbols and Society.* Ed. Joseph R. Gusfield. Chicago and London: University of Chicago Press, 1989.

Clasen, C.P. *Anabaptism: A Social History.* Ithaca: Cornell University Press, 1972.

Conquest, Robert. *The Great Terror: Stalin's Purge of the Thirties.* London: Macmillan, 1968.

Davies. R.W. "The Gulag Accounts." *Wilson Quarterly* 20.2 (Spring 1996): 142 ff.

Dyck, Cornelius J. *An Introduction to Mennonite History: A Popular History of the Anabaptists and the Mennonites.* Scottdale, PA: Herald Press, 1981.

Epp, David. *Sketches from the Pioneer Years of the Industry in the Mennonite Settlements of South Russia.* Trans. J.P. Penner. Leamington, ON: *Der Bote*, 1972.

_____. "The Emergence of German Industry in the South Russian Colonies." Trans. J.B. Toews. *Mennonite Quarterly Review* 55 (1981): 139-43.

Epp, Frank H. *Mennonite Exodus: The Rescue and Resettlement of the Russian Mennonites Since the Communist Revolution.* Altona, Manitoba: D.W. Friesen, 1962.

Epp, Marlene. *Women Without Men: Mennonite Refugees of the Second World War.* Toronto: University of Toronto Press, 2002.

Fairclough, Norman. *Discourse and Social Change.* Cambridge: Polity Press, 1992.

Fleischhauer, Ingeborg and Benjamin Pinkus. *The Soviet Germans: Past and Present.* London: C. Hurst, 1986.

Friesen, P.M. *The Mennonite Brotherhood in Russia (1789-1910).* Fresno, CA: General Conference of Mennonite Brethren Churches, 1978.

Friesen, Rudy, P. and Sergey Shmakin. *Into the Past: Buildings of the Mennonite Commonwealth.* Winnipeg: Christian Press, 1996.

*Glossary of Russian Abbreviations and Acronyms.* Washington, DC: Library of Congress, 1967.

Kelly, Catriona. "Introduction: Iconoclasm and Commemorating the Past." *Constructing Russian Identity in the Age of Revolution: 1881-1940.* Eds. C. Kelly and D. Shepherd. Oxford: Oxford University Press, 1998. 227-37.

Loewen, Harry. *Between Worlds: Reflections of a Soviet-born Canadian Mennonite.* Kitchener, ON: Pandora Press, 2006.

Loewen, Harry. *Road to Freedom: Mennonites Escape the Land of Suffering.* Kitchener, ON: Pandora Press, 2000.

Martin, Terry. *The Affirmative Action Empire: Nations and Nationalism in the Soviet Union, 1923-1939.* Ithaca and London: Cornell University Press, 2001.

*Mennonite Encyclopedia.* Scottdale, PA: Mennonite Publishing House, 1955.

Neufeld, Dietrich. *A Russian Dance of Death: Revolution and Civil War in the Ukraine.* Trans. Al Reimer. Winnipeg: Hyperion Press, 1977.

Plett, Delbert. *Saints and Sinners: The Kleine Gemeinde in Imperial Russia.* Rosenort, MB: Country Graphics and Printing, 1999.

Regehr, Ted D. *For Everything There is a Season: A History of the Alexanderkrone Zentralschule.* Winnipeg: CMBC Publications, 1988.

Reimer, A. "The Print Culture of the Russian Mennonites 1870-1930." *Mennonites in Russia: Essays in Honour of Gerhard Lorenz.* Ed. J. Friesen. Winnipeg: CMBC Publications, 1989. 221-37.

Rempel, David G. "The Mennonite Colonies in New Russia: A Study of their Settlement and Economic Development from 1789-1914." PhD dissertation, Stanford University, 1933.

Rupert, Raphael. *A Hidden World.* Ed. Anthony Rhodes. London: Collins Press, 1963.

Thernstrom, Stephen (ed). *Harvard Encyclopedia of American Ethnic Groups.* Cambridge: Harvard University Press, 1980. 1076.

Thurston, Robert W. *Life and Terror in Stalin's Russia 1934-1941.* New Haven and London: Yale University Press, 1996.

## Interviews

Bargen, Peter. Personal interview. Edmonton, AB. 3 June 2004.

Eggert, Richard and Erma. Personal interview. Abbotsford, BC. 13 June 2001.

Epp, Helen. Personal interview. Langley, BC. 4 Apr. 2003

Fleming-Loewen, Anna. Personal interview. Abbotsford, BC. 14 Nov. 2001.

Hempler, Ida. Personal interview. Vancouver, BC. 19 July 2001.

Hempler, Ida. Personal interview. Maple Ridge, BC. 9 Sept. 2001.

Hempler, Ida. Personal interview. Maple Ridge, BC. 16 July 2002.

Mantler, Maria Bargen. Personal interview, Winnipeg, MB. 18 Nov. 2006.

Loewen, Walter. Personal interview. Abbotsford, BC. 14 Nov. 2001.

Neufeldt, Julia. Personal interview. Winnipeg, MB. 20 Aug. 2003.

Regehr, John. Personal interview. Kelowna, BC. 22 July 2006.

Regehr Dirksen, Lena. Telephone interview. Vancouver, BC. 7 June 2005.

Regehr Dirksen, Lena. Personal interviews. Cologne, Germany. 8-11 Oct. 2005.

Plett, Peter. Personal interview. Vancouver, BC. July 11, 2007.

Sawatsky, Jakob. Personal interview. White Rock, BC. 14 July 2000.

Sawatsky, Jakob. Personal interview. White Rock, BC. 17 Nov. 2001.

Sawatsky, Jakob. Personal interview. White Rock, BC. 31 July 2003.

Sawatsky, Jakob. Personal interview. White Rock, BC. 15 Aug. 2003.

Wiebe, Walter. Personal interview. Langley, BC. 7 Sept. 2003.

## Correspondence

Applebaum, Anne. Electronic letter. 7 Nov. 2005.

Applebaum, Anne. Electronic letter. 5 Dec. 2006.

Bargen, Peter. Electronic letter. 6 Mar. 2000.

Bargen, Peter. Electronic letter. 6 Jan. 2003.

Bargen, Peter. Electronic letter. 14 Jan. 2003.

Bargen, Peter. Electronic letter. 28 May 2004.

Bergen, Price. Electronic letter. 11 October 2006.

Martin, Terry. Electronic Letter, 8 Nov. 2005.

Siegelbaum, Lewis. Electronic letter. 22 Jan. 2003.